Geoffrey Moore is Professor of American Literature and Head of the Department of American Studies at the University of Hull. Since 1951, when he returned from four years' teaching at Wisconsin and Tulane Universities, he has devoted himself to writing and talking about American subjects: first, as a broadcaster, television producer, and regular contributor to *The Times Literary Supplement* and, subsequently, as an academic. In 1955 he became the first full-time lecturer in American Literature in England (at Manchester University) moving on to Hull in 1962. During the past quarter of a century he has returned many times to North America.

The editor of *The Penguin Book of Modern American Verse* (1954) – 'one of the very few creative and wholly satisfying anthologies of verse published since the thirties' (Roy Fuller) – Geoffrey Moore has also published *Poetry from Cambridge in Wartime* (1947), *Poetry Today* (1958), *American Literature and the American Imagination* (1964), *American Literature* (1964) and numerous articles in literary and scholarly journals.

The Penguin Book of
American Verse

Edited with an Introduction by
Geoffrey Moore

PENGUIN BOOKS

Penguin Books Ltd, Harmondsworth, Middlesex, England
Penguin Books, 625 Madison Avenue, New York, New York 10022, U.S.A.
Penguin Books Australia Ltd, Ringwood, Victoria, Australia
Penguin Books Canada Ltd, 2801 John Street, Markham, Ontario, Canada L3R 1B4
Penguin Books (N.Z.) Ltd, 182–190 Wairau Road, Auckland 10, New Zealand

—

First published by Penguin Books 1977
Reprinted 1979

—

Copyright © Geoffrey Moore, 1977
All rights reserved

—

Made and printed in Great Britain
by Richard Clay (The Chaucer Press), Ltd
Bungay, Suffolk
Set in Monotype Bembo

*The Acknowledgements which appear
on pages 639–45 should be
regarded as an extension of the
copyright page*

Contents

CONTENTS

CONTENTS

CONTENTS

8

CONTENTS

CONTENTS

CONTENTS

CONTENTS

CONTENTS

CONTENTS

CONTENTS

CONTENTS

Introduction

For *The Penguin Book of Modern American Verse*, published in 1954, I selected fifty-eight poets to represent the period between Emily Dickinson and W. S. Merwin. In this anthology the number is one hundred and one, and the period spanned has been enlarged to include the major poets of the seventeenth, eighteenth and nineteenth centuries as well as the twentieth.

The aim of the earlier book was to introduce to the general public in the United Kingdom the wide variety of American poetic talent in the first half of the twentieth century. This time, however, I felt that a different kind of collection was called for – one which would not only cover the whole of American verse from its beginnings but also pay special attention to the extraordinarily vital period which has elapsed since the early fifties.

No anthology can be ideal. It is not possible to include everyone; it is certainly not possible to include all the poems one might wish. The economics of the market: restrictions on length, amount available for permissions fees, cooperation or non-cooperation of the poet or his publisher – all these things, at least partly, dictate the shape of an anthology. Within these limits, however, it is a reflection of the editor's critical judgement, and the selection both of poets and of poems must stand or fall on its own merit. Nevertheless, the reader may be interested in the principles behind this selection.

I have tried to bear in mind two considerations: that of making a book which could be used as a 'teaching anthology' (i.e. one which includes generous selections from the poets normally taught in university courses) and that of making a book which would be representative, so that the full range of American poetry might be brought before the reader unfamiliar with the subject as a whole. For the past twenty years there has been a tendency in American anthologies to be restrictive – a reaction, no doubt, against the older principle of including as many authors as possible. My own solution is a compromise. I have cut the 'classic American poets' to a minimum, and given greater weight to the major figures of the between-wars period and to those poets who have emerged since the Second World War. I have also included a number of ballads and parodies, and even a sample or two of 'public' verse, such as 'The Star-Spangled Banner' and 'Battle-Hymn of the Republic'. Comic poets, or the comic side of poets, also have their place, for poetry is not always a matter of 'O altitudo'.

American literature begins with the literary products of the colonists, for in the seventeenth century may be found the key to much of what follows later. Regardless of the historical importance of the Southern colonies it is the Puritan ethic which has formed, possibly warped, the American soul. This is fully reflected in American poetry. The North-eastern colonists of the seventeenth century wrote pietistic verse which is far removed from the intellectual sophistication of Donne, Herbert or Marvell. They wrote for a purpose, and writing for a purpose has coloured the whole of American literature.

I have selected from the wealth of material provided by Jantz, Meserole, Morison and others a sample of what I consider to be the best verse of Anne Bradstreet and Edward Taylor, adding a dash of Michael Wigglesworth – for 'The Day of Doom' is an interesting historical document and also provides unwittingly entertaining reading. Contrary to the usual practice, I have allowed slightly more space to Anne Bradstreet than to Edward Taylor, for although Taylor is intellectually more substantial, his verses make hard going for all but the most dedicated reader. Anne Bradstreet's tender humanity is nearer to my heart. Earlier than Katherine Philips ('the matchless Orinda'), she is the first woman poet in the English language and her response to pioneer conditions is of documentary as well as poetic value.

Unlike Anne Bradstreet, Edward Taylor wrote in what might be called a metaphysical style – the result of isolation since he was, in fact, born eleven years after Dryden. Typically, he is the one poet who is rescued from the meagre pickings of seventeenth-century New England verse by American editors who compile anthologies with such titles as *Masters of American Literature*. To my mind, however, he is not a great poet and it does American literature a disservice to claim that he is so. As well as being physician to his community, Taylor was a Puritan preacher, and the range of his thought was limited by his embattled and lonely situation. His verse does not have the striking appeal and challenge of the English metaphysicals, whose style of far-fetched conceits he adopted. The seventeenth-century American could not afford to let any chink be seen in his armour. Otherwise there might penetrate not only lust and sloth, but Arminianism, Antinomianism, Quakerism, the terrifying possibility of there being an alternative attitude to life.

All this is revealed by a comparison of the poems of Bradstreet, Taylor, Wigglesworth, Tompson and the rest with the wealth of English poetry in the seventeenth century. Culturally speaking, colonies cannot be expected to compete with the motherland – that is self-evident, and one only suggests the comparison in order to let it be seen what Americans have had to contend with in becoming aware of – indeed developing – their own tradition. Perhaps the most important consequence of the peculiarly American combination of colonialism and Puritanism was that irony was scarcely available to the early Americans. There is no note in American poetry in the seventeenth century comparable to that of Herbert's 'The Pulley'. Not the making but the message primarily concerned the Puritan poet. From these seeds a garden was to grow, to which in time the seeds of other strains were added. But still the original Puritan plant persists, pervading the whole garden in which, perhaps, like Rappacini, only the American can exist unscathed.

In the eighteenth century there is still little enough to choose from in American poetry except Freneau, Barlow and the 'Connecticut Wits'. 'The Hasty Pudding' obviously owes something to 'The Rape of the Lock', but it has a robust, breezy quality which is quite unlike the waspishness of Pope. In Freneau we may also see the beginning of a conscious awareness of being American. He was one of the first to assert – even to the point of chauvinism – that the United States ought to draw upon her own strengths and not imitate the products of 'that damnable place'. Concealed beneath his eighteenth-century poetic diction there is a power of sympathy which is very far from the sentiments of the earlier Americans towards the 'black man' of the forests. Curiously enough, although the style is, like Taylor's, an anachronism (in an age of Crabbe, Blake, and Burns he has more in common with Prior, Pope or Gay), the sentiments are advanced for his age.

Building on Freneau's example, the first American poet of the nineteenth century, William Cullen Bryant, made one important contribution: he hymned the grandeur of the American forests and prairies. For the rest, he illustrates a strain in American poetry which could have been its downfall. 'Thanatopsis', that favourite anthology piece (replaced here by the superior 'The Prairies'), is curiously insipid, vaguely stoical. It is linked in tone with Emerson's transcendentalism rather than with the trenchant empiricism of Wordsworth's *Preface to the Lyrical Ballads*. In his lack of vitality, Bryant is also like Emerson and the rest of that race of gentle American aesthetes. There was an emotional anaemia in early nineteenth-century artistic and intellectual America which persisted long after the Civil War, even though in Whitman the vitality of American poetry had become clearly evident.

Nevertheless, the minor poets of the nineteenth century are important in their own special way. Poe, who wrote 'out of Time, out of mind', did so much for French poetry that he became that well-known French poet 'Edgarpo'. Bryant, Emerson and Thoreau, and those four designated by George Arms in *The Fields Were Green* as 'the Schoolroom Poets' (Longfellow, Whittier, Holmes and Lowell), also show another side of the American character. The latter two, in particular, are representative of what Holmes himself called the 'harmless, inoffensive, aristocracy of New England'. Their poetry shows that ability to convey a tone which I. A. Richards noted in Longfellow's 'In the Churchyard at Cambridge' when he said:

. . . if there is any character in poetry that modern readers – who derive their ideas of it rather from the best known poems of Wordsworth, Shelley and Keats or from our contemporaries, than from Dryden,

Pope or Cowper – are unprepared to encounter, it is this social, urbane, highly cultivated, self-confident, temperate and easy kind of humour.

This quality is something which is not easily found in the lusher pastures of the English nineteenth-century scene and cannot be discarded as merely a throwback to the English mood of the eighteenth century, for it is classicism in a nineteenth-century key – with an admixture of Yankee directness, good sense and honesty. Richards's perception gives considerable point to Auden's observation that: 'From Bryant on there is scarcely one American poet whose work, if unsigned, could be mistaken for that of an Englishman.' Even so, the distinctions are fine; only with Whitman does the difference between English and American verse become both dramatic and obvious.

As Mark Twain is the most American of American novelists so Whitman is the most American of American poets. It is not only a matter of tone or vocabulary; Whitman did not have 'poetic subjects'; he had something to say, the strength of which fills his work with such buoyant confidence that, despite his lapses and outrageous coinings, we are carried along on the wave of his rhetoric. Only an American poet would have had the gall to strike such an attitude and not care. As Randall Jarrell said in *Poetry and the Age*, 'Walt Whitman, he had his nerve.' Jarrell also spelt out the details of Whitman's more subtle achievements, how one must look behind the so-called 'catalogues' to the nature of the words themselves. So analysed, Whitman is revealed as a writer of great delicacy and deep human sympathy. This, combined with the enormous range of his reference and his capacity for detail, make him the first great original of the American scene. Charles Feidelson extended Americans' awareness of their own poetic individuality by making clear the nature of Whitman's symbolic act, the significance in his work of 'the voyaging ego'. When Whitman says 'See steamers steaming through my poems' he gives us these things; we become them. Not 'talking about' but presenting in living detail is the American artist's contribution to literature.

Emily Dickinson's work also exhibits in a quite remarkable way another aspect of the American contribution: the ability to shock us into an awareness of the extremity of human experience with a single phrase. She expresses the joys and sorrows of a single life, and such was her strength and such her insight that it is our lives which she mirrors.

A measure of Emily Dickinson's strength may be seen by comparing her work with that of the English woman poet who was born in the same year: Christina Georgina Rossetti. Rossetti's verse sings; it has a pleasing musical element. But in spite of the (no doubt) freshness of Rossetti's original perceptions, her verse is trifling, full of paraphernalia, images thought up to illustrate poetic attitudes. Emily Dickinson's concentrated phrases startle and shock the reader with their harshness. Not even Emily Brontë could approach this, for the English Emily – despite the fact that she was of the same stamp as Emily Dickinson and had a far harder life – never expressed in verse that jarring combination of terrifying atmosphere and exactly right sentiment which was Emily Dickinson's achievement.

Twentieth-century American poetry begins with Edwin Arlington Robinson. His contribution to the development of a native American style may be found in such poems as 'Isaac and Archibald' which, but for its excessive length, I should have included in this volume. As an exemplar, this poem is interesting both as a product of New England ten years before the freer style of the 'Chicago Renaissance' and as a forerunner of the conversational manner represented half a century later by Robert Mezey's 'My Mother' or Charles Bukowski's 'don't come round but if you do'. Robinson's diction is nearer to the note of American speech than the hypnotic Biblical cadences of Whitman. In prose, this note is found in *Huckleberry Finn* which – as Hemingway was fond of telling us – was the one book out of which all subsequent American literature came. Certainly, it is the heart-note of American utterance, the making over into memorable speech of what Tocqueville was referring to when he said: 'It is not then to the written but to the spoken language that attention must be paid if we would detect the modification which the idiom of an aristocratic people may undergo when it becomes the language of a democracy.'

This is the main line of American writing, in verse as much as in prose. American literature may have its other facet: the contribution of Henry James or of Wallace Stevens, but, in reverse of history, the redskins – to use Philip Rahv's half-ironical categories – seem to have triumphed over the palefaces. This fact might confidently have been predicted from the beginning by a process of deduction such as Tocqueville so brilliantly formulated, but it is the inductive examination of the historical facts which supplies the proof. Even at their most sophisticated, the Americans are more down-to-earth, less 'literary' than the English. In this context Robert Frost's deceptively quiet verse marks a further step towards the achievement of a native American voice in poetry.

Apart from the work of Robinson and Frost, the major American contribution in the early years of the twentieth century lay in the pioneering work of Pound and Eliot. They were the great instigators of 'modern' poetry; they made available a new poetic style, different in its range and cultural references from anything which had gone before.

Part of what they stood for may be found in the manifesto of Imagism, an Anglo–American literary movement produced under the aegis of another influential literary figure of the years before the First World War, Amy Lowell:

(1) To use the language of common speech, but to employ always the exact word, not the merely decorative word.

(2) To create new rhythms – as the expression of new moods. We do not insist upon 'free verse' as the only method of writing poetry ... We do believe that the individuality of a poet may often be better expressed in free verse than in conventional forms.

(3) To allow absolute freedom in the choice of subject.

(4) To present an image (hence the name 'Imagist'). We are not a school of painters, but we believe that poetry should render particulars exactly and not deal in vague generalities however magnificent and sonorous.

(5) To produce poetry that is hard and clear, never blurred or indefinite.

(6) Finally, most of us believe that concentration is the very essence of poetry.

Pound's spirit, however, could not – any more than Wordsworth's in his time – be bounded by the rigidity of a theory. Only perhaps in the work of H. D. do we find Imagism unsullied by personality. But personality, T. S. Eliot notwithstanding, is what makes the work of a poet distinctive. Pound's distinction could be seen from the first. He 'struck through the mask'; he showed that poetry was life and not merely a part of life; and he insisted on the greatest models and the highest traditions. He was – like so many other American literary artists – the teacher *par excellence*; he came, like some poetic messiah, to show the way.

And show the way he did, to a generation of poets who did not wish to cling to the outworn conventions and stereotyped subjects of the past. One in particular who was indebted to him was T. S. Eliot, for whom he was '*il miglior fabbro*', the man who helped forge 'The Waste Land'. But there were others who had reason to be grateful to Pound, and not merely in a literary way. He was the great befriender, scornful of hypocrisy, but genuinely helpful to all who needed help. Whether his un-American activities during the Second World War and his anti-Semitism were errors of judgement or morality, one cannot fault him in friendship or generosity.

The young Pound maintained a constant communication both with the advanced and experimental writers of continental Europe and with those back home who were working for the same cause. In Chicago, for example, Harriet Monroe had founded *Poetry* in 1912 and was doing her best to encourage creative activity in middle-America. Not that her taste was always Pound's taste. It is not, for example, recorded that Pound had much of an opinion of the poets of the so-called 'Middle Western Renaissance': Vachel Lindsay, Edgar Lee Masters and Carl Sandburg.

Rebecca West wrote an appreciative little book about Sandburg in the twenties and it is true that, in the light of the insipid neo-Georgian-ism and Sitwellian play-acting which seemed to dominate the English scene, there was a certain brash mixture of the laconic and the histrionic about Sandburg which must have been appealing. There has always been an attraction for the English in the kind of personality which Sandburg represented. He was a great 'character', who celebrated the might of Chicago, 'the broad acres' and the people of the Middle West. Yet in retrospect it is Masters (of the *Spoon River Anthology*) who is revealed as being the most important of the three; even Vachel Lindsay's thundering metres ('The Congo', 'Simon Legree', 'General William Booth Enters Into Heaven') now seem more acceptable than Sandburg's hollow invocations or folksy anecdotes.

The real strength of poetry in the United States, however, lay not in regionalism but in the degree to which her major poets could make an impact on the international scene. In this connection no others were so important in the twenties as Pound and Eliot. Robinson was well-known only in America, and Frost, at first, only in England. As time went by, however, it was to become increasingly clear that two more had to be reckoned as major. The first was Wallace Stevens; the second William Carlos Williams.

In the thirties, a decade after Stevens's first book, *Harmonium*, was published, Louis Untermeyer could assert that his poems had 'little relation to any human struggle'. On the contrary; Stevens's contribution goes very deep. All his life he was interested in the profoundest problems of human existence, problems which transcend national boundaries or immediate social necessities: the nature of apprehended reality and its relation to the creative imagination, and the problem of belief and order. He was a meditative poet and while he was capable of the most vivid sensual images he never used them at random or in excess of their immediate poetic relevance. His images, like his thought, are complex and relate closely to the syntax of his verse – and so his clear grammatical structure and exact use of words are a great help in understanding the more difficult poems.

A lawyer for an insurance firm in Hartford, Connecticut for nearly forty years of his life, Stevens negotiated the world of business with the same authority which invests his poems. Behind what seemed to Untermeyer a charming example of Connecticut rococo, there stands a toughness and seriousness of mind that is equalled only by T. S. Eliot. His poetic manner runs from the extravagant rhetoric of 'The Comedian as the Letter C' to the subtle seriousness of 'Notes Toward a Supreme Fiction'.

This long and difficult poem deals with the basic philosophical and spiritual imperatives towards which Stevens had been moving all his life. The imagination, in its attempt to abstract truth, brings up the idea of 'major man' – not the exceptional man, like the 'MacCullough', but the best in every man. Change, as Stevens pointed out in 'Sunday Morning', is not merely a bringer of death, but a source of vital freshness. We must celebrate life by a constant and amazed delight in the unexpectedness of each moment. The 'order' that we seek must be flexible, organic, partaking of the freshness of transformation. Through the aesthetic experience Stevens explored the possibility of a new epistemology, pushing the boundaries of poetic communication to a new limit. His poetry is a controlled jugglery of parenthetical, qualifying, and extending impressions, to which no commentary could do justice for, as Stevens saw so clearly, poetry 'is the subject of the poem', it 'must defeat the intelligence almost successfully'. Whatever qualifications one might feel called upon to make about Stevens's final contribution, his poetry begins where other good verse leaves us, in a state of heightened awareness.

To come from Stevens to the world of Williams is like coming from Parnassus into the market place. Williams wrote the kind of verse which the average man would have written if the average man could write. His poems read like notes or, as they sometimes were, jottings on the back of a prescription pad:

> *This Is Just to Say*
> I have eaten
> the plums
> that were in
> the icebox
>
> and which
> you were probably
> saving
> for breakfast
>
> Forgive me
> they were delicious
> so sweet
> and so cold

From this poem follows so much of the writing of the sixties and seventies; but it took a long time for the message to get through. Although Williams had been publishing since 1909 it was only after the Second World War, with the appearance of *Paterson*, Book I in 1946 and the *Collected Later Poems* and *Collected Earlier Poems* of 1950 and 1951 that it became clear that Williams was a force to be reckoned with in a far more radical way than had previously been supposed. This was at least true in the United States – less so in England, where to many his verse still 'tasted like sawdust in the mouth'.

The difficulty lay in the rhythm and form of communication. Although it was not quite true that Williams got his speech 'from the mouths of Polish mothers', as he maintained, he certainly followed his own voice-pattern, as later American poets (e.g. Olson and Creeley) have been doing. This, of course, was a radical departure for, in spite of the advances which had been made in the art of poetic communication since Robinson and Frost, Pound and Eliot, a certain transformation had always been felt necessary in order to turn what men actually said or thought into 'literature'. And with the art of 'making into literature' there had gone the idea of memorable utterance, a series of phrase-patterns which had some relation to what had always been regarded as the 'poetic line'. Not that modern poets (not good ones, anyway) ever attempted to write like Milton or Keats, but at least there was still an idea of a certain kind of 'beauty' at the back of their minds. Williams makes no compromise whatsoever with beauty. His verse is 'anti-poetic': factual, visual, simple – sometimes banal, un-mellifluous to the point of being prosy, if not prosaic. The form is direct; it makes no concession to 'poetic music'. Dr Williams was in more senses than one an 'objectivist'. Not only did he put objects in his poems; he also had his eye on the object, on the thing to be said. The way in which that thing was said emerged organically, like a Henry Moore sculpture from the grain of the stone.

Like Williams, E. E. Cummings, born a generation later, embraced nature and naturalness, although, unlike Williams, he retained to the end a certain element of whimsy. Some of the most celebrated poems, like 'my father moved through dooms of love', are not entirely free from this strain. He was also a little too ready to use 'stock response' emotive words. R. P. Blackmur counted 'flower' forty-eight times in Cummings's first book, *Tulips and Chimneys* (1923), and twenty-one times in *Etcetera* (1925). His conclusion was that 'it must contain for him an almost unlimited variety and extent of meaning ... The question is whether or not the reader can possibly have shared the experience which Mr Cummings has had of the word.' Words like 'thrilling', 'delicious', or 'bright' also come very readily to Cummings's pen.

Cummings is at his best in the poems which reflect, without pressure on the reader, his ear for common speech. A good example is the one which begins 'ygUDuh'. Others are 'plato told', 'my sweet old etcetera', and the touching 'this little bride & groom are'. Right through his poetic career he could at his best achieve the perfection of the late 'the little horse is newLY', in which he conveys a simple yet powerful emotional state skilfully and poignantly. Where his contribution may be most important for the poetry of the seventies, however, is in the typographical experiments. Here the typography is part of the poem itself, so that we have an early twentieth-century example of 'concrete poetry' (an antecedent may be the emblematic poems of the seventeenth century). In many cases the poem cannot be read aloud at all; it must be seen on the page.

Another poet who has especial significance for the contemporary period is Marianne Moore. T. S. Eliot compared Miss Moore's verse with certain eighteenth-century poetry like Gray's 'Elegy', in which 'the scene described is a point of departure for meditations on one thing or another'. What appeals today is not merely her dry scholarly wit but, more particularly, her syllabic counting and the engagingly matter-of-fact tone of her educated speech rhythms:

> There is a great amount of poetry in unconscious
> fastidiousness. Certain Ming
>   products, imperial floor-coverings of coach-
> wheel yellow, are well enough in their way but I have
>   seen something
> that I like better – a
>   mere childish attempt to make an imperfectly
>   ballasted animal stand up,

> similar determination to make a pup
> eat his meat from the plate.

Miss Moore, it will be seen, was also, like Stevens, a proponent of the '*ding an sich*', or perhaps – in her call for poets to be 'literalists of the imagination' and to present 'imaginary gardens with real toads in them' – nearer to the 'no ideas but in things' theory of Williams.

One or two other names from the rich period of the twenties must be mentioned before we pass on to the poetry of the thirties. The 'Fugitives' were a group who took their name from a little magazine, *The Fugitive*, edited in Nashville, Tennessee from 1922–5. The founders of the 'movement' were John Crowe Ransom, Allen Tate, Donald Davidson, and Merrill Moore. Later, there came 'Agrarianism', a call for the South to defend its own values, the founding of the *Southern Review*, edited at Baton Rouge, Louisiana by Cleanth Brooks and Robert Penn Warren, and then the *Kenyon Review*, edited by Ransom from Kenyon College, Gambier, Ohio. From this group also sprang the 'New Criticism' and the textbooks of Brooks and Warren, which were to have such an effect on American university education in the years immediately following the Second World War. Of the 'Fugitives', Warren continues to mine a rich vein of verse. *Incarnations* (1968) shows that Warren – who is of course well-known as a novelist – was writing better poetry in his sixties than he was in his thirties.

A radically different poet, Hart Crane, however, emerged in the later twenties. Born in 1899 in Garrettsville, Ohio, the son of a well-to-do manufacturer, he had an unhappy home life and little formal education. He committed suicide in 1932 by jumping overboard from a ship returning from Mexico. His first book came at a time when 'The Waste Land' was making its greatest impact and Crane's reaction was that he wished to 'move toward a more positive, or (if I may put it so in a sceptical age) ecstatic goal'. 'When I speak,' he wrote to Harriet Monroe, 'of "adagios of islands" the reference is to the motion of the boat through islands clustered thickly ... And it seems a much more direct and creative statement than any more "logical" employment of words such as "coasting slowly through the islands".' The battle had already been won – by Rimbaud, by Mallarmé, by the Dadaists and Surrealists – but writing as Crane was in an American context, he had to fight the good fight all over again. The result of his isolation was, at times, too much verbiage, a wildness which arises from a subconscious attempt to counteract the residual pieties of Puritanism.

The Bridge was a peculiarly American compromise. It arose out of Crane's sense of the grandeur of man's material achievements in the twentieth century; yet he tried also to express his sense of an accompanying flowering of the spirit. The ostensible subject is Brooklyn Bridge, but the bridge of Crane's vision is also a bridge between centuries and between men, a Whitmanesque dream of brotherhood. 'I found,' said Crane, 'that I was really building a bridge between so-called classical experience and many divergent realities of our seething confused cosmos of today.' In eight parts he presents an array of panoramas and insights ranging from the time of Captain John Smith to the Depression.

There is something in the cultural atmosphere of the United States which has made Americans try the big thing. It can be seen in the novel, from *Moby-Dick* to *Of Time and the River*, and in poetry, from *The Columbiad*, through 'Song of Myself', the *Cantos* and *The Bridge* to *Paterson*. In their different forms these poems have the impertinence to speak for humanity. One is awed as much by the pretension as by the effort that it cost. Crane, of course, with his half-baked symbolism and his attitudinizing ('I am Baudelaire, I am Whitman, I am Christopher Marlowe, I am Christ') has more bravado and less justification for it than his masters. Nevertheless, it is surprising how much he was able to get away with and how good he could be when he was not trying too hard, as in the lyrics of 'Voyages'.

The importance of Pound, Eliot, Stevens and Williams, of E. E. Cummings, Marianne Moore and Hart Crane, tends to obscure the fact that Conrad Aiken, H. D. and Robinson Jeffers made their own special contribution. Although – apart from H. D. – they have become unfashionable in the seventies, they are by no means negligible poets. Jeffers, in particular, has great power and individuality. Living and writing in California, the hawk and the rock became his symbols ('I'd sooner, except the penalties, kill a man than a hawk . . .'). He reacted violently against certain aspects of twentieth-century life ('The orange-peel, eggshells, papers, pieces of clothing, the clots/Of dung in corners of the rock . . .'). Beside the 'intense and terrible beauty of nature' he saw man, in his present state, to be futile and depraved.

Finally, there cannot go unrecorded the phenomenon of the 'Harlem Renaissance'. Although, technically, there is nothing new about the poets who emerged from this movement, what is important is that, for the first time, the black man in America showed a militant racial consciousness. Langston Hughes and Countee Cullen were the forerunners of the highly vocal Etheridge Knight, Imamu Amiri Baraka, Don L. Lee, Sonia Sanchez and Nikki Giovanni.

There is little in American poetry of the thirties to parallel the political commitment of the so-called 'Pylon Poets' in England. It is true that many American writers turned to radicalism, or even joined the Communist Party, but they were for the most part not poets. There are no Audens, Spenders, Day Lewises, or MacNeices on the American scene; only Archibald MacLeish, invoking the 'social muse', and Kenneth Fearing, the Ring Lardner of American verse. Like Lardner, Fearing avoids sentimentality, in 'Dirge' celebrating a Depression death with:

> Denouement to denouement, he took a personal pride in the
>   certain, certain way he lived his own, private life,
> But nevertheless, they shut off his gas; nevertheless, the bank
>   foreclosed; nevertheless, the landlord called; nevertheless,
>   the radio broke,

In the forties the chief 'war poets' were Richard Eberhart, Karl Shapiro and Randall Jarrell. Shapiro's *V-Letter*, written when he was a soldier in the Pacific, won a Pulitzer Prize in 1944. Jarrell's 'The Death of the Ball Turret Gunner' is as stark a comment as any to emerge from the Second World War:

From my mother's sleep I fell into the State,
And I hunched in its belly till my wet fur froze.
Six miles from earth, loosed from its dream of life,
I woke to black flak and the nightmare fighters.
When I died they washed me out of the turret with a hose.

Like Elizabeth Bishop, Theodore Roethke and Delmore Schwartz, these poets also wrote well on subjects unconnected with the war. But newer, younger poets were emerging who were to appear the brightest talents of the fifties: John Berryman, Robert Lowell and Richard Wilbur. This was the age of 'fine writing', when, it seemed, no American poet could write badly, and when Wallace Stevens was the hero of the American scene.

Below the surface in the fifties, however, a revolution was taking shape. Under the leadership of Charles Olson, rector of Black Mountain College in North Carolina, a number of poets including Robert Creeley, Robert Duncan, Ed Dorn and Paul Blackburn developed an 'open-field' verse which they saw to be the answer to the domination of the 'New Criticism'. For the Black Mountain poets Pound and Williams were the chief gods. At the same time the 'Beat' poets, although subscribing, like those of the Black Mountain, to the idea of a more 'open' verse, sounded a more ecstatic, apocalyptic note. In their opposition to authority and formalism Allen Ginsberg, Gregory Corso and Lawrence Ferlinghetti followed Williams more than Pound. Ferlinghetti established the City Lights Press so that the work of the 'Beats' might gain the audience which it could not find in the literary magazines, just as the Black Mountain poets sought their own outlets in the *Black Mountain Review* and *Origin*. Olson's 'Maximus' poems were first published by Jonathan Williams's Jargon Press. Throughout this period such prestigious reviews as *Hudson* and *Sewanee* refused to admit that anything except 'academic' verse could be critically acceptable – at least, that is how the story is told by the Beat and Black Mountain poets.

The Beats, originally from New York, established themselves in San Francisco, where Kenneth Rexroth had been publishing for many years. Robert Duncan also became associated with this group and, later, Gary Snyder, who was to spend some time in Japan. The new note was sounded by Ginsberg's 'Howl'. The experiences of which the Beats wrote were private, visionary. They openly embraced drugs and hallucination, using words and experiences which were shocking to an audience accustomed to good taste and felicity of expression.

In New York in the fifties a quite different group of poets were mounting their own attack on good taste. The leaders of the 'New York School' were Kenneth Koch, Frank O'Hara and John Ashbery. Intensely interested in the art of Pollock and de Kooning, like them they attacked accepted styles and received values. Koch parodied Robert Frost in 'Mending Sump'. In 'To the Film Industry in Crisis' O'Hara ('Not you, lean quarterlies and swarthy periodicals . . .') ends his first verse with an invocation to:

> . . . you, Motion Picture Industry,
> it's you I love!

It was during this period that Robert Lowell made a distinction between poetry which was 'cooked' and poetry which came 'raw'. But the proponents of the 'cooked' – Robert Lowell himself among them – acknowledged the dawn of a new era by changing their styles to accommodate the new taste for 'open verse'. The difference between the highly wrought 'The Quaker Graveyard at Nantucket' and almost any of the poems in *Life Studies* (1959) is dramatic. Also, in the latter volume Lowell made use of the material of his own life, inviting the description of 'confessional' poet.

Most of the poets who were accepted as important in the fifties seem to have gained something from the Beat and Black Mountain initiative. Theodore Roethke's style became more open and discursive; Richard Wilbur was found to be using, in *Walking to Sleep* (1969), the broken line of William Carlos Williams; John Berryman seemed sometimes to be competing with Lowell (or vice versa) in his haste to change from the tortured style of *The Dispossessed*. Not that the superb *Dream Songs* bear any overt resemblance to the products of the Black Mountain or the Beat poets; the influences were as subtle as they were profound. It was something in the conditions of American life that these poets were becoming attuned to, something which the Black Mountain and Beat poets had picked up earlier and responded to more wildly and extremely.

During the sixties the Beats, who had at first seemed so outrageous, settled into the public consciousness. They no longer had to be published by small presses. In fact, as a group they ceased to have any real existence, Ginsberg emerging clearly as the outstanding talent. In a similar way, after the end of Black Mountain College as an experiment in the later fifties, the Black Mountain poets took on separate identities. Robert Creeley, Robert Duncan and Ed Dorn have their own special – and probably different – followings. Olson, in particular, has become a cult-figure, a rallying-point for those who are as much interested in the reform of society as in literature.

Olson is a difficult case. He was, in every sense, a big man and if a man has the confidence to think and act big he will almost certainly have followers. Taking his lead from Pound's *Cantos* and Williams's *Paterson*, Olson wrote the Maximus poems, based on Gloucester, Massachusetts. As Maximus he uses his Gloucester base to explore the geography, history, anthropology and archaeology of the region. Unfortunately, however, he did not have Pound's power or Williams's human sympathy – or the talent of either of them, so that the result too often reads like *pastiche*. It is perhaps not remarkable that he acquired a following in the universities since, if the reader lack the sensibility to tell the real from the imitation, there is always the *study* of poetry – and that can be undertaken without critical discrimination. For such readers what Olson is saying seems to be eminently on the right lines and, in the light of what they take to be the 'true' nature and direction of verse in our time, his essay on 'Projective Verse' (1950) is a key document. It is not easy to follow Olson into all the ramifications of his argument. However, the main points are as follows.

Olson begins by making a distinction between 'open' or 'projective' verse on the one hand and 'closed' or 'non-projective' verse on the other. 'Closed' verse is verse 'which print bred'. It requires a different 'stance toward reality' from 'composition by field'. From the moment a poet ventures into FIELD COMPOSITION he can 'go by no track other than the one the poem under hand declares for itself'.

Form, for the projective poet, is 'NEVER MORE THAN AN EXTENSION OF CONTENT'; that is the principle. The process can be 'boiled down to one statement,' says Olson, '(first pounded into my head by Edward Dahlberg): ONE PERCEPTION MUST IMMEDIATELY AND DIRECTLY LEAD TO A FURTHER PERCEPTION.'

The poetic line, Olson maintains, comes 'from the breath, from the breathing of the man who writes, at the moment that he writes'. He speaks of the LAW OF THE LINE which projective verse creates and which must be 'hewn to, obeyed'. The conventions 'which logic has forced on syntax must be broken open as quietly as must the too set feet of the old line'.

Twenty years after Olson wrote this essay a new generation of theorists has emerged. Among the most outspoken of them is David Antin who, in support of Olson's theory and practice, directs his main attack against 'modernism'. Olson's importance has not been recognized until now, he maintains, because unlike 'Eliot, Tate, Lowell, and so on' he did not 'occupy a trivial moral space'.

The followers of Olson are both exclusive and full of moral fervour; they have the fanaticism of Maoists. When one turns from their theories to the artefacts which they support, however, there is some discrepancy. Olson, according to Antin:

will seek to articulate vowel music, to play upon patterned contrasts between tense and lax vowels, or compact and diffuse vowels, or vowels with higher and/or lower pitched prominent formants, to dispose of these under varying conditions of tenseness or laxness, or brevity or length in the environment of differentially closed, or closed versus open, syllables, under varying accentual conditions resulting from different position in words, in word groups, in sentences and whole segments of discourse. To this Olson adds a final discrimination in the notation of pausal juncture, and of shifts of attention and general speaking tempo and pulse.

Yet Olson's poetry is often as opaque to the feelings as it is to the intelligence. There is an illogicality at the heart of the argument. This is that the adoption of the 'correct techniques', the 'right stance' towards literature in our time will necessarily produce good verse. Underlying this assumption is a socio-politico-economic view of writing. With literature as an art in itself, with quality of sensibility, with understanding of the divine power of the creator to produce a poem which transcends theories and philosophies it is not concerned. If this is the spirit of the age into which we are being led then literature is to be the handmaiden of ideas. Worthy as the political aim may be ('a poetry broad enough and deep enough to embody the universal condition', 'the consideration of the poetry of non-literate and partially literate cultures') it might be doubted whether the product so insisted upon would always be guaranteed to create in us that sense of truth and delight which has been the mark of the best poetry for two thousand years.

At the same time, however, it would be foolish to deny the influence of the followers of 'projective verse'. When Leslie Fiedler calls for a 'Post Modernist' criticism he is recognizing the importance of the shift which has taken place since the fifties, not a little of it due to the Black Mountain school – some also to the example of the Beat poets. We have, says Fiedler: 'entered quite another time, apocalyptic, anti-rational, blatantly romantic and sentimental; an age dedicated to joyous and prophetic irresponsibility; one, at any rate, distasteful of self-protective irony and too great self-awareness.'

The key to this observation may be found in the last phrase. However exaggerated the theories of Olson and Antin may be, it is clear that contemporary American poetry owes little to the poetry and criticism of T. S. Eliot or to the theory and practice of the 'New Critics' who dominated the American poetic scene in the forties and fifties.

For my own part, as a follower neither of the 'projective verse' school nor of any other, I acknowledge their importance only in so far as they have cleared the air and liberated American poets, whatever their affiliations. It is poets who matter. In the end, I suspect, it is William Carlos Williams and he alone who is responsible for the great change which has come over American verse. However important Pound may have been, one cannot write 'like' Pound – as Olson has clearly shown. One can write like Williams – not always very well, perhaps, but sometimes not all that badly. It is his example, his 'reply to Greek and Latin with the bare hands', which in the end, after fifty or more years, has shown the way for a generation of poets who in their differing styles project the American voice in poetry.

This 'new' American poetry is not musical in the traditional English sense. It does not have what Eliot called 'auditory imagination'; it creates a different kind of reverberation in the mind, projecting the sound of American speech: harsh, direct, ironical, obtaining its effects by timing, catching the cultural echoes and references which the tang of idiom brings with it. It is not calculated to appeal to the English ear. Although it is written in what seems to be the same language, it has different references, different cadences and pitches. Its echoes may be found in Ginsberg, in the throw-away line, the laconic phrase which connotes a much wider area of sensibility than it denotes:

> America I'm putting my queer shoulder to the wheel.

or

> I saw you, Walt Whitman, childless, lonely old grubber,
> poking among the meats in the refrigerator and eyeing
> the grocery boys . . .

They may be found in the fractured idiom of Berryman:

> There sat down, once, a thing on Henry's heart
> só heavy, if he had a hundred years
> & more, & weeping, sleepless, in all them time
> Henry could not make good.
> Starts again always in Henry's ears
> the little cough somewhere, an odour, a chime.

or Creeley's 'The Operation':

> By Saturday I said you would be better on Sunday
> The insistence was a part of a reconciliation.
>
> Your eyes bulged, the grey
> light hung on you, you were hideous.

My involvement is just an old
habitual relationship.

Cruel, cruel to describe
what there is no reason to describe.

However, I find what I am seeking to define as clearly in less cele-
brated contemporary poets – in William Stafford, for example, in
Weldon Kees, in Reed Whittemore, in Robert Bly, Galway Kinnell,
James Wright, Gary Snyder, and in Charles Bukowski:

I mean if I don't answer
I don't answer, and the reason is
that I am not yet ready to kill you
or love you, or even accept you,
it means I don't want to talk
I am busy, I am mad, I am glad
or maybe I'm stringing up a rope;
so even if the lights are on
and you hear sound
like breathing or praying or singing
a radio or the roll of dice
or typing –
go away, it is not the day
the night, the hour;
it is not the ignorance of impoliteness
I wish to hurt nothing, not even a bug
but sometimes I gather evidence of a kind
that takes some sorting,
and your blue eyes, be they blue
and your hair, if you have some
or your mind – they cannot enter
until the rope is cut or knotted
or until I have shaven into
new mirrors, until the wound is
stopped or opened
                    forever

I would not claim for any of the poems quoted that they gave evidence of greatness in the old sense. That is not the point. What I am talking about is the language which they use, the vehicle which they provide for a kind of poetic communication which is not yet possible in Britain. Perhaps, before it is, society itself must change. British poets – with one or two honourable exceptions – go to one extreme or the other, producing either a false chumminess or a form of poetic language which arises from striking an attitude. Whichever way, the note is off-key. We are told by little-Englanders that the chief thing wrong with our society is that it has been 'Americanized', as if Americans were responsible for all the ills of the world. Perhaps what is wrong is that it has not been Americanized enough, if by 'American' is meant the ability to communicate without pretension, without self-consciousness and with perfect assurance of the truth and value of what is being said. As W. H. Auden put it: 'One comes across passages, even in very fine English poets, which make one think: "Yes, very effective, but does he believe what he is saying?": in American poetry such passages are extremely rare.'

The University of Hull
1976   GEOFFREY MOORE

ACKNOWLEDGEMENTS

I should like to express my gratitude to Mrs Christine Gibbons for preparing the manuscript with typical care and accuracy and to Michael Woolf for his unfailing willingness to help in the early stages of the book. My special thanks are due to Peter Easy, without whose devoted assistance with the texts, bibliographies and proofs my task would have been immeasurably more arduous.   G.M.

Note on the Text

I have followed American texts throughout, using those of the most accurate scholarly editions wherever available. In the great majority of poems, therefore, spellings follow the American pattern. If there are occasional inconsistencies, this is because the poets are inconsistent. Some, like Pound and Lowell, use English spellings; others, like Allen Tate, employ English and American interchangeably – sometimes even in the same poem. Wherever else the reader finds oddities of spelling or punctuation (e.g. Whitman's 'naivetè' and 'Kanadian' and some of the usages of the seventeenth century poets), this is what the poet wrote. This is also true of such later poets as Emily Dickinson, whose idiosyncrasies of syntax and punctuation are not merely quaint but meaningful.

Anne Bradstreet 1612—72

The Author to her Book

Thou ill-form'd offspring of my feeble brain,
Who after birth did'st by my side remain,
Till snatcht from thence by friends, less wise then true
Who thee abroad expos'd to publick view,
Made thee in raggs, halting to th' press to trudg,
Where errors were not lessened (all may judg)
At thy return my blushing was not small,
My rambling brat (in print) should mother call,
I cast thee by as one unfit for light,
Thy Visage was so irksome in my sight;
Yet being mine own, at length affection would
Thy blemishes amend, if so I could:
I wash'd thy face, but more defects I saw
And rubbing off a spot, still made a flaw.
I stretcht thy joynts to make thee even feet,
Yet still thou run'st more hobling then is meet;
In better dress to trim thee was my mind,
But nought save home-spun Cloth, i'th' house I find
In this array, 'mongst Vulgars mayst thou roam
In Criticks hands, beware thou dost not come;
And take thy way where yet thou art not known,
If for thy Father askt, say, thou hadst none:
And for thy Mother, she alas is poor,
Which caus'd her thus to send thee out of door.

The Flesh and the Spirit

In secret place where once I stood
Close by the Banks of *Lacrim* flood
I heard two sisters reason on
Things that are past, and things to come;
One flesh was call'd, who had her eye
On worldly wealth and vanity;
The other Spirit, who did rear
Her thoughts unto a higher sphere:
Sister, quoth Flesh, what liv'st thou on
Nothing but Meditation?
Doth Contemplation feed thee so
Regardlesly to let earth goe?
Can Speculation satisfy
Notion without Reality?
Dost dream of things beyond the Moon
And dost thou hope to dwell there soon?
Hast treasures there laid up in store
That all in th' world thou count'st but poor?
Art fancy sick; or turn'd a Sot
To catch at shadowes which are not?
Come, come, Ile shew unto thy sence,
Industry hath its recompence.
What canst desire, but thou maist see
True substance in variety?
Doth honour like? acquire the same,
As some to their immortal fame:
And trophyes to thy name erect
Which wearing time shall ne're deject.
For riches dost thou long full sore?
Behold enough of precious store.
Earth hath more silver, pearls and gold,
Then eyes can see, or hands can hold.
Affect's thou pleasure? take thy fill,

Earth hath enough of what you will.
Then let not goe, what thou maist find,
For things unknown, only in mind.
Spir: Be still thou unregenerate part,
Disturb no more my setled heart,
For I have vow'd (and so will doe)
Thee as a foe, still to pursue.
And combate with thee will and must,
Untill I see thee laid in th' dust.
Sisters we are, ye[a] twins we be,
Yet deadly feud 'twixt thee and me;
For from one father are we not,
Thou by old Adam wast begot,
But my arise is from above,
Whence my dear father I do love.
Thou speakst me fair, but hatst me sore,
Thy flatt'ring shews Ile trust no more.
How oft thy slave, hast thou me made,
When I believ'd, what thou hast said,
And never had more cause of woe
Then when I did what thou bad'st doe.
Ile stop mine ears at these thy charms,
And count them for my deadly harms.
Thy sinfull pleasures I doe hate,
Thy riches are to me no bait,
Thine honours doe, nor will I love;
For my ambition lyes above.
My greatest honour it shall be
When I am victor over thee,
And triumph shall, with laurel head,
When thou my Captive shalt be led,
How I do live, thou need'st not scoff,
For I have meat thou know'st not off;
The hidden Manna I doe eat,
The word of life it is my meat.
My thoughts do yield me more content

Then can thy hours in pleasure spent.
Nor are they shadows which I catch,
Nor fancies vain at which I snatch,
But reach at things that are so high,
Beyond thy dull Capacity;
Eternal substance I do see,
With which inriched I would be:
Mine Eye doth pierce the heavens, and see
What is Invisible to thee.
My garments are not silk nor gold,
Nor such like trash which Earth doth hold,
But Royal Robes I shall have on,
More glorious then the glistring Sun;
My Crown not Diamonds, Pearls, and gold,
But such as Angels heads infold.
The City where I hope to dwell,
There's none on Earth can parallel;
The stately Walls both high and strong,
Are made of pretious *Jasper* stone;
The Gates of Pearl, both rich and clear,
And Angels are for Porters there;
The Streets thereof transparent gold,
Such as no Eye did e're behold,
A Chrystal River there doth run,
Which doth proceed from the Lambs Throne:
Of Life, there are the waters sure,
Which shall remain for ever pure,
Nor Sun, nor Moon, they have no need,
For glory doth from God proceed:
No Candle there, nor yet Torch light,
For there shall be no darksome night.
From sickness and infirmity,
For evermore they shall be free,
Nor withering age shall e're come there,
But beauty shall be bright and clear;
This City pure is not for thee,

For things unclean there shall not be:
If I of Heaven may have my fill,
Take thou the world, and all that will.

From *Contemplations*

18

When I behold the heavens as in their prime,
And then the earth (though old) stil clad in green,
The stones and trees, insensible of time,
Nor age nor wrinkle on their front are seen;
If winter come, and greeness then do fade,
A Spring returns, and they more youthfull made;
But Man grows old, lies down, remains where once he's laid.

20 [19]

By birth more noble then those creatures all,
Yet seems by nature and by custome curs'd,
No sooner born, but grief and care makes fall
That state obliterate he had at first:
Nor youth, nor strength, nor wisdom spring again
Nor habitations long their names retain,
But in oblivion to the final day remain.

20

Shall I then praise the heavens, the trees, the earth
Because their beauty and their strength last longer
Shall I wish there, or never to had birth,
Because they're bigger, and their bodyes stronger?
Nay, they shall darken, perish, fade and dye,
And when unmade, so ever shall they lye,
But man was made for endless immortality.

To My Dear and Loving Husband

If ever two were one, then surely we.
If ever man were lov'd by wife, then thee;
If ever wife was happy in a man,
Compare with me ye women if you can.
I prize thy love more than whole Mines of gold,
Or all the riches that the East doth hold.
My love is such that Rivers cannot quench,
Nor ought but love from thee, give recompence.
Thy love is such I can no way repay,
The heavens reward thee manifold I pray.
Then while we live, in love lets so persever,
That when we live no more, we may live ever.

Here followes some verses upon the burning of our House, July 10th, 1666. Copyed out of a loose Paper

In silent night when rest I took,
For sorrow neer I did not look,
I waken'd was with thundring nois
And Piteous shreiks of dreadfull voice.
That fearfull sound of fire and fire,
Let no man know is my Desire.

I, starting up, the light did spye,
And to my God my heart did cry
To strengthen me in my Distresse
And not to leave me succourlesse.
Then coming out beheld a space,
The flame consume my dwelling place.

And, when I could no longer look,
I blest his Name that gave and took,

That layd my goods now in the dust:
Yea so it was, and so 'twas just.
It was his own: it was not mine;
Far be it that I should repine.

He might of All justly bereft,
But yet sufficient for us left.
When by the Ruines oft I past,
My sorrowing eyes aside did cast,
And here and there the places spye
Where oft I sate, and long did lye.

Here stood that Trunk, and there that chest;
There lay that store I counted best:
My pleasant things in ashes lye,
And them behold no more shall I.
Under thy roof no guest shall sitt,
Nor at thy Table eat a bitt.

No pleasant tale shall 'ere be told,
Nor things recounted done of old.
No Candle 'ere shall shine in Thee,
Nor bridegroom's voice ere heard shall bee.
In silence ever shalt thou lye;
Adeiu, Adeiu; All's vanity.

Then streight I 'gin my heart to chide,
And did thy wealth on earth abide?
Didst fix thy hope on mouldring dust,
The arm of flesh didst make thy trust?
Raise up thy thoughts above the skye
That dunghill mists away may flie.

Thou hast an house on high erect,
Fram'd by that mighty Architect,
With glory richly furnished,

Stands permanent though this bee fled.
It's purchased, and paid for too
By him who hath enough to doe.

A Prise so vast as is unknown,
Yet, by his Gift, is made thine own.
Ther's wealth enough, I need no more;
Farewell my Pelf, farewell my Store.
The world no longer let me Love,
My hope and Treasure lyes Above.

Michael Wigglesworth 1631 – 1705

From *The Day of Doom*

1

The Security
of the World
before Christ's
coming to
Judgment.
Luk. 12:19

Still was the night, Serene and Bright,
　　when all Men sleeping lay;
Calm was the season, and carnal reason
　　thought so 'twould last for ay.
Soul, take thine ease, let sorrow cease,
　　much good thou hast in store:
This was their Song, their Cups among,
　　the Evening before.

2

Wallowing in all kind of sin,
　　vile wretches lay secure:
The best of men had scarcely then
　　their Lamps kept in good ure.

Mat. 25:5

Virgins unwise, who through disguise
　　amongst the best were number'd,
Had clos'd their eyes; yea, and the wise
　　through sloth and frailty slumber'd.

3

Like as of old, when Men grow bold

Mat. 24:37, 38

　　Gods threatnings to contemn,
Who stopt their Ear, and would not hear,
　　when Mercy warned them:
But took their course, without remorse,
　　til God began to powre
Destruction the World upon
　　in a tempestuous showre.

4

They put away the evil day,
    and drown'd their care and fears,
Till drown'd were they, and swept away
    by vengeance unawares:

I Thes. 5:3

So at the last, whilst Men sleep fast
    in their security,
Surpriz'd they are in such a snare
    as cometh suddenly.

5

The Suddenness,
Majesty, and
Terror of
Christ's
appearing.
Mat. 25:6
II Pet. 3:10

For at midnight brake forth a Light,
    which turn'd the night to day,
And speedily an hideous cry
    did all the world dismay.
Sinners awake, their hearts do ake,
    trembling their loynes surprizeth;
Amaz'd with fear, by what they hear,
    each one of them ariseth.

6

They rush from Beds with giddy heads,
    and to their windows run,
Viewing this light, which shines more bright

Mat. 24:29, 30

    then doth the Noon-day Sun.
Straightway appears (they see't with tears)
    the Son of God most dread;
Who with his Train comes on amain
    To Judge both Quick and Dead.

7

Before his face the Heav'ns gave place,

II Pet. 3:10

    and Skies are rent asunder,
With mighty voice, and hideous noise,
    more terrible than Thunder.

His brightness damps heav'ns glorious lamps
    and makes them hide their heads,
As if afraid and quite dismay'd,
    they quit their wonted steads.

8

Ye sons of men that durst contemn
    the Threatnings of Gods Word,
How cheer you now? your hearts, I trow,
    are thrill'd as with a sword.
Now Atheist blind, whose brutish mind
    a God could never see,
Dost thou perceive, dost now believe,
    that Christ thy Judge shall be?

9

Stout Courages, (whose hardiness
    could Death and Hell out-face)
Are you as bold now you behold
    your Judge draw near apace?
They cry, no, no: Alas! and wo!
    our Courage all is gone:
Our hardiness (fool hardiness)
    hath us undone, undone.

10

No heart so bold, but now grows cold
    and almost dead with fear:
Rev. 6:16   No eye so dry, but now can cry,
    and pour out many a tear.
Earths Potentates and pow'rful States,
    Captains and Men of Might,
Are quite abasht, their courage dasht
    at this most dreadful sight.

11

Mean men lament, great men do rent
   their Robes, and tear their hair:

Mat. 24:30   They do not spare their flesh to tear
   through horrible despair.
All Kindreds wail: all hearts do fail:
   horror the world doth fill
With weeping eyes, and loud out-cries,
   yet knows not how to kill.

12

Rev. 6:15, 16   Some hide themselves in Caves and Delves,
   in places under ground:
Some rashly leap into the Deep,
   to scape by being drown'd:
Some to the Rocks (O sensless blocks!)
   and woody Mountains run,
That there they might this fearful sight,
   and dreaded Presence shun.

Edward Taylor 1645 – 1729

From *Preparatory Meditations*, First Series

38. MEDITATION. 1 JOH. 2.1. AN ADVOCATE WITH THE FATHER

Oh! What a thing is Man? Lord, Who am I?
  That thou shouldst give him Law (Oh! golden Line)
To regulate his Thoughts, Words, Life thereby.
    And judge him Wilt thereby too in thy time.
  A Court of Justice thou in heaven holdst
  To try his Case while he's here housd on mould.

How do thy Angells lay before thine eye
  My Deeds both White, and Black I dayly doe?
How doth thy Court thou Pannellst there them try?
  But flesh complains. What right for this? let's know.
For right, or wrong I can't appeare unto't.
  And shall a sentence Pass on such a suite?

Soft; blemish not this golden Bench, or place.
  Here is no Bribe, nor Colourings to hide
Nor Pettifogger to befog the Case
  But Justice hath her Glory here well tri'de.
  Her spotless Law all spotted Cases tends.
  Without Respect or Disrespect them ends.

God's Judge himselfe: and Christ Atturny is,
  The Holy Ghost Regesterer is founde.
Angells the sergeants are, all Creatures kiss
  The booke, and doe as Evidences abounde.
  All Cases pass according to pure Law
  And in the sentence is no Fret, nor flaw.

What saist, my soule? Here all thy Deeds are tri'de.
. Is Christ thy Advocate to pleade thy Cause?
Art thou his Client? Such shall never slide.
   He never lost his Case: he pleads such Laws
   As Carry do the same, nor doth refuse
   The Vilest sinners Case that doth him Choose.

This is his Honour, not Dishonour: nay
   No Habeas–Corpus against his Clients came
For all their Fines his Purse doth make down pay.
   He Non-Suites Satan's Suite or Casts the Same.
   He'l plead thy Case, and not accept a Fee.
   He'l plead Sub Forma Pauperis for thee.

My Case is bad. Lord, be my Advocate.
   My sin is red: I'me under Gods Arrest.
Thou hast the Hint of Pleading; plead my State.
   Although it's bad thy Plea will make it best.
   If thou wilt plead my Case before the King:
   I'le Waggon Loads of Love, and Glory bring.

[When] Let by Rain

Ye Flippering Soule,
  Why dost between the Nippers dwell?
Not stay, nor goe. Not yea, nor yet Controle.
  Doth this doe well?
    Rise journy'ng when the skies fall weeping Showers.
    Not o're nor under th'Clouds and Cloudy Powers.

Not yea, nor noe:
  On tiptoes thus? Why sit on thorns?
Resolve the matter: Stay thyselfe or goe.
  Be n't both wayes born.
    Wager thyselfe against thy surplice, see,
    And win thy Coate: or let thy Coate Win thee.

Is this th'Effect,
  To leaven thus my Spirits all?
To make my heart a Crabtree Cask direct?
  A Verjuicte Hall?
    As Bottle Ale, whose Spirits prisond nurst
    When jog'd, the bung with Violence doth burst?

Shall I be made
  A sparkling Wildfire Shop
Where my dull Spirits at the Fireball trade
  Do frisk and hop?
    And while the Hammer doth the Anvill pay,
    The fireball matter sparkles ery way.

One sorry fret,
  An anvill Sparke, rose higher
And in thy Temple falling almost set
  The house on fire.
    Such fireballs droping in the Temple Flame
    Burns up the building: Lord forbid the same.

Upon a Spider Catching a Fly

Thou sorrow, venom Elfe.
  Is this thy play,
To spin a web out of thyselfe
    To Catch a Fly?
      For Why?

I saw a pettish wasp
  Fall foule therein.
Whom yet thy Whorle pins did not clasp
    Lest he should fling
      His sting.

But as affraid, remote
  Didst stand hereat
And with thy little fingers stroke
    And gently tap
      His back.

Thus gently him didst treate
  Lest he should pet,
And in a froppish, waspish heate
    Should greatly fret
      Thy net.

Whereas the silly Fly,
  Caught by its leg
Thou by the throate tookst hastily
    And 'hinde the head
      Bite Dead.

This goes to pot, that not
  Nature doth call.
Strive not above what strength hath got
    Lest in the brawle
      Thou fall.

This Frey seems thus to us.
 Hells Spider gets
His intrails spun to whip Cords thus
 And wove to nets
  And sets.

To tangle Adams race
 In's stratigems
To their Destructions, spoil'd, made base
 By venom things
  Damn'd Sins.

But mighty, Gracious Lord
 Communicate
Thy Grace to breake the Cord, afford
 Us Glorys Gate
  And State.

We'l Nightingaile sing like
 When pearcht on high
In Glories Cage, thy glory, bright,
 And thankfully,
  For joy.

Huswifery

Make me, O Lord, thy Spining Wheele compleate.
 Thy Holy Worde my Distaff make for mee.
Make mine Affections thy Swift Flyers neate
 And make my Soule thy holy Spoole to bee.
 My Conversation make to be thy Reele
 And reele the yarn thereon spun of thy Wheele.

Make me thy Loome then, knit therein this Twine:
   And make thy Holy Spirit, Lord, winde quills:
Then weave the Web thyselfe. The yarn is fine.
   Thine Ordinances make my Fulling Mills.
   Then dy the same in Heavenly Colours Choice,
   All pinkt with Varnisht Flowers of Paradise.

Then cloath therewith mine Understanding, Will,
   Affections, Judgment, Conscience, Memory
My Words, and Actions, that their shine may fill
   My wayes with glory and thee glorify.
   Then mine apparell shall display before yee
   That I am Cloathd in Holy robes for glory.

Philip Freneau 1752 – 1832

The Indian Student

OR, FORCE OF NATURE

From Susquehanna's farthest springs
Where savage tribes pursue their game,
(His blanket tied with yellow strings,)
A shepherd of the forest came.

Not long before, a wandering priest
Expressed his wish, with visage sad –
'Ah, why (he cried) in Satan's waste,
'Ah, why detain so fine a lad?

'In white-man's land there stands a town
'Where learning may be purchased low –
'Exchange his blanket for a gown,
'And let the lad to college go.' –

From long debate the council rose,
And viewing Shalum's tricks with joy
To Cambridge Hall,★ o'er wastes of snows,
They sent the copper-coloured boy.

One generous chief a bow supplied,
This gave a shaft, and that a skin;
The feathers, in vermillion dyed,
Himself did from a turkey win:

★Harvard College, at Cambridge in Massachusetts – *Freneau's note, edition* 1788.

Thus dressed so gay, he took his way
O'er barren hills, alone, alone!
His guide a star, he wandered far,
His pillow every night a stone.

At last he came, with foot so lame,
Where learned men talk heathen Greek,
And Hebrew lore is gabbled o'er,
To please the Muses, – twice a week.

Awhile he writ, awhile he read,
Awhile he conned their grammar rules –
(An Indian savage so well bred
Great credit promised to the schools.)

Some thought he would in law excel,
Some said in physic he would shine;
And one that knew him, passing well,
Beheld, in him, a sound Divine.

But those of more discerning eye
Even then could other prospects show,
And saw him lay his Virgil by
To wander with his dearer bow.

The tedious hours of study spent,
The heavy-moulded lecture done,
He to the woods a hunting went,
Through lonely wastes he walked, he run.

No mystic wonders fired his mind;
He sought to gain no learned degree,
But only sense enough to find
The squirrel in the hollow tree.

The shady bank, the purling stream,
The woody wild his heart possessed,

The dewy lawn, his morning dream
In fancy's gayest colours dressed.

'And why (he cried) did I forsake
'My native wood for gloomy walls;
'The silver stream, the limpid lake
'For musty books and college halls.

'A little could my wants supply –
'Can wealth and honour give me more;
'Or, will the sylvan god deny
'The humble treat he gave before?

'Let seraphs gain the bright abode,
'And heaven's sublimest mansions see –
'I only bow to Nature's God –
'The land of shades will do for me.

'These dreadful secrets of the sky
'Alarm my soul with chilling fear –
'Do planets in their orbits fly,
'And is the earth, indeed, a sphere?

'Let planets still their course pursue,
'And comets to the centre run –
'In Him my faithful friend I view,
'The image of my God – the Sun.

'Where Nature's ancient forests grow,
'And mingled laurel never fades,
'My heart is fixed; – and I must go
'To die among my native shades.'

He spoke, and to the western springs,
(His gown discharged, his money spent,
His blanket tied with yellow strings,)
The shepherd of the forest went.

Joel Barlow 1754 – 1812

From *The Hasty-Pudding*

CANTO I

Ye Alps audacious, thro' the Heavens that rise,
To cramp the day and hide me from the skies;
Ye Gallic flags, that o'er their heights unfurl'd,
Bear death to kings, and freedom to the world,
I sing not you. A softer theme I chuse,
A virgin theme, unconscious of the Muse,
But fruitful, rich, well suited to inspire
The purest frenzy of poetic fire.

Despise it not, ye Bards to terror steel'd,
Who hurl'd your thunders round the epic field;
Nor ye who strain your midnight throats to sing
Joys that the vineyard and the still-house bring;
Or on some distant fair your notes employ,
And speak of raptures that you ne'er enjoy.
I sing the sweets I know, the charms I feel,
My morning incense, and my evening meal,
The sweets of Hasty-Pudding. Come, dear bowl,
Glide o'er my palate, and inspire my soul.
The milk beside thee, smoking from the kine,
Its substance mingled, married in with thine,
Shall cool and temper thy superior heat,
And save the pains of blowing while I eat.

Oh! could the smooth, the emblematic song
Flow like thy genial juices o'er my tongue,
Could those mild morsels in my numbers chime,

And, as they roll in substance, roll in rhyme,
No more thy aukward unpoetic name
Should shun the Muse, or prejudice thy fame;
But rising grateful to th' accustom'd ear,
All Bards should catch it, and all realms revere!

    Assist me first with pious toil to trace
Thro' wrecks of time thy lineage and thy race;
Declare what lovely squaw, in days of yore,
(Ere great Columbus sought thy native shore)
First gave thee to the world; her works of fame
Have liv'd indeed, but liv'd without a name.
Some tawny Ceres, goddess of her days,
First learn'd with stones to crack the well-dry'd maize,
Thro' the rough sieve to shake the golden show'r,
In boiling water stir the yellow flour:
The yellow flour, bestrew'd and stir'd with haste,
Swells in the flood and thickens to a paste,
Then puffs and wallops, rises to the brim,
Drinks the dry knobs that on the surface swim:
The knobs at last the busy ladle breaks,
And the whole mass its true consistence takes.

    Could but her sacred name, unknown so long,
Rise like her labors, to the song of song,
To her, to them, I'd consecrate my lays,
And blow her pudding with the breath of praise.
If 'twas Oella, whom I sang before,
I here ascribe her one great virtue more.
Not thro' the rich Peruvian realms alone
The fame of Sol's sweet daughter should be known,
But o'er the world's wide climes should live secure,
Far as his rays extend, as long as they endure.

    Dear Hasty-Pudding, what unpromis'd joy
Expands my heart, to meet thee in Savoy!

Doom'd o'er the world thro' devious paths to roam,
Each clime my country, and each house my home,
My soul is sooth'd, my cares have found an end,
I greet my long-lost, unforgotten friend.

For thee thro' Paris, that corrupted town,
How long in vain I wandered up and down,
Where shameless Bacchus, with his drenching hoard
Cold from his cave usurps the morning board.
London is lost in smoke and steep'd in tea;
No Yankee there can lisp the name of thee;
The uncouth word, a libel on the town,
Would call a proclamation from the crown.
For climes oblique, that fear the sun's full rays,
Chill'd in their fogs, exclude the generous maize;
A grain whose rich luxurient growth requires
Short gentle showers, and bright etherial fires.

Francis Scott Key 1779 – 1843

The Star-Spangled Banner

O say, can you see, by the dawn's early light,
  What so proudly we hailed at the twilight's last gleaming –
Whose broad stripes and bright stars, through the clouds of the fight,
  O'er the ramparts we watched were so gallantly streaming!
And the rocket's red glare, the bombs bursting in air,
Gave proof through the night that our flag was still there;
O! say, does that star-spangled banner yet wave
O'er the land of the free, and the home of the brave?

On that shore dimly seen through the mists of the deep,
  Where the foe's haughty host in dread silence reposes,
What is that which the breeze, o'er the towering steep,
  As it fitfully blows, now conceals, now discloses?
Now it catches the gleam of the morning's first beam,
In full glory reflected now shines on the stream;
Tis the star-spangled banner; O long may it wave
O'er the land of the free, and the home of the brave!

And where is that band who so vauntingly swore
  That the havoc of war and the battle's confusion
A home and a country should leave us no more?
  Their blood has washed out their foul footsteps' pollution.
No refuge could save the hireling and slave
From the terror of flight, or the gloom of the grave;
And the star-spangled banner in triumph doth wave
O'er the land of the free, and the home of the brave.

O! thus be it ever, when freemen shall stand
  Between their loved homes and the war's desolation!
Blest with victory and peace, may the heav'n-rescued land
  Praise the power that hath made and preserved us a nation.
Then conquer we must, when our cause it is just,
And this be our motto – '*In God is our trust*':
And the star-spangled banner in triumph shall wave
O'er the land of the free, and the home of the brave.

William Cullen Bryant 1794 – 1878

The Prairies

These are the gardens of the Desert, these
The unshorn fields, boundless and beautiful,
For which the speech of England has no name –
The Prairies. I behold them for the first,
And my heart swells, while the dilated sight
Takes in the encircling vastness. Lo! they stretch,
In airy undulations, far away,
As if the ocean, in his gentlest swell,
Stood still, with all his rounded billows fixed,
And motionless forever. – Motionless? –
No – they are all unchained again. The clouds
Sweep over with their shadows, and, beneath,
The surface rolls and fluctuates to the eye;
Dark hollows seem to glide along and chase
The sunny ridges. Breezes of the South!
Who toss the golden and the flame-like flowers,
And pass the prairie-hawk that, poised on high,
Flaps his broad wings, yet moves not – ye have played
Among the palms of Mexico and vines
Of Texas, and have crisped the limpid brooks
That from the fountains of Sonora glide
Into the calm Pacific – have ye fanned
A nobler or a lovelier scene than this?
Man hath no power in all this glorious work:
The hand that built the firmament hath heaved
And smoothed these verdant swells, and sown their slopes
With herbage, planted them with island groves,
And hedged them round with forests. Fitting floor

For this magnificent temple of the sky –
With flowers whose glory and whose multitude
Rival the constellations! The great heavens
Seem to stoop down upon the scene in love, –
A nearer vault, and of a tenderer blue,
Than that which bends above our eastern hills.

As o'er the verdant waste I guide my steed,
Among the high rank grass that sweeps his sides
The hollow beating of his footstep seems
A sacrilegious sound. I think of those
Upon whose rest he tramples. Are they here –
The dead of other days? – and did the dust
Of these fair solitudes once stir with life
And burn with passion? Let the mighty mounds
That overlook the rivers, or that rise
In the dim forest crowded with old oaks,
Answer. A race, that long has passed away,
Built them; – a disciplined and populous race
Heaped, with long toil, the earth, while yet the Greek
Was hewing the Pentelicus to forms
Of symmetry, and rearing on its rock
The glittering Parthenon. These ample fields
Nourished their harvests, here their herds were fed,
When haply by their stalls the bison lowed,
And bowed his manèd shoulder to the yoke.
All day this desert murmured with their toils,
Till twilight blushed, and lovers walked, and wooed
In a forgotten language, and old tunes,
From instruments of unremembered form,
Gave the soft winds a voice. The red man came –
The roaming hunter tribes, warlike and fierce,
And the mound-builders vanished from the earth.
The solitude of centuries untold
Has settled where they dwelt. The prairie-wolf
Hunts in their meadows, and his fresh-dug den

Yawns by my path. The gopher mines the ground
Where stood their swarming cities. All is gone;
All – save the piles of earth that hold their bones,
The platforms where they worshipped unknown gods,
The barriers which they builded from the soil
To keep the foe at bay – till o'er the walls
The wild beleaguerers broke, and, one by one,
The strongholds of the plain were forced, and heaped
With corpses. The brown vultures of the wood
Flocked to those vast uncovered sepulchres,
And sat unscared and silent at their feast.
Haply some solitary fugitive,
Lurking in marsh and forest, till the sense
Of desolation and of fear became
Bitterer than death, yielded himself to die.
Man's better nature triumphed then. Kind words
Welcomed and soothed him; the rude conquerors
Seated the captive with their chiefs; he chose
A bride among their maidens, and at length
Seemed to forget – yet ne'er forgot – the wife
Of his first love, and her sweet little ones,
Butchered, amid their shrieks, with all his race.

Thus change the forms of being. Thus arise
Races of living things, glorious in strength,
And perish, as the quickening breath of God
Fills them, or is withdrawn. The red man, too,
Has left the blooming wilds he ranged so long,
And, nearer to the Rocky Mountains, sought
A wilder hunting-ground. The beaver builds
No longer by these streams, but far away,
On waters whose blue surface ne'er gave back
The white man's face – among Missouri's springs,
And pools whose issues swell the Oregon –
He rears his little Venice. In these plains
The bison feeds no more. Twice twenty leagues

Beyond remotest smoke of hunter's camp,
Roams the majestic brute, in herds that shake
The earth with thundering steps – yet here I meet
His ancient footprints stamped beside the pool.

Still this great solitude is quick with life.
Myriads of insects, gaudy as the flowers
They flutter over, gentle quadrupeds,
And birds, that scarce have learned the fear of man,
Are here, and sliding reptiles of the ground,
Startlingly beautiful. The graceful deer
Bounds to the wood at my approach. The bee,
A more adventurous colonist than man,
With whom he came across the eastern deep,
Fills the savannas with his murmurings,
And hides his sweets, as in the golden age,
Within the hollow oak. I listen long
To his domestic hum, and think I hear
The sound of that advancing multitude
Which soon shall fill these deserts. From the ground
Comes up the laugh of children, the soft voice
Of maidens, and the sweet and solemn hymn
Of Sabbath worshippers. The low of herds
Blends with the rustling of the heavy grain
Over the dark brown furrows. All at once
A fresher wind sweeps by, and breaks my dream,
And I am in the wilderness alone.

Ralph Waldo Emerson 1803 – 82

The Rhodora:

ON BEING ASKED, WHENCE IS THE FLOWER?

In May, when sea-winds pierced our solitudes,
I found the fresh Rhodora in the woods,
Spreading its leafless blooms in a damp nook,
To please the desert and the sluggish brook.
The purple petals, fallen in the pool,
Made the black water with their beauty gay;
Here might the red-bird come his plumes to cool,
And court the flower that cheapens his array.
Rhodora! if the sages ask thee why
This charm is wasted on the earth and sky,
Tell them, dear, that if eyes were made for seeing,
Then Beauty is its own excuse for being:
Why thou wert there, O rival of the rose!
I never thought to ask, I never knew:
But, in my simple ignorance, suppose
The self-same Power that brought me there brought you.

Each and All

Little thinks, in the field, yon red-cloaked clown
Of thee from the hill-top looking down;
The heifer that lows in the upland farm,
Far-heard, lows not thine ear to charm;
The sexton, tolling his bell at noon,
Deems not that great Napoleon

Stops his horse, and lists with delight,
Whilst his files sweep round yon Alpine height;
Nor knowest thou what argument
Thy life to thy neighbor's creed has lent.
All are needed by each one;
Nothing is fair or good alone.
I thought the sparrow's note from heaven,
Singing at dawn on the alder bough;
I brought him home, in his nest, at even;
He sings the song, but it cheers not now,
For I did not bring home the river and sky; –
He sang to my ear, – they sang to my eye.
The delicate shells lay on the shore;
The bubbles of the latest wave
Fresh pearls to their enamel gave,
And the bellowing of the savage sea
Greeted their safe escape to me.
I wiped away the weeds and foam,
I fetched my sea-born treasures home;
But the poor, unsightly, noisome things
Had left their beauty on the shore
With the sun and the sand and the wild uproar.
The lover watched his graceful maid,
As 'mid the virgin train she strayed,
Nor knew her beauty's best attire
Was woven still by the snow-white choir.
At last she came to his hermitage,
Like the bird from the woodlands to the cage; –
The gay enchantment was undone,
A gentle wife, but fairy none.
Then I said, 'I covet truth;
Beauty is unripe childhood's cheat;
I leave it behind with the games of youth:' –
As I spoke, beneath my feet
The ground-pine curled its pretty wreath,
Running over the club-moss burrs;

I inhaled the violet's breath;
Around me stood the oaks and firs;
Pine-cones and acorns lay on the ground;
Over me soared the eternal sky,
Full of light and of deity;
Again I saw, again I heard,
The rolling river, the morning bird; –
Beauty through my senses stole;
I yielded myself to the perfect whole.

The Problem

I like a church; I like a cowl;
I love a prophet of the soul;
And on my heart monastic aisles
Fall like sweet strains, or pensive smiles;
Yet not for all his faith can see
Would I that cowlèd churchman be.

Why should the vest on him allure,
Which I could not on me endure?

Not from a vain or shallow thought
His awful Jove young Phidias brought;
Never from lips of cunning fell
The thrilling Delphic oracle;
Out from the heart of nature rolled
The burdens of the Bible old;
The litanies of nations came,
Like the volcano's tongue of flame,
Up from the burning core below, –
The canticles of love and woe:
The hand that rounded Peter's dome
And groined the aisles of Christian Rome

Wrought in a sad sincerity;
Himself from God he could not free;
He builded better than he knew; –
The conscious stone to beauty grew.

Know'st thou what wove yon woodbird's nest
Of leaves, and feathers from her breast?
Or how the fish outbuilt her shell,
Painting with morn each annual cell?
Or how the sacred pine-tree adds
To her old leaves new myriads?
Such and so grew these holy piles,
Whilst love and terror laid the tiles.
Earth proudly wears the Parthenon,
As the best gem upon her zone,
And Morning opes with haste her lids
To gaze upon the Pyramids;
O'er England's abbeys bends the sky,
As on its friends, with kindred eye;
For out of Thought's interior sphere
These wonders rose to upper air;
And Nature gladly gave them place,
Adopted them into her race,
And granted them an equal date
With Andes and with Ararat.

These temples grew as grows the grass;
Art might obey, but not surpass.
The passive Master lent his hand
To the vast soul that o'er him planned;
And the same power that reared the shrine
Bestrode the tribes that knelt within.
Ever the fiery Pentecost
Girds with one flame the countless host,
Trances the heart through chanting choirs,
And through the priest the mind inspires.

The word unto the prophet spoken
Was writ on tables yet unbroken;
The word by seers or sibyls told,
In groves of oak, or fanes of gold,
Still floats upon the morning wind,
Still whispers to the willing mind.
One accent of the Holy Ghost
The heedless world hath never lost.
I know what say the fathers wise, –
The Book itself before me lies,
Old *Chrysostom*, best Augustine,
And he who blent both in his line,
The younger *Golden Lips* or mines,
Taylor, the Shakspeare of divines.
His words are music in my ear,
I see his cowlèd portrait dear;
And yet, for all his faith could see,
I would not the good bishop be.

The Snow-Storm

Announced by all the trumpets of the sky,
Arrives the snow, and, driving o'er the fields,
Seems nowhere to alight: the whited air
Hides hills and woods, the river, and the heaven,
And veils the farm-house at the garden's end.
The sled and traveller stopped, the courier's feet
Delayed, all friends shut out, the housemates sit
Around the radiant fireplace, enclosed
In a tumultuous privacy of storm.

Come see the north wind's masonry.
Out of an unseen quarry evermore
Furnished with tile, the fierce artificer

Curves his white bastions with projected roof
Round every windward stake, or tree, or door.
Speeding, the myriad-handed, his wild work
So fanciful, so savage, nought cares he
For number or proportion. Mockingly,
On coop or kennel he hangs Parian wreaths;

A swan-like form invests the hidden thorn;
Fills up the farmer's lane from wall to wall,
Maugre the farmer's sighs; and at the gate
A tapering turret overtops the work.
And when his hours are numbered, and the world
Is all his own, retiring, as he were not,
Leaves, when the sun appears, astonished Art
To mimic in slow structures, stone by stone,
Built in an age, the mad wind's night-work,
The frolic architecture of the snow.

Blight

Give me truths;
For I am weary of the surfaces,
And die of inanition. If I knew
Only the herbs and simples of the wood,
Rue, cinquefoil, gill, vervain and agrimony,
Blue-vetch and trillium, hawkweed, sassafras,
Milkweeds and murky brakes, quaint pipes and sundew,
And rare and virtuous roots, which in these woods
Draw untold juices from the common earth,
Untold, unknown, and I could surely spell
Their fragrance, and their chemistry apply
By sweet affinities to human flesh,
Driving the foe and stablishing the friend, –
O, that were much, and I could be a part

Of the round day, related to the sun
And planted world, and full executor
Of their imperfect functions.
But these young scholars, who invade our hills,
Bold as the engineer who fells the wood,
And travelling often in the cut he makes,
Love not the flower they pluck, and know it not,
And all their botany is Latin names.
The old men studied magic in the flowers,
And human fortunes in astronomy,
And an omnipotence in chemistry,
Preferring things to names, for these were men,
Were unitarians of the united world,
And, wheresoever their clear eye-beams fell,
They caught the footsteps of the SAME. Our eyes
Are armed, but we are strangers to the stars,
And strangers to the mystic beast and bird,
And strangers to the plant and to the mine.
The injured elements say, 'Not in us;'
And night and day, ocean and continent,
Fire, plant and mineral say, 'Not in us;'
And haughtily return us stare for stare.
For we invade them impiously for gain;
We devastate them unreligiously,
And coldly ask their pottage, not their love.
Therefore they shove us from them, yield to us
Only what to our griping toil is due;
But the sweet affluence of love and song,
The rich results of the divine consents
Of man and earth, of world beloved and lover,
The nectar and ambrosia, are withheld;
And in the midst of spoils and slaves, we thieves
And pirates of the universe, shut out
Daily to a more thin and outward rind,
Turn pale and starve. Therefore, to our sick eyes,
The stunted trees look sick, the summer short,

Clouds shade the sun, which will not tan our hay,
And nothing thrives to reach its natural term;
And life, shorn of its venerable length,
Even at its greatest space is a defeat,
And dies in anger that it was a dupe;
And, in its highest noon and wantonness,
Is early frugal, like a beggar's child;
Even in the hot pursuit of the best aims
And prizes of ambition, checks its hand,
Like Alpine cataracts frozen as they leaped,
Chilled with a miserly comparison
Of the toy's purchase with the length of life.

Hamatreya

Bulkeley, Hunt, Willard, Hosmer, Meriam, Flint,
Possessed the land which rendered to their toil
Hay, corn, roots, hemp, flax, apples, wool and wood.
Each of these landlords walked amidst his farm,
Saying, ''T is mine, my children's and my name's.
How sweet the west wind sounds in my own trees!
How graceful climb those shadows on my hill!
I fancy these pure waters and the flags
Know me, as does my dog: we sympathise;
And, I affirm, my actions smack of the soil.'

Where are these men? Asleep beneath their grounds:
And strangers, fond as they, their furrows plough.
Earth laughs in flowers, to see her boastful boys
Earth-proud, proud of the earth which is not theirs;
Who steer the plough, but cannot steer their feet
Clear of the grave.
They added ridge to valley, brook to pond,
And sighed for all that bounded their domain;

'This suits me for a pasture; that's my park;
We must have clay, lime, gravel, granite-ledge,
And misty lowland, where to go for peat.
The land is well, – lies fairly to the south.
'T is good, when you have crossed the sea and back,
To find the sitfast acres where you left them.'
Ah! the hot owner sees not Death, who adds
Him to his land, a lump of mould the more.
Hear what the Earth says:–

EARTH-SONG

'Mine and yours;
Mine, not yours.
Earth endures;
Stars abide –
Shine down in the old sea;
Old are the shores;
But where are old men?
I who have seen much,
Such have I never seen.

'The lawyer's deed
Ran sure,
In tail,
To them, and to their heirs
Who shall succeed,
Without fail,
Forevermore.

'Here is the land,
Shaggy with wood,
With its old valley,
Mound and flood.

But the heritors?
Fled like the flood's foam. –
The lawyer, and the laws,
And the kingdom,
Clean swept herefrom.

'They called me theirs,
Who so controlled me;
Yet every one
Wished to stay, and is gone,
How am I theirs,
If they cannot hold me,
But I hold them?'

When I heard the Earth-song
I was no longer brave;
My avarice cooled
Like lust in the chill of the grave.

Days

Daughters of Time, the hypocritic Days,
Muffled and dumb like barefoot dervishes,
And marching single in an endless file,
Bring diadems and fagots in their hands.
To each they offer gifts after his will,
Bread, kingdoms, stars, and sky that holds
     them all.
I, in my pleached garden, watched the pomp,
Forgot my morning wishes, hastily
Took a few herbs and apples, and the Day
Turned and departed silent. I, too late,
Under her solemn fillet saw the scorn.

Henry Wadsworth Longfellow
1807 – 82

In the Churchyard at Cambridge

In the village churchyard she lies,
Dust is in her beautiful eyes,
  No more she breathes, nor feels, nor stirs;
At her feet and at her head
Lies a slave to attend the dead,
  But their dust is white as hers.

Was she, a lady of high degree,
So much in love with the vanity
  And foolish pomp of this world of ours?
Or was it Christian charity,
And lowliness and humility,
  The richest and rarest of all dowers?

Who shall tell us? No one speaks;
No color shoots into those cheeks,
  Either of anger or of pride,
At the rude question we have asked;
Nor will the mystery be unmasked
  By those who are sleeping at her side.

Hereafter? – And do you think to look
On the terrible pages of that Book
  To find her failings, faults, and errors?
Ah, you will then have other cares,
In your own shortcomings and despairs,
  In your own secret sins and terrors!

The Day is Done

The day is done, and the darkness
  Falls from the wings of Night,
As a feather is wafted downward
  From an eagle in his flight.

I see the lights of the village
  Gleam through the rain and the mist,
And a feeling of sadness comes o'er me
  That my soul cannot resist:

A feeling of sadness and longing,
  That is not akin to pain,
And resembles sorrow only
  As the mist resembles the rain.

Come, read to me some poem,
  Some simple and heartfelt lay,
That shall soothe this restless feeling,
  And banish the thoughts of day.

Not from the grand old masters,
  Not from the bards sublime,
Whose distant footsteps echo
  Through the corridors of Time.

For, like strains of martial music,
  Their mighty thoughts suggest
Life's endless toil and endeavor;
  And to-night I long for rest.

Read from some humbler poet,
  Whose songs gushed from his heart,
As showers from the clouds of summer,
  Or tears from the eyelids start;

Who, through long days of labor,
  And nights devoid of ease,
Still heard in his soul the music
  Of wonderful melodies.

Such songs have power to quiet
  The restless pulse of care,
And come like the benediction
  That follows after prayer.

Then read from the treasured volume
  The poem of thy choice,
And lend to the rhyme of the poet
  The beauty of thy voice.

And the night shall be filled with music,
  And the cares, that infest the day,
Shall fold their tents, like the Arabs,
  And as silently steal away.

The Jewish Cemetery at Newport

How strange it seems! These Hebrews in their graves,
  Close by the street of this fair seaport town,
Silent beside the never-silent waves,
  At rest in all this moving up and down!

The trees are white with dust, that o'er their sleep
  Wave their broad curtains in the south wind's breath,
While underneath these leafy tents they keep
  The long, mysterious Exodus of Death.

And these sepulchral stones, so old and brown,
   That pave with level flags their burial-place,
Seem like the tablets of the Law, thrown down
   And broken by Moses at the mountain's base.

The very names recorded here are strange,
   Of foreign accent, and of different climes;
Alvares and Rivera interchange
   With Abraham and Jacob of old times.

'Blessed be God! for he created Death!'
   The mourners said, 'and Death is rest and peace;'
Then added, in the certainty of faith,
   'And giveth Life that nevermore shall cease.'

Closed are portals of their Synagogue,
   No Psalms of David now the silence break,
No Rabbi reads the ancient Decalogue
   In the grand dialect the Prophets spake.

Gone are the living, but the dead remain,
   And not neglected; for a hand unseen,
Scattering its bounty, like a summer rain,
   Still keeps their graves and their remembrance green.

How came they here? What burst of Christian hate,
   What persecution, merciless and blind,
Drove o'er the sea – that desert desolate –
   These Ishmaels and Hagars of mankind?

They lived in narrow streets and lanes obscure,
   Ghetto and Judenstrass, in mirk and mire;
Taught in the school of patience to endure
   The life of anguish and the death of fire.

All their lives long, with the unleavened bread
　　And bitter herbs of exile and its fears,
The wasting famine of the heart they fed,
　　And slaked its thirst with marah of their tears.

Anathema maranatha! was the cry
　　That rang from town to town, from street to street;
At every gate the accursed Mordecai
　　Was mocked and jeered, and spurned by Christian feet.

Pride and humiliation hand in hand
　　Walked with them through the world where'er they went;
Trampled and beaten were they as the sand,
　　And yet unshaken as the continent.

For in the background figures vague and vast
　　Of patriarchs and of prophets rose sublime,
And all the great traditions of the Past
　　They saw reflected in the coming time.

And thus forever with reverted look
　　The mystic volume of the world they read,
Spelling it backward, like a Hebrew book,
　　Till life became a Legend of the Dead.

But ah! what once has been shall be no more!
　　The groaning earth in travail and in pain
Brings forth its races, but does not restore,
　　And the dead nations never rise again.

Chaucer

An old man in a lodge within a park;
　　The chamber walls depicted all around
　　　With portraitures of huntsman, hawk, and hound,
　　And the hurt deer. He listeneth to the lark,

Whose song comes with the sunshine through the dark
  Of painted glass in leaden lattice bound;
  He listeneth and he laugheth at the sound,
Then writeth in a book like any clerk.
He is the poet of the dawn, who wrote
  The Canterbury Tales, and his old age
  Made beautiful with song; and as I read
I hear the crowing cock, I hear the note
  Of lark and linnet, and from every page
  Rise odors of ploughed field or flowery mead.

The Tide Rises, the Tide Falls

The tide rises, the tide falls,
The twilight darkens, the curlew calls;
Along the sea-sands damp and brown
The traveller hastens toward the town,
  And the tide rises, the tide falls.

Darkness settles on roofs and walls,
But the sea, the sea in the darkness calls;
The little waves, with their soft, white hands,
Efface the footprints in the sands,
  And the tide rises, the tide falls.

The morning breaks; the steeds in their stalls
Stamp and neigh, as the hostler calls;
The day returns, but nevermore
Returns the traveller to the shore,
  And the tide rises, the tide falls.

From *The Song of Hiawatha*

HIAWATHA'S DEPARTURE

By the shore of Gitche Gumee,
By the shining Big-Sea-Water,
At the doorway of his wigwam,
In the pleasant Summer morning,
Hiawatha stood and waited.
All the air was full of freshness,
All the earth was bright and joyous,
And before him, through the sunshine,
Westward toward the neighboring forest
Passed in golden swarms the Ahmo,
Passed the bees, the honey-makers,
Burning, singing in the sunshine.

Bright above him shone the heavens,
Level spread the lake before him;
From its bosom leaped the sturgeon,
Sparkling, flashing in the sunshine;
On its margin the great forest
Stood reflected in the water,
Every tree-top had its shadow,
Motionless beneath the water.

From the brow of Hiawatha
Gone was every trace of sorrow,
As the fog from off the water,
As the mist from off the meadow.
With a smile of joy and triumph,
With a look of exultation,
As of one who in a vision
Sees what is to be, but is not,
Stood and waited Hiawatha.

Toward the sun his hands were lifted,
Both the palms spread out against it,

And between the parted fingers
Fell the sunshine on his features,
Flecked with light his naked shoulders,
As it falls and flecks an oak-tree
Through the rifted leaves and branches.

O'er the water floating, flying,
Something in the hazy distance,
Something in the mists of morning,
Loomed and lifted from the water,
Now seemed floating, now seemed flying,
Coming nearer, nearer, nearer.

Was it Shingebis the diver?
Or the pelican, the Shada?
Or the heron, the Shuh-shuh-gah?
Or the white goose, Waw-be-wawa,
With the water dripping, flashing,
From its glossy neck and feathers?

It was neither goose nor diver,
Neither pelican nor heron,
O'er the water floating, flying,
Through the shining mist of morning,
But a birch canoe with paddles,
Rising, sinking on the water,
Dripping, flashing in the sunshine;
And within it came a people
From the distant land of Wabun,
From the farthest realms of morning
Came the Black-Robe chief, the Prophet,
He the Priest of Prayer, the Pale-face,
With his guides and his companions.

And the noble Hiawatha,
With his hands aloft extended,
Held aloft in sign of welcome,
Waited, full of exultation,
Till the birch canoe with paddles
Grated on the shining pebbles,

Stranded on the sandy margin,
Till the Black-Robe chief, the Pale-face,
With the cross upon his bosom,
Landed on the sandy margin.

   Then the joyous Hiawatha
Cried aloud and spake in this wise:
'Beautiful is the sun, O strangers,
When you come so far to see us!
All our town in peace awaits you,
All our doors stand open for you;
You shall enter all our wigwams,
For the heart's right hand we give you.

   'Never bloomed the earth so gayly,
Never shone the sun so brightly,
As to-day they shine and blossom
When you come so far to see us!
Never was our lake so tranquil,
Nor so free from rocks and sand-bars;
For your birch canoe in passing
Has removed both rock and sand-bar.

   'Never before had our tobacco
Such a sweet and pleasant flavor,
Never the broad leaves of our cornfields
Were so beautiful to look on,
As they seem to us this morning,
When you come so far to see us!'

   And the Black-Robe chief made answer,
Stammered in his speech a little,
Speaking words yet unfamiliar:
'Peace be with you, Hiawatha,
Peace be with you and your people,
Peace of prayer, and peace of pardon,
Peace of Christ, and joy of Mary!'

   Then the generous Hiawatha
Led the strangers to his wigwam,
Seated them on skins of bison,

Seated them on skins of ermine,
And the careful old Nokomis
Brought them food in bowls of basswood,
Water brought in birchen dippers,
And the calumet, the peace-pipe,
Filled and lighted for their smoking.

All the old men of the village,
All the warriors of the nation,
All the Jossakeeds, the Prophets,
The magicians, the Wabenos,
And the Medicine-men, the Medas,
Came to bid the strangers welcome;
'It is well,' they said, 'O brothers,
That you come so far to see us!'

In a circle round the doorway,
With their pipes they sat in silence,
Waiting to behold the strangers,
Waiting to receive their message;
Till the Black-Robe chief, the Pale-face,
From the wigwam came to greet them,
Stammering in his speech a little,
Speaking words yet unfamiliar;
'It is well,' they said, 'O brother,
That you come so far to see us!'

Then the Black-Robe chief, the Prophet,
Told his message to the people,
Told the purport of his mission,
Told them of the Virgin Mary,
And her blessed Son, the Saviour,
How in distant lands and ages
He had lived on earth as we do;
How he fasted, prayed, and labored;
How the Jews, the tribe accursed,
Mocked him, scourged him, crucified him;
How he rose from where they laid him,
Walked again with his disciples,

And ascended into heaven.

    And the chiefs made answer, saying:
'We have listened to your message,
We have heard your words of wisdom,
We will think on what you tell us.
It is well for us, O brothers,
That you come so far to see us!'

    Then they rose up and departed
Each one homeward to his wigwam,
To the young men and the women
Told the story of the strangers
Whom the Master of Life had sent them
From the shining land of Wabun.

    Heavy with the heat and silence
Grew the afternoon of Summer;
With a drowsy sound the forest
Whispered round the sultry wigwam,
With a sound of sleep the water
Rippled on the beach below it;
From the cornfields shrill and ceaseless
Sang the grasshopper, Pah-puk-keena;
And the guests of Hiawatha,
Weary with the heat of Summer,
Slumbered in the sultry wigwam.

    Slowly o'er the simmering landscape
Fell the evening's dusk and coolness,
And the long and level sunbeams
Shot their spears into the forest,
Breaking through its shields of shadow,
Rushed into each secret ambush,
Searched each thicket, dingle, hollow;
Still the guests of Hiawatha
Slumbered in the silent wigwam.

    From his place rose Hiawatha,
Bade farewell to old Nokomis,
Spake in whispers, spake in this wise,

Did not wake the guests, that slumbered:
  'I am going, O Nokomis,
On a long and distant journey,
To the portals of the Sunset,
To the regions of the home-wind,
Of the Northwest-Wind, Keewaydin.
But these guests I leave behind me,
In your watch and ward I leave them;
See that never harm comes near them,
See that never fear molests them,
Never danger nor suspicion,
Never want of food or shelter,
In the lodge of Hiawatha!'

  Forth into the village went he,
Bade farewell to all the warriors,
Bade farewell to all the young men,
Spake persuading, spake in this wise:
  'I am going, O my people,
On a long and distant journey;
Many moons and many winters
Will have come, and will have vanished,
Ere I come again to see you.
But my guests I leave behind me;
Listen to their words of wisdom,
Listen to the truth they tell you,
For the Master of Life has sent them
From the land of light and morning!'

  On the shore stood Hiawatha,
Turned and waved his hand at parting;
On the clear and luminous water
Launched his birch canoe for sailing,
From the pebbles of the margin
Shoved it forth into the water;
Whispered to it, 'Westward! westward!'
And with speed it darted forward.

  And the evening sun descending

Set the clouds on fire with redness,
Burned the broad sky, like a prairie,
Left upon the level water
One long track and trail of splendor,
Down whose stream, as down a river,
Westward, westward Hiawatha
Sailed into the fiery sunset,
Sailed into the purple vapors,
Sailed into the dusk of evening.

 And the people from the margin
Watched him floating, rising, sinking,
Till the birch canoe seemed lifted
High into that sea of splendor,
Till it sank into the vapors
Like the new moon slowly, slowly
Sinking in the purple distance.

 And they said, 'Farewell forever!'
Said, 'Farewell, O Hiawatha!'
And the forests, dark and lonely,
Moved through all their depths of darkness,
Sighed, 'Farewell, O Hiawatha!'
And the waves upon the margin
Rising, rippling on the pebbles,
Sobbed, 'Farewell, O Hiawatha!'
And the heron, the Shuh-shuh-gah,
From her haunts among the fen-lands,
Screamed, 'Farewell, O Hiawatha!'

 Thus departed Hiawatha,
Hiawatha the Beloved,
In the glory of the sunset,
In the purple mists of evening,
To the regions of the home-wind,
Of the Northwest-Wind, Keewaydin,
To the Islands of the Blessed,
To the kingdom of Ponemah,
To the land of the Hereafter!

John Greenleaf Whittier 1807 – 92

Skipper Ireson's Ride

Of all the rides since the birth of time,
Told in story or sung in rhyme, –
On Apuleius's Golden Ass,
Or one-eyed Calendar's horse of brass,
Witch astride of a human back,
Islam's prophet on Al-Borák, –
The strangest ride that ever was sped
Was Ireson's, out from Marblehead!
  Old Floyd Ireson, for his hard heart,
  Tarred and feathered and carried in a cart
    By the women of Marblehead!

Body of turkey, head of owl,
Wings a-droop like a rained-on fowl,
Feathered and ruffled in every part,
Skipper Ireson stood in the cart.
Scores of women, old and young,
Strong of muscle, and glib of tongue,
Pushed and pulled up the rocky lane,
Shouting and singing the shrill refrain:
  'Here's Flud Oirson, fur his horrd horrt,
  Torr'd an' futherr'd an' corr'd in a corrt
    By the women o' Morble'ead!'

Wrinkled scolds with hands on hips,
Girls in bloom of cheek and lips,
Wild-eyed, free-limbed, such as chase
Bacchus round some antique vase,

Brief of skirt, with ankles bare,
Loose of kerchief and loose of hair,
With conch-shells blowing and fish-horns' twang,
Over and over the Mænads sang:
  'Here's Flud Oirson, fur his horrd horrt,
   Torr'd an' futherr'd an' corr'd in a corrt
      By the women o' Morble'ead!'

Small pity for him! – He sailed away
From a leaking ship, in Chaleur Bay, –
Sailed away from a sinking wreck,
With his own town's-people on her deck!
'Lay by! lay by!' they called to him.
Back he answered, 'Sink or swim!
Brag of your catch of fish again!'
And off he sailed through the fog and rain!
  Old Floyd Ireson, for his hard heart,
  Tarred and feathered and carried in a cart
      By the women of Marblehead!

Fathoms deep in dark Chaleur
That wreck shall lie forevermore.
Mother and sister, wife and maid,
Looked from the rocks of Marblehead
Over the moaning and rainy sea, –
Looked for the coming that might not be!
What did the winds and the sea-birds say
Of the cruel captain who sailed away? –
  Old Floyd Ireson, for his hard heart,
  Tarred and feathered and carried in a cart
      By the women of Marblehead!

Through the street, on either side,
Up flew windows, doors swung wide;
Sharp-tongued spinsters, old wives gray,
Treble lent the fish-horn's bray.

Sea-worn grandsires, cripple-bound,
Hulks of old sailors run aground,
Shook head, and fist, and hat, and cane,
And cracked with curses the hoarse refrain:
  'Here's Flud Oirson, fur his horrd horrt,
    Torr'd an' futherr'd an' corr'd in a corrt
      By the women o' Morble'ead!'

Sweetly along the Salem road
Bloom of orchard and lilac showed.
Little the wicked skipper knew
Of the fields so green and the sky so blue.
Riding there in his sorry trim,
Like an Indian idol glum and grim,
Scarcely he seemed the sound to hear
Of voices shouting, far and near:
  'Here's Flud Oirson, fur his horrd horrt,
    Torr'd an' futherr'd an' corr'd in a corrt
      By the women o' Morble'ead!'

'Hear me, neighbors!' at last he cried, –
'What to me is this noisy ride?
What is the shame that clothes the skin
To the nameless horror that lives within?
Waking or sleeping, I see a wreck,
And hear a cry from a reeling deck!
Hate me and curse me, – I only dread
The hand of God and the face of the dead!'
  Said old Floyd Ireson, for his hard heart,
    Tarred and feathered and carried in a cart
      By the women of Marblehead!

Then the wife of the skipper lost at sea
Said, 'God has touched him! why should we?'
Said an old wife mourning her only son,
'Cut the rogue's tether and let him run!'

So with soft relentings and rude excuse,
Half scorn, half pity, they cut him loose,
And gave him a cloak to hide him in,
And left him alone with his shame and sin.
  Poor Floyd Ireson, for his hard heart,
   Tarred and feathered and carried in a cart
   By the women of Marblehead!

Barbara Frietchie

Up from the meadows rich with corn,
Clear in the cool September morn,

The clustered spires of Frederick stand
Green-walled by the hills of Maryland.

Round about them orchards sweep,
Apple and peach tree fruited deep,

Fair as the garden of the Lord
To the eyes of the famished rebel horde,

On that pleasant morn of the early fall
When Lee marched over the mountain wall;

Over the mountains winding down,
Horse and foot, into Frederick town.

Forty flags with their silver stars,
Forty flags with their crimson bars,

Flapped in the morning wind: the sun
Of noon looked down, and saw not one.

Up rose old Barbara Frietchie then,
Bowed with her fourscore years and ten;

Bravest of all in Frederick town,
She took up the flag the men hauled down;

In her attic window the staff she set,
To show that one heart was loyal yet.

Up the street came the rebel tread,
Stonewall Jackson riding ahead.

Under his slouched hat left and right
He glanced; the old flag met his sight.

'Halt!' – the dust-brown ranks stood fast.
'Fire!' – out blazed the rifle-blast.

It shivered the window, pane and sash;
It rent the banner with seam and gash.

Quick, as it fell, from the broken staff
Dame Barbara snatched the silken scarf.

She leaned far out on the window-sill,
And shook it forth with a royal will.

'Shoot, if you must, this old gray head,
But spare your country's flag,' she said.

A shade of sadness, a blush of shame,
Over the face of the leader came;

The nobler nature within him stirred
To life at that woman's deed and word:

'Who touches a hair of yon gray head
Dies like a dog! March on!' he said.

All day long through Frederick street
Sounded the tread of marching feet:

All day long that free flag tost
Over the heads of the rebel host.

Ever its torn folds rose and fell
On the loyal winds that loved it well;

And through the hill-gaps sunset light
Shone over it with a warm good-night.

Barbara Frietchie's work is o'er,
And the Rebel rides on his raids no more.

Honor to her! and let a tear
Fall, for her sake, on Stonewall's bier.

Over Barbara Frietchie's grave,
Flag of Freedom and Union, wave!

Peace and order and beauty draw
Round thy symbol of light and law;

And ever the stars above look down
On thy stars below in Frederick town!

Edgar Allan Poe 1809–49

A Dream within a Dream

Take this kiss upon the brow!
And, in parting from you now,
Thus much let me avow –
You are not wrong, who deem
That my days have been a dream;
Yet if Hope has flown away
In a night, or in a day,
In a vision, or in none,
Is it therefore the less *gone*?
All that we see or seem
Is but a dream within a dream.

I stand amid the roar
Of a surf-tormented shore,
And I hold within my hand
Grains of the golden sand –
How few! yet how they creep
Through my fingers to the deep,
While I weep – while I weep!
Oh God! can I not grasp
Them with a tighter clasp?
O God! can I not save
One from the pitiless wave?
Is *all* that we see or seem
But a dream within a dream?

To Helen

Helen, thy beauty is to me
   Like those Nicéan barks of yore,
That gently, o'er a perfumed sea,
   The weary, way-worn wanderer bore
   To his own native shore.

On desperate seas long wont to roam,
   Thy hyacinth hair, thy classic face,
Thy Naiad airs have brought me home
   To the glory that was Greece,
And the grandeur that was Rome.

Lo! in yon brilliant window-niche
   How statue-like I see thee stand,
   The agate lamp within thy hand!
Ah, Psyche, from the regions which
   Are Holy Land!

The City in the Sea

Lo! Death has reared himself a throne
In a strange city lying alone
Far down within the dim West,
Where the good and the bad and the worst and the best
Have gone to their eternal rest.
There shrines and palaces and towers
(Time-eaten towers that tremble not!)
Resemble nothing that is ours.
Around, by lifting winds forgot,
Resignedly beneath the sky
The melancholy waters lie.

No rays from the holy heaven come down
On the long night-time of that town;
But light from out the lurid sea
Streams up the turrets silently –
Gleams up the pinnacles far and free –
Up domes – up spires – up kingly halls –
Up fanes – up Babylon-like walls –
Up shadowy long-forgotten bowers
Of sculptured ivy and stone flowers –
Up many and many a marvellous shrine
Whose wreathéd friezes intertwine
The viol, the violet, and the vine.

Resignedly beneath the sky
The melancholy waters lie.
So blend the turrets and shadows there
That all seem pendulous in air,
While from a proud tower in the town
Death looks gigantically down.

There open fanes and gaping graves
Yawn level with the luminous waves;
But not the riches there that lie
In each idol's diamond eye –
Not the gaily-jewelled dead
Tempt the waters from their bed;
For no ripples curl, alas!
Along that wilderness of glass –
No swellings tell that winds may be
Upon some far-off happier sea –
No heavings hint that winds have been
On seas less hideously serene.

But lo, a stir is in the air!
The wave – there is a movement there!

As if the towers had thrust aside,
In slightly sinking, the dull tide –
As if their tops had feebly given
A void within the filmy Heaven.
The waves have now a redder glow –
The hours are breathing faint and low –
And when, amid no earthly moans,
Down, down that town shall settle hence,
Hell, rising from a thousand thrones,
Shall do it reverence.

To One in Paradise

Thou wast that all to me, love,
  For which my soul did pine –
A green isle in the sea, love,
  A fountain and a shrine,
All wreathed with fairy fruits and flowers,
  And all the flowers were mine.

Ah, dream too bright to last!
  Ah, starry Hope! that didst arise
But to be overcast!
  A voice from out the Future cries,
'On! on!' – but o'er the Past
  (Dim gulf!) my spirit hovering lies
Mute, motionless, aghast!

For, alas! alas! with me
  The light of Life is o'er!
No more – no more – no more –
  (Such language holds the solemn sea
To the sands upon the shore)
  Shall bloom the thunder-blasted tree,
Or the stricken eagle soar!

And all my days are trances,
　　And all my nightly dreams
Are where thy grey eye glances,
　　And where thy footstep gleams –
In what ethereal dances,
　　By what eternal streams.

The Conqueror Worm

Lo! 't is a gala night
　　Within the lonesome latter years!
An angel throng, bewinged, bedight
　　In veils, and drowned in tears,
Sit in a theatre, to see
　　A play of hopes and fears,
While the orchestra breathes fitfully
　　The music of the spheres.

Mimes, in the form of God on high,
　　Mutter and mumble low,
And hither and thither fly –
　　Mere puppets they, who come and go
At bidding of vast formless things
　　That shift the scenery to and fro,
Flapping from out their Condor wings
　　Invisible Wo!

That motley drama – oh, be sure
　　It shall not be forgot!
With its Phantom chased for evermore
　　By a crowd that seize it not,
Through a circle that ever returneth in
　　To the self-same spot,
And much of Madness, and more of Sin,
　　And Horror the soul of the plot.

But see, amid the mimic rout,
  A crawling shape intrude!
A blood-red thing that writhes from out
  The scenic solitude!
It writhes! – it writhes! – with mortal pangs
  The mimes become its food,
And seraphs sob at vermin fangs
  In human gore imbued.

Out – out are the lights – out all!
  And, over each quivering form,
The curtain, a funeral pall,
  Comes down with the rush of a storm,
While the angels, all pallid and wan,
  Uprising, unveiling, affirm
That the play is the tragedy, 'Man',
  And its hero, the Conqueror Worm.

For Annie

Thank Heaven! the crisis,
  The danger, is past,
And the lingering illness
  Is over at last –
And the fever called 'Living'
  Is conquered at last.

Sadly, I know
  I am shorn of my strength,
And no muscle I move
  As I lie at full length –
But no matter! – I feel
  I am better at length.

And I rest so composedly,
  Now, in my bed,
That any beholder
  Might fancy me dead –
Might start at beholding me,
  Thinking me dead.

The moaning and groaning,
  The sighing and sobbing,
Are quieted now,
  With that horrible throbbing
At heart: – ah, that horrible,
  Horrible throbbing!

The sickness – the nausea –
  The pitiless pain –
Have ceased, with the fever
  That maddened my brain –
With the fever called 'Living'
  That burned in my brain.

And oh! of all tortures
  That torture the worst
Has abated – the terrible
  Torture of thirst
For the naphthaline river
  Of Passion accurst: –
I have drank of a water
  That quenches all thirst: –

Of a water that flows,
  With a lullaby sound,
From a spring but a very few
  Feet under ground –
From a cavern not very far
  Down under ground.

And ah! let it never
   Be foolishly said
That my room it is gloomy
   And narrow my bed;
For man never slept
   In a different bed –
And, to *sleep*, you must slumber
   In just such a bed.

My tantalized spirit
   Here blandly reposes,
Forgetting, or never
   Regretting, its roses –
Its old agitations
   Of myrtles and roses:

For now, while so quietly
   Lying, it fancies
A holier odor
   About it, of pansies –
A rosemary odor,
   Commingled with pansies –
With rue and the beautiful
   Puritan pansies.

And so it lies happily,
   Bathing in many
A dream of the truth
   And the beauty of Annie –
Drowned in a bath
   Of the tresses of Annie.

She tenderly kissed me,
   She fondly caressed,

And then I fell gently
   To sleep on her breast –
Deeply to sleep
   From the heaven of her breast.

When the light was extinguished,
   She covered me warm,
And she prayed to the angels
   To keep me from harm –
To the queen of the angels
   To shield me from harm.

And I lie so composedly,
   Now, in my bed,
(Knowing her love),
   That you fancy me dead –
And I rest so contentedly,
   Now, in my bed
(With her love at my breast),
   That you fancy me dead –
That you shudder to look at me,
   Thinking me dead: –

But my heart it is brighter
   Than all of the many
Stars in the sky,
   For it sparkles with Annie –
It glows with the light
   Of the love of my Annie –
With the thought of the light
   Of the eyes of my Annie.

Annabel Lee

It was many and many a year ago,
   In a kingdom by the sea,
That a maiden there lived whom you may know
   By the name of Annabel Lee;
And this maiden she lived with no other thought
   Than to love and be loved by me.

She was a child and *I* was a child,
   In this kingdom by the sea,
But we loved with a love that was more than love –
   I and my Annabel Lee –
With a love that the wingéd seraphs of Heaven
   Coveted her and me.

And this was the reason that, long ago,
   In this kingdom by the sea,
A wind blew out of a cloud, by night
   Chilling my Annabel Lee;
So that her highborn kinsmen came
   And bore her away from me,
To shut her up in a sepulchre
   In this kingdom by the sea.

The angels, not half so happy in Heaven,
   Went envying her and me: –
Yes! – that was the reason (as all men know,
   In this kingdom by the sea)
That the wind came out of the cloud, chilling
   And killing my Annabel Lee.

But our love it was stronger by far than the love
   Of those who were older than we –
   Of many far wiser than we –

And neither the angels in Heaven above
  Nor the demons down under the sea,
Can ever dissever my soul from the soul
  Of the beautiful Annabel Lee: –

For the moon never beams, without bringing me dreams
  Of the beautiful Annabel Lee;
And the stars never rise but I see the bright eyes
  Of the beautiful Annabel Lee:
And so, all the night-tide, I lie down by the side
Of my darling, my darling, my life and my bride,
  In the sepulchre there by the sea –
  In her tomb by the side of the sea.

Oliver Wendell Holmes 1809–94

From *Wind-Clouds and Star-Drifts*

MANHOOD

I claim the right of knowing whom I serve,
Else is my service idle; He that asks
My homage asks it from a reasoning soul.
To crawl is not to worship; we have learned
A drill of eyelids, bended neck and knee,
Hanging our prayers on hinges, till we ape
The flexures of the many-jointed worm.
Asia has taught her Allahs and salaams
To the world's children, – we have grown to men!
We who have rolled the sphere beneath our feet
To find a virgin forest, as we lay
The beams of our rude temple, first of all
Must frame its doorway high enough for man
To pass unstooping; knowing as we do
That He who shaped us last of living forms
Has long enough been served by creeping things,
Reptiles that left their footprints in the sand
Of old sea-margins that have turned to stone,
And men who learned their ritual; we demand
To know Him first, then trust Him and then love
When we have found Him worthy of our love,
Tried by our own poor hearts and not before;
He must be truer than the truest friend,
He must be tenderer than a woman's love,
A father better than the best of sires;
Kinder than she who bore us, though we sin
Oftener than did the brother we are told

We – poor ill-tempered mortals – must forgive,
Though seven times sinning threescore times and ten.

This is the new world's gospel: Be ye men!
Try well the legends of the children's time;
Ye are the chosen people, God has led
Your steps across the desert of the deep
As now across the desert of the shore;
Mountains are cleft before you as the sea
Before the wandering tribe of Israel's sons;
Still onward rolls the thunderous caravan,
Its coming printed on the western sky,
A cloud by day, by night a pillared flame;
Your prophets are a hundred unto one
Of them of old who cried, 'Thus saith the Lord';
They told of cities that should fall in heaps,
But yours of mightier cities that shall rise
Where yet the lonely fishers spread their nets,
Where hides the fox and hoots the midnight owl;
The tree of knowledge in your garden grows
Not single, but at every humble door;
Its branches lend you their immortal food,
That fills you with the sense of what ye are,
No servants of an altar hewed and carved
From senseless stone by craft of human hands,
Rabbi, or dervish, brahmin, bishop, bonze,
But masters of the charm with which they work
To keep your hands from that forbidden tree!

Ye that have tasted that divinest fruit,
Look on this world of yours with opened eyes!
Ye are as gods! Nay, makers of your gods, –
Each day ye break an image in your shrine
And plant a fairer image where it stood:
Where is the Moloch of your fathers' creed,
Whose fires of torment burned for span-long babes?

Fit object for a tender mother's love!
Why not? It was a bargain duly made
For these same infants through the surety's act
Intrusted with their all for earth and heaven,
By Him who chose their guardian, knowing well
His fitness for the task, – this, even this,
Was the true doctrine only yesterday
As thoughts are reckoned, – and to-day you hear
In words that sound as if from human tongues
Those monstrous, uncouth horrors of the past
That blot the blue of heaven and shame the earth
As would the saurians of the age of slime,
Awaking from their stony sepulchres
And wallowing hateful in the eye of day!

Jones Very 1813–80

The Dead

I see them, – crowd on crowd they walk the earth,
Dry, leafless trees no autumn wind laid bare;
And in their nakedness find cause for mirth,
And all unclad would winter's rudeness dare;
No sap doth through their clattering branches flow,
Whence springing leaves and blossoms bright appear;
Their hearts the living God have ceased to know,
Who gives the springtime to th'expectant year;
They mimic life, as if from him to steal
His glow of health to paint the livid cheek;
They borrow words for thoughts they cannot feel,
That with a seeming heart their tongue may speak;
And in their show of life more dead they live
Than those that to the earth with many tears they give.

Soul-Sickness

How many of the body's health complain,
When they some deeper malady conceal;
Some unrest of the soul, some secret pain,
Which thus its presence doth to them reveal.
Vain would we seek, by the physician's aid,
A name for this soul-sickness e'er to find;
A remedy for health and strength decayed,
Whose cause and cure are wholly of the mind.
To higher nature is the soul allied,

And restless seeks its being's Source to know;
Finding nor health nor strength in aught beside;
How often vainly sought in things below,
Whether in sunny clime, or sacred stream,
Or plant of wondrous powers of which we dream!

Henry David Thoreau 1817–62

Great God, I ask Thee for No Meaner Pelf

Great God, I ask thee for no meaner pelf
Than that I may not disappoint myself,
That in my action I may soar as high,
As I can now discern with this clear eye.

And next in value, which thy kindness lends,
That I may greatly disappoint my friends,
Howe'er they think or hope that it may be,
They may not dream how thou'st distinguished me.

That my weak hand may equal my firm faith,
And my life practice more than my tongue saith;
That my low conduct may not show,
Nor my relenting lines,
That I thy purpose did not know,
Or overrated thy designs.

I am a Parcel of Vain Strivings Tied

I am a parcel of vain strivings tied
  By a chance bond together,
    Dangling this way and that, their links
   Were made so loose and wide,
     Methinks,
    For milder weather.

A bunch of violets without their roots,
   And sorrel intermixed,
  Encircled by a wisp of straw
    Once coiled about their shoots,
      The law
    By which I'm fixed.

A nosegay which Time clutched from out
   Those fair Elysian fields,
  With weeds and broken stems, in haste,
   Doth make the rabble rout
     That waste
    The day he yields.

And here I bloom for a short hour unseen,
   Drinking my juices up,
  With no root in the land
   To keep my branches green,
     But stand
    In a bare cup.

Some tender buds were left upon my stem
   In mimicry of life,
  But ah! the children will not know,
   Till time has withered them,
     The woe
    With which they're rife.

But now I see I was not plucked for naught,
   And after in life's vase
  Of glass set while I might survive,
   But by a kind hand brought
     Alive
    To a strange place.

That stock thus thinned will soon redeem its hours,
  And by another year,
Such as God knows, with freer air,
  More fruits and fairer flowers
    Will bear,
  While I droop here.

James Russell Lowell 1819–91

From *A Fable for Critics*

EMERSON

'There comes Emerson first, whose rich words, every one,
Are like gold nails in temples to hang trophies on,
Whose prose is grand verse, while his verse, the Lord knows,
Is some of it pr– No, 'tis not even prose;
I'm speaking of metres; some poems have welled
From those rare depths of soul that have ne'er been excelled;
They're not epics, but that doesn't matter a pin,
In creating, the only hard thing's to begin;
A grass-blade's no easier to make than an oak;
If you've once found the way, you've achieved the grand stroke;
In the worst of his poems are mines of rich matter,
But thrown in a heap with a crash and a clatter;
Now it is not one thing nor another alone
Makes a poem, but rather the general tone,
The something pervading, uniting the whole,
The before unconceived, unconceivable soul,
So that just in removing this trifle or that, you
Take away, as it were, a chief limb of the statue;
Roots, wood, bark, and leaves singly perfect may be,
But, clapt hodge-podge together, they don't make a tree.

'But, to come back to Emerson (whom, by the way,
I believe we left waiting), – his is, we may say,
A Greek head on right Yankee shoulders, whose range
Has Olympus for one pole, for t'other the Exchange;
He seems, to my thinking (although I'm afraid
The comparison must, long ere this, have been made),

A Plotinus–Montaigne, where the Egyptian's gold mist
And the Gascon's shrewd wit cheek-by-jowl coexist;
All admire, and yet scarcely six converts he's got
To I don't (nor they either) exactly know what;
For though he builds glorious temples, 'tis odd
He leaves never a doorway to get in a god.
'Tis refreshing to old-fashioned people like me
To meet such a primitive Pagan as he,
In whose mind all creation is duly respected
As parts of himself – just a little projected;
And who's willing to worship the stars and the sun,
A convert to – nothing but Emerson.
So perfect a balance there is in his head,
That he talks of things sometimes as if they were dead;
Life, nature, love, God, and affairs of that sort,
He looks at as merely ideas; in short,
As if they were fossils stuck round in a cabinet,
Of such vast extent that our earth's a mere dab in it;
Composed just as he is inclined to conjecture her,
Namely, one part pure earth, ninety-nine parts pure lecturer;
You are filled with delight at his clear demonstration,
Each figure, word, gesture, just fits the occasion,
With the quiet precision of science he'll sort 'em,
But you can't help suspecting the whole a *post mortem*.

'There are persons, mole-blind to the soul's make and style,
Who insist on a likeness 'twixt him and Carlyle;
To compare him with Plato would be vastly fairer,
Carlyle's the more burly, but E. is the rarer;
He sees fewer objects, but clearlier, truelier,
If C.'s as original, E.'s more peculiar;
That he's more of a man you might say of the one,
Of the other he's more of an Emerson;
C.'s the Titan, as shaggy of mind as of limb, –
E. the clear-eyed Olympian, rapid and slim;
The one's two thirds Norseman, the other half Greek,

Where the one's most abounding, the other's to seek;
C.'s generals require to be seen in the mass, –
E.'s specialties gain if enlarged by the glass;
C. gives nature and God his own fits of the blues,
And rims common-sense things with mystical hues, –
E. sits in a mystery calm and intense,
And looks coolly around him with sharp common-sense;
C. shows you how every-day matters unite
With the dim transdiurnal recesses of night, –
While E., in a plain, preternatural way,
Makes mysteries matters of mere every day;
C. draws all his characters quite *à la* Fuseli, –
Not sketching their bundles of muscles and thews illy,
He paints with a brush so untamed and profuse,
They seem nothing but bundles of muscles and thews;
E. is rather like Flaxman, lines strait and severe,
And a colorless outline, but full, round, and clear; –
To the men he thinks worthy he frankly accords
The design of a white marble statue in words.
C. labors to get at the centre, and then
Takes a reckoning from there of his actions and men;
E. calmly assumes the said centre as granted,
And, given himself, has whatever is wanted.'

POE AND LONGFELLOW

'There comes Poe, with his raven, like Barnaby Rudge,
Three fifths of him genius and two fifths sheer fudge,
Who talks like a book of iambs and pentameters,
In a way to make people of common sense damn metres,
Who has written some things quite the best of their kind,
But the heart somehow seems all squeezed out by the mind,
Who – But hey-day! What's this? Messieurs Mathews and Poe,
You mustn't fling mud-balls at Longfellow so,

Does it make a man worse that his character's such
As to make his friends love him (as you think) too much?
Why, there is not a bard at this moment alive
More willing than he that his fellows should thrive;
While you are abusing him thus, even now
He would help either one of you out of a slough;
You may say that he's smooth and all that till you're hoarse,
But remember that elegance also is force;
After polishing granite as much as you will,
The heart keeps its tough old persistency still;
Deduct all you can, *that* still keeps you at bay;
Why, he'll live till men weary of Collins and Gray.
I'm not over-fond of Greek metres in English,
To me rhyme's a gain, so it be not too jinglish,
And your modern hexameter verses are no more
Like Greek ones than sleek Mr Pope is like Homer;
As the roar of the sea to the coo of a pigeon is,
So, compared to your moderns, sounds old Melesigenes;
I may be too partial, the reason, perhaps, o't is
That I've heard the old blind man recite his own rhapsodies,
And my ear with that music impregnate may be,
Like the poor exiled shell with the soul of the sea,
Or as one can't bear Strauss when his nature is cloven
To its deeps within deeps by the stroke of Beethoven;
But, set that aside, and 'tis truth that I speak,
Had Theocritus written in English, not Greek,
I believe that his exquisite sense would scarce change a line
In that rare, tender, virgin-like pastoral Evangeline.
That's not ancient nor modern, its place is apart
Where time has no sway, in the realm of pure Art,
'Tis a shrine of retreat from Earth's hubbub and strife
As quiet and chaste as the author's own life.'

Herman Melville 1819–91

Misgivings

When ocean-clouds over inland hills
   Sweep storming in late autumn brown,
And horror the sodden valley fills,
   And the spire falls crashing in the town,
I muse upon my country's ills –
The tempest bursting from the waste of Time
On the world's fairest hope linked with man's foulest crime.

Nature's dark side is heeded now –
   (Ah! optimist-cheer disheartened flown) –
A child may read the moody brow
   Of yon black mountain lone.
With shouts the torrents down the gorges go,
And storms are formed behind the storm we feel:
The hemlock shakes in the rafter, the oak in the driving keel.

Shiloh

A REQUIEM
(APRIL 1862)

Skimming lightly, wheeling still,
   The swallows fly low
Over the field in clouded days,
   The forest-field of Shiloh –
Over the field where April rain
Solaced the parched one stretched in pain
Through the pause of night
That followed the Sunday fight

Around the church of Shiloh –
The church so lone, the log-built one,
That echoed to many a parting groan
    And natural prayer
Of dying foemen mingled there –
Foemen at morn, but friends at eve –
  Fame or country least their care:
(What like a bullet can undeceive!)
  But now they lie low,
While over them the swallows skim
  And all is hushed at Shiloh.

Monody

To have known him, to have loved him
  After loneness long;
And then to be estranged in life,
  And neither in the wrong;
And now for death to set his seal –
  Ease me, a little ease, my song!

By wintry hills his hermit-mound
  The sheeted snow-drifts drape,
And houseless there the snow-bird flits
  Beneath the fir-trees' crape:
Glazed now with ice the cloistral vine
  That hid the shyest grape.

Walt Whitman 1819—92

Song of Myself

1

I celebrate myself, and sing myself,
And what I assume you shall assume,
For every atom belonging to me as good belongs to you.

I loafe and invite my soul,
I lean and loafe at my ease observing a spear of summer grass.

My tongue, every atom of my blood, form'd from this soil, this air,
Born here of parents born here from parents the same, and their
    parents the same,
I, now thirty-seven years old in perfect health begin,
Hoping to cease not till death.

Creeds and schools in abeyance,
Retiring back a while sufficed at what they are, but never forgotten,
I harbor for good or bad, I permit to speak at every hazard,
Nature without check with original energy.

2

Houses and rooms are full of perfumes, the shelves are crowded with
    perfumes,
I breathe the fragrance myself and know it and like it,
The distillation would intoxicate me also, but I shall not let it.

The atmosphere is not a perfume, it has no taste of the distillation, it
    is odorless,
It is for my mouth forever, I am in love with it,
I will go to the bank by the wood and become undisguised and naked,

I am mad for it to be in contact with me.

The smoke of my own breath

Echoes, ripples, buzz'd whispers, love-root, silk-thread, crotch and vine,

My respiration and inspiration, the beating of my heart, the passing of blood and air through my lungs,

The sniff of green leaves and dry leaves, and of the shore and dark-color'd sea-rocks, and of hay in the barn,

The sound of the belch'd words of my voice loos'd to the eddies of the wind,

A few light kisses, a few embraces, a reaching around of arms,

The play of shine and shade on the trees as the supple boughs wag,

The delight alone or in the rush of the streets, or along the fields and hill-sides,

The feeling of health, the full-noon trill, the song of me rising from bed and meeting the sun.

Have you reckon'd a thousand acres much? have you reckon'd the earth much?

Have you practis'd so long to learn to read?

Have you felt so proud to get at the meaning of poems?

Stop this day and night with me and you shall possess the origin of all poems,

You shall possess the good of the earth and sun, (there are millions of suns left,)

You shall no longer take things at second or third hand, nor look through the eyes of the dead, nor feed on the spectres in books,

You shall not look through my eyes either, nor take things from me,

You shall listen to all sides and filter them from your self.

3

I have heard what the talkers were talking, the talk of the beginning and the end,

But I do not talk of the beginning or the end.

There was never any more inception than there is now,
Nor any more youth or age than there is now,
And will never be any more perfection than there is now,
Nor any more heaven or hell than there is now.

Urge and urge and urge,
Always the procreant urge of the world.

Out of the dimness opposite equals advance, always substance and
    increase, always sex,
Always a knit of identity, always distinction, always a breed of life.

To elaborate is no avail, learn'd and unlearn'd feel that it is so.

Sure as the most certain sure, plumb in the uprights, well entretied,
    braced in the beams,
Stout as a horse, affectionate, haughty, electrical,
I and this mystery here we stand.

Clear and sweet is my soul, and clear and sweet is all that is not my
    soul.

Lack one lacks both, and the unseen is proved by the seen,
Till that becomes unseen and receives proof in its turn.

Showing the best and dividing it from the worst age vexes age,
Knowing the perfect fitness and equanimity of things, while they
    discuss I am silent, and go bathe and admire myself.

Welcome is every organ and attribute of me, and of any man hearty
    and clean,
Not an inch nor a particle of an inch is vile, and none shall be less
    familiar than the rest.

I am satisfied – I see, dance, laugh, sing;
As the hugging and loving bed-fellow sleeps at my side through the
    night, and withdraws at the peep of the day with stealthy tread,

Leaving me baskets cover'd with white towels swelling the house
    with their plenty,
Shall I postpone my acceptation and realization and scream at my eyes,
That they turn from gazing after and down the road,
And forthwith cipher and show me to a cent,
Exactly the value of one and exactly the value of two, and which is
    ahead?

4

Trippers and askers surround me,
People I meet, the effect upon me of my early life or the ward and
    city I live in, or the nation,
The latest dates, discoveries, inventions, societies, authors old and
    new,
My dinner, dress, associates, looks, compliments, dues,
The real or fancied indifference of some man or woman I love,
The sickness of one of my folks or of myself, or ill-doing or loss or
    lack of money, or depressions or exaltations,
Battles, the horrors of fratricidal war, the fever of doubtful news, the
    fitful events;
These come to me days and nights and go from me again,
But they are not the Me myself.

Apart from the pulling and hauling stands what I am,
Stands amused, complacent, compassionating, idle, unitary,
Looks down, is erect, or bends an arm on an impalpable certain rest,
Looking with side-curved head curious what will come next,
Both in and out of the game and watching and wondering at it.

Backward I see in my own days where I sweated through fog with
    linguists and contenders,
I have no mockings or arguments, I witness and wait.

5

I believe in you my soul, the other I am must not abase itself to you,
And you must not be abased to the other.

Loafe with me on the grass, loose the stop from your throat,
Not words, not music or rhyme I want, not custom or lecture, not
    even the best,
Only the lull I like, the hum of your valvèd voice.

I mind how once we lay such a transparent summer morning,
How you settled your head athwart my hips and gently turn'd over
    upon me,
And parted the shirt from my bosom-bone, and plunged your tongue
    to my bare-stript heart,
And reach'd till you felt my beard, and reach'd till you held my feet.

Swiftly arose and spread around me the peace and knowledge that
    pass all the argument of the earth,
And I know that the hand of God is the promise of my own,
And I know that the spirit of God is the brother of my own,
And that all the men ever born are also my brothers, and the women
    my sisters and lovers,
And that a kelson of the creation is love,
And limitless are leaves stiff or drooping in the fields,
And brown ants in the little wells beneath them,
And mossy scabs of the worm fence, heap'd stones, elder, mullein
    and poke-weed.

6

A child said *What is the grass?* fetching it to me with full hands;
How could I answer the child? I do not know what it is any more
    than he.

I guess it must be the flag of my disposition, out of hopeful green
    stuff woven.

Or I guess it is the handkerchief of the Lord,
A scented gift and remembrancer designedly dropt,
Bearing the owner's name someway in the corners, that we may see
    and remark, and say *Whose?*

Or I guess the grass is itself a child, the produced babe of the
    vegetation.

Or I guess it is a uniform hieroglyphic,
And it means, Sprouting alike in broad zones and narrow zones,
Growing among black folks as among white,
Kanuck, Tuckahoe, Congressman, Cuff, I give them the same, I
    receive them the same.

And now it seems to me the beautiful uncut hair of graves.

Tenderly will I use you curling grass,
It may be you transpire from the breasts of young men,
It may be if I had known them I would have loved them,
It may be you are from old people, or from offspring taken soon out
    of their mothers' laps,
And here you are the mothers' laps.

This grass is very dark to be from the white heads of old mothers,
Darker than the colorless beards of old men,
Dark to come from under the faint red roofs of mouths.

O I perceive after all so many uttering tongues,
And I perceive they do not come from the roofs of mouths for
    nothing.

I wish I could translate the hints about the dead young men and
    women,
And the hints about old men and mothers, and the offspring taken
    soon out of their laps.

What do you think has become of the young and old men?
And what do you think has become of the women and children?

They are alive and well somewhere,
The smallest sprout shows there is really no death,

And if ever there was it led forward life, and does not wait at the end
    to arrest it,
And ceas'd the moment life appear'd.

All goes onward and outward, nothing collapses,
And to die is different from what any one supposed, and luckier.

7

Has any one supposed it lucky to be born?
I hasten to inform him or her it is just as lucky to die, and I know it.

I pass death with the dying and birth with the new-wash'd babe, and
    am not contain'd between my hat and boots,
And peruse manifold objects, no two alike and every one good,
The earth good and the stars good, and their adjuncts all good.

I am not an earth nor an adjunct of an earth,
I am the mate and companion of people, all just as immortal and
    fathomless as myself,
(They do not know how immortal, but I know.)

Every kind for itself and its own, for me mine male and female,
For me those that have been boys and that love women,
For me the man that is proud and feels how it stings to be slighted,
For me the sweet-heart and the old maid, for me mothers and the
    mothers of mothers,
For me lips that have smiled, eyes that have shed tears,
For me children and the begetters of children.

Undrape! you are not guilty to me, nor stale nor discarded,
I see through the broadcloth and gingham whether or no,
And am around, tenacious, acquisitive, tireless, and cannot be shaken
    away.

8

The little one sleeps in its cradle,
I lift the gauze and look a long time, and silently brush away flies
    with my hand.

The youngster and the red-faced girl turn aside up the busy hill,
I peeringly view them from the top.

The suicide sprawls on the bloody floor of the bedroom,
I witness the corpse with its dabbled hair, I note where the pistol has
    fallen.

The blab of the pave, tires of carts, sluff of boot-soles, talk of the
    promenaders,
The heavy omnibus, the driver with his interrogating thumb, the
    clank of the shod horses on the granite floor,
The snow-sleighs, clinking, shouted jokes, pelts of snow-balls,
The hurrahs for popular favorites, the fury of rous'd mobs,
The flap o f the curtain'd litter, a sick man inside borne to the hospital,
The meeting of enemies, the sudden oath, the blows and fall,
The excited crowd, the policeman with his star quickly working his
    passage to the centre of the crowd,
The impassive stones that receive and return so many echoes,
What groans of over-fed or half-starv'd who fall sunstruck or in fits,
What exclamations of women taken suddenly who hurry home and
    give birth to babes,
What living and buried speech is always vibrating here, what howls
    restrain'd by decorum,
Arrests of criminals, slights, adulterous offers made, acceptances,
    rejections with convex lips,
I mind them or the show or resonance of them – I come and I depart.

9

The big doors of the country barn stand open and ready,
The dried grass of the harvest-time loads the slow-drawn wagon,

The clear light plays on the brown gray and green intertinged,
The armfuls are pack'd to the sagging mow.

I am there, I help, I came stretch'd atop of the load,
I felt its soft jolts, one leg reclined on the other,
I jump from the cross-beams and seize the clover and timothy,
And roll head over heels and tangle my hair full of wisps.

10

Alone far in the wilds and mountains I hunt,
Wandering amazed at my own lightness and glee,
In the late afternoon choosing a safe spot to pass the night,
Kindling a fire and broiling the fresh-kill'd game,
Falling asleep on the gather'd leaves with my dog and gun by my
    side.

The Yankee clipper is under her sky-sails, she cuts the sparkle and
    scud,
My eyes settle the land, I bend at her prow or shout joyously from
    the deck.

The boatmen and clam-diggers arose early and stopt for me,
I tuck'd my trowser-ends in my boots and went and had a good time;
You should have been with us that day round the chowder-kettle.

I saw the marriage of the trapper in the open air in the far west, the
    bride was a red girl,
Her father and his friends sat near cross-legged and dumbly smoking,
    they had moccasins to their feet and large thick blankets hanging
    from their shoulders,
On a bank lounged the trapper, he was drest mostly in skins, his
    luxuriant beard and curls protected his neck, he held his bride by
    the hand,
She had long eyelashes, her head was bare, her coarse straight locks
    descended upon her voluptuous limbs and reach'd to her feet.

The runaway slave came to my house and stopt outside,
I heard his motions crackling the twigs of the woodpile,
Through the swung half-door of the kitchen I saw him limpsy and
    weak,
And went where he sat on a log and led him in and assured him,
And brought water and fill'd a tub for his sweated body and bruis'd
    feet,
And gave him a room that enter'd from my own, and gave him some
    coarse clean clothes,
And remember perfectly well his revolving eyes and his awkwardness,
And remember putting plasters on the galls of his neck and ankles;
He staid with me a week before he was recuperated and pass'd north
I had him sit next me at table, my fire-lock lean'd in the cornre.

11

Twenty-eight young men bathe by the shore,
Twenty-eight young men and all so friendly;
Twenty-eight years of womanly life and all so lonesome.

She owns the fine house by the rise of the bank,
She hides handsome and richly drest aft the blinds of the window.

Which of the young men does she like the best?
Ah the homeliest of them is beautiful to her.

Where are you off to, lady? for I see you,
You splash in the water there, yet stay stock still in your room.

Dancing and laughing along the beach came the twenty-ninth bather,
The rest did not see her, but she saw them and loved them.

The beards of the young men glisten'd with wet, it ran from their
    long hair,
Little streams pass'd all over their bodies.

An unseen hand also pass'd over their bodies,
It descended tremblingly from their temples and ribs.

The young men float on their backs, their white bellies bulge to the
    sun, they do not ask who seizes fast to them,
They do not know who puffs and declines with pendant and bending
    arch,
They do not think whom they souse with spray.

12

The butcher-boy puts off his killing-clothes, or sharpens his knife at
    the stall in the market,
I loiter enjoying his repartee and his shuffle and break-down.

Blacksmiths with grimed and hairy chests environ the anvil,
Each has his main-sledge, they are all out, there is a great heat in the
    fire.

From the cinder-strew'd threshold I follow their movements,
The lithe sheer of their waists plays even with their massive arms,
Overhand the hammers swing, overhand so slow, overhand so sure,
They do not hasten, each man hits in his place.

13

The negro holds firmly the reins of his four horses, the block swags
    underneath on its tied-over chain,
The negro that drives the long dray of the stone-yard, steady and tall
    he stands pois'd on one leg on the string-piece,
His blue shirt exposes his ample neck and breast and loosens over his
    hip-band,
His glance is calm and commanding, he tosses the slouch of his hat
    away from his forehead,
The sun falls on his crispy hair and mustache, falls on the black of his
    polish'd and perfect limbs.

I behold the picturesque giant and love him, and I do not stop there,
I go with the team also.

In me the caresser of life wherever moving, backward as well as
    forward sluing,
To niches aside and junior bending, not a person or object missing,
Absorbing all to myself and for this song.

Oxen that rattle the yoke and chain or halt in the leafy shade, what is
    that you express in your eyes?
It seems to me more than all the print I have read in my life.

My tread scares the wood-drake and wood-duck on my distant and
    day-long ramble,
They rise together, they slowly circle around.

I believe in those wing'd purposes,
And acknowledge red, yellow, white, playing within me,
And consider green and violet and the tufted crown intentional,
And do not call the tortoise unworthy because she is not something
    else,
And the jay in the woods never studied the gamut, yet trills pretty
    well to me,
And the look of the bay mare shames silliness out of me.

14

The wild gander leads his flock through the cool night,
Ya-honk he says, and sounds it down to me like an invitation,
The pert may suppose it meaningless, but I listening close,
Find its purpose and place up there toward the wintry sky.

The sharp-hoof'd moose of the north, the cat on the house-sill, the
    chickadee, the prairie-dog,
The litter of the grunting sow as they tug at her teats,
The brood of the turkey-hen and she with her half-spread wings,
I see in them and myself the same old law.

The press of my foot to the earth springs a hundred affections,
They scorn the best I can do to relate them.

I am enamour'd of growing out-doors,
Of men that live among cattle or taste of the ocean or woods,
Of the builders and steerers of ships and the wielders of axes and
    mauls, and the drivers of horses,
I can eat and sleep with them week in and week out.

What is commonest, cheapest, nearest, easiest, is Me,
Me going in for my chances, spending for vast returns,
Adorning myself to bestow myself on the first that will take me,
Not asking the sky to come down to my good will,
Scattering it freely forever.

15

The pure contralto sings in the organ loft,
The carpenter dresses his plank, the tongue of his foreplane whistles
    its wild ascending lisp,
The married and unmarried children ride home to their Thanks-
    giving dinner,
The pilot seizes the king-pin, he heaves down with a strong arm,
The mate stands braced in the whale-boat, lance and harpoon are
    ready,
The duck-shooter walks by silent and cautious stretches,
The deacons are ordain'd with cross'd hands at the altar,
The spinning-girl retreats and advances to the hum of the big
    wheel,
The farmer stops by the bars as he walks on a First-day loafe and looks
    at the oats and rye,
The lunatic is carried at last to the asylum a confirm'd case,
(He will never sleep any more as he did in the cot in his mother's
    bed-room;)
The jour printer with gray head and gaunt jaws works at his case,
He turns his quid of tobacco while his eyes blurr with the manuscript;
The malform'd limbs are tied to the surgeon's table,
What is removed drops horribly in a pail;
The quadroon girl is sold at the auction-stand, the drunkard nods by
    the bar-room stove,

The machinist rolls up his sleeves, the policeman travels his beat, the
gate-keeper marks who pass,

The young fellow drives the express-wagon, (I love him, though I do
not know him;)

The half-breed straps on his light boots to compete in the race,

The western turkey-shooting draws old and young, some lean on
their rifles, some sit on logs,

Out from the crowd steps the marksman, takes his position, levels his
piece;

The groups of newly-come immigrants cover the wharf or levee,

As the woolly-pates hoe in the sugar-field, the overseer views them
from his saddle,

The bugle calls in the ball-room, the gentlemen run for their partners,
the dancers bow to each other,

The youth lies awake in the cedar-roof'd garret and harks to the
musical rain,

The Wolverine sets traps on the creek that helps fill the Huron,

The squaw wrapt in her yellow-hemm'd cloth is offering moccasins
and bead-bags for sale,

The connoisseur peers along the exhibition-gallery with half-shut
eyes bent sideways,

As the deck-hands make fast the steamboat the plank is thrown for
the shore-going passengers,

The young sister holds out the skein while the elder sister winds it off
in a ball, and stops now and then for the knots,

The one-year wife is recovering and happy having a week ago borne
her first child,

The clean-hair'd Yankee girl works with her sewing-machine or in
the factory or mill,

The paving-man leans on his two-handed rammer, the reporter's
lead flies swiftly over the note-book, the sign-painter is lettering
with blue and gold,

The canal boy trots on the tow-path, the book-keeper counts at his
desk, the shoemaker waxes his thread,

The conductor beats time for the band and all the performers follow
him,

The child is baptized, the convert is making his first professions,
The regatta is spread on the bay, the race is begun, (how the white
  sails sparkle!)
The drover watching his drove sings out to them that would stray,
The pedler sweats with his pack on his back, (the purchaser higgling
  about the odd cent;)
The bride unrumples her white dress, the minute-hand of the clock
  moves slowly,
The opium-eater reclines with rigid head and just-open'd lips,
The prostitute draggles her shawl, her bonnet bobs on her tipsy and
  pimpled neck,
The crowd laugh at her blackguard oaths, the men jeer and wink to
  each other,
(Miserable! I do not laugh at your oaths nor jeer you;)
The President holding a cabinet council is surrounded by the great
  Secretaries,
On the piazza walk three matrons stately and friendly with twined
  arms,
The crew of the fish-smack pack repeated layers of halibut in the hold,
The Missourian crosses the plains toting his wares and his cattle,
As the fare-collector goes through the train he gives notice by the
  jingling of loose change,
The floor-men are laying the floor, the tinners are tinning the roof,
  the masons are calling for mortar,
In single file each shouldering his hod pass onward the laborers;
Seasons pursuing each other the indescribable crowd is gather'd, it is
  the fourth of Seventh-month, (what salutes of cannon and
  small arms!)
Seasons pursuing each other the plougher ploughs, the mower mows,
  and the winter-grain falls in the ground;
Off on the lakes the pike-fisher watches and waits by the hole in the
  frozen surface,
The stumps stand thick round the clearing, the squatter strikes deep
  with his axe,
Flatboatmen make fast towards dusk near the cotton-wood or
  pecan-trees,

Coon-seekers go through the regions of the Red river or through
those drain'd by the Tennessee, or through those of the
Arkansas,

Torches shine in the dark that hangs on the Chattahooche or
Altamahaw,

Patriarchs sit at supper with sons and grandsons and great-grandsons
around them,

In walls of adobie, in canvas tents, rest hunters and trappers after their
day's sport,

The city sleeps and the country sleeps,

The living sleep for their time, the dead sleep for their time,

The old husband sleeps by his wife and the young husband sleeps by
his wife;

And these tend inward to me, and I tend outward to them,

And such as it is to be of these more or less I am,

And of these one and all I weave the song of myself.

16

I am of old and young, of the foolish as much as the wise,

Regardless of others, ever regardful of others,

Maternal as well as paternal, a child as well as a man,

Stuff'd with the stuff that is coarse and stuff'd with the stuff that
is fine,

One of the Nation of many nations, the smallest the same and the
largest the same,

A Southerner soon as a Northerner, a planter nonchalant and
hospitable down by the Oconee I live,

A Yankee bound my own way ready for trade, my joints the
limberest joints on earth and the sternest joints on earth,

A Kentuckian walking the vale of the Elkhorn in my deer-skin
leggings, a Louisianian or Georgian,

A boatman over lakes or bays or along coasts, a Hoosier, Badger,
Buckeye;

At home on Kanadian snow-shoes or up in the bush, or with fisher-
men off Newfoundland,

At home in the fleet of ice-boats, sailing with the rest and tacking,

At home on the hills of Vermont or in the woods of Maine, or the
    Texan ranch,
Comrade of Californians, comrade of free North-Westerners, (loving
    their big proportions,)
Comrade of raftsmen and coalmen, comrade of all who shake hands
    and welcome to drink and meat,
A learner with the simplest, a teacher of the thoughtfullest,
A novice beginning yet experient of myriads of seasons,
Of every hue and caste am I, of every rank and religion,
A farmer, mechanic, artist, gentleman, sailor, quaker,
Prisoner, fancy-man, rowdy, lawyer, physician, priest.

I resist any thing better than my own diversity,
Breathe the air but leave plenty after me,
And am not stuck up, and am in my place.

(The moth and the fish-eggs are in their place,
The bright suns I see and the dark suns I cannot see are in their place,
The palpable is in its place and the impalpable is in its place.)

17

These are really the thoughts of all men in all ages and lands, they are
    not original with me,
If they are not yours as much as mine they are nothing, or next to
    nothing,
If they are not the riddle and the untying of the riddle they are
    nothing,
If they are not just as close as they are distant they are nothing.

This is the grass that grows wherever the land is and the water is,
This the common air that bathes the globe.

18

With music strong I come, with my cornets and my drums,
I play not marches for accepted victors only, I play marches for
    conquer'd and slain persons.

Have you heard that it was good to gain the day?
I also say it is good to fall, battles are lost in the same spirit in which
   they are won.

I beat and pound for the dead,
I blow through my embouchures my loudest and gayest for them.

Vivas to those who have fail'd!
And to those whose war-vessels sank in the sea!
And to those themselves who sank in the sea!
And to all generals that lost engagements, and all overcome heroes!
And the numberless unknown heroes equal to the greatest heroes
   known!

19

This is the meal equally set, this the meat for natural hunger,
It is for the wicked just the same as the righteous, I make appointments
   with all,
I will not have a single person slighted or left away,
The kept-woman, sponger, thief, are hereby invited,
The heavy-lipp'd slave is invited, the venerealee is invited;
There shall be no difference between them and the rest.

This is the press of a bashful hand, this the float and odor of hair,
This the touch of my lips to yours, this the murmur of yearning,
This the far-off depth and height reflecting my own face,
This the thoughtful merge of myself, and the outlet again.

Do you guess I have some intricate purpose?
Well I have, for the Fourth-month showers have, and the mica on
   the side of a rock has.

Do you take it I would astonish?
Does the daylight astonish? does the early redstart twittering through
   the woods?
Do I astonish more than they?

This hour I tell things in confidence,
I might not tell everybody, but I will tell you.

20

Who goes there? hankering, gross, mystical, nude;
How is it I extract strength from the beef I eat?

What is a man anyhow? what am I? what are you?

All I mark as my own you shall offset it with your own,
Else it were time lost listening to me.

I do not snivel that snivel the world over,
That months are vacuums and the ground but wallow and filth.

Whimpering and truckling fold with powders for invalids, con-
    formity, goes to the fourth-remov'd,
I wear my hat as I please indoors or out.

Why should I pray? why should I venerate and be ceremonious?

Having pried through the strata, analyzed to a hair, counsel'd with
    doctors and calculated close,
I find no sweeter fat than sticks to my own bones.

In all people I see myself, none more and not one a barley-corn less,
And the good or bad I say of myself I say of them.

I know I am solid and sound,
To me the converging objects of the universe perpetually flow,
All are written to me, and I must get what the writing means.

I know I am deathless,
I know this orbit of mine cannot be swept by a carpenter's compass,
I know I shall not pass like a child's carlacue cut with a burnt stick at
    night.

I know I am august,
I do not trouble my spirit to vindicate itself or be understood,
I see that the elementary laws never apologize,
(I reckon I behave no prouder than the level I plant my house by,
    after all.)

I exist as I am, that is enough,
If no other in the world be aware I sit content,
And if each and all be aware I sit content.

One world is aware and by far the largest to me, and that is myself,
And whether I come to my own to-day or in ten thousand or ten
    million years,
I can cheerfully take it now, or with equal cheerfulness I can wait.

My foothold is tenon'd and mortis'd in granite,
I laugh at what you call dissolution,
And I know the amplitude of time.

21

I am the poet of the Body and I am the poet of the Soul,
The pleasures of heaven are with me and the pains of hell are with me,
The first I graft and increase upon myself, the latter I translate into a
    new tongue.

I am the poet of the woman the same as the man,
And I say it is as great to be a woman as to be a man,
And I say there is nothing greater than the mother of men.

I chant the chant of dilation or pride,
We have had ducking and deprecating about enough,
I show that size is only development.

Have you outstript the rest? are you the President?
It is a trifle, they will more than arrive there every one, and still
    pass on.

I am he that walks with the tender and growing night,
I call to the earth and sea half-held by the night.

Press close bare-bosom'd night – press close magnetic nourishing
 night!
Night of south winds – night of the large few stars!
Still nodding night – mad naked summer night.

Smile O voluptuous cool-breath'd earth!
Earth of the slumbering and liquid trees!
Earth of departed sunset – earth of the mountains misty-topt!
Earth of the vitreous pour of the full moon just tinged with blue!
Earth of shine and dark mottling the tide of the river!
Earth of the limpid gray of clouds brighter and clearer for my sake!
Far-swooping elbow'd earth – rich apple-blossom'd earth!
Smile, for your lover comes.

Prodigal, you have given me love – therefore I to you give love!
O unspeakable passionate love.

22

You sea! I resign myself to you also – I guess what you mean,
I behold from the beach your crooked inviting fingers,
I believe you refuse to go back without feeling of me,
We must have a turn together, I undress, hurry me out of sight of
 the land,
Cushion me soft, rock me in billowy drowse,
Dash me with amorous wet, I can repay you.

Sea of stretch'd ground-swells,
Sea breathing broad and convulsive breaths,
Sea of the brine of life and of unshovell'd yet always-ready graves,
Howler and scooper of storms, capricious and dainty sea,
I am integral with you, I too am of one phase and of all phases.

Partaker of influx and efflux I, extoller of hate and conciliation,
Extoller of amies and those that sleep in each others' arms.

I am he attesting sympathy,
(Shall I make my list of things in the house and skip the house that
    supports them?)

I am not the poet of goodness only, I do not decline to be the poet of
    wickedness also.

What blurt is this about virtue and about vice?
Evil propels me and reform of evil propels me, I stand indifferent,
My gait is no fault-finder's or rejecter's gait,
I moisten the roots of all that has grown.

Did you fear some scrofula out of the unflagging pregnancy?
Did you guess the celestial laws are yet to be work'd over and
    rectified?

I find one side a balance and the antipodal side a balance,
Soft doctrine as steady help as stable doctrine,
Thoughts and deeds of the present our rouse and early start.

This minute that comes to me over the past decillions,
There is no better than it and now.

What behaved well in the past or behaves well to-day is not such a
    wonder,
The wonder is always and always how there can be a mean man or an
    infidel.

23

Endless unfolding of words of ages!
And mine a word of the modern, the word En-Masse.

A word of the faith that never balks,
Here or henceforward it is all the same to me, I accept Time absolutely.

It alone is without flaw, it alone rounds and completes all,
That mystic baffling wonder alone completes all.

I accept Reality and dare not question it,
Materialism first and last imbuing.

Hurrah for positive science! long live exact demonstration!
Fetch stonecrop mixt with cedar and branches of lilac,
This is the lexicographer, this the chemist, this made a grammar of
    the old cartouches,
These mariners put the ship through dangerous unknown seas,
This is the geologist, this works with the scalpel, and this is a
    mathematician.

Gentlemen, to you the first honors always!
Your facts are useful, and yet they are not my dwelling,
I but enter by them to an area of my dwelling.

Less the reminders of properties told my words,
And more the reminders they of life untold, and of freedom and
    extrication,
And make short account of neuters and geldings, and favor men and
    women fully equipt,
And beat the gong of revolt, and stop with fugitives and them that
    plot and conspire.

24

Walt Whitman, a kosmos, of Manhattan the son,
Turbulent, fleshy, sensual, eating, drinking and breeding,
No sentimentalist, no stander above men and women or apart from
    them,
No more modest than immodest.

Unscrew the locks from the doors!
Unscrew the doors themselves from their jambs!

Whoever degrades another degrades me,
And whatever is done or said returns at last to me.

Through me the afflatus surging and surging, through me the current
and index.

I speak the pass-word primeval, I give the sign of democracy,
By God! I will accept nothing which all cannot have their counterpart
of on the same terms.

Through me many long dumb voices,
Voices of the interminable generations of prisoners and slaves,
Voices of the diseas'd and despairing and of thieves and dwarfs,
Voices of cycles of preparation and accretion,
And of the threads that connect the stars, and of wombs and of the
father-stuff,
And of the rights of them the others are down upon,
Of the deform'd, trivial, flat, foolish, despised,
Fog in the air, beetles rolling balls of dung.

Through me forbidden voices,
Voices of sexes and lusts, voices veil'd and I remove the veil,
Voices indecent by me clarified and transfigur'd.

I do not press my fingers across my mouth,
I keep as delicate around the bowels as around the head and heart,
Copulation is no more rank to me than death is.

I believe in the flesh and the appetites,
Seeing, hearing, feeling, are miracles, and each part and tag of me is
a miracle.

Divine am I inside and out, and I make holy whatever I touch or am
touch'd from,
The scent of these arm-pits aroma finer than prayer,
This head more than churches, bibles, and all the creeds.

If I worship one thing more than another it shall be the spread of my
own body, or any part of it,

Translucent mould of me it shall be you!
Shaded ledges and rests it shall be you!
Firm masculine colter it shall be you!
Whatever goes to the tilth of me it shall be you!
You my rich blood! your milky stream pale strippings of my
    life!
Breast that presses against other breasts it shall be you!
My brain it shall be your occult convolutions!
Root of wash'd sweet-flag! timorous pond-snipe! nest of guarded
    duplicate eggs! it shall be you!
Mix'd tussled hay of head, beard, brawn, it shall be you!
Trickling sap of maple, fibre of manly wheat, it shall be you!
Sun so generous it shall be you!
Vapors lighting and shading my face it shall be you!
You sweaty brooks and dews it shall be you!
Winds whose soft-tickling genitals rub against me it shall be
    you!
Broad muscular fields, branches of live oak, loving lounger in my
    winding paths, it shall be you!
Hands I have taken, face I have kiss'd, mortal I have ever touch'd, it
    shall be you.

I dote on myself, there is that lot of me and all so luscious,
Each moment and whatever happens thrills me with joy,
I cannot tell how my ankles bend, nor whence the cause of my
    faintest wish,
Nor the cause of the friendship I emit, nor the cause of the friendship
    I take again.

That I walk up my stoop, I pause to consider if it really be,
A morning-glory at my window satisfies me more than the meta-
    physics of books.

To behold the day-break!
The little light fades the immense and diaphanous shadows,
The air tastes good to my palate.

Hefts of the moving world at innocent gambols silently rising freshly
    exuding,
Scooting obliquely high and low.

Something I cannot see puts upward libidinous prongs,
Seas of bright juice suffuse heaven.

The earth by the sky staid with, the daily close of their junction,
The heav'd challenge from the east that moment over my head,
The mocking taunt, See then whether you shall be master!

25

Dazzling and tremendous how quick the sun-rise would kill me,
If I could not now and always send sun-rise out of me.

We also ascend dazzling and tremendous as the sun,
We found our own O my soul in the calm and cool of the day-break.

My voice goes after what my eyes cannot reach,
With the twirl of my tongue I encompass worlds and volumes of
    worlds.

Speech is the twin of my vision, it is unequal to measure itself,
It provokes me forever, it says sarcastically,
Walt you contain enough, why don't you let it out then?

Come now I will not be tantalized, you conceive too much of
    articulation,
Do you not know O speech how the buds beneath you are folded?
Waiting in gloom, protected by frost,
The dirt receding before my prophetical screams,
I underlying causes to balance them at last,
My knowledge my live parts, it keeping tally with the meaning of
    all things,
Happiness, (which whoever hears me let him or her set out in search
    of this day.)

My final merit I refuse you, I refuse putting from me what I really am,
Encompass worlds, but never try to encompass me,
I crowd your sleekest and best by simply looking toward you.

Writing and talk do not prove me,
I carry the plenum of proof and every thing else in my face,
With the hush of my lips I wholly confound the skeptic.

26

Now I will do nothing but listen,
To accrue what I hear into this song, to let sounds contribute toward it.

I hear bravuras of birds, bustle of growing wheat, gossip of flames,
    clack of sticks cooking my meals,
I hear the sound I love, the sound of the human voice,
I hear all sounds running together, combined, fused or following,
Sounds of the city and sounds out of the city, sounds of the day and
    night,
Talkative young ones to those that like them, the loud laugh of
    work-people at their meals,
The angry base of disjointed friendship, the faint tones of the sick,
The judge with hands tight to the desk, his pallid lips pronouncing a
    death-sentence,
The heave'e'yo of stevedores unlading ships by the wharves, the
    refrain of the anchor-lifters,
The ring of alarm-bells, the cry of fire, the whirr of swift-streaking
    engines and hose-carts with premonitory tinkles and color'd
    lights,
The steam-whistle, the solid roll of the train of approaching cars,
The slow march play'd at the head of the association marching two
    and two,
(They go to guard some corpse, the flag-tops are draped with black
    muslin.)

I hear the violoncello, ('tis the young man's heart's complaint,)
I hear the key'd cornet, it glides quickly in through my ears,
It shakes mad-sweet pangs through my belly and breast.

I hear the chorus, it is a grand opera,
Ah this indeed is music – this suits me.

A tenor large and fresh as the creation fills me,
The orbic flex of his mouth is pouring and filling me full.

I hear the train'd soprano (what work with hers is this?)
The orchestra whirls me wider than Uranus flies,
It wrenches such ardors from me I did not know I possess'd them,
It sails me, I dab with bare feet, they are lick'd by the indolent waves,
I am cut by bitter and angry hail, I lose my breath,
Steep'd amid honey'd morphine, my windpipe throttled in fakes of
    death,
At length let up again to feel the puzzle of puzzles,
And that we call Being.

27

To be in any form, what is that?
(Round and round we go, all of us, and ever come back thither,)
If nothing lay more develop'd the quahaug in its callous shell were
    enough.

Mine is no callous shell,
I have instant conductors all over me whether I pass or stop,
They seize every object and lead it harmlessly through me.

I merely stir, press, feel with my fingers, and am happy,
To touch my person to some one else's is about as much as I can stand.

28

Is this then a touch? quivering me to a new identity,
Flames and ether making a rush for my veins,
Treacherous tip of me reaching and crowding to help them,
My flesh and blood playing out lightning to strike what is hardly
    different from myself,
On all sides prurient provokers stiffening my limbs,

Straining the udder of my heart for its withheld drip,
Behaving licentious toward me, taking no denial,
Depriving me of my best as for a purpose,
Unbuttoning my clothes, holding me by the bare waist,
Deluding my confusion with the calm of the sunlight and pasture-
     fields,
Immodestly sliding the fellow-senses away,
They bribed to swap off with touch and go and graze at the edges
     of me,
No consideration, no regard for my draining strength or my anger,
Fetching the rest of the herd around to enjoy them a while,
Then all uniting to stand on a headland and worry me.

The sentries desert every other part of me,
They have left me helpless to a red marauder,
They all come to the headland to witness and assist against me.

I am given up by traitors,
I talk wildly, I have lost my wits, I and nobody else am the greatest
     traitor,
I went myself first to the headland, my own hands carried me there.

You villain touch! what are you doing? my breath is tight in its
     throat,
Unclench your floodgates, you are too much for me.

29

Blind loving wrestling touch, sheath'd hooded sharp-tooth'd touch!
Did it make you ache so, leaving me?

Parting track'd by arriving, perpetual payment of perpetual loan,
Rich showering rain, and recompense richer afterward.

Sprouts take and accumulate, stand by the curb prolific and vital,
Landscapes projected masculine, full-sized and golden.

30

All truths wait in all things,
They neither hasten their own delivery nor resist it,
They do not need the obstetric forceps of the surgeon,
The insignificant is as big to me as any,
(What is less or more than a touch?)

Logic and sermons never convince,
The damp of the night drives deeper into my soul.

(Only what proves itself to every man and woman is so,
Only what nobody denies is so.)

A minute and a drop of me settle my brain,
I believe the soggy clods shall become lovers and lamps,
And a compend of compends is the meat of a man or woman,
And a summit and flower there is the feeling they have for each
    other,
And they are to branch boundlessly out of that lesson until it becomes
    omnific,
And until one and all shall delight us, and we them.

31

I believe a leaf of grass is no less than the journey-work of the stars,
And the pismire is equally perfect, and a grain of sand, and the egg of
    the wren,
And the tree-toad is a chef-d'œuvre for the highest,
And the running blackberry would adorn the parlors of heaven,
And the narrowest hinge in my hand puts to scorn all machinery,
And the cow crunching with depress'd head surpasses any statue,
And a mouse is miracle enough to stagger sextillions of infidels.

I find I incorporate gneiss, coal, long-threaded moss, fruits, grains,
    esculent roots,
And am stucco'd with quadrupeds and birds all over,

And have distanced what is behind me for good reasons,
But call any thing back again when I desire it.

In vain the speeding or shyness,
In vain the plutonic rocks send their old heat against my approach,
In vain the mastodon retreats beneath its own powder'd bones,
In vain objects stand leagues off and assume manifold shapes,
In vain the ocean settling in hollows and the great monsters lying
     low,
In vain the buzzard houses herself with the sky,
In vain the snake slides through the creepers and logs,
In vain the elk takes to the inner passes of the woods,
In vain the razor-bill'd auk sails far north to Labrador,
I follow quickly, I ascend to the nest in the fissure of the cliff.

32

I think I could turn and live with animals, they are so placid and
     self-contain'd,
I stand and look at them long and long.

They do not sweat and whine about their condition,
They do not lie awake in the dark and weep for their sins,
They do not make me sick discussing their duty to God,
Not one is dissatisfied, not one is demented with the mania of owning
     things,
Not one kneels to another, nor to his kind that lived thousands of
     years ago,
Not one is respectable or unhappy over the whole earth.

So they show their relations to me and I accept them,
They bring me tokens of myself, they evince them plainly in their
     possession.

I wonder where they get those tokens,
Did I pass that way huge times ago and negligently drop them?

Myself moving forward then and now and forever,
Gathering and showing more always and with velocity,
Infinite and omnigenous, and the like of these among them,
Not too exclusive toward the reachers of my remembrancers,
Picking out here one that I love, and now go with him on brotherly
    terms.

A gigantic beauty of a stallion, fresh and responsive to my caresses,
Head high in the forehead, wide between the ears,
Limbs glossy and supple, tail dusting the ground,
Eyes full of sparkling wickedness, ears finely cut, flexibly moving.

His nostrils dilate as my heels embrace him,
His well-built limbs tremble with pleasure as we race around and
    return.
I but use you a minute, then I resign you, stallion,
Why do I need your paces when I myself out-gallop them?
Even as I stand or sit passing faster than you.

33

Space and Time! now I see it is true, what I guess'd at,
What I guess'd when I loaf'd on the grass,
What I guess'd while I lay alone in my bed,
And again as I walk'd the beach under the paling stars of the morning.

My ties and ballasts leave me, my elbows rest in sea-gaps,
I skirt sierras, my palms cover continents,
I am afoot with my vision.

By the city's quadrangular houses – in log huts, camping with
    lumbermen,
Along the ruts of the turnpike, along the dry gulch and rivulet bed,
Weeding my onion-patch or hoeing rows of carrots and parsnips,
    crossing savannas, trailing in forests,
Prospecting, gold-digging, girdling the trees of a new purchase,

Scorch'd ankle-deep by the hot sand, hauling by boat down the
    shallow river,
Where the panther walks to and fro on a limb overhead, where the
    buck turns furiously at the hunter,
Where the rattlesnake suns his flabby length on a rock, where the
    otter is feeding on fish,
Where the alligator in his tough pimples sleeps by the bayou,
Where the black bear is searching for roots or honey, where the
    beaver pats the mud with his paddle-shaped tail;
Over the growing sugar, over the yellow-flower'd cotton plant, over
    the rice in its low moist field,
Over the sharp-peak'd farm house, with its scallop'd scum and
    slender shoots from the gutters,
Over the western persimmon, over the long-leav'd corn, over the
    delicate blue-flower flax,
Over the white and brown buckwheat, a hummer and buzzer there
    with the rest,
Over the dusky green of the rye as it ripples and shades in the breeze;
Scaling mountains, pulling myself cautiously up, holding on by low
    scragged limbs,
Walking the path worn in the grass and beat through the leaves of
    the brush,
Where the quail is whistling betwixt the woods and the wheat-lot,
Where the bat flies in the Seventh-month eve, where the great gold-
    bug drops through the dark,
Where the brook puts out of the roots of the old tree and flows to
    the meadow,
Where cattle stand and shake away flies with the tremulous shuddering
    of their hides,
Where the cheese-cloth hangs in the kitchen, where andirons straddle
    the hearth-slab, where cobwebs fall in festoons from the
    rafters;
Where trip-hammers crash, where the press is whirling its cylinders,
Wherever the human heart beats with terrible throes under its ribs,
Where the pear-shaped balloon is floating aloft, (floating in it myself
    and looking composedly down,)

Where the life-car is drawn on the slip-noose, where the heat hatches
    pale-green eggs in the dented sand,
Where the she-whale swims with her calf and never forsakes it,
Where the steam-ship trails hind-ways its long pennant of smoke,
Where the fin of the shark cuts like a black chip out of the water,
Where the half-burn'd brig is riding on unknown currents,
Where shells grow to her slimy deck, where the dead are corrupting
    below;
Where the dense-starr'd flag is borne at the head of the regiments,
Approaching Manhattan up by the long-stretching island,
Under Niagara, the cataract falling like a veil over my countenance,
Upon a door-step, upon the horse-block of hard wood outside,
Upon the race-course, or enjoying picnics or jigs or a good game of
    baseball,
At he-festivals, with blackguard gibes, ironical license, bull-dances,
    drinking, laughter,
At the cider-mill tasting the sweets of the brown mash, sucking the
    juice through a straw,
At apple-peelings wanting kisses for all the red fruit I find,
At musters, beach-parties, friendly bees, huskings, house-raisings;
Where the mocking-bird sounds his delicious gurgles, cackles,
    screams, weeps,
Where the hay-rick stands in the barn-yard, where the dry-stalks are
    scatter'd, where the brood-cow waits in the hovel,
Where the bull advances to do his masculine work, where the stud
    to the mare, where the cock is treading the hen,
Where the heifers browse, where geese nip their food with short
    jerks,
Where sun-down shadows lengthen over the limitless and lonesome
    prairie,
Where herds of buffalo make a crawling spread of the square miles
    far and near,
Where the humming-bird shimmers, where the neck of the long-
    lived swan is curving and winding,
Where the laughing-gull scoots by the shore, where she laughs her
    near-human laugh,

Where bee-hives range on a gray bench in the garden half hid by the high weeds,

Where band-neck'd partridges roost in a ring on the ground with their heads out,

Where burial coaches enter the arch'd gates of a cemetery,

Where winter wolves bark amid wastes of snow and icicled trees,

Where the yellow-crown'd heron comes to the edge of the marsh at night and feeds upon small crabs,

Where the splash of swimmers and divers cools the warm noon,

Where the katy-did works her chromatic reed on the walnut-tree over the well,

Through patches of citrons and cucumbers with silver-wired leaves,

Through the salt-lick or orange glade, or under conical firs,

Through the gymnasium, through the curtain'd saloon, through the office or public hall;

Pleas'd with the native and pleas'd with the foreign, pleas'd with the new and old,

Pleas'd with the homely woman as well as the handsome,

Pleas'd with the quakeress as she puts off her bonnet and talks melodiously,

Pleas'd with the tune of the choir of the whitewash'd church,

Pleas'd with the earnest words of the sweating Methodist preacher, impress'd seriously at the camp-meeting;

Looking in at the shop windows of Broadway the whole forenoon, flatting the flesh of my nose on the thick plate glass,

Wandering the same afternoon with my face turn'd up to the clouds, or down a lane or along the beach,

My right and left arms round the sides of two friends, and I in the middle;

Coming home with the silent and dark-cheek'd bush-boy, (behind me he rides at the drape of the day,)

Far from the settlements studying the print of animals' feet, or the moccasin print,

By the cot in the hospital reaching lemonade to a feverish patient,

Nigh the coffin'd corpse when all is still, examining with a candle;

Voyaging to every port to dicker and adventure,

Hurrying with the modern crowd as eager and fickle as any,
Hot toward one I hate, ready in my madness to knife him,
Solitary at midnight in my back yard, my thoughts gone from me a
    long while,
Walking the old hills of Judæa with the beautiful gentle God by my
    side,
Speeding through space, speeding through heaven and the stars,
Speeding amid the seven satellites and the broad ring, and the
    diameter of eighty thousand miles,
Speeding with tail'd meteors, throwing fire-balls like the rest,
Carrying the crescent child that carries its own full mother in its
    belly,
Storming, enjoying, planning, loving, cautioning,
Backing and filling, appearing and disappearing,
I tread day and night such roads.

I visit the orchards of spheres and look at the product,
And look at quintillions ripen'd and look at quintillions green.

I fly those flights of a fluid and swallowing soul,
My course runs below the soundings of plummets.

I help myself to material and immaterial,
No guard can shut me off, no law prevent me.

I anchor my ship for a little while only,
My messengers continually cruise away or bring their returns to me.

I go hunting polar furs and the seal, leaping chasms with a pike-
    pointed staff, clinging to topples of brittle and blue.

I ascend to the foretruck,
I take my place late at night in the crow's-nest,
We sail the arctic sea, it is plenty light enough,
Through the clear atmosphere I stretch around on the wonderful
    beauty,

The enormous masses of ice pass me and I pass them, the scenery is
    plain in all directions,
The white-topt mountains show in the distance, I fling out my fancies
    toward them,
We are approaching some great battle-field in which we are soon to
    be engaged,
We pass the colossal outposts of the encampment, we pass with still
    feet and caution,
Or we are entering by the suburbs some vast and ruin'd city,
The blocks and fallen architecture more than all the living cities of
    the globe.

I am a free companion, I bivouac by invading watchfires,
I turn the bridegroom out of bed and stay with the bride myself,
I tighten her all night to my thighs and lips.

My voice is the wife's voice, the screech by the rail of the stairs,
They fetch my man's body up dripping and drown'd.

I understand the large hearts of heroes,
The courage of present times and all times,
How the skipper saw the crowded and rudderless wreck of the steam-
    ship, and Death chasing it up and down the storm,
How he knuckled tight and gave not back an inch, and was faithful
    of days and faithful of nights,
And chalk'd in large letters on a board, *Be of good cheer, we will not
    desert you;*
How he follow'd with them and tack'd with them three days and
    would not give it up,
How he saved the drifting company at last,
How the lank loose-gown'd women look'd when boated from the
    side of their prepared graves,
How the silent old-faced infants and the lifted sick, and the sharp-
    lipp'd unshaved men;
All this I swallow, it tastes good, I like it well, it becomes mine,
I am the man, I suffer'd, I was there.

The disdain and calmness of martyrs,

The mother of old, condemn'd for a witch, burnt with dry wood,
    her children gazing on,

The hounded slave that flags in the race, leans by the fence, blowing,
    cover'd with sweat,

The twinges that sting like needles his legs and neck, the murderous
    buckshot and the bullets,

All these I feel or am.

I am the hounded slave, I wince at the bite of the dogs,

Hell and despair are upon me, crack and again crack the marksmen,

I clutch the rails of the fence, my gore dribs, thinn'd with the ooze
    of my skin,

I fall on the weeds and stones,

The riders spur their unwilling horses, haul close,

Taunt my dizzy ears and beat me violently over the head with
    whip-stocks.

Agonies are one of my changes of garments,

I do not ask the wounded person how he feels, I myself become the
    wounded person,

My hurts turn livid upon me as I lean on a cane and observe.

I am the mash'd fireman with breast-bone broken,

Tumbling walls buried me in their debris,

Heat and smoke I inspired, I heard the yelling shouts of my comrades,

I heard the distant click of their picks and shovels,

They have clear'd the beams away, they tenderly lift me forth.

I lie in the night air in my red shirt, the pervading hush is for my
    sake,

Painless after all I lie exhausted but not so unhappy,

White and beautiful are the faces around me, the heads are bared of
    their fire-caps,

The kneeling crowd fades with the light of the torches.

Distant and dead resuscitate,
They show as the dial or move as the hands of me, I am the clock
     myself.

I am an old artillerist, I tell of my fort's bombardment,
I am there again.

Again the long roll of the drummers,
Again the attacking cannon, mortars,
Again to my listening ears the cannon responsive.

I take part, I see and hear the whole,
The cries, curses, roar, the plaudits for well-aim'd shots,
The ambulanza slowly passing trailing its red drip,
Workmen searching after damages, making indispensable repairs,
The fall of grenades through the rent roof, the fan-shaped explosion,
The whizz of limbs, heads, stone, wood, iron, high in the air.

Again gurgles the mouth of my dying general, he furiously waves
     with his hand,
He gasps through the clot *Mind not me – mind – the entrenchments.*

34

Now I tell what I knew in Texas in my early youth,
(I tell not the fall of Alamo,
Not one escaped to tell the fall of Alamo,
The hundred and fifty are dumb yet at Alamo,)
'Tis the tale of the murder in cold blood of four hundred and twelve
     young men.

Retreating they had form'd in a hollow square with their baggage for
     breastworks,
Nine hundred lives out of the surrounding enemy's, nine times their
     number, was the price they took in advance,
Their colonel was wounded and their ammunition gone,
They treated for an honorable capitulation, receiv'd writing and seal,
     gave up their arms and march'd back prisoners of war.

They were the glory of the race of rangers,
Matchless with horse, rifle, song, supper, courtship,
Large, turbulent, generous, handsome, proud, and affectionate,
Bearded, sunburnt, drest in the free costume of hunters,
Not a single one over thirty years of age.

The second First-day morning they were brought out in squads and
    massacred, it was beautiful early summer,
The work commenced about five o'clock and was over by eight.

None obey'd the command to kneel,
Some made a mad and helpless rush, some stood stark and straight,
A few fell at once, shot in the temple or heart, the living and dead lay
    together,
The maim'd and mangled dug in the dirt, the new-comers saw them
    there,
Some half-kill'd attempted to crawl away,
These were despatch'd with bayonets or batter'd with the blunts of
    muskets,
A youth not seventeen years old seiz'd his assassin till two more came
    to release him,
The three were all torn and cover'd with the boy's blood.

At eleven o'clock began the burning of the bodies;
That is the tale of the murder of the four hundred and twelve young
    men.

35

Would you hear of an old-time sea-fight?
Would you learn who won by the light of the moon and stars?
List to the yarn, as my grandmother's father the sailor told it to me.

Our foe was no skulk in his ship I tell you, (said he,)
His was the surly English pluck, and there is no tougher or truer,
    and never was, and never will be;
Along the lower'd eve he came horribly raking us.

We closed with him, the yards entangled, the cannon touch'd,
My captain lash'd fast with his own hands.

We had receiv'd some eighteen pound shots under the water,
On our lower-gun-deck two large pieces had burst at the first fire,
    killing all around and blowing up overhead.

Fighting at sun-down, fighting at dark,
Ten o'clock at night, the full moon well up, our leaks on the gain,
    and five feet of water reported,
The master-at-arms loosing the prisoners confined in the after-hold
    to give them a chance for themselves.

The transit to and from the magazine is now stopt by the sentinels,
They see so many strange faces they do not know whom to trust.

Our frigate takes fire,
The other asks if we demand quarter?
If our colors are struck and the fighting done?

Now I laugh content, for I hear the voice of my little captain,
We have not struck, he composedly cries, *we have just begun our part of*
    the fighting.

Only three guns are in use,
One is directed by the captain himself against the enemy's main-mast,
Two well serv'd with grape and canister silence his musketry and
    clear his decks.

The tops alone second the fire of this little battery, especially the main-
    top,
They hold out bravely during the whole of the action.

Not a moment's cease,
The leaks gain fast on the pumps, the fire eats toward the powder-
    magazine.

One of the pumps has been shot away, it is generally thought we are
    sinking.

Serene stands the little captain,
He is not hurried, his voice is neither high nor low,
His eyes give more light to us than our battle-lanterns.

Toward twelve there in the beams of the moon they surrender to us.

36

Stretch'd and still lies the midnight,
Two great hulls motionless on the breast of the darkness,
Our vessel riddled and slowly sinking, preparations to pass to the one
    we have conquer'd,
The captain on the quarter-deck coldly giving his orders through a
    countenance white as a sheet,
Near by the corpse of the child that serv'd in the cabin,
The dead face of an old salt with long white hair and carefully curl'd
    whiskers,
The flames spite of all that can be done flickering aloft and
    below,
The husky voices of the two or three officers yet fit for duty,
Formless stacks of bodies and bodies by themselves, dabs of flesh upon
    the masts and spars,
Cut of cordage, dangle of rigging, slight shock of the soothe of
    waves,
Black and impassive guns, litter of powder-parcels, strong scent,
A few large stars overhead, silent and mournful shining,
Delicate sniffs of sea-breeze, smells of sedgy grass and fields by the
    shore, death-messages given in charge to survivors,
The hiss of the surgeon's knife, the gnawing teeth of his saw,
Wheeze, cluck, swash of falling blood, short wild scream, and long,
    dull, tapering groan,
These so, these irretrievable.

37

You laggards there on guard! look to your arms!
In at the conquer'd doors they crowd! I am possess'd!
Embody all presences outlaw'd or suffering,
See myself in prison shaped like another man,
And feel the dull unintermitted pain.

For me the keepers of convicts shoulder their carbines and keep
    watch,
It is I let out in the morning and barr'd at night.

Not a mutineer walks handcuff'd to jail but I am handcuff'd to him
    and walk by his side,
(I am less the jolly one there, and more the silent one with sweat on
    my twitching lips.)

Not a youngster is taken for larceny but I go up too, and am tried
    and sentenced.

Not a cholera patient lies at the last gasp but I also lie at the last gasp,
My face is ash-color'd, my sinews gnarl, away from me people
    retreat.

Askers embody themselves in me and I am embodied in them,
I project my hat, sit shame-faced, and beg.

38

Enough! enough! enough!
Somehow I have been stunn'd. Stand back!
Give me a little time beyond my cuff'd head, slumbers, dreams,
    gaping,
I discover myself on the verge of a usual mistake.

That I could forget the mockers and insults!
That I could forget the trickling tears and the blows of the bludgeons
    and hammers!
That I could look with a separate look on my own crucifixion and
    bloody crowning.

I remember now,
I resume the overstaid fraction,
The grave of rock multiplies what has been confided to it, or to any
    graves,
Corpses rise, gashes heal, fastenings roll from me.

I troop forth replenish'd with supreme power, one of an average
    unending procession,
Inland and sea-coast we go, and pass all boundary lines,
Our swift ordinances on their way over the whole earth,
The blossoms we wear in our hats the growth of thousands of years.

Eleves, I salute you! come forward!
Continue your annotations, continue your questionings.

39

The friendly and flowing savage, who is he?
Is he waiting for civilization, or past it and mastering it?

Is he some Southwesterner rais'd out-doors? is he Kanadian?
Is he from the Mississippi country? Iowa, Oregon, California?
The mountains? prairie-life, bush-life? or sailor from the sea?

Wherever he goes men and women accept and desire him,
They desire he should like them, touch them, speak to them, stay
    with them.

Behavior lawless as snow-flakes, words simple as grass, uncomb'd
    head, laughter, and naiveté,

Slow-stepping feet, common features, common modes and emana-
tions,
They descend in new forms from the tips of his fingers,
They are wafted with the odor of his body or breath, they fly out of
the glance of his eyes.

40

Flaunt of the sunshine I need not your bask – lie over!
You light surfaces only, I force surfaces and depths also.

Earth! you seem to look for something at my hands,
Say, old top-knot, what do you want?

Man or woman, I might tell how I like you, but cannot,
And might tell what it is in me and what it is in you, but cannot,
And might tell that pining I have, that pulse of my nights and days.

Behold, I do not give lectures or a little charity,
When I give I give myself.

You there, impotent, loose in the knees,
Open your scarf'd chops till I blow grit within you,
Spread your palms and lift the flaps of your pockets,
I am not to be denied, I compel, I have stores plenty and to spare,
And any thing I have I bestow.

I do not ask who you are, that is not important to me,
You can do nothing and be nothing but what I will infold you.

To cotton-field drudge or cleaner of privies I lean,
On his right cheek I put the family kiss,
And in my soul I swear I never will deny him.

On women fit for conception I start bigger and nimbler babes,
(This day I am jetting the stuff of far more arrogant republics.)

To any one dying, thither I speed and twist the knob of the door,
Turn the bed-clothes toward the foot of the bed,
Let the physician and the priest go home.

I seize the descending man and raise him with resistless will,
O despairer, here is my neck,
By God, you shall not go down! hang your whole weight upon me.

I dilate you with tremendous breath, I buoy you up,
Every room of the house do I fill with an arm'd force,
Lovers of me, bafflers of graves.

Sleep – I and they keep guard all night,
Not doubt, not decease shall dare to lay finger upon you,
I have embraced you, and henceforth possess you to myself,
And when you rise in the morning you will find what I tell you is so.

41

I am he bringing help for the sick as they pant on their backs,
And for strong upright men I bring yet more needed help.

I heard what was said of the universe,
Heard it and heard it of several thousand years;
It is middling well as far as it goes – but is that all?

Magnifying and applying come I,
Outbidding at the start the old cautious hucksters,
Taking myself the exact dimensions of Jehovah,
Lithographing Kronos, Zeus his son, and Hercules his grandson,
Buying drafts of Osiris, Isis, Belus, Brahma, Buddha,
In my portfolio placing Manito loose, Allah on a leaf, the crucifix
    engraved,
With Odin and the hideous-faced Mexitli and every idol and image,
Taking them all for what they are worth and not a cent more,
Admitting they were alive and did the work of their days,

(They bore mites as for unfledg'd birds who have now to rise and fly
and sing for themselves,)

Accepting the rough deific sketches to fill out better in myself,
bestowing them freely on each man and woman I see,

Discovering as much or more in a framer framing a house,

Putting higher claims for him there with his roll'd-up sleeves driving
the mallet and chisel,

Not objecting to special revelations, considering a curl of smoke or a
hair on the back of my hand just as curious as any revelation,

Lads ahold of fire-engines and hook-and-ladder ropes no less to me
than the gods of the antique wars,

Minding their voices peal through the crash of destruction,

Their brawny limbs passing safe over charr'd laths, their white
foreheads whole and unhurt out of the flames;

By the mechanic's wife with her babe at her nipple interceding for
every person born,

Three scythes at harvest whizzing in a row from three lusty angels
with shirts bagg'd out at their waists,

The snag-tooth'd hostler with red hair redeeming sins past and to
come,

Selling all he possesses, traveling on foot to fee lawyers for his brother
and sit by him while he is tried for forgery;

What was strewn in the amplest strewing the square rod about me,
and not filling the square rod then,

The bull and the bug never worshipp'd half enough,

Dung and dirt more admirable than was dream'd,

The supernatural of no account, myself waiting my time to be one of
the supremes,

The day getting ready for me when I shall do as much good as the
best, and be as prodigious;

By my life-lumps! becoming already a creator,

Putting myself here and now to the ambush'd womb of the shadows.

42

A call in the midst of the crowd,
My own voice, orotund sweeping and final.

Come my children,
Come my boys and girls, my women, household and intimates,
Now the performer launches his nerve, he has pass'd his prelude on
    the reeds within.

Easily written loose-finger'd chords – I feel the thrum of your climax
    and close.

My head slues round on my neck,
Music rolls, but not from the organ,
Folks are around me, but they are no household of mine.

Ever the hard unsunk ground,
Ever the eaters and drinkers, ever the upward and downward sun,
    ever the air and the ceaseless tides,
Ever myself and my neighbors, refreshing, wicked, real,
Ever the old inexplicable query, ever that thorn'd thumb, that breath
    of itches and thirsts,
Ever the vexer's *hoot! hoot!* till we find where the sly one hides and
    bring him forth,
Ever love, ever the sobbing liquid of life,
Ever the bandage under the chin, ever the trestles of death.

Here and there with dimes on the eyes walking,
To feed the greed of the belly the brains liberally spooning,
Tickets buying, taking, selling, but in to the feast never once going,
Many sweating, ploughing, thrashing, and then the chaff for payment
    receiving,
A few idly owning, and they the wheat continually claiming.

This is the city and I am one of the citizens,
Whatever interests the rest interests me, politics, wars, markets,
    newspapers, schools,
The mayor and councils, banks, tariffs, steamships, factories, stocks,
    stores, real estate and personal estate.

The little plentiful manikins skipping around in collars and tail'd
    coats,
I am aware who they are, (they are positively not worms or fleas,)
I acknowledge the duplicates of myself, the weakest and shallowest is
    deathless with me,
What I do and say the same waits for them,
Every thought that flounders in me the same flounders in them.

I know perfectly well my own egotism,
Know my omnivorous lines and must not write any less,
And would fetch you whoever you are flush with myself.

Not words of routine this song of mine,
But abruptly to question, to leap beyond yet nearer bring;
This printed and bound book – but the printer and the printing-
    office boy?
The well-taken photographs – but your wife or friend close and solid
    in your arms?
The black ship mail'd with iron, her mighty guns in her turrets – but
    the pluck of the captain and engineers?
In the houses the dishes and fare and furniture – but the host and
    hostess, and the look out of their eyes?
The sky up there – yet here or next door, or across the way?
The saints and sages in history – but you yourself?
Sermons, creeds, theology – but the fathomless human brain,
And what is reason? and what is love? and what is life?

43

I do not despise you priests, all time, the world over,
My faith is the greatest of faiths and the least of faiths,
Enclosing worship ancient and modern and all between ancient and
    modern,
Believing I shall come again upon the earth after five thousand years,
Waiting responses from oracles, honoring the gods, saluting the sun,
Making a fetich of the first rock or stump, powowing with sticks in
    the circle of obis,

Helping the llama or brahmin as he trims the lamps of the idols,

Dancing yet through the streets in a phallic procession, rapt and austere in the woods a gymnosophist,

Drinking mead from the skull-cap, to Shastas and Vedas admirant, minding the Koran,

Walking the teokallis, spotted with gore from the stone and knife, beating the serpent-skin drum,

Accepting the Gospels, accepting him that was crucified, knowing assuredly that he is divine,

To the mass kneeling or the puritan's prayer rising, or sitting patiently in a pew,

Ranting and frothing in my insane crisis, or waiting dead-like till my spirit arouses me,

Looking forth on pavement and land, or outside of pavement and land,

Belonging to the winders of the circuit of circuits.

One of that centripetal and centrifugal gang I turn and talk like a man leaving charges before a journey.

Down-hearted doubters dull and excluded,

Frivolous, sullen, moping, angry, affected, dishearten'd, atheistical,

I know every one of you, I know the sea of torment, doubt, despair and unbelief.

How the flukes splash!

How they contort rapid as lightning, with spasms and spouts of blood!

Be at peace bloody flukes of doubters and sullen mopers,

I take my place among you as much as among any,

The past is the push of you, me, all, precisely the same,

And what is yet untried and afterward is for you, me, all, precisely the same.

I do not know what is untried and afterward,

But I know it will in its turn prove sufficient, and cannot fail.

Each who passes is consider'd, each who stops is consider'd, not a
　　single one can it fail.

It cannot fail the young man who died and was buried,
Nor the young woman who died and was put by his side,
Nor the little child that peep'd in at the door, and then drew back and
　　was never seen again,
Nor the old man who has lived without purpose, and feels it with
　　bitterness worse than gall,
Nor him in the poor house tubercled by rum and the bad disorder,
Nor the numberless slaughter'd and wreck'd, nor the brutish koboo
　　call'd the ordure of humanity,
Nor the sacs merely floating with open mouths for food to slip in,
Nor any thing in the earth, or down in the oldest graves of the earth,
Nor any thing in the myriads of spheres, nor the myriads of myriads
　　that inhabit them,
Nor the present, nor the least wisp that is known.

44

It is time to explain myself – let us stand up.

What is known I strip away,
I launch all men and women forward with me into the Unknown.

The clock indicates the moment – but what does eternity indicate?

We have thus far exhausted trillions of winters and summers,
There are trillions ahead, and trillions ahead of them.

Births have brought us richness and variety,
And other births will bring us richness and variety.

I do not call one greater and one smaller,
That which fills its period and place is equal to any.

Were mankind murderous or jealous upon you, my brother, my
    sister?
I am sorry for you, they are not murderous or jealous upon me,
All has been gentle with me, I keep no account with lamentation,
(What have I to do with lamentation?)

I am an acme of things accomplish'd, and I am encloser of things to be.

My feet strike an apex of the apices of the stairs,
On every step bunches of ages, and larger bunches between the steps,
All below duly travel'd, and still I mount and mount.

Rise after rise bow the phantoms behind me,
Afar down I see the huge first Nothing, I know I was even there,
I waited unseen and always, and slept through the lethargic mist,
And took my time, and took no hurt from the fetid carbon.

Long I was hugg'd close – long and long.

Immense have been the preparations for me,
Faithful and friendly the arms that have help'd me.

Cycles ferried my cradle, rowing and rowing like cheerful boatmen,
For room to me stars kept aside in their own rings,
They sent influences to look after what was to hold me.

Before I was born out of my mother generations guided me,
My embryo has never been torpid, nothing could overlay it.

For it the nebula cohered to an orb,
The long slow strata piled to rest it on,
Vast vegetables gave it sustenance,
Monstrous sauroids transported it in their mouths and deposited it
    with care.

All forces have been steadily employ'd to complete and delight me,
Now on this spot I stand with my robust soul.

45

O span of youth! ever-push'd elasticity!
O manhood, balanced, florid and full.

My lovers suffocate me,
Crowding my lips, thick in the pores of my skin,
Jostling me through streets and public halls, coming naked to me at
    night,
Crying by day *Ahoy!* from the rocks of the river, swinging and
    chirping over my head,
Calling my name from flower-beds, vines, tangled underbrush,
Lighting on every moment of my life,
Bussing my body with soft balsamic busses,
Noiselessly passing handfuls out of their hearts and giving them to be
    mine.

Old age superbly rising! O welcome, ineffable grace of dying days!

Every condition promulges not only itself, it promulges what grows
    after and out of itself,
And the dark hush promulges as much as any.

I open my scuttle at night and see the far-sprinkled systems,
And all I see multiplied as high as I can cipher edge but the rim of the
    farther systems.

Wider and wider they spread, expanding, always expanding,
Outward and outward and forever outward.

My sun has his sun and round him obediently wheels,
He joins with his partners a group of superior circuit,
And greater sets follow, making specks of the greatest inside them.

There is no stoppage and never can be stoppage,
If I, you, and the worlds, and all beneath or upon their surfaces, were
  this moment reduced back to a pallid float, it would not avail in
  the long run,
We should surely bring up again where we now stand,
And surely go as much farther, and then farther and farther.

A few quadrillions of eras, a few octillions of cubic leagues, do not
  hazard the span or make it impatient,
They are but parts, any thing is but a part.

See ever so far, there is limitless space outside of that,
Count ever so much, there is limitless time around that.

My rendezvous is appointed, it is certain,
The Lord will be there and wait till I come on perfect terms,
The great Camerado, the lover true for whom I pine will be there.

46

I know I have the best of time and space, and was never measured and
  never will be measured.

I tramp a perpetual journey, (come listen all!)
My signs are a rain-proof coat, good shoes, and a staff cut from the
  woods,
No friend of mine takes his ease in my chair,
I have no chair, no church, no philosophy,
I lead no man to a dinner-table, library, exchange,
But each man and each woman of you I lead upon a knoll,
My left hand hooking you round the waist,
My right hand pointing to landscapes of continents and the public
  road.

Not I, not any one else can travel that road for you,
You must travel it for yourself.

It is not far, it is within reach,
Perhaps you have been on it since you were born and did not know,
Perhaps it is everywhere on water and on land.

Shoulder your duds dear son, and I will mine, and let us hasten forth,
Wonderful cities and free nations we shall fetch as we go.

If you tire, give me both burdens, and rest the chuff of your hand on
    my hip,
And in due time you shall repay the same service to me,
For after we start we never lie by again.

This day before dawn I ascended a hill and look'd at the crowded
    heaven,
And I said to my spirit *When we become the enfolders of those orbs, and
    the pleasure and knowledge of every thing in them, shall we be fill'd
    and satisfied then?*
And my spirit said *No, we but level that lift to pass and continue beyond.*

You are also asking me questions and I hear you,
I answer that I cannot answer, you must find out for yourself.

Sit a while dear son,
Here are biscuits to eat and here is milk to drink,
But as soon as you sleep and renew yourself in sweet clothes, I kiss
    you with a good-by kiss and open the gate for your egress hence.

Long enough have you dream'd contemptible dreams,
Now I wash the gum from your eyes,
You must habit yourself to the dazzle of the light and of every moment
    of your life.

Long have you timidly waded holding a plank by the shore,
Now I will you to be a bold swimmer,
To jump off in the midst of the sea, rise again, nod to me, shout, and
    laughingly dash with your hair.

47

I am the teacher of athletes,
He that by me spreads a wider breast than my own proves the width
    of my own,
He most honors my style who learns under it to destroy the teacher.

The boy I love, the same becomes a man not through derived power,
    but in his own right,
Wicked rather than virtuous out of conformity or fear,
Fond of his sweetheart, relishing well his steak,
Unrequited love or a slight cutting him worse than sharp steel cuts,
First-rate to ride, to fight, to hit the bull's eye, to sail a skiff, to sing
    a song or play on the banjo,
Preferring scars and the beard and faces pitted with small-pox over
    all latherers,
And those well-tann'd to those that keep out of the sun.

I teach straying from me, yet who can stray from me?
I follow you whoever you are from the present hour,
My words itch at your ears till you understand them.

I do not say these things for a dollar or to fill up the time while I
    wait for a boat,
(It is you talking just as much as myself, I act as the tongue of you,
Tied in your mouth, in mine it begins to be loosen'd.)

I swear I will never again mention love or death inside a house,
And I swear I will never translate myself at all, only to him or her
    who privately stays with me in the open air.

If you would understand me go to the heights or water-shore,
The nearest gnat is an explanation, and a drop or motion of waves a
    key,
The maul, the oar, the hand-saw, second my words.

No shutter'd room or school can commune with me,
But roughs and little children better than they.

The young mechanic is closest to me, he knows me well,
The woodman that takes his axe and jug with him shall take me with
    him all day,
The farm-boy ploughing in the field feels good at the sound of my
    voice,
In vessels that sail my words sail, I go with fishermen and seamen and
    love them.

The soldier camp'd or upon the march is mine,
On the night ere the pending battle many seek me, and I do not fail
    them,
On that solemn night (it may be their last) those that know me seek me.

My face rubs to the hunter's face when he lies down alone in his
    blanket,
The driver thinking of me does not mind the jolt of his wagon,
The young mother and old mother comprehend me,
The girl and the wife rest the needle a moment and forget where
    they are,
They and all would resume what I have told them.

48

I have said that the soul is not more than the body,
And I have said that the body is not more than the soul,
And nothing, not God, is greater to one than one's self is,
And whoever walks a furlong without sympathy walks to his own
    funeral drest in his shroud,
And I or you pocketless of a dime may purchase the pick of the earth,
And to glance with an eye or show a bean in its pod confounds the
    learning of all times,
And there is no trade or employment but the young man following
    it may become a hero,

And there is no object so soft but it makes a hub for the wheel'd
    universe,
And I say to any man or woman, Let your soul stand cool and
    composed before a million universes.

And I say to mankind, Be not curious about God,
For I who am curious about each am not curious about God,
(No array of terms can say how much I am at peace about God and
    about death.)

I hear and behold God in every object, yet understand God not in
    the least,
Nor do I understand who there can be more wonderful than myself.

Why should I wish to see God better than this day?
I see something of God each hour of the twenty-four, and each
    moment then,
In the faces of men and women I see God, and in my own face in
    the glass,
I find letters from God dropt in the street, and every one is sign'd by
    God's name,
And I leave them where they are, for I know that wheresoe'er I go,
Others will punctually come for ever and ever.

49

And as to you Death, and you bitter hug of mortality, it is idle to
    try to alarm me.

To his work without flinching the accoucheur comes,
I see the elder-hand pressing receiving supporting,
I recline by the sills of the exquisite flexible doors,
And mark the outlet, and mark the relief and escape.

And as to you Corpse I think you are good manure, but that does
    not offend me,
I smell the white roses sweet-scented and growing,
I reach to the leafy lips, I reach to the polish'd breasts of melons.

And as to you Life I reckon you are the leavings of many deaths,
(No doubt I have died myself ten thousand times before.)

I hear you whispering there O stars of heaven,
O suns – O grass of graves – O perpetual transfers and promotions,
If you do not say any thing how can I say any thing?

Of the turbid pool that lies in the autumn forest,
Of the moon that descends the steeps of the soughing twilight,
Toss, sparkles of day and dusk – toss on the black stems that decay in
    the muck,
Toss to the moaning gibberish of the dry limbs.

I ascend from the moon, I ascend from the night,
I perceive that the ghastly glimmer is noonday sunbeams reflected,
And debouch to the steady and central from the offspring great or
    small.

50

There is that in me – I do not know what it is – but I know it is in me.

Wrench'd and sweaty – calm and cool then my body becomes,
I sleep – I sleep long.

I do not know it – it is without name – it is a word unsaid,
It is not in any dictionary, utterance, symbol.

Something it swings on more than the earth I swing on,
To it the creation is the friend whose embracing awakes me.

Perhaps I might tell more. Outlines! I plead for my brothers and
    sisters.

Do you see O my brothers and sisters?
It is not chaos or death – it is form, union, plan – it is eternal life – it
    is Happiness.

51

The past and present wilt – I have fill'd them, emptied them,
And proceed to fill my next fold of the future.

Listener up there! what have you to confide to me?
Look in my face while I snuff the sidle of evening,
(Talk honestly, no one else hears you, and I stay only a minute
    longer.)

Do I contradict myself?
Very well then I contradict myself,
(I am large, I contain multitudes.)

I concentrate toward them that are nigh, I wait on the door-slab.

Who has done his day's work? who will soonest be through with his
    supper?
Who wishes to walk with me?

Will you speak before I am gone? will you prove already too late?

52

The spotted hawk swoops by and accuses me, he complains of my
    gab and my loitering.

I too am not a bit tamed, I too am untranslatable,
I sound my barbaric yawp over the roofs of the world.

The last scud of day holds back for me,
It flings my likeness after the rest and true as any on the shadow'd
    wilds,
It coaxes me to the vapor and the dusk.

I depart as air, I shake my white locks at the runaway sun,
I effuse my flesh in eddies, and drift it in lacy jags.

I bequeath myself to the dirt to grow from the grass I love,
If you want me again look for me under your boot-soles.

You will hardly know who I am or what I mean,
But I shall be good health to you nevertheless,
And filter and fibre your blood.

Failing to fetch me at first keep encouraged,
Missing me one place search another,
I stop somewhere waiting for you.

From *Calamus*

SCENTED HERBAGE OF MY BREAST

Scented herbage of my breast,
Leaves from you I glean, I write, to be perused best afterwards,
Tomb-leaves, body-leaves growing up above me above death,
Perennial roots, tall leaves, O the winter shall not freeze you delicate
    leaves,
Every year shall you bloom again, out from where you retired you
    shall emerge again;
O I do not know whether many passing by will discover you or
    inhale your faint odor, but I believe a few will;
O slender leaves! O blossoms of my blood! I permit you to tell in
    your own way of the heart that is under you,
O I do not know what you mean there underneath yourselves, you
    are not happiness,
You are often more bitter than I can bear, you burn and sting me,
Yet you are beautiful to me you faint tinged roots, you make me
    think of death,
Death is beautiful from you, (what indeed is finally beautiful except
    death and love?)
O I think it is not for life I am chanting here my chant of lovers, I
    think it must be for death,

For how calm, how solemn it grows to ascend to the atmosphere of
    lovers,

Death or life I am then indifferent, my soul declines to prefer,

(I am not sure but the high soul of lovers welcomes death most,)

Indeed O death, I think now these leaves mean precisely the same as
    you mean,

Grow up taller sweet leaves that I may see! grow up out of my
    breast!

Spring away from the conceal'd heart there!

Do not fold yourself so in your pink-tinged roots timid leaves!

Do not remain down there so ashamed, herbage of my breast!

Come I am determin'd to unbare this broad breast of mine, I have
    long enough stifled and choked;

Emblematic and capricious blades I leave you, now you serve me not,

I will say what I have to say by itself,

I will sound myself and comrades only, I will never again utter a call
    only their call,

I will raise with it immortal reverberations through the States,

I will give an example to lovers to take permanent shape and will
    through the States,

Through me shall the words be said to make death exhilarating,

Give me your tone therefore O death, that I may accord with it,

Give me yourself, for I see that you belong to me now above all,
    and are folded inseparably together, you love and death are,

Nor will I allow you to balk me any more with what I was calling
    life,

For now it is convey'd to me that you are the purports essential,

That you hide in these shifting forms of life, for reasons, and that
    they are mainly for you,

That you beyond them come forth to remain, the real reality,

That behind the mask of materials you patiently wait, no matter
    how long,

That you will one day perhaps take control of all,

That you will perhaps dissipate this entire show of appearance,

That may-be you are what it is all for, but it does not last so very long,

But you will last very long.

From *Drum-Taps*

WHEN LILACS LAST IN THE DOORYARD BLOOM'D

1

When lilacs last in the dooryard bloom'd,
And the great star early droop'd in the western sky in the night,
I mourn'd, and yet shall mourn with ever-returning spring.

Ever-returning spring, trinity sure to me you bring,
Lilac blooming perennial and drooping star in the west,
And thought of him I love.

2

O powerful western fallen star!
O shades of night – O moody, tearful night!
O great star disappear'd – O the black murk that hides the star!
O cruel hands that hold me powerless – O helpless soul of me!
O harsh surrounding cloud that will not free my soul.

3

In the dooryard fronting an old farm-house near the white-wash'd
    palings,
Stands the lilac-bush tall-growing with heart-shaped leaves of rich
    green,
With many a pointed blossom rising delicate, with the perfume
    strong I love,
With every leaf a miracle – and from this bush in the dooryard,
With delicate-color'd blossoms and heart-shaped leaves of rich green,
A sprig with its flower I break.

4

In the swamp in secluded recesses,
A shy and hidden bird is warbling a song.

Solitary the thrush,
The hermit withdrawn to himself, avoiding the settlements,
Sings by himself a song.

Song of the bleeding throat,
Death's outlet song of life, (for well dear brother I know,
If thou wast not granted to sing thou would'st surely die.)

5

Over the breast of the spring, the land, amid cities,
Amid lanes and through old woods, where lately the violets peep'd
    from the ground, spotting the gray debris,
Amid the grass in the fields each side of the lanes, passing the endless
    grass,
Passing the yellow-spear'd wheat, every grain from its shroud in the
    dark-brown fields uprisen,
Passing the apple-tree blows of white and pink in the orchards,
Carrying a corpse to where it shall rest in the grave,
Night and day journeys a coffin.

6

Coffin that passes through lanes and streets,
Through day and night with the great cloud darkening the land,
With the pomp of the inloop'd flags with the cities draped in black,
With the show of the States themselves as of crape-veil'd women
    standing,
With processions long and winding and the flambeaus of the night,
With the countless torches lit, with the silent sea of faces and the
    unbared heads,
With the waiting depot, the arriving coffin, and the sombre faces,
With dirges through the night, with the thousand voices rising strong
    and solemn,
With all the mournful voices of the dirges pour'd around the coffin,
The dim-lit churches and the shuddering organs – where amid these
    you journey,

With the tolling tolling bells' perpetual clang,
Here, coffin that slowly passes,
I give you my sprig of lilac.

7

(Nor for you, for one alone,
Blossoms and branches green to coffins all I bring,
For fresh as the morning, thus would I chant a song for you O sane
    and sacred death.

All over bouquets of roses,
O death, I cover you over with roses and early lilies,
But mostly and now the lilac that blooms the first,
Copious I break, I break the sprigs from the bushes,
With loaded arms I come, pouring for you,
For you and the coffins all of you O death.)

8

O western orb sailing the heaven,
Now I know what you must have meant as a month since I walk'd,
As I walk'd in silence the transparent shadowy night,
As I saw you had something to tell as you bent to me night after
    night,
As you droop'd from the sky low down as if to my side, (while the
    other stars all look'd on,)
As we wander'd together the solemn night, (for something I know
    not what kept me from sleep,)
As the night advanced, and I saw on the rim of the west how full
    you were of woe,
As I stood on the rising ground in the breeze in the cool transparent
    night,
As I watch'd where you pass'd and was lost in the netherward black
    of the night,
As my soul in its trouble dissatisfied sank, as where you sad orb,
Concluded, dropt in the night, and was gone.

9

Sing on there in the swamp,
O singer bashful and tender, I hear your notes, I hear your call,
I hear, I come presently, I understand you,
But a moment I linger, for the lustrous star has detain'd me,
The star my departing comrade holds and detains me.

10

O how shall I warble myself for the dead one there I loved?
And how shall I deck my song for the large sweet soul that has gone?
And what shall my perfume be for the grave of him I love?

Sea-winds blown from east and west,
Blown from the Eastern sea and blown from the Western sea, till
  there on the prairies meeting,
These and with these and the breath of my chant,
I'll perfume the grave of him I love.

11

O what shall I hang on the chamber walls?
And what shall the pictures be that I hang on the walls,
To adorn the burial-house of him I love?

Pictures of growing spring and farms and homes,
With the Fourth-month eve at sundown, and the gray smoke lucid
  and bright,
With floods of the yellow gold of the gorgeous, indolent, sinking
  sun, burning, expanding the air,
With the fresh sweet herbage under foot, and the pale green leaves of
  the trees prolific,
In the distance the flowing glaze, the breast of the river, with a
  wind-dapple here and there,
With ranging hills on the banks, with many a line against the sky,
  and shadows,

And the city at hand with dwellings so dense, and stacks of chimneys,
And all the scenes of life and the workshops, and the workmen
   homeward returning.

12

Lo, body and soul – this land,
My own Manhattan with spires, and the sparkling and hurrying tides,
   and the ships,
The varied and ample land, the South and the North in the light,
   Ohio's shores and flashing Missouri,
And ever the far-spreading prairies cover'd with grass and corn.

Lo, the most excellent sun so calm and haughty,
The violet and purple morn with just-felt breezes,
The gentle soft-born measureless light,
The miracle spreading bathing all, the fulfill'd noon,
The coming eve delicious, the welcome night and the stars,
Over my cities shining all, enveloping man and land.

13

Sing on, sing on you gray-brown bird,
Sing from the swamps, the recesses, pour your chant from the bushes,
Limitless out of the dusk, out of the cedars and pines.

Sing on dearest brother, warble your reedy song,
Loud human song, with voice of uttermost woe.

O liquid and free and tender!
O wild and loose to my soul – O wondrous singer!
You only I hear – yet the star holds me, (but will soon depart,)
Yet the lilac with mastering odor holds me.

14

Now while I sat in the day and look'd forth,
In the close of the day with its light and the fields of spring, and the
   farmers preparing their crops,

In the large unconscious scenery of my land with its lakes and forests,
In the heavenly aerial beauty, (after the perturb'd winds and the
storms,)
Under the arching heavens of the afternoon swift passing, and the
voices of children and women,
The many-moving sea-tides, and I saw the ships how they sail'd,
And the summer approaching with richness, and the fields all busy
with labor,
And the infinite separate houses, how they all went on, each with its
meals and minutia of daily usages,
And the streets how their throbbings throbb'd, and the cities pent –
lo, then and there,
Falling upon them all and among them all, enveloping me with the
rest,
Appear'd the cloud, appear'd the long black trail,
And I knew death, its thought, and the sacred knowledge of death.

Then with the knowledge of death as walking one side of me,
And the thought of death close-walking the other side of me,
And I in the middle as with companions, and as holding the hands
of companions,
I fled forth to the hiding receiving night that talks not,
Down to the shores of the water, the path by the swamp in the
dimness,
To the solemn shadowy cedars and ghostly pines so still.

And the singer so shy to the rest receiv'd me,
The gray-brown bird I know receiv'd us comrades three,
And he sang the carol of death, and a verse for him I love.

From deep secluded recesses,
From the fragrant cedars and the ghostly pines so still,
Came the carol of the bird.

And the charm of the carol rapt me,
As I held as if by their hands my comrades in the night,
And the voice of my spirit tallied the song of the bird.

Come lovely and soothing death,
Undulate round the world, serenely arriving, arriving,
In the day, in the night, to all, to each,
Sooner or later delicate death.

Prais'd be the fathomless universe,
For life and joy, and for objects and knowledge curious,
And for love, sweet love – but praise! praise! praise!
For the sure-enwinding arms of cool-enfolding death.

Dark mother always gliding near with soft feet,
Have none chanted for thee a chant of fullest welcome?
Then I chant it for thee, I glorify thee above all,
I bring thee a song that when thou must indeed come, come unfalteringly.

Approach strong deliveress,
When it is so, when thou hast taken them I joyously sing the dead,
Lost in the loving floating ocean of thee,
Laved in the flood of thy bliss O death.

From me to thee glad serenades,
Dances for thee I propose saluting thee, adornments and feastings for thee,
And the sights of the open landscape and the high-spread sky are fitting,
And life and the fields, and the huge and thoughtful night.

The night in silence under many a star,
The ocean shore and the husky whispering wave whose voice I know,
And the soul turning to thee O vast and well-veil'd death,
And the body gratefully nestling close to thee.

Over the tree-tops I float thee a song,
Over the rising and sinking waves, over the myriad fields and the prairies
    wide,
Over the dense-pack'd cities all and the teeming wharves and ways,
I float this carol with joy, with joy to thee O death.

15

To the tally of my soul,
Loud and strong kept up the gray-brown bird,
With pure deliberate notes spreading filling the night.

Loud in the pines and cedars dim,
Clear in the freshness moist and the swamp-perfume,
And I with my comrades there in the night.

While my sight that was bound in my eyes unclosed,
As to long panoramas of visions.

And I saw askant the armies,
I saw as in noiseless dreams hundreds of battle-flags,
Borne through the smoke of the battles and pierc'd with missiles I
    saw them,
And carried hither and yon through the smoke, and torn and bloody,
And at last but a few shreds left on the staffs, (and all in silence,)
And the staffs all splinter'd and broken.

I saw battle-corpses, myriads of them,
And the white skeletons of young men, I saw them,
I saw the debris and debris of all the slain soldiers of the war,
But I saw they were not as was thought,
They themselves were fully at rest, they suffer'd not,
The living remain'd and suffer'd, the mother suffer'd,
And the wife and the child and the musing comrade suffer'd,
And the armies that remain'd suffer'd.

16

Passing the visions, passing the night,
Passing, unloosing the hold of my comrades' hands,
Passing the song of the hermit bird and the tallying song of my soul,
Victorious song, death's outlet song, yet varying ever-altering song,

As low and wailing, yet clear the notes, rising and falling, flooding
    the night,
Sadly sinking and fainting, as warning and warning, and yet again
    bursting with joy,
Covering the earth and filling the spread of the heaven,
As that powerful psalm in the night I heard from recesses,
Passing, I leave thee lilac with heart-shaped leaves,
I leave thee there in the door-yard, blooming, returning with spring.

I cease from my song for thee,
From my gaze on thee in the west, fronting the west, communing
    with thee,
O comrade lustrous with silver face in the night.

Yet each to keep and all, retrievements out of the night,
The song, the wondrous chant of the gray-brown bird,
And the tallying chant, the echo arous'd in my soul,
With the lustrous and drooping star with the countenance full of woe,
With the holders holding my hand nearing the call of the bird,
Comrades mine and I in the midst, and their memory ever to keep,
    for the dead I loved so well,
For the sweetest, wisest soul of all my days and lands – and this for
    his dear sake,
Lilac and star and bird twined with the chant of my soul,
There in the fragrant pines and the cedars dusk and dim.

Good-bye My Fancy!

Good-bye my Fancy!
Farewell dear mate, dear love!
I'm going away, I know not where,
Or to what fortune, or whether I may ever see you again,
So Good-bye my Fancy.

Now for my last – let me look back a moment;
The slower fainter ticking of the clock is in me,
Exit, nightfall, and soon the heart-thud stopping.

Long have we lived, joy'd, caress'd together;
Delightful! – now separation – Good-bye my Fancy.

Yet let me not be too hasty,
Long indeed have we lived, slept, filter'd, become really blended
    into one;
Then if we die we die together, (yes, we'll remain one,)
If we go anywhere we'll go together to meet what happens,
May-be we'll be better off and blither, and learn something,
May-be it is yourself now really ushering me to the true songs,
    (who knows?)
May-be it is you the mortal knob really undoing, turning – so now
    finally,
Good-bye – and hail! my Fancy.

Julia Ward Howe 1819–1910

Battle-Hymn of the Republic

Mine eyes have seen the glory of the coming of the Lord:
He is trampling out the vintage where the grapes of wrath are stored;
He hath loosed the fateful lightning of His terrible swift sword;
      His truth is marching on.

I have seen Him in the watch-fires of a hundred circling camps;
They have builded Him an altar in the evening dews and damps;
I can read His righteous sentence by the dim and flaring lamps:
      His day is marching on.

I have read a fiery gospel writ in burnished rows of steel:
'As ye deal with my contemners, so with you my grace shall deal;
Let the Hero, born of woman, crush the serpent with his heel,
      Since God is marching on.'

He has sounded forth the trumpet that shall never call retreat;
He is sifting out the hearts of men before His judgment-seat;
Oh, be swift, my soul, to answer Him! be jubilant, my feet!
      Our God is marching on.

In the beauty of the lilies Christ was born across the sea,
With a glory in his bosom that transfigures you and me:
As he died to make men holy, let us die to make men free,
      While God is marching on.

Frederick Goddard Tuckerman
1821–73

From *Sonnets*, Fourth Series

VIII 'NOR STRANGE IT IS, TO US WHO WALK IN BONDS'

Nor strange it is, to us who walk in bonds
Of flesh and time, if virtue's self awhile
Gleam dull like sunless ice; whilst graceful guile –
Blood-flecked like hamatite or diamonds
With a red inward spark – to reconcile
Beauty and evil seems and corresponds
So well with good that the mind joys to have
Full wider jet and scope: nor swings and sleeps
Forever in one cradle wearily
Like those vast weeds that off d'Acunha's isle
Wash with the surf and flap their mighty fronds
Mournfully to the dipping of the wave,
Yet cannot be disrupted from their deeps
By the whole heave and settle of the sea.

From *Sonnets*, Fifth Series

IV 'BUT MAN FINDS MEANS, GRANT HIM BUT PLACE AND ROOM'

But man finds means, grant him but place and room,
To gauge the depths and views a wonder dawn,
Sees all the worlds in utmost space withdrawn
In shape and structure like a honeycomb,

Locates his sun and grasps the universe
Or to their bearings bids the orbs disperse;
Now seems to stand like that great angel girt
With moon and stars: now, sick for shelter even,
Craves but a roof to turn the thunder-rain –
Or finds his vaunted reach and wisdom vain,
Lost in the myriad meaning of a word,
Or starts at its bare import, panic-stirred:
For earth is earth or hearth or dearth or dirt,
The sky heaved over our faint heads is heaven.

Emily Dickinson 1830–86

67 'Success is counted sweetest'

Success is counted sweetest
By those who ne'er succeed.
To comprehend a nectar
Requires sorest need.

Not one of all the purple Host
Who took the Flag today
Can tell the definition
So clear of Victory

As he defeated – dying –
On whose forbidden ear
The distant strains of triumph
Burst agonized and clear!

214 'I taste a liquor never brewed'

I taste a liquor never brewed –
From Tankards scooped in Pearl –
Not all the Vats upon the Rhine
Yield such an Alcohol!

Inebriate of Air – am I –
And Debauchee of Dew –
Reeling – thro endless summer days –
From inns of Molten Blue –

When 'Landlords' turn the drunken Bee
Out of the Foxglove's door –
When Butterflies – renounce their 'drams' –
I shall but drink the more!

Till Seraphs swing their snowy Hats –
And Saints – to windows run –
To see the little Tippler
Leaning against the – Sun –

216 'Safe in their Alabaster Chambers'

VERSION OF 1861

Safe in their Alabaster Chambers –
Untouched by Morning –
And untouched by Noon –
Lie the meek members of the Resurrection –
Rafter of Satin – and Roof of Stone!

Grand go the Years – in the Crescent – above them –
Worlds scoop their Arcs –
And Firmaments – row –
Diadems – drop – and Doges – surrender –
Soundless as dots – on a Disc of Snow –

241 'I like a look of Agony'

I like a look of Agony,
Because I know it's true –
Men do not sham Convulsion,
Nor simulate, a Throe –

The Eyes glaze once – and that is Death –
Impossible to feign
The Beads upon the Forehead
By homely Anguish strung.

258 'There's a certain Slant of light'

There's a certain Slant of light,
Winter Afternoons –
That oppresses, like the Heft
Of Cathedral Tunes –

Heavenly Hurt, it gives us –
We can find no scar,
But internal difference,
Where the Meanings, are –

None may teach it – Any –
'Tis the Seal Despair –
An imperial affliction
Sent us of the Air –

When it comes, the Landscape listens –
Shadows – hold their breath –
When it goes, 'tis like the Distance
On the look of Death –

303 'The Soul selects her own Society'

The Soul selects her own Society –
Then – shuts the Door –
To her divine Majority –
Present no more –

Unmoved – she notes the Chariots – pausing –
At her low Gate –
Unmoved – an Emperor be kneeling
Upon her Mat –

I've known her – from an ample nation –
Choose One –
Then – close the Valves of her attention –
Like Stone –

328 'A Bird came down the Walk'

A Bird came down the Walk –
He did not know I saw –
He bit an Angleworm in halves
And ate the fellow, raw,

And then he drank a Dew
From a convenient Grass –
And then hopped sidewise to the Wall
To let a Beetle pass –

He glanced with rapid eyes
That hurried all around –
They looked like frightened Beads, I thought –
He stirred his Velvet Head

Like one in danger, Cautious,
I offered him a Crumb
And he unrolled his feathers
And rowed him softer home –

Than Oars divide the Ocean,
Too silver for a seam –
Or Butterflies, off Banks of Noon
Leap, plashless as they swim.

341 'After great pain, a formal feeling comes'

After great pain, a formal feeling comes –
The Nerves sit ceremonious, like Tombs –
The stiff Heart questions was it He, that bore,
And Yesterday, or Centuries before?

The Feet, mechanical, go round –
Of Ground, or Air, or Ought –
A Wooden way
Regardless grown,
A Quartz contentment, like a stone –

This is the Hour of Lead –
Remembered, if outlived,
As Freezing persons, recollect the Snow –
First – Chill – then Stupor – then the letting go –

401 'What Soft – Cherubic Creatures'

What Soft – Cherubic Creatures –
These Gentlewomen are –
One would as soon assault a Plush –
Or violate a Star –

Such Dimity Convictions –
A Horror so refined
Of freckled Human Nature –
Of Deity – ashamed –

It's such a common – Glory –
A Fisherman's – Degree –
Redemption – Brittle Lady –
Be so – ashamed of Thee –

449 'I died for Beauty – but was scarce'

I died for Beauty – but was scarce
Adjusted in the Tomb
When One who died for Truth, was lain
In an adjoining Room –

He questioned softly 'Why I failed'?
'For Beauty', I replied –
'And I – for Truth – Themself are One –
We Bretheren, are', He said –

And so, as Kinsmen, met a Night –
We talked between the Rooms –
Until the Moss had reached our lips –
And covered up – our names –

465 'I heard a Fly buzz – when I died'

I heard a Fly buzz – when I died –
The Stillness in the Room
Was like the Stillness in the Air –
Between the Heaves of Storm –

The Eyes around – had wrung them dry –
And Breaths were gathering firm
For that last Onset – when the King
Be witnessed – in the Room –

I willed my Keepsakes – Signed away
What portion of me be
Assignable – and then it was
There interposed a Fly –

With Blue – uncertain stumbling Buzz –
Between the light – and me –
And then the Windows failed – and then
I could not see to see –

510 'It was not Death, for I stood up'

It was not Death, for I stood up,
And all the Dead, lie down –
It was not Night, for all the Bells
Put out their Tongues, for Noon.

It was not Frost, for on my Flesh
I felt Siroccos – crawl –
Nor Fire – for just my Marble feet
Could keep a Chancel, cool –

And yet, it tasted, like them all,
The Figures I have seen
Set orderly, for Burial,
Reminded me, of mine –

As if my life were shaven,
And fitted to a frame,
And could not breathe without a key,
And 'twas like Midnight, some –

When everything that ticked – has stopped –
And Space stares all around –
Or Grisly frosts – first Autumn morns,
Repeal the Beating Ground –

But, most, like Chaos – Stopless – cool –
Without a Chance, or Spar –
Or even a Report of Land –
To justify – Despair.

547 'I've seen a Dying Eye'

I've seen a Dying Eye
Run round and round a Room –
In search of Something – as it seemed –
Then Cloudier become –
And then – obscure with Fog –
And then – be soldered down
Without disclosing what it be
'Twere blessed to have seen –

585 'I like to see it lap the Miles'

I like to see it lap the Miles –
And lick the Valleys up –
And stop to feed itself at Tanks –
And then – prodigious step

Around a Pile of Mountains –
And supercilious peer
In Shanties – by the sides of Roads –
And then a Quarry pare

To fit its Ribs –
And crawl between
Complaining all the while
In horrid – hooting stanza –
Then chase itself down Hill –

And neigh like Boanerges –
Then – punctual as a Star
Stop – docile and omnipotent
At its own stable door –

640 'I cannot live with You'

I cannot live with You –
It would be Life –
And Life is over there –
Behind the Shelf

The Sexton keeps the Key to –
Putting up
Our Life – His Porcelain –
Like a Cup –

Discarded of the Housewife –
Quaint – or Broke –
A newer Sevres pleases –
Old Ones crack –

I could not die – with You –
For One must wait
To shut the Other's Gaze down –
You – could not –

And I – Could I stand by
And see You – freeze –
Without my Right of Frost –
Death's privilege?

Nor could I rise – with You –
Because Your Face
Would put out Jesus' –
That New Grace

Glow plain – and foreign
On my homesick Eye –
Except that You than He
Shone closer by –

They'd judge Us – How –
For You – served Heaven – You know,
Or sought to –
I could not –

Because You saturated Sight –
And I had no more Eyes
For sordid excellence
As Paradise

And were You lost, I would be –
Though My Name
Rang loudest
On the Heavenly fame –

And were You – saved –
And I – condemned to be
Where You were not –
That self – were Hell to Me –

So We must meet apart –
You there – I – here –
With just the Door ajar
That Oceans are – and Prayer –
And that White Sustenance –
Despair –

712 *'Because I could not stop for Death'*

Because I could not stop for Death –
He kindly stopped for me –
The Carriage held but just Ourselves –
And Immortality.

We slowly drove – He knew no haste
And I had put away
My labor and my leisure too,
For His Civility –

We passed the School, where Children strove
At Recess – in the Ring –
We passed the Fields of Gazing Grain –
We passed the Setting Sun –

Or rather – He passed Us –
The Dews drew quivering and chill –
For only Gossamer, my Gown –
My Tippet – only Tulle –

We paused before a House that seemed
A Swelling of the Ground –
The Roof was scarcely visible –
The Cornice – in the Ground –

Since then – 'tis Centuries – and yet
Feels shorter than the Day
I first surmised the Horses' Heads
Were toward Eternity –

829 'Ample make this Bed'

Ample make this Bed –
Make this Bed with Awe –
In it wait till Judgment break
Excellent and Fair.

Be its Mattress straight –
Be its Pillow round –
Let no Sunrise' yellow noise
Interrupt this Ground –

986 'A narrow Fellow in the Grass'

A narrow Fellow in the Grass
Occasionally rides –
You may have met Him – did you not
His notice sudden is –

The Grass divides as with a Comb –
A spotted shaft is seen –
And then it closes at your feet
And opens further on –

He likes a Boggy Acre
A Floor too cool for Corn –
Yet when a Boy, and Barefoot –
I more than once at Noon
Have passed, I thought, a Whip lash
Unbraiding in the Sun
When stooping to secure it
It wrinkled, and was gone –

Several of Nature's People
I know, and they know me –
I feel for them a transport
Of cordiality –

But never met this Fellow
Attended, or alone
Without a tighter breathing
And Zero at the Bone –

1624 'Apparently with no surprise'

Apparently with no surprise
To any happy Flower
The Frost beheads it at its play –
In accidental power –
The blonde Assassin passes on –
The Sun proceeds unmoved
To measure off another Day
For an Approving God.

1732 'My life closed twice before its close'

My life closed twice before its close –
It yet remains to see
If Immortality unveil
A third event to me

So huge, so hopeless to conceive
As these that twice befell.
Parting is all we know of heaven,
And all we need of hell.

George A. Strong 1832–1912

From *The Song of Milkanwatha*

'WHEN HE KILLED THE MUDJOKIVIS'

When he killed the Mudjokivis,
Of the skin he made him mittens,
Made them with the fur side inside,
Made them with the skin side outside,
He, to get the warm side inside
Put the inside skin side outside;
He, to get the cold side outside,
Put the warm side fur side inside.
That's why he put fur side inside,
Why he put the skin side outside,
Why he turned them inside outside.

Francis Bret Harte 1836–1902

Plain Language from Truthful James

TABLE MOUNTAIN, 1870

Which I wish to remark,
   And my language is plain,
That for ways that are dark
   And for tricks that are vain,
The heathen Chinee is peculiar,
   Which the same I would rise to explain.

Ah Sin was his name;
   And I shall not deny,
In regard to the same,
   What that name might imply;
But his smile it was pensive and childlike,
   As I frequent remarked to Bill Nye.

It was August the third,
   And quite soft was the skies:
Which it might be inferred
   That Ah Sin was likewise;
Yet he played it that day upon William
   And me in a way I despise.

Which we had a small game,
   And Ah Sin took a hand:
It was Euchre. The same
   He did not understand;
But he smiled as he sat by the table,
   With the smile that was childlike and bland.

Yet the cards they were stocked
  In a way that I grieve,
And my feelings were shocked
  At the state of Nye's sleeve,
Which was stuffed full of aces and bowers,
  And the same with intent to deceive.

But the hands that were played
  By that heathen Chinee,
And the points that he made,
  Were quite frightful to see, –
Till at last he put down a right bower,
  Which the same Nye had dealt unto me.

Then I looked up at Nye,
  And he gazed upon me;
And he rose with a sigh,
  And said, 'Can this be?
We are ruined by Chinese cheap labor,' –
  And he went for that heathen Chinee.

In the scene that ensued
  I did not take a hand,
But the floor it was strewed
  Like the leaves on the strand
With the cards that Ah Sin had been hiding,
  In the game 'he did not understand.'

In his sleeves, which were long,
  He had twenty-four packs, –
Which was coming it strong,
  Yet I state but the facts;
And we found on his nails, which were taper,
  What is frequent in tapers, – that's wax.

Which is why I remark,
　　And my language is plain,
That for ways that are dark
　　And for tricks that are vain,
The heathen Chinee is peculiar, –
　　Which the same I am free to maintain.

Anonymous

The Old Chisholm Trail

Come along, boys, and listen to my tale,
I'll tell you of my troubles on the old Chisholm Trail.

(*Refrain*)
   Coma ti yi youpy, youpy yea, youpy yea,
   Coma ti yi youpy, youpy yea.

I started up the trail October twenty-third,
I started up the trail with the 2-U herd.

Oh, a ten-dollar hoss and a forty-dollar saddle,
And I'm goin' to punchin' Texas cattle.

I woke up one morning on the old Chisholm Trail,
Rope in my hand and a cow by the tail.

I'm up in the mornin' afore daylight
And afore I sleep the moon shines bright.

Old Ben Bolt was a blamed good boss,
But he'd go to see the girls on a sore-backed hoss.

Old Ben Bolt was a fine old man
And you'd know there was whiskey wherever he'd land.

It's cloudy in the West, a-looking like rain,
And my damned old slicker's in the wagon again.

Crippled my hoss, I don't know how,
Ropin' at the horns of a 2-U cow.

We hit Caldwell and we hit her on the fly,
We bedded down the cattle on the hill close by.

No chaps, no slicker, and it's pouring down rain,
And I swear, by god, I'll never night-herd again.

Feet in the stirrups and seat in the saddle,
I hung and rattled with them long-horn cattle.

Last night I was on guard and the leader broke the ranks,
I hit my horse down the shoulders, and I spurred him in the flanks.

The wind commenced to blow, and the rain began to fall,
Hit looked, by grab, like we was goin' to lose 'em all.

Foot in the stirrup and hand on the horn,
Best damned cowboy ever was born.

We rounded 'em up and put 'em on the cars,
And that was the last of the old Two Bars.

Oh it's bacon and beans most every day, –
I'd as soon be a-eatin' prairie hay.

I'm on my best horse and I'm goin' at a run,
I'm the quickest shootin' cowboy that ever pulled a gun.

I went to the wagon to get my roll,
To come back to Texas, dad-burn my soul.

I went to the boss to draw my roll,
He had it figgered out I was nine dollars in the hole.

With my knees in the saddle and my seat in the sky,
I'll quit punching cows in the sweet by and by.

  Coma ti yi youpy, youpy yea, youpy yea,
  Coma ti yi youpy, youpy yea.

John Henry

John Henry was a li'l baby, uh-huh,
He sat on his daddy's knee;
Said: 'De Big Bend Tunnel on de C. & O. road
Gonna cause de death of me,
Lawd, Lawd, gonna cause de death of me.'

Cap'n says to John Henry,
'Gonna bring me a steam drill 'round,
Gonna take dat steam drill out on de job,
Gonna whop dat steel on down,
Lawd, Lawd, gonna whop dat steel on down.'

John Henry tol' his cap'n
Dat a man wuz a natural man,
An' befo' he'd let dat steam drill run him down,
He'd fall dead wid a hammer in his han',
He'd fall dead wid a hammer in his han'.

John Henry sez to his cap'n:
'Send me a twelve-poun' hammer aroun',
A twelve-poun' hammer wid a fo'-foot handle,
An' I beat yo' steam drill down,
An' I beat yo' steam drill down.'

John Henry started on de right han',
De steam drill started on de lef' –
'Before I'd let dis steam drill beat me down,
I'd hammer my fool self to death,
Lawd, Lawd, I'd hammer my fool self to death.'

Sun shine hot an' burnin',
Wer'n't no breeze a-tall,
Sweat ran down like water down a hill,
Dat day John Henry let his hammer fall,
Lawd, Lawd, dat day John Henry let his hammer fall.

White man tol' John Henry,
'Nigger, damn yo' soul,
You might beat dis steam an' drill of mine,
When de rocks in dis mountain turn to gol',
Lawd, Lawd, when de rocks in dis mountain turn to gol'.'

John Henry hammered in de mountains,
An' his hammer was strikin' fire,
He drove so hard till he broke his pore heart,
An' he lied down his hammer an' he died,
Lawd, Lawd, he lied down his hammer an' he died.

John Henry had a li'l baby,
Hel' him in de palm of his han'.
De las' words I heard de pore boy say:
'Son, yo're gonna be a steel-drivin' man,
Son, yo're gonna be a steel-drivin' man!'

John Henry had a pretty li'l 'ooman,
An' de dress she wo' was blue,
An' de las' words she said to him:
'John Henry, I've been true to you,
Lawd, Lawd, John Henry, I've been true to you.'

John Henry had anothah 'ooman,
De dress she wo' wuz red.
De las' words I heard de pore gal say:
'I'm goin' w'eah mah man drapt daid,
I'm goin' w'eah mah man drapt daid!'

'Oh, who's gonna shoe yo' li'l feetses,
An' who's gonna glub yo' han's,
An' who's gonna kiss yo' rosy, rosy lips,
An' who's gonna be yo' man,
Lawd, Lawd, an' who's gonna be yo' man?'

Dey took John Henry to de graveyard,
An' dey buried him in de san',
An' every locomotive come roarin' by,
Says, 'Dere lays a steel-drivin' man,
Lawd, Lawd, dere lays a steel-drivin' man.'

Frankie and Johnny

Frankie and Johnny were lovers, O lordy how they could love.
Swore to be true to each other, true as the stars above;
He was her man, but he done her wrong.

Frankie she was his woman, everybody knows.
She spent one hundred dollars for a suit of Johnny's clothes.
He was her man, but he done her wrong.

Frankie and Johnny went walking, Johnny in his bran' new suit,
'O good Lawd,' says Frankie, 'but don't my Johnny look cute?'
He was her man, but he done her wrong.

Frankie went down to Memphis; she went on the evening train.
She paid one hundred dollars for Johnny a watch and chain.
He was her man, but he done her wrong.

Frankie went down to the corner, to buy a glass of beer;
She says to the fat bartender, 'Has my loving man been here?
He was my man, but he done me wrong.'

'Ain't going to tell you no story, ain't going to tell you no lie,
I seen your man 'bout an hour ago with a girl named Alice Bly –
If he's your man, he's doing you wrong.'

Frankie went back to the hotel, she didn't go there for fun,
Under her long red kimono she toted a forty-four gun.
He was her man, but he done her wrong.

Frankie went down to the hotel, looked in the window so high,
There was her lovin' Johnny a-lovin' up Alice Bly;
He was her man, but he done her wrong.

Frankie went down to the hotel, she rang that hotel bell,
'Stand back all of you floozies or I'll blow you all to hell,
I want my man, he's doin' me wrong.'

Frankie threw back her kimono; took out the old forty-four;
Roota-toot-toot, three times she shot, right through that hotel door.
She shot her man, 'cause he done her wrong.

Johnny grabbed off his Stetson. 'O good Lawd, Frankie, don't
    shoot.'
But Frankie put her finger on the trigger, and the gun went roota-
    toot-toot.
He was her man, but she shot him down.

'Roll me over easy, roll me over slow,
Roll me over easy, boys, 'cause my wounds are hurting me so,
I was her man, but I done her wrong.'

With the first shot Johnny staggered; with the second shot he fell;
When the third bullet hit him, there was a new man's face in hell.
He was her man, but he done her wrong.

Frankie heard a rumbling away down under the ground.
Maybe it was Johnny where she had shot him down.
He was her man, and she done him wrong.

'Oh, bring on your rubber-tired hearses, bring on your rubber-tired
    hacks,
They're takin' my Johnny to the buryin' groun' but they'll never
    bring him back.
He was my man, but he done me wrong.'

The judge he said to the jury, 'It's plain as plain can be.
This woman shot her man, so it's murder in the second degree.
He was her man, though he done her wrong.'

Now it wasn't murder in the second degree, it wasn't murder in the
    third.
Frankie simply dropped her man, like a hunter drops a bird.
He was her man, but he done her wrong.

'Oh, put me in that dungeon. Oh, put me in that cell.
Put me where the northeast wind blows from the southeast corner of
    hell.
I shot my man 'cause he done me wrong.'

Frankie walked up to the scaffold, as calm as a girl could be,
She turned her eyes to heaven and said, 'Good Lord, I'm coming to
    thee.
He was my man, and I done him wrong.'

Edgar Lee Masters 1869–1950

The Hill

Where are Elmer, Herman, Bert, Tom and Charley,
The weak of will, the strong of arm, the clown, the boozer, the
    fighter?
All, all, are sleeping on the hill.

One passed in a fever,
One was burned in a mine,
One was killed in a brawl,
One died in a jail,
One fell from a bridge toiling for children and wife –
All, all are sleeping, sleeping, sleeping on the hill.

Where are Ella, Kate, Mag, Lizzie and Edith,
The tender heart, the simple soul, the loud, the proud, the happy
    one? –
All, all, are sleeping on the hill.

One died in shameful child-birth,
One of a thwarted love,
One at the hands of a brute in a brothel,
One of a broken pride, in the search for heart's desire,
One after life in far-away London and Paris
Was brought to her little space by Ella and Kate and Mag –
All, all are sleeping, sleeping, sleeping on the hill.

Where are Uncle Isaac and Aunt Emily,
And old Towny Kincaid and Sevigne Houghton,
And Major Walker who had talked
With venerable men of the revolution? –
All, all, are sleeping on the hill.

They brought them dead sons from the war,
And daughters whom life had crushed,
And their children fatherless, crying –
All, all are sleeping, sleeping, sleeping on the hill.

Where is Old Fiddler Jones
Who played with life all his ninety years,
Braving the sleet with bared breast,
Drinking, rioting, thinking neither of wife nor kin,
Nor gold, nor love, nor heaven?
Lo! he babbles of the fish-frys of long ago,
Of the horse-races of long ago at Clary's Grove,
Of what Abe Lincoln said
One time at Springfield.

Elsa Wertman

I was a peasant girl from Germany,
Blue-eyed, rosy, happy and strong.
And the first place I worked was at Thomas Greene's.
On a summer's day when she was away
He stole into the kitchen and took me
Right in his arms and kissed me on my throat,
I turning my head. Then neither of us
Seemed to know what happened.
And I cried for what would become of me.
And cried and cried as my secret began to show.
One day Mrs Greene said she understood,
And would make no trouble for me,
And, being childless, would adopt it.
(He had given her a farm to be still.)
So she hid in the house and sent out rumors,
As if it were going to happen to her.
And all went well and the child was born – They were so kind to me.

Later I married Gus Wertman, and years passed.
But – at political rallies when sitters-by thought I was crying
At the eloquence of Hamilton Greene –
That was not it.
No! I wanted to say:
That's my son! That's my son!

Editor Whedon

To be able to see every side of every question;
To be on every side, to be everything, to be nothing long;
To pervert truth, to ride it for a purpose,
To use great feelings and passions of the human family
For base designs, for cunning ends,
To wear a mask like the Greek actors –
Your eight-page paper – behind which you huddle,
Bawling through the megaphone of big type:
'This is I, the giant.'
Thereby also living the life of a sneak-thief,
Poisoned with the anonymous words
Of your clandestine soul.
To scratch dirt over scandal for money,
And exhume it to the winds for revenge,
Or to sell papers,
Crushing reputations, or bodies, if need be,
To win at any cost, save your own life.
To glory in demoniac power, ditching civilization,
As a paranoiac boy puts a log on the track
And derails the express train.
To be an editor, as I was.
Then to lie here close by the river over the place
Where the sewage flows from the village,
And the empty cans and garbage are dumped,
And abortions are hidden.

'Butch' Weldy

After I got religion and steadied down
They gave me a job in the canning works,
And every morning I had to fill
The tank in the yard with gasoline,
That fed the blow-fires in the sheds
To heat the soldering irons.
And I mounted a rickety ladder to do it,
Carrying buckets full of the stuff.
One morning, as I stood there pouring,
The air grew still and seemed to heave,
And I shot up as the tank exploded,
And down I came with both legs broken,
And my eyes burned crisp as a couple of eggs.
For someone left a blow-fire going,
And something sucked the flame in the tank.
The Circuit Judge said whoever did it
Was a fellow-servant of mine, and so
Old Rhodes' son didn't have to pay me.
And I sat on the witness stand as blind
As Jack the Fiddler, saying over and over,
'I didn't know him at all.'

Edwin Arlington Robinson 1869–1935

Reuben Bright

Because he was a butcher and thereby
Did earn an honest living (and did right),
I would not have you think that Reuben Bright
Was any more a brute than you or I;
For when they told him that his wife must die,
He stared at them, and shook with grief and fright,
And cried like a great baby half that night,
And made the women cry to see him cry.

And after she was dead, and he had paid
The singers and the sexton and the rest,
He packed a lot of things that she had made
Most mournfully away in an old chest
Of hers, and put some chopped-up cedar boughs
In with them, and tore down the slaughterhouse.

Miniver Cheevy

Miniver Cheevy, child of scorn,
    Grew lean while he assailed the seasons;
He wept that he was ever born,
    And he had reasons.

Miniver loved the days of old
    When swords were bright and steeds were prancing;
The vision of a warrior bold
    Would set him dancing.

Miniver sighed for what was not,
   And dreamed, and rested from his labors;
He dreamed of Thebes and Camelot,
   And Priam's neighbors.

Miniver mourned the ripe renown
   That made so many a name so fragrant;
He mourned Romance, now on the town,
   And Art, a vagrant.

Miniver loved the Medici,
   Albeit he had never seen one;
He would have sinned incessantly
   Could he have been one.

Miniver cursed the commonplace
   And eyed a khaki suit with loathing;
He missed the mediæval grace
   Of iron clothing.

Miniver scorned the gold he sought,
   But sore annoyed was he without it;
Miniver thought, and thought, and thought,
   And thought about it.

Miniver Cheevy, born too late,
   Scratched his head and kept on thinking;
Miniver coughed, and called it fate,
   And kept on drinking.

Richard Cory

Whenever Richard Cory went down town,
We people on the pavement looked at him:
He was a gentleman from sole to crown,
Clean favored, and imperially slim.

And he was always quietly arrayed,
And he was always human when he talked;
But still he fluttered pulses when he said,
'Good-morning,' and he glittered when he walked.

And he was rich – yes, richer than a king –
And admirably schooled in every grace:
In fine, we thought that he was everything
To make us wish that we were in his place.

So on we worked, and waited for the light,
And went without the meat, and cursed the bread;
And Richard Cory, one calm summer night,
Went home and put a bullet through his head.

Eros Turannos

She fears him, and will always ask
    What fated her to choose him;
She meets in his engaging mask
    All reasons to refuse him;
But what she meets and what she fears
Are less than are the downward years,
Drawn slowly to the foamless weirs
    Of age, were she to lose him.

Between a blurred sagacity
    That once had power to sound him,
And Love, that will not let him be
    The Judas that she found him,
Her pride assuages her almost,
As if it were alone the cost. –
He sees that he will not be lost,
    And waits and looks around him.

A sense of ocean and old trees
   Envelops and allures him;
Tradition, touching all he sees,
   Beguiles and reassures him;
And all her doubts of what he says
Are dimmed with what she knows of days –
Till even prejudice delays
   And fades, and she secures him.

The falling leaf inaugurates
   The reign of her confusion;
The pounding wave reverberates
   The dirge of her illusion;
And home, where passion lived and died,
Becomes a place where she can hide,
While all the town and harbor side
   Vibrate with her seclusion.

We tell you, tapping on our brows,
   The story as it should be, –
As if the story of a house
   Were told, or ever could be;
We'll have no kindly veil between
Her visions and those we have seen, –
As if we guessed what hers have been,
   Or what they are or would be.

Meanwhile we do no harm; for they
   That with a god have striven,
Not hearing much of what we say,
   Take what the god has given;
Though like waves breaking it may be,
Or like a changed familiar tree,
Or like a stairway to the sea
   Where down the blind are driven.

Mr Flood's Party

Old Eben Flood, climbing alone one night
Over the hill between the town below
And the forsaken upland hermitage
That held as much as he should ever know
On earth again of home, paused warily.
The road was his with not a native near;
And Eben, having leisure, said aloud,
For no man else in Tilbury Town to hear:

'Well, Mr Flood, we have the harvest moon
Again, and we may not have many more;
The bird is on the wing, the poet says,
And you and I have said it here before.
Drink to the bird.' He raised up to the light
The jug that he had gone so far to fill,
And answered huskily: 'Well, Mr Flood,
Since you propose it, I believe I will.'

Alone, as if enduring to the end
A valiant armor of scarred hopes outworn,
He stood there in the middle of the road
Like Roland's ghost winding a silent horn.
Below him, in the town among the trees,
Where friends of other days had honored him,
A phantom salutation of the dead
Rang thinly till old Eben's eyes were dim.

Then, as a mother lays her sleeping child
Down tenderly, fearing it may awake,
He set the jug down slowly at his feet
With trembling care, knowing that most things break;
And only when assured that on firm earth

234

It stood, as the uncertain lives of men
Assuredly did not, he paced away,
And with his hand extended paused again:

'Well, Mr Flood, we have not met like this
In a long time; and many a change has come
To both of us, I fear, since last it was
We had a drop together. Welcome home!'
Convivially returning with himself,
Again he raised the jug up to the light;
And with an acquiescent quaver said:
'Well, Mr Flood, if you insist, I might.

'Only a very little, Mr Flood –
For auld lang syne. No more, sir; that will do.'
So, for the time, apparently it did,
And Eben evidently thought so too;
For soon amid the silver loneliness
Of night he lifted up his voice and sang,
Secure, with only two moons listening,
Until the whole harmonious landscape rang –

'For auld lang syne.' The weary throat gave out,
The last word wavered, and the song was done.
He raised again the jug regretfully
And shook his head, and was again alone.
There was not much that was ahead of him,
And there was nothing in the town below –
Where strangers would have shut the many doors
That many friends had opened long ago.

Stephen Crane 1871–1900

From *The Black Riders*

III 'IN THE DESERT'

In the desert
I saw a creature, naked, bestial,
Who, squatting upon the ground,
Held his heart in his hands,
And ate of it.
I said, 'Is it good, friend?'
'It is bitter – bitter,' he answered;
'But I like it
Because it is bitter,
And because it is my heart.'

From *War is Kind*

XII 'A NEWSPAPER IS A COLLECTION OF HALF-INJUSTICES'

A newspaper is a collection of half-injustices
Which, bawled by boys from mile to mile,
Spreads its curious opinion
To a million merciful and sneering men,
While families cuddle the joys of the fireside
When spurred by tale of dire lone agony.
A newspaper is a court
Where every one is kindly and unfairly tried
By a squalor of honest men.

A newspaper is a market
Where wisdom sells its freedom
And melons are crowned by the crowd.
A newspaper is a game
Where his error scores the player victory
While another's skill wins death.
A newspaper is a symbol;
It is feckless life's chronicle,
A collection of loud tales
Concentrating eternal stupidities,
That in remote ages lived unhaltered,
Roaming through a fenceless world.

Amy Lowell 1874–1925

Meeting-House Hill

I must be mad, or very tired,
When the curve of a blue bay beyond a railroad track
Is shrill and sweet to me like the sudden springing of a tune,
And the sight of a white church above thin trees in a city square
Amazes my eyes as though it were the Parthenon.
Clear, reticent, superbly final,
With the pillars of its portico refined to a cautious elegance,
It dominates the weak trees,
And the shot of its spire
Is cool, and candid,
Rising into an unresisting sky.
Strange meeting-house
Pausing a moment upon a squalid hill-top.
I watch the spire sweeping the sky,
I am dizzy with the movement of the sky,
I might be watching a mast
With its royals set full
Straining before a two-reef breeze.
I might be sighting a tea-clipper,
Tacking into the blue bay,
Just back from Canton
With her hold full of green and blue porcelain,
And a Chinese coolie leaning over the rail
Gazing at the white spire
With dull, sea-spent eyes.

Anonymous

'I sometimes think I'd rather crow'

I sometimes think I'd rather crow
And be a rooster than to roost
And be a crow. But I dunno.

A rooster he can roost also,
Which don't seem fair when crows can't crow.
Which may help some. Still I dunno.

Crows should be glad of one thing though;
Nobody thinks of eating crow,
While roosters they are good enough
For anyone unless they're tough.

There're lots of tough old roosters though,
And anyway a crow can't crow,
So mebby roosters stand more show.
It looks that way. But I dunno.

Robert Frost 1874–1963

The Tuft of Flowers

I went to turn the grass once after one
Who mowed it in the dew before the sun.

The dew was gone that made his blade so keen
Before I came to view the leveled scene.

I looked for him behind an isle of trees;
I listened for his whetstone on the breeze.

But he had gone his way, the grass all mown,
And I must be, as he had been, – alone,

'As all must be,' I said within my heart,
'Whether they work together or apart.'

But as I said it, swift there passed me by
On noiseless wing a bewildered butterfly,

Seeking with memories grown dim o'er night
Some resting flower of yesterday's delight.

And once I marked his flight go round and round,
As where some flower lay withering on the ground.

And then he flew as far as eye could see,
And then on tremulous wing came back to me.

I thought of questions that have no reply,
And would have turned to toss the grass to dry;

But he turned first, and led my eye to look
At a tall tuft of flowers beside a brook,

A leaping tongue of bloom the scythe had spared
Beside a reedy brook the scythe had bared.

The mower in the dew had loved them thus,
By leaving them to flourish, not for us,

Nor yet to draw one thought of ours to him,
But from sheer morning gladness at the brim.

The butterfly and I had lit upon,
Nevertheless, a message from the dawn,

That made me hear the wakening birds around,
And hear his long scythe whispering to the ground,

And feel a spirit kindred to my own;
So that henceforth I worked no more alone;

But glad with him, I worked as with his aid,
And weary, sought at noon with him the shade;

And dreaming, as it were, held brotherly speech
With one whose thought I had not hoped to reach.

'Men work together,' I told him from the heart,
'Whether they work together or apart.'

Mending Wall

Something there is that doesn't love a wall,
That sends the frozen-ground-swell under it,
And spills the upper boulders in the sun;

And makes gaps even two can pass abreast.
The work of hunters is another thing:
I have come after them and made repair
Where they have left not one stone on a stone,
But they would have the rabbit out of hiding,
To please the yelping dogs. The gaps I mean,
No one has seen them made or heard them made,
But at spring mending-time we find them there.
I let my neighbor know beyond the hill;
And on a day we meet to walk the line
And set the wall between us once again.
We keep the wall between us as we go.
To each the boulders that have fallen to each.
And some are loaves and some so nearly balls
We have to use a spell to make them balance:
'Stay where you are until our backs are turned!'
We wear our fingers rough with handling them.
Oh, just another kind of outdoor game,
One on a side. It comes to little more:
There where it is we do not need the wall:
He is all pine and I am apple orchard.
My apple trees will never get across
And eat the cones under his pines, I tell him.
He only says, 'Good fences make good neighbors.'
Spring is the mischief in me, and I wonder
If I could put a notion in his head:
'*Why* do they make good neighbors? Isn't it
Where there are cows? But here there are no cows.
Before I built a wall I'd ask to know
What I was walling in or walling out,
And to whom I was like to give offense.
Something there is that doesn't love a wall,
That wants it down.' I could say 'Elves' to him,
But it's not elves exactly, and I'd rather
He said it for himself. I see him there
Bringing a stone grasped firmly by the top

In each hand, like an old-stone savage armed.
He moves in darkness as it seems to me,
Not of woods only and the shade of trees.
He will not go behind his father's saying,
And he likes having thought of it so well
He says again, 'Good fences make good neighbors.'

The Death of the Hired Man

Mary sat musing on the lamp-flame at the table
Waiting for Warren. When she heard his step,
She ran on tip-toe down the darkened passage
To meet him in the doorway with the news
And put him on his guard. 'Silas is back.'
She pushed him outward with her through the door
And shut it after her. 'Be kind,' she said.
She took the market things from Warren's arms
And set them on the porch, then drew him down
To sit beside her on the wooden steps.

'When was I ever anything but kind to him ?
But I'll not have the fellow back,' he said.
'I told him so last haying, didn't I?
If he left then, I said, that ended it.
What good is he? Who else will harbor him
At his age for the little he can do?
What help he is there's no depending on.
Off he goes always when I need him most.
He thinks he ought to earn a little pay,
Enough at least to buy tobacco with,
So he won't have to beg and be beholden.
"All right," I say, "I can't afford to pay
Any fixed wages, though I wish I could."
"Someone else can." "Then someone else will have to."

I shouldn't mind his bettering himself
If that was what it was. You can be certain,
When he begins like that, there's someone at him
Trying to coax him off with pocket-money, –
In haying time, when any help is scarce.
In winter he comes back to us. I'm done.'

'Sh! not so loud: he'll hear you,' Mary said.

'I want him to: he'll have to soon or late.'

'He's worn out. He's asleep beside the stove.
When I came up from Rowe's I found him here,
Huddled against the barn-door fast asleep,
A miserable sight, and frightening, too –
You needn't smile – I didn't recognize him –
I wasn't looking for him – and he's changed.
Wait till you see.'

                              'Where did you say he'd been?'

'He didn't say. I dragged him to the house,
And gave him tea and tried to make him smoke.
I tried to make him talk about his travels.
Nothing would do: he just kept nodding off.'

'What did he say? Did he say anything?'

'But little.'

                    'Anything? Mary, confess
He said he'd come to ditch the meadow for me.'

'Warren!'

                    'But did he? I just want to know.'

'Of course he did. What would you have him say?
Surely you wouldn't grudge the poor old man
Some humble way to save his self-respect.
He added, if you really care to know,
He meant to clear the upper pasture, too.
That sounds like something you have heard before?
Warren, I wish you could have heard the way
He jumbled everything. I stopped to look
Two or three times – he made me feel so queer –
To see if he was talking in his sleep.
He ran on Harold Wilson – you remember –
The boy you had in haying four years since.
He's finished school, and teaching in his college.
Silas declares you'll have to get him back.
He says they two will make a team for work:
Between them they will lay this farm as smooth!
The way he mixed that in with other things.
He thinks young Wilson a likely lad, though daft
On education – you know how they fought
All through July under the blazing sun,
Silas up on the cart to build the load,
Harold along beside to pitch it on.'

'Yes, I took care to keep well out of earshot.'

'Well, those days trouble Silas like a dream.
You wouldn't think they would. How some things linger!
Harold's young college boy's assurance piqued him.
After so many years he still keeps finding
Good arguments he sees he might have used.
I sympathize. I know just how it feels
To think of the right thing to say too late.
Harold's associated in his mind with Latin.
He asked me what I thought of Harold's saying
He studied Latin like the violin
Because he liked it – that an argument!

He said he couldn't make the boy believe
He could find water with a hazel prong –
Which showed how much good school had ever done him.
He wanted to go over that. But most of all
He thinks if he could have another chance
To teach him how to build a load of hay –'

'I know, that's Silas' one accomplishment.
He bundles every forkful in its place,
And tags and numbers it for future reference,
So he can find and easily dislodge it
In the unloading. Silas does that well.
He takes it out in bunches like big birds' nests.
You never see him standing on the hay
He's trying to lift, straining to lift himself.'

'He thinks if he could teach him that, he'd be
Some good perhaps to someone in the world.
He hates to see a boy the fool of books.
Poor Silas, so concerned for other folk,
And nothing to look backward to with pride,
And nothing to look forward to with hope,
So now and never any different.'

Part of a moon was falling down the west,
Dragging the whole sky with it to the hills.
Its light poured softly in her lap. She saw it
And spread her apron to it. She put out her hand
Among the harp-like morning-glory strings,
Taut with the dew from garden bed to eaves,
As if she played unheard some tenderness
That wrought on him beside her in the night.
'Warren,' she said, 'he has come home to die:
You needn't be afraid he'll leave you this time.'

'Home,' he mocked gently.
                                        'Yes, what else but home?

It all depends on what you mean by home.
Of course he's nothing to us, any more
Than was the hound that came a stranger to us
Out of the woods, worn out upon the trail.'

'Home is the place where, when you have to go there,
They have to take you in.'

                                     'I should have called it
Something you somehow haven't to deserve.'

Warren leaned out and took a step or two,
Picked up a little stick, and brought it back
And broke it in his hand and tossed it by.
'Silas has better claim on us you think
Than on his brother? Thirteen little miles
As the road winds would bring him to his door.
Silas has walked that far no doubt today.
Why doesn't he go there? His brother's rich,
A somebody – director in the bank.'

'He never told us that.'

                           'We know it though.'

'I think his brother ought to help, of course.
I'll see to that if there is need. He ought of right
To take him in, and might be willing to –
He may be better than appearances.
But have some pity on Silas. Do you think
If he had any pride in claiming kin
Or anything he looked for from his brother,
He'd keep so still about him all this time?'

'I wonder what's between them.'

'I can tell you.
Silas is what he is – we wouldn't mind him –
But just the kind that kinsfolk can't abide.
He never did a thing so very bad.
He don't know why he isn't quite as good
As anybody. Worthless though he is,
He won't be made ashamed to please his brother.'

'*I* can't think Si ever hurt anyone.'

'No, but he hurt my heart the way he lay
And rolled his old head on that sharp-edged chairback.
He wouldn't let me put him on the lounge.
You must go in and see what you can do.
I made the bed up for him there tonight.
You'll be surprised at him – how much he's broken.
His working days are done; I'm sure of it.'

'I'd not be in a hurry to say that.'

'I haven't been. Go, look, see for yourself.
But, Warren, please remember how it is:
He's come to help you ditch the meadow.
He has a plan. You mustn't laugh at him.
He may not speak of it, and then he may.
I'll sit and see if that small sailing cloud
Will hit or miss the moon.'

It hit the moon.
Then there were three there, making a dim row,
The moon, the little silver cloud, and she.

Warren returned – too soon, it seemed to her,
Slipped to her side, caught up her hand and waited.
'Warren?' she questioned.

'Dead,' was all he answered.

After Apple-Picking

My long two-pointed ladder's sticking through a tree
Toward heaven still,
And there's a barrel that I didn't fill
Beside it, and there may be two or three
Apples I didn't pick upon some bough.
But I am done with apple-picking now.
Essence of winter sleep is on the night,
The scent of apples: I am drowsing off.
I cannot rub the strangeness from my sight
I got from looking through a pane of glass
I skimmed this morning from the drinking trough
And held against the world of hoary grass.
It melted, and I let it fall and break.
But I was well
Upon my way to sleep before it fell,
And I could tell
What form my dreaming was about to take.
Magnified apples appear and disappear,
Stem end and blossom end,
And every fleck of russet showing clear.
My instep arch not only keeps the ache,
It keeps the pressure of a ladder-round.
I feel the ladder sway as the boughs bend.
And I keep hearing from the cellar bin
The rumbling sound
Of load on load of apples coming in.
For I have had too much
Of apple-picking: I am overtired
Of the great harvest I myself desired.
There were ten thousand thousand fruit to touch,
Cherish in hand, lift down, and not let fall.
For all
That struck the earth,

No matter if not bruised or spiked with stubble,
Went surely to the cider-apple heap
As of no worth.
One can see what will trouble
This sleep of mine, whatever sleep it is.
Were he not gone,
The woodchuck could say whether it's like his
Long sleep, as I describe its coming on,
Or just some human sleep.

For Once, Then, Something

Others taunt me with having knelt at well-curbs
Always wrong to the light, so never seeing
Deeper down in the well than where the water
Gives me back in a shining surface picture
Me myself in the summer heaven godlike
Looking out of a wreath of fern and cloud puffs.
Once, when trying with chin against a well-curb,
I discerned, as I thought, beyond the picture,
Through the picture, a something white, uncertain,
Something more of the depths – and then I lost it.
Water came to rebuke the too clear water.
One drop fell from a fern, and lo, a ripple
Shook whatever it was lay there at bottom,
Blurred it, blotted it out. What was that whiteness?
Truth? A pebble of quartz? For once, then, something.

'Out, Out –'

The buzz saw snarled and rattled in the yard
And made dust and dropped stove-length sticks of wood,
Sweet-scented stuff when the breeze drew across it.

And from there those that lifted eyes could count
Five mountain ranges one behind the other
Under the sunset far into Vermont.
And the saw snarled and rattled, snarled and rattled,
As it ran light, or had to bear a load.
And nothing happened: day was all but done.
Call it a day, I wish they might have said
To please the boy by giving him the half hour
That a boy counts so much when saved from work.
His sister stood beside them in her apron
To tell them 'Supper'. At the word, the saw,
As if to prove saws knew what supper meant,
Leaped out at the boy's hand, or seemed to leap –
He must have given the hand. However it was,
Neither refused the meeting. But the hand!
The boy's first outcry was a rueful laugh,
As he swung toward them holding up the hand
Half in appeal, but half as if to keep
The life from spilling. Then the boy saw all –
Since he was old enough to know, big boy
Doing a man's work, though a child at heart –
He saw all spoiled. 'Don't let him cut my hand off –
The doctor, when he comes. Don't let him, sister!'
So. But the hand was gone already.
The doctor put him in the dark of ether.
He lay and puffed his lips out with his breath.
And then – the watcher at his pulse took fright.
No one believed. They listened at his heart.
Little – less – nothing! – and that ended it.
No more to build on there. And they, since they
Were not the one dead, turned to their affairs.

Stopping by Woods on a Snowy Evening

Whose woods these are I think I know.
His house is in the village though;
He will not see me stopping here
To watch his woods fill up with snow.

My little horse must think it queer
To stop without a farmhouse near
Between the woods and frozen lake
The darkest evening of the year.

He gives his harness bells a shake
To ask if there is some mistake.
The only other sound's the sweep
Of easy wind and downy flake.

The woods are lovely, dark and deep,
But I have promises to keep,
And miles to go before I sleep,
And miles to go before I sleep.

Bereft

Where had I heard this wind before
Change like this to a deeper roar?
What would it take my standing there for,
Holding open a restive door,
Looking down hill to a frothy shore?
Summer was past and day was past.
Sombre clouds in the west were massed.
Out in the porch's sagging floor,
Leaves got up in a coil and hissed,
Blindly struck at my knee and missed.

Something sinister in the tone
Told me my secret must be known:
Word I was in the house alone
Somehow must have gotten abroad,
Word I was in my life alone,
Word I had no one left but God.

Neither Out Far Nor In Deep

The people along the sand
All turn and look one way.
They turn their back on the land.
They look at the sea all day.

As long as it takes to pass
A ship keeps raising its hull;
The wetter ground like glass
Reflects a standing gull.

The land may vary more;
But wherever the truth may be –
The water comes ashore,
And the people look at the sea.

They cannot look out far.
They cannot look in deep.
But when was that ever a bar
To any watch they keep?

Provide, Provide

The witch that came (the withered hag)
To wash the steps with pail and rag,
Was once the beauty Abishag,

The picture pride of Hollywood.
Too many fall from great and good
For you to doubt the likelihood.

Die early and avoid the fate.
Or if predestined to die late,
Make up your mind to die in state.

Make the whole stock exchange your own!
If need be occupy a throne,
Where nobody can call *you* crone.

Some have relied on what they knew;
Others on being simply true.
What worked for them might work for you.

No memory of having starred
Atones for later disregard,
Or keeps the end from being hard.

Better to go down dignified
With boughten friendship at your side
Than none at all. Provide, provide!

Design

I found a dimpled spider, fat and white,
On a white heal-all, holding up a moth
Like a white piece of rigid satin cloth –
Assorted characters of death and blight
Mixed ready to begin the morning right,
Like the ingredients of a witches' broth –
A snow-drop spider, a flower like a froth,
And dead wings carried like a paper kite.

What had that flower to do with being white,
The wayside blue and innocent heal-all?
What brought the kindred spider to that height,
Then steered the white moth thither in the night?
What but design of darkness to appall? –
If design govern in a thing so small.

Don Marquis 1878–1937

pete the parrot and shakespeare

i got acquainted with
a parrot named pete recently
who is an interesting bird
pete says he used
to belong to the fellow
that ran the mermaid tavern
in london then i said
you must have known
shakespeare know him said pete
poor mutt i knew him well
he called me pete and i called him
bill but why do you say poor mutt
well said pete bill was a
disappointed man and was always
boring his friends about what
he might have been and done
if he only had a fair break
two or three pints of sack
and sherris and the tears
would trickle down into his
beard and his beard would get
soppy and wilt his collar

i remember one night when
bill and ben jonson and
frankie beaumont
were sopping it up

here i am ben says bill
nothing but a lousy playwright
and with anything like luck
in the breaks i might have been
a fairly decent sonnet writer
i might have been a poet
if i had kept away from the theatre

yes says ben i ve often
thought of that bill
but one consolation is
you are making pretty good money
out of the theatre

money money says bill what the hell
is money what i want is to be
a poet not a business man
these damned cheap shows
i turn out to keep the
theatre running break my heart
slap stick comedies and
blood and thunder tragedies
and melodramas say i wonder
if that boy heard you order
another bottle frankie
the only compensation is that i get
a chance now and then
to stick in a little poetry
when nobody is looking
but hells bells that isn t
  what i want to do
  i want to write sonnets and
  songs and spenserian stanzas
  and i might have done it too
if i hadn t got
into this frightful show game

business business business
grind grind grind
what a life for a man
that might have been a poet

well says frankie beaumont
why don t you cut it bill
i can t says bill
i need the money i ve got
a family to support down in
the country well says frankie
anyhow you write pretty good
plays bill any mutt can write
plays for this london public
says bill if he puts enough
murder in them what they want
is kings talking like kings
never had sense enough to talk
and stabbings and stranglings
and fat men making love
and clowns basting each
other with clubs and cheap puns
and off color allusions to all
the smut of the day oh i know
what the low brows want
and i give it to them

well says ben jonson
don t blubber into the drink
brace up like a man
and quit the rotten business
i can t i can t says bill
i ve been at it too long i ve got to
the place now where i can t
write anything else
but this cheap stuff

i m ashamed to look an honest
young sonneteer in the face
i live a hell of a life i do
the manager hands me some mouldy old
manuscript and says
bill here s a plot for you
this is the third of the month
by the tenth i want a good
script out of this that we
can start rehearsals on
not too big a cast
and not too much of your
damned poetry either
you know your old
familiar line of hokum
they eat up that falstaff stuff
of yours ring him in again
and give them a good ghost
or two and remember we gotta
have something dick burbage can get
his teeth into and be sure
and stick in a speech
somewhere the queen will take
for a personal compliment and if
you get in a line or two somewhere
about the honest english yeoman
it s always good stuff
and it s a pretty good stunt
bill to have the heavy villain
a moor or a dago or a jew
or something like that and say
i want another
comic welshman in this
but i don t need to tell
you bill you know this game
just some of your ordinary

hokum and maybe you could
kill a little kid or two a prince
or something they like
a little pathos along with
the dirt now you better see burbage
tonight and see what he wants
in that part oh says bill
to think i am
debasing my talents with junk
like that oh god what i wanted
was to be a poet
and write sonnet serials
like a gentleman should

well says i pete
bill s plays are highly
esteemed to this day
is that so says pete
poor mutt little he would
care what poor bill wanted
was to be a poet
                              archy

Carl Sandburg 1878–1967

Limited

I am riding on a limited express, one of the crack trains of the nation.
Hurtling across the prairie into blue haze and dark air go fifteen all-
　　steel coaches holding a thousand people.
(All the coaches shall be scrap and rust and all the men and women
　　laughing in the diners and sleepers shall pass to ashes.)
I ask a man in the smoker where he is going and he answers: 'Omaha'.

From *The People, Yes*

THE COPPERFACES, THE RED MEN

The copperfaces, the red men, handed us tobacco,
the weed for the pipe of friendship,
also the bah-tah-to, the potato, the spud.
Sunflowers came from Peruvians in ponchos.
Early Italians taught us of chestnuts,
walnuts and peaches being Persian mementos,
Siberians finding for us what rye might do,
Hindus coming through with the cucumber,
Egyptians giving us the onion, the pea,
Arabians handing advice with one gift:
'Some like it, some say it's just spinach.'
　　To the Chinese we have given
　　kerosene, bullets, Bibles
and they have given us radishes, soy beans, silk,
poems, paintings, proverbs, porcelain, egg foo yong,
gunpowder, Fourth of July firecrackers, fireworks,

and labor gangs for the first Pacific railways.
    Now we may thank these people
    or reserve our thanks
    and speak of them as outsiders
    and imply the request,
'Would you just as soon get off the earth?'
holding ourselves aloof in pride of distinction
saying to ourselves this costs us nothing
as though hate has no cost
as though hate ever grew anything worth growing.
Yes we may say this trash is beneath our notice
or we may hold them in respect and affection
as fellow creepers on a commodious planet
saying, 'Yes you too you too are people.'

Vachel Lindsay 1879–1931

Bryan, Bryan, Bryan, Bryan

THE CAMPAIGN OF EIGHTEEN NINETY-SIX,
AS VIEWED AT THE TIME BY
A SIXTEEN-YEAR-OLD, ETC.

I

In a nation of one hundred fine, mob-hearted, lynching, relenting,
    repenting millions,
There are plenty of sweeping, swinging, stinging, gorgeous things
    to shout about,
And knock your old blue devils out.

I brag and chant of Bryan, Bryan, Bryan,
Candidate for president who sketched a silver Zion,
The one American Poet who could sing outdoors,
He brought in tides of wonder, of unprecedented splendor,
Wild roses from the plains, that made hearts tender,
All the funny circus silks
Of politics unfurled,
Bartlett pears of romance that were honey at the cores,
And torchlights down the street, to the end of the world.

There were truths eternal in the gab and tittle-tattle.
There were real heads broken in the fustian and the rattle.
There were real lines drawn:
Not the silver and the gold,
But Nebraska's cry went eastward against the dour and old,
The mean and cold.

It was eighteen ninety-six, and I was just sixteen
And Altgeld ruled in Springfield, Illinois,
When there came from the sunset Nebraska's shout of joy:
In a coat like a deacon, in a black Stetson hat
He scourged the elephant plutocrats
With barbed wire from the Platte.
The scales dropped from their mighty eyes.
They saw that summer's noon
A tribe of wonders coming
To a marching tune.

Oh, the longhorns from Texas,
The jay hawks from Kansas,
The plop-eyed bungaroo and giant giassicus,
The varmint, chipmunk, bugaboo,
The horned-toad, prairie-dog and ballyhoo,
From all the newborn states arow,
Bidding the eagles of the west fly on,
Bidding the eagles of the west fly on.
The fawn, prodactyl and thing-a-ma-jig,
The rakaboor, the hellangone,
The whangdoodle, batfowl and pig,
The coyote, wild-cat and grizzly in a glow,
In a miracle of health and speed, the whole breed abreast,
They leaped the Mississippi, blue border of the West,
From the Gulf to Canada, two thousand miles long: –
Against the towns of Tubal Cain,
Ah, – sharp was their song.
Against the ways of Tubal Cain, too cunning for the young,
The longhorn calf, the buffalo and wampus gave tongue.

These creatures were defending things Mark Hanna never dreamed:
The moods of airy childhood that in desert dews gleamed,
The gossamers and whimsies,
The monkeyshines and didoes
Rank and strange

Of the canyons and the range,
The ultimate fantastics
Of the far western slope,
And of prairie schooner children
Born beneath the stars,
Beneath falling snows,
Of the babies born at midnight
In the sod huts of lost hope,
With no physician there,
Except a Kansas prayer,
With the Indian raid a howling through the air.

And all these in their helpless days
By the dour East oppressed,
Mean paternalism
Making their mistakes for them,
Crucifying half the West,
Till the whole Atlantic coast
Seemed a giant spiders' nest.

And these children and their sons
At last rode through the cactus,
A cliff of mighty cowboys
On the lope,
With gun and rope.
And all the way to frightened Maine the old East heard them call,
And saw our Bryan by a mile lead the wall
Of men and whirling flowers and beasts,
The bard and the prophet of them all.
Prairie avenger, mountain lion,
Bryan, Bryan, Bryan, Bryan,
Gigantic troubadour, speaking like a siege gun,
Smashing Plymouth Rock with his boulders from the West,
And just a hundred miles behind, tornadoes piled across the sky,
Blotting out sun and moon,
A sign on high.

Headlong, dazed and blinking in the weird green light,
The scalawags made moan,
Afraid to fight.

II

When Bryan came to Springfield, and Altgeld gave him greeting,
Rochester was deserted, Divernon was deserted,
Mechanicsburg, Riverton, Chickenbristle, Cotton Hill;
Empty: for all Sangamon drove to the meeting –
In silver-decked racing cart,
Buggy, buckboard, carryall,
Carriage, phaeton, whatever would haul,
And silver-decked farm-wagons gritted, banged and rolled,
With the new tale of Bryan by the iron tires told.

The State House loomed afar,
A speck, a hive, a football,
A captive balloon!
And the town was all one spreading wing of bunting, plumes, and
       sunshine,
Every rag and flag, and Bryan picture sold,
When the rigs in many a dusty line
Jammed our streets at noon,
And joined the wild parade against the power of gold.

We roamed, we boys from High School,
With mankind,
While Springfield gleamed,
Silk-lined.
Oh, Tom Dines, and Art Fitzgerald,
And the gangs that they could get!
I can hear them yelling yet.
Helping the incantation,
Defying aristocracy,
With every bridle gone,
Ridding the world of the low down mean,

Bidding the eagles of the West fly on,
Bidding the eagles of the West fly on,
We were bully, wild and woolly,
Never yet curried below the knees.
We saw flowers in the air,
Fair as the Pleiades, bright as Orion,
– Hopes of all mankind,
Made rare, resistless, thrice refined.
Oh, we bucks from every Springfield ward!
Colts of democracy –
Yet time-winds out of Chaos from the star-fields of the Lord.

The long parade rolled on. I stood by my best girl.
She was a cool young citizen, with wise and laughing eyes.
With my necktie by my ear, I was stepping on my dear,
But she kept like a pattern, without a shaken curl.

She wore in her hair a brave prairie rose.
Her gold chums cut her, for that was not the pose.
No Gibson Girl would wear it in that fresh way.
But we were fairy Democrats, and this was our day.

The earth rocked like the ocean, the sidewalk was a deck.
The houses for the moment were lost in the wide wreck.
And the bands played strange and stranger music as they trailed along.
Against the ways of Tubal Cain,
Ah, sharp was their song!
The demons in the bricks, the demons in the grass,
The demons in the bank-vaults peered out to see us pass,
And the angels in the trees, the angels in the grass,
The angels in the flags, peered out to see us pass.
And the sidewalk was our chariot, and the flowers bloomed higher,
And the street turned to silver and the grass turned to fire,
And then it was but grass, and the town was there again,
A place for women and men.

III

Then we stood where we could see
Every band,
And the speaker's stand.
And Bryan took the platform.
And he was introduced.
And he lifted his hand
And cast a new spell.
Progressive silence fell
In Springfield,
In Illinois,
Around the world.
Then we heard these glacial boulders across the prairie rolled:
'*The people have a right to make their own mistakes* . . .
You shall not crucify mankind
Upon a cross of gold.'

And everybody heard him –
In the streets and State House yard.
And everybody heard him
In Springfield,
In Illinois,
Around and around and around the world,
That danced upon its axis
And like a darling broncho whirled.

IV

July, August, suspense.
Wall Street lost to sense.
August, September, October,
More suspense,
And the whole East down like a wind-smashed fence.

Then Hanna to the rescue,
Hanna of Ohio,
Rallying the roller-tops,

Rallying the bucket-shops.
Threatening drouth and death,
Promising manna,
Rallying the trusts against the bawling flannelmouth;
Invading misers' cellars,
Tin-cans, socks,
Melting down the rocks,
Pouring out the long green to a million workers,
Spondulix by the mountain-load, to stop each new tornado
And beat the cheapskate, blatherskite,
Populistic, anarchistic,
Deacon – desperado.

V

Election night at midnight:
Boy Bryan's defeat.
Defeat of western silver.
Defeat of the wheat.
Victory of letterfiles
And plutocrats in miles
With dollar signs upon their coats,
Diamond watchchains on their vests
And spats on their feet.
Victory of custodians,
Plymouth Rock,
And all that inbred landlord stock.
Victory of the neat.
Defeat of the aspen groves of Colorado valleys,
The blue bells of the Rockies,
And blue bonnets of old Texas,
By the Pittsburg alleys.
Defeat of alfalfa and the Mariposa lily.
Defeat of the Pacific and the long Mississippi.
Defeat of the young by the old and silly.
Defeat of tornadoes by the poison vats supreme.
Defeat of my boyhood, defeat of my dream.

VI

Where is McKinley, that respectable McKinley,
The man without an angle or a tangle,
Who soothed down the city man and soothed down the farmer,
The German, the Irish, the Southerner, the Northerner,
Who climbed every greasy pole, and slipped through every crack;
Who soothed down the gambling hall, the bar-room, the church,
The devil vote, the angel vote, the neutral vote,
The desperately wicked, and their victims on the rack,
The gold vote, the silver vote, the brass vote, the lead vote,
Every vote? . . .

Where is McKinley, Mark Hanna's McKinley,
His slave, his echo, his suit of clothes?
Gone to join the shadows, with the pomps of that time,
And the flame of that summer's prairie rose.

Where is Cleveland whom the Democratic platform
Read from the party in a glorious hour,
Gone to join the shadows with pitchfork Tillman,
And sledge-hammer Altgeld who wrecked his power.

Where is Hanna, bulldog Hanna,
Low-browed Hanna, who said: 'Stand pat'?
Gone to his place with old Pierpont Morgan.
Gone somewhere . . . with lean rat Platt.

Where is Roosevelt, the young dude cowboy,
Who hated Bryan, then aped his way?
Gone to join the shadows with mighty Cromwell
And tall King Saul, till the Judgment day.

Where is Altgeld, brave as the truth,
Whose name the few still say with tears?
Gone to join the ironies with Old John Brown,
Whose fame rings loud for a thousand years.

Where is that boy, that Heaven-born Bryan,
That Homer Bryan, who sang from the West?
Gone to join the shadows with Altgeld the Eagle,
Where the kings and the slaves and the troubadours rest.

Wallace Stevens 1879–1955

A High-Toned Old Christian Woman

Poetry is the supreme fiction, madame.
Take the moral law and make a nave of it
And from the nave build haunted heaven. Thus,
The conscience is converted into palms,
Like windy citherns hankering for hymns.
We agree in principle. That's clear. But take
The opposing law and make a peristyle,
And from the peristyle project a masque
Beyond the planets. Thus, our bawdiness,
Unpurged by epitaph, indulged at last,
Is equally converted into palms,
Squiggling like saxophones. And palm for palm,
Madame, we are where we began. Allow,
Therefore, that in the planetary scene
Your disaffected flagellants, well-stuffed,
Smacking their muzzy bellies in parade,
Proud of such novelties of the sublime,
Such tink and tank and tunk-a-tunk-tunk,
May, merely may, madame, whip from themselves
A jovial hullabaloo among the spheres.
This will make widows wince. But fictive things
Wink as they will. Wink most when widows wince.

Sunday Morning

I

Complacencies of the peignoir, and late
Coffee and oranges in a sunny chair,
And the green freedom of a cockatoo
Upon a rug mingle to dissipate
The holy hush of ancient sacrifice.
She dreams a little, and she feels the dark
Encroachment of that old catastrophe,
As a calm darkens among water-lights.
The pungent oranges and bright, green wings
Seem things in some procession of the dead,
Winding across wide water, without sound.
The day is like wide water, without sound,
Stilled for the passing of her dreaming feet
Over the seas, to silent Palestine,
Dominion of the blood and sepulchre.

II

Why should she give her bounty to the dead?
What is divinity if it can come
Only in silent shadows and in dreams?
Shall she not find in comforts of the sun,
In pungent fruit and bright, green wings, or else
In any balm or beauty of the earth,
Things to be cherished like the thought of heaven?
Divinity must live within herself:
Passions of rain, or moods in falling snow;
Grievings in loneliness, or unsubdued
Elations when the forest blooms; gusty
Emotions on wet roads on autumn nights;
All pleasures and all pains, remembering
The bough of summer and the winter branch.
These are the measures destined for her soul.

III

Jove in the clouds had his inhuman birth.
No mother suckled him, no sweet land gave
Large-mannered motions to his mythy mind.
He moved among us, as a muttering king,
Magnificent, would move among his hinds,
Until our blood, commingling, virginal,
With heaven, brought such requital to desire
The very hinds discerned it, in a star.
Shall our blood fail? Or shall it come to be
The blood of paradise? And shall the earth
Seem all of paradise that we shall know?
The sky will be much friendlier then than now,
A part of labor and a part of pain,
And next in glory to enduring love,
Not this dividing and indifferent blue.

IV

She says, 'I am content when wakened birds,
Before they fly, test the reality
Of misty fields, by their sweet questionings;
But when the birds are gone, and their warm fields
Return no more, where, then, is paradise?'
There is not any haunt of prophecy,
Nor any old chimera of the grave,
Neither the golden underground, nor isle
Melodious, where spirits gat them home,
Nor visionary south, nor cloudy palm
Remote on heaven's hill, that has endured
As April's green endures; or will endure
Like her remembrance of awakened birds,
Or her desire for June and evening, tipped
By the consummation of the swallow's wings.

V

She says, 'But in contentment I still feel
The need of some imperishable bliss.'
Death is the mother of beauty; hence from her,
Alone, shall come fulfilment to our dreams
And our desires. Although she strews the leaves
Of sure obliteration on our paths,
The path sick sorrow took, the many paths
Where triumph rang its brassy phrase, or love
Whispered a little out of tenderness,
She makes the willow shiver in the sun
For maidens who were wont to sit and gaze
Upon the grass, relinquished to their feet.
She causes boys to pile new plums and pears
On disregarded plate. The maidens taste
And stray impassioned in the littering leaves.

VI

Is there no change of death in paradise?
Does ripe fruit never fall? Or do the boughs
Hang always heavy in that perfect sky,
Unchanging, yet so like our perishing earth,
With rivers like our own that seek for seas
They never find, the same receding shores
That never touch with inarticulate pang?
Why set the pear upon those river-banks
Or spice the shores with odors of the plum?
Alas, that they should wear our colors there,
The silken weavings of our afternoons,
And pick the strings of our insipid lutes!
Death is the mother of beauty, mystical,
Within whose burning bosom we devise
Our earthly mothers waiting, sleeplessly.

VII

Supple and turbulent, a ring of men
Shall chant in orgy on a summer morn
Their boisterous devotion to the sun,
Not as a god, but as a god might be,
Naked among them, like a savage source.
Their chant shall be a chant of paradise,
Out of their blood, returning to the sky;
And in their chant shall enter, voice by voice,
The windy lake wherein their lord delights,
The trees, like serafin, and echoing hills,
That choir among themselves long afterward.
They shall know well the heavenly fellowship
Of men that perish and of summer morn.
And whence they came and whither they shall go
The dew upon their feet shall manifest.

VIII

She hears, upon that water without sound,
A voice that cries, 'The tomb in Palestine
Is not the porch of spirits lingering.
It is the grave of Jesus, where he lay.'
We live in an old chaos of the sun,
Or old dependency of day and night,
Or island solitude, unsponsored, free,
Of that wide water, inescapable.
Deer walk upon our mountains, and the quail
Whistle about us their spontaneous cries;
Sweet berries ripen in the wilderness;
And, in the isolation of the sky,
At evening, casual flocks of pigeons make
Ambiguous undulations as they sink,
Downward to darkness, on extended wings.

Le Monocle de Mon Oncle

'Mother of heaven, regina of the clouds,
O sceptre of the sun, crown of the moon,
There is not nothing, no, no, never nothing,
Like the clashed edges of two words that kill.'
And so I mocked her in magnificent measure.
Or was it that I mocked myself alone?
I wish that I might be a thinking stone.
The sea of spuming thought foists up again
The radiant bubble that she was. And then
A deep up-pouring from some saltier well
Within me, bursts its watery syllable.

II

A red bird flies across the golden floor.
It is a red bird that seeks out his choir
Among the choirs of wind and wet and wing.
A torrent will fall from him when he finds.
Shall I uncrumple this much-crumpled thing?
I am a man of fortune greeting heirs;
For it has come that thus I greet the spring.
These choirs of welcome choir for me farewell.
No spring can follow past meridian.
Yet you persist with anecdotal bliss
To make believe a starry *connaissance*.

III

Is it for nothing, then, that old Chinese
Sat tittivating by their mountain pools
Or in the Yangtse studied out their beards?
I shall not play the flat historic scale.
You know how Utamaro's beauties sought
The end of love in their all-speaking braids.
You know the mountainous coiffures of Bath.

Alas! Have all the barbers lived in vain
That not one curl in nature has survived?
Why, without pity on these studious ghosts,
Do you come dripping in your hair from sleep?

IV

This luscious and impeccable fruit of life
Falls, it appears, of its own weight to earth.
When you were Eve, its acrid juice was sweet,
Untasted, in its heavenly, orchard air.
An apple serves as well as any skull
To be the book in which to read a round,
And is as excellent, in that it is composed
Of what, like skulls, comes rotting back to ground.
But it excels in this, that as the fruit
Of love, it is a book too mad to read
Before one merely reads to pass the time.

V

In the high west there burns a furious star.
It is for fiery boys that star was set
And for sweet-smelling virgins close to them.
The measure of the intensity of love
Is measure, also, of the verve of earth.
For me, the firefly's quick, electric stroke
Ticks tediously the time of one more year.
And you? Remember how the crickets came
Out of their mother grass, like little kin,
In the pale nights, when your first imagery
Found inklings of your bond to all that dust.

VI

If men at forty will be painting lakes
The ephemeral blues must merge for them in one,
The basic slate, the universal hue.
There is a substance in us that prevails.
But in our amours amorists discern

Such fluctuations that their scrivening
Is breathless to attend each quirky turn.
When amorists grow bald, then amours shrink
Into the compass and curriculum
Of introspective exiles, lecturing.
It is a theme for Hyacinth alone.

VII

The mules that angels ride come slowly down
The blazing passes, from beyond the sun.
Descensions of their tinkling bells arrive.
These muleteers are dainty of their way.
Meantime, centurions guffaw and beat
Their shrilling tankards on the table-boards.
This parable, in sense, amounts to this:
The honey of heaven may or may not come,
But that of earth both comes and goes at once.
Suppose these couriers brought amid their train
A damsel heightened by eternal bloom.

VIII

Like a dull scholar, I behold, in love,
An ancient aspect touching a new mind.
It comes, it blooms, it bears its fruit and dies.
This trivial trope reveals a way of truth.
Our bloom is gone. We are the fruit thereof.
Two golden gourds distended on our vines,
Into the autumn weather, splashed with frost,
Distorted by hale fatness, turned grotesque.
We hang like warty squashes, streaked and rayed,
The laughing sky will see the two of us
Washed into rinds by rotting winter rains.

IX

In verses wild with motion, full of din,
Loudened by cries, by clashes, quick and sure

As the deadly thought of men accomplishing
Their curious fates in war, come, celebrate
The faith of forty, ward of Cupido.
Most venerable heart, the lustiest conceit
Is not too lusty for your broadening.
I quiz all sounds, all thoughts, all everything
For the music and manner of the paladins
To make oblation fit. Where shall I find
Bravura adequate to this great hymn?

X

The fops of fancy in their poems leave
Memorabilia of the mystic spouts,
Spontaneously watering their gritty soils.
I am a yeoman, as such fellows go.
I know no magic trees, no balmy boughs,
No silver-ruddy, gold-vermilion fruits.
But, after all, I know a tree that bears
A semblance to the thing I have in mind.
It stands gigantic, with a certain tip
To which all birds come sometime in their time.
But when they go that tip still tips the tree.

XI

If sex were all, then every trembling hand
Could make us squeak, like dolls, the wished-for words.
But note the unconscionable treachery of fate,
That makes us weep, laugh, grunt and groan, and shout
Doleful heroics, pinching gestures forth
From madness or delight, without regard
To that first, foremost law. Anguishing hour!
Last night, we sat beside a pool of pink,
Clippered with lilies scudding the bright chromes,
Keen to the point of starlight, while a frog
Boomed from his very belly odious chords.

XII

A blue pigeon it is, that circles the blue sky,
On sidelong wing, around and round and round.
A white pigeon it is, that flutters to the ground,
Grown tired of flight. Like a dark rabbi, I
Observed, when young, the nature of mankind,
In lordly study. Every day, I found
Man proved a gobbet in my mincing world.
Like a rose rabbi, later, I pursued,
And still pursue, the origin and course
Of love, but until now I never knew
That fluttering things have so distinct a shade.

Disillusionment of Ten o'Clock

The houses are haunted
By white night-gowns.
None are green,
Or purple with green rings,
Or green with yellow rings,
Or yellow with blue rings.
None of them are strange,
With socks of lace
And beaded ceintures.
People are not going
To dream of baboons and periwinkles.
Only, here and there, an old sailor,
Drunk and asleep in his boots,
Catches tigers
In red weather.

Sad Strains of a Gay Waltz

The truth is that there comes a time
When we can mourn no more over music
That is so much motionless sound.

There comes a time when the waltz
Is no longer a mode of desire, a mode
Of revealing desire and is empty of shadows.

Too many waltzes have ended. And then
There's that mountain-minded Hoon,
For whom desire was never that of the waltz,

Who found all form and order in solitude,
For whom the shapes were never the figures of men.
Now, for him, his forms have vanished.

There is order in neither sea nor sun.
The shapes have lost their glistening.
There are these sudden mobs of men,

These sudden clouds of faces and arms,
An immense suppression, freed,
These voices crying without knowing for what,

Except to be happy, without knowing how,
Imposing forms they cannot describe,
Requiring order beyond their speech.

Too many waltzes have ended. Yet the shapes
For which the voices cry, these, too, may be
Modes of desire, modes of revealing desire.

Too many waltzes – The epic of disbelief
Blares oftener and soon, will soon be constant.
Some harmonious skeptic soon in a skeptical music

Will unite these figures of men and their shapes
Will glisten again with motion, the music
Will be motion and full of shadows.

The Idea of Order at Key West

She sang beyond the genius of the sea.
The water never formed to mind or voice,
Like a body wholly body, fluttering
Its empty sleeves; and yet its mimic motion
Made constant cry, caused constantly a cry,
That was not ours although we understood,
Inhuman, of the veritable ocean.

The sea was not a mask. No more was she.
The song and water were not medleyed sound
Even if what she sang was what she heard,
Since what she sang was uttered word by word.
It may be that in all her phrases stirred
The grinding water and the gasping wind;
But it was she and not the sea we heard.

For she was the maker of the song she sang.
The ever-hooded, tragic-gestured sea
Was merely a place by which she walked to sing.
Whose spirit is this? we said, because we knew
It was the spirit that we sought and knew
That we should ask this often as she sang.

If it was only the dark voice of the sea
That rose, or even colored by many waves;
If it was only the outer voice of sky
And cloud, of the sunken coral water-walled,
However clear, it would have been deep air,
The heaving speech of air, a summer sound
Repeated in a summer without end
And sound alone. But it was more than that,
More even than her voice, and ours, among
The meaningless plungings of water and the wind,
Theatrical distances, bronze shadows heaped
On high horizons, mountainous atmospheres
Of sky and sea.
                                    It was her voice that made
The sky acutest at its vanishing.
She measured to the hour its solitude.
She was the single artificer of the world
In which she sang. And when she sang, the sea,
Whatever self it had, became the self
That was her song, for she was the maker. Then we,
As we beheld her striding there alone,
Knew that there never was a world for her
Except the one she sang and, singing, made.

Ramon Fernandez, tell me, if you know,
Why, when the singing ended and we turned
Toward the town, tell why the glassy lights,
The lights in the fishing boats at anchor there,
As the night descended, tilting in the air,
Mastered the night and portioned out the sea,
Fixing emblazoned zones and fiery poles,
Arranging, deepening, enchanting night.

Oh! Blessed rage for order, pale Ramon,
The maker's rage to order words of the sea,

Words of the fragrant portals, dimly-starred,
And of ourselves and of our origins,
In ghostlier demarcations, keener sounds.

Credences of Summer

I

Now in midsummer come and all fools slaughtered
And spring's infuriations over and a long way
To the first autumnal inhalations, young broods
Are in the grass, the roses are heavy with a weight
Of fragrance and the mind lays by its trouble.

Now the mind lays by its trouble and considers.
The fidgets of remembrance come to this.
This is the last day of a certain year
Beyond which there is nothing left of time.
It comes to this and the imagination's life.

There is nothing more inscribed nor thought nor felt
And this must comfort the heart's core against
Its false disasters – these fathers standing round,
These mothers touching, speaking, being near,
These lovers waiting in the soft dry grass.

II

Postpone the anatomy of summer, as
The physical pine, the metaphysical pine.
Let's see the very thing and nothing else.
Let's see it with the hottest fire of sight.
Burn everything not part of it to ash.

Trace the gold sun about the whitened sky
Without evasion by a single metaphor.

Look at it in its essential barrenness
And say this, this is the centre that I seek.
Fix it in an eternal foliage

And fill the foliage with arrested peace,
Joy of such permanence, right ignorance
Of change still possible. Exile desire
For what is not. This is the barrenness
Of the fertile thing that can attain no more.

III

It is the natural tower of all the world,
The point of survey, green's green apogee,
But a tower more precious than the view beyond,
A point of survey squatting like a throne,
Axis of everything, green's apogee

And happiest folk-land, mostly marriage-hymns.
It is the mountain on which the tower stands,
It is the final mountain. Here the sun,
Sleepless, inhales his proper air, and rests.
This is the refuge that the end creates.

It is the old man standing on the tower,
Who reads no book. His ruddy ancientness
Absorbs the ruddy summer and is appeased,
By an understanding that fulfils his age,
By a feeling capable of nothing more.

IV

One of the limits of reality
Presents itself in Oley when the hay,
Baked through long days, is piled in mows. It is
A land too ripe for enigmas, too serene.
There the distant fails the clairvoyant eye

And the secondary senses of the ear
Swarm, not with secondary sounds, but choirs,
Not evocations but last choirs, last sounds
With nothing else compounded, carried full,
Pure rhetoric of a language without words.

Things stop in that direction and since they stop
The direction stops and we accept what is
As good. The utmost must be good and is
And is our fortune and honey hived in the trees
And mingling of colors at a festival.

V

One day enriches a year. One woman makes
The rest look down. One man becomes a race,
Lofty like him, like him perpetual.
Or do the other days enrich the one?
And is the queen humble as she seems to be,

The charitable majesty of her whole kin?
The bristling soldier, weather-foxed, who looms
In the sunshine is a filial form and one
Of the land's children, easily born, its flesh,
Not fustian. The more than casual blue

Contains the year and other years and hymns
And people, without souvenir. The day
Enriches the year, not as embellishment.
Stripped of remembrance, it displays its strength –
The youth, the vital son, the heroic power.

VI

The rock cannot be broken. It is the truth.
It rises from land and sea and covers them.
It is a mountain half way green and then,
The other immeasurable half, such rock
As placid air becomes. But it is not

A hermit's truth nor symbol in hermitage.
It is the visible rock, the audible,
The brilliant mercy of a sure repose,
On this present ground, the vividest repose,
Things certain sustaining us in certainty.

It is the rock of summer, the extreme,
A mountain luminous half way in bloom
And then half way in the extremest light
Of sapphires flashing from the central sky,
As if twelve princes sat before a king.

VII

Far in the woods they sang their unreal songs,
Secure. It was difficult to sing in face
Of the object. The singers had to avert themselves
Or else avert the object. Deep in the woods
They sang of summer in the common fields.

They sang desiring an object that was near,
In face of which desire no longer moved,
Nor made of itself that which it could not find . . .
Three times the concentred self takes hold, three times
The thrice concentred self, having possessed

The object, grips it in savage scrutiny,
Once to make captive, once to subjugate
Or yield to subjugation, once to proclaim
The meaning of the capture, this hard prize,
Fully made, fully apparent, fully found.

VIII

The trumpet of morning blows in the clouds and through
The sky. It is the visible announced,
It is the more than visible, the more
Than sharp, illustrious scene. The trumpet cries
This is the successor of the invisible.

This is its substitute in stratagems
Of the spirit. This, in sight and memory,
Must take its place, as what is possible
Replaces what is not. The resounding cry
Is like ten thousand tumblers tumbling down

To share the day. The trumpet supposes that
A mind exists, aware of division, aware
Of its cry as clarion, its diction's way
As that of a personage in a multitude:
Man's mind grown venerable in the unreal.

IX

Fly low, cock bright, and stop on a bean pole. Let
Your brown breast redden, while you wait for warmth.
With one eye watch the willow, motionless.
The gardener's cat is dead, the gardener gone
And last year's garden grows salacious weeds.

A complex of emotions falls apart,
In an abandoned spot. Soft, civil bird,
The decay that you regard: of the arranged
And of the spirit of the arranged, *douceurs*,
Tristesses, the fund of life and death, suave bush

And polished beast, this complex falls apart.
And on your bean pole, it may be, you detect
Another complex of other emotions, not
So soft, so civil, and you make a sound,
Which is not part of the listener's own sense.

X

The personae of summer play the characters
Of an inhuman author, who meditates
With the gold bugs, in blue meadows, late at night.
He does not hear his characters talk. He sees
Them mottled, in the moodiest costumes,

Of blue and yellow, sky and sun, belted
And knotted, sashed and seamed, half pales of red,
Half pales of green, appropriate habit for
The huge decorum, the manner of the time,
Part of the mottled mood of summer's whole,

In which the characters speak because they want
To speak, the fat, the roseate characters,
Free, for a moment, from malice and sudden cry,
Complete in a completed scene, speaking
Their parts as in a youthful happiness.

The World as Meditation

J'ai passé trop de temps à travailler mon violon, à voyager. Mais l'exercice essentiel du compositeur – la méditation – rien ne l'a jamais suspendu en moi . . . Je vis un rêve permanent, qui ne s'arrête ni nuit ni jour.

– Georges Enesco

Is it Ulysses that approaches from the east,
The interminable adventurer? The trees are mended.
That winter is washed away. Someone is moving

On the horizon and lifting himself up above it.
A form of fire approaches the cretonnes of Penelope,
Whose mere savage presence awakens the world in which she dwells.

She has composed, so long, a self with which to welcome him,
Companion to his self for her, which she imagined,
Two in a deep-founded sheltering, friend and dear friend.

The trees had been mended, as an essential exercise
In an inhuman meditation, larger than her own.
No winds like dogs watched over her at night.

She wanted nothing he could not bring her by coming alone.
She wanted no fetchings. His arms would be her necklace
And her belt, the final fortune of their desire.

But was it Ulysses? Or was it only the warmth of the sun
On her pillow? The thought kept beating in her like her heart.
The two kept beating together. It was only day.

It was Ulysses and it was not. Yet they had met,
Friend and dear friend and a planet's encouragement.
The barbarous strength within her would never fail.

She would talk a little to herself as she combed her hair.
Repeating his name with its patient syllables,
Never forgetting him that kept coming constantly so near.

William Carlos Williams 1883–1963

Spring and All

By the road to the contagious hospital
under the surge of the blue
mottled clouds driven from the
northeast – a cold wind. Beyond, the
waste of broad, muddy fields
brown with dried weeds, standing and fallen

patches of standing water
the scattering of tall trees

All along the road the reddish
purplish, forked, upstanding, twiggy
stuff of bushes and small trees
with dead, brown leaves under them
leafless vines –

Lifeless in appearance, sluggish
dazed spring approaches –

They enter the new world naked,
cold, uncertain of all
save that they enter. All about them
the cold, familiar wind –

Now the grass, tomorrow
the stiff curl of wildcarrot leaf
One by one objects are defined –
It quickens: clarity, outline of leaf

But now the stark dignity of
entrance – Still, the profound change
has come upon them: rooted, they
grip down and begin to awaken

The Red Wheelbarrow

so much depends
upon

a red wheel
barrow

glazed with rain
water

beside the white
chickens.

This Is Just to Say

I have eaten
the plums
that were in
the icebox

and which
you were probably
saving
for breakfast

Forgive me
they were delicious
so sweet
and so cold

Proletarian Portrait

A big young bareheaded woman
in an apron

Her hair slicked back standing
on the street

One stockinged foot toeing
the sidewalk

Her shoe in her hand. Looking
intently into it

She pulls out the paper insole
to find the nail

That has been hurting her

To a Poor Old Woman

munching a plum on
the street a paper bag
of them in her hand

They taste good to her
They taste good
to her. They taste
good to her

You can see it by
the way she gives herself
to the one half
sucked out in her hand

Comforted
a solace of ripe plums
seeming to fill the air
They taste good to her

An Elegy for D. H. Lawrence

Green points on the shrub
and poor Lawrence dead.
The night damp and misty
and Lawrence no more in the world
to answer April's promise
with a fury of labor
against waste, waste and life's
coldness.

Once he received a letter –
he never answered it –
praising him: so English
he had thereby raised himself
to an unenglish greatness.
Dead now and it grows clearer
what bitterness drove him.

This is the time.
The serpent in the grotto
water dripping from the stone
into a pool.
Mediterranean evenings. Ashes
of Cretan fires. And to the north
forsythia hung with
yellow bells in the cold.

Poor Lawrence
worn with a fury of sad labor
to create summer from
spring's decay. English
women. Men driven not to love
but to the ends of the earth.
The serpent turning his
stone-like head,
the fixed agate eyes turn also.

And unopened jonquils
hang their folded heads. No
summer. But for Lawrence
full praise in this
half cold half season –
before trees are in leaf and
tufted grass stars
unevenly the bare ground.

Slowly the serpent leans
to drink by the tinkling water
the forked tongue alert,
Then fold after fold,
glassy strength, passing
a given point,
as by desire drawn
forward bodily, he glides
smoothly in.

To stand by the sea or walk
again along a river's bank and talk
with a companion, to halt
watching where the edge of water
meets and lies upon
the unmoving shore –
Flood waters rise, and will rise,

rip the quiet valley
trap the gypsy and the girl
She clings drowning to
a bush in flower.

Remember, now, Lawrence dead.
Blue squills in bloom – to
the scorched aridity of
the Mexican plateau. Or baked
public squares in the cities of
Mediterranean islands
where one waits for busses and
boats come slowly along the water
arriving.

But the sweep of spring over
temperate lands, meadows and woods
where the young walk and talk
incompletely,
straining to no summer,
hearing the frogs, speaking of
birds and insects –

Febrile spring moves not to heat
but always more slowly,
burdened by a weight of leaves.
Nothing now
to burst the bounds –
remains confined by them. Heat,
heat! Unknown. Poor Lawrence,
dead and only the drowned
fallen dancing from the deck
of a pleasure boat
unfading desire.

Rabbits, imaginings, the
drama, literature, satire.
The serpent cannot move
his stony eyes, scarcely sees
but touching the air
with his forked tongue surmises
and his body which dipped
into the cold water
is gone.

Violently the satiric sun
that leads April not to
the panting dance but to stillness
in, into the brain, dips
and is gone also.
And sisters return
through the dusk
to the measured rancor
of their unbending elders.

Greep, greep, greep the cricket
chants where the snake
with agate eyes leaned to the water.
Sorrow to the young
that Lawrence has passed
unwanted from England.
And in the gardens forsythia
and in the woods
now the crinkled spice-bush
in flower.

From *Paterson*

THE FALLS

What common language to unravel?
The Falls, combed into straight lines
from that rafter of a rock's
lip. Strike in! the middle of

some trenchant phrase, some
well packed clause. Then . . .
This is my plan. 4 sections: First,
the archaic persons of the drama.

An eternity of bird and bush,
resolved. An unraveling:
the confused streams aligned, side
by side, speaking! Sound

married to strength, a strength
of falling – from a height! The wild
voice of the shirt-sleeved
Evangelist rivaling, Hear

me! I am the Resurrection
and the Life! echoing
among the bass and pickerel, slim
eels from Barbados, Sargasso

Sea, working up the coast to that
bounty, ponds and wild streams –
Third, the old town: Alexander Hamilton
working up from St Croix,

from that sea! and a deeper, whence
he came! stopped cold
by that unmoving roar, fastened
there: the rocks silent

but the water, married to the stone,
voluble, though frozen; the water
even when and though frozen
still whispers and moans –

And in the brittle air
a factory bell clangs, at dawn, and
snow whines under their feet. Fourth,
the modern town, a

disembodied roar! the cataract and
its clamor broken apart – and from
all learning, the empty
ear struck from within, roaring . . .

EPISODE 17

Beat hell out of it
  Beautiful Thing
  spotless cap
and crossed white straps
over the dark rippled cloth –
  Lift the stick
above that easy head
where you sit by the ivied
church, one arm
  buttressing you
long fingers spread out
among the clear grass prongs –
  and drive it down
  Beautiful Thing

that your caressing body kiss
   and kiss again
that holy lawn –

And again: obliquely –
legs curled under you as a
   deer's leaping –
pose of supreme indifference
   sacrament
to a summer's day
   Beautiful Thing
in the unearned suburbs
   then pause
   the arm fallen –
what memories
of what forgotten face
brooding upon that lily stem?

   The incredible
nose straight from the brow
   the empurpled lips
and dazzled half-sleepy eyes
   Beautiful Thing
of some trusting animal
   makes a temple
of its place of savage slaughter
   revealing
the damaged will incites still
   to violence
consummately beautiful thing
and falls about your resting
   shoulders –

Gently! Gently!
as in all things an opposite
   that awakes

the fury, conceiving
    knowledge
by way of despair that has
    no place
to lay its glossy head –
Save only – Not alone!
    Never, if possible
alone! to escape the accepted
    chopping block
and a square hat! –

And as reverie gains and
    your joints loosen
    the trick's done!
Day is covered and we see you –
    but not alone!
drunk and bedraggled to release
the strictness of beauty
under a sky full of stars
    Beautiful Thing
and a slow moon –

                            The car
    had stopped long since
    when the others
came and dragged those out
    who had you there
    indifferent
to whatever the anesthetic
    Beautiful Thing
might slum away the bars –
Reek of it!
    What does it matter?
    could set free
only the one thing –
But you!

– in your white lace dress
　'the dying swan'
and high heeled slippers – tall
as you already were –
　till your head
through fruitful exaggeration
was reaching the sky and the
prickles of its ecstasy
　Beautiful Thing!

And the guys from Paterson
　beat up
the guys from Newark and told
them to stay the hell out
of their territory and then
socked you one
　across the nose
　Beautiful Thing
for good luck and emphasis
　cracking it
till I must believe that all
desired women have had each
　in the end
　a busted nose
and live afterward marked up
　Beautiful Thing
　for memory's sake
to be credible in their deeds

Then back to the party!
　and they maled
and femaled you jealously
　Beautiful Thing
as if to discover when and
　by what miracle
there should escape what?

still to be possessed
out of what part
   Beautiful Thing
should it look?
   or be extinguished –
Three days in the same dress
   up and down –
   It would take
a Dominie to be patient
   Beautiful Thing
with you –

The stroke begins again –
   regularly
automatic
   contrapuntal to
the flogging
like the beat of famous lines
in the few excellent poems
woven to make you
   gracious
and on frequent occasions
   foul drunk
   Beautiful Thing
pulse of release
   to the attentive
and obedient mind.

The Dance

In Breughel's great picture, The Kermess,
the dancers go round, they go round and
around, the squeal and the blare and the
tweedle of bagpipes, a bugle and fiddles

tipping their bellies (round as the thick-
sided glasses whose wash they impound)
their hips and their bellies off balance
to turn them. Kicking and rolling about
the Fair Grounds, swinging their butts, those
shanks must be sound to bear up under such
rollicking measures, prance as they dance
in Breughel's great picture, The Kermess.

To Ford Madox Ford in Heaven

Is it any better in Heaven, my friend Ford,
    than you found it in Provence?

I don't think so for you made Provence a
    heaven by your praise of it
to give a foretaste of what might be
    your joy in the present circumstances.
It was Heaven you were describing there
    transubstantiated from its narrowness
to resemble the paths and gardens of a
greater world where you now reside.
But, dear man, you have taken a major
    part of it from us.
      Provence that you
praised so well will never be the same
    Provence to us
      now you are gone.

A heavenly man you seem to me now, never
    having been for me a saintly one.
It lived about you, a certain grossness that
    was not like the world.

The world is cleanly, polished and well
    made but heavenly man
is filthy with his flesh and corrupt that
    loves to eat and drink and whore –
to laugh at himself and not be afraid of
    himself knowing well he has
no possessions and opinions that are worth
    caring a broker's word about
and that all he is, but one thing, he feeds
    as one will feed a pet dog.

So roust and love and dredge the belly full
    in Heaven's name!
I laugh to think of you wheezing in Heaven.
    Where is Heaven? But why
do I ask that, since you showed the way?
    I don't care a damn for it
other than for that better part lives beside
    me here so long as I
live and remember you. Thank God you
    were not delicate, you let the world in
and lied! damn it you lied grossly
    sometimes. But it was all, I
see now, a carelessness, the part of a man
    that is homeless here on earth.

Provence, the fat assed Ford will never
    again strain the chairs of your cafés
pull and pare for his dish your sacred garlic,
    grunt and sweat and lick
his lips. Gross as the world he has left to
    us he has become
a part of that of which you were the known
    part, Provence, he loved so well.

The Ivy Crown

The whole process is a lie,
   unless,
      crowned by excess,
it break forcefully,
   one way or another,
      from its confinement –
or find a deeper well.
   Anthony and Cleopatra
     were right;
they have shown
   the way. I love you
     or I do not live
at all.
Daffodil time
   is past. This is
     summer, summer!
the heart says,
   and not even the full of it.
     no doubts
are permitted –
   though they will come
     and may
before our time
   overwhelm us.
     We are only mortal
but being mortal
   can defy our fate.
     We may
by an outside chance
   even win! We do not
     look to see
ionquils and violets
   come again

            but there are,
still,
         the roses!
Romance has no part in it.
         The business of love is
              cruelty which,
by our wills,
         we transform
            to live together.
It has its seasons,
         for and against,
            whatever the heart
fumbles in the dark
         to assert
            toward the end of May.
Just as the nature of briars
         is to tear flesh,
            I have proceeded
through them.
         Keep
            the briars out,
they say.
         You cannot live
            and keep free of
briars.
Children pick flowers.
         Let them.
            Though having them
in hand they have
         no further use for them
            but leave them crumpled
at the curb's edge.
At our age the imagination
         across the sorry facts
            lifts us
to make roses

       stand before thorns.
               Sure
love is cruel
         and selfish
                and totally obtuse –
at least, blinded by the light,
         young love is.
                But we are older,
I to love
         and you to be loved,
            we have,
no matter how,
         by our wills survived
            to keep
the jeweled prize
         always
              at our finger tips.
We will it so
         and so it is
             past all accident.

Ezra Pound 1885 – 1972

The Seafarer

FROM THE ANGLO-SAXON

May I for my own self song's truth reckon,
Journey's jargon, how I in harsh days
Hardship endured oft.
Bitter breast-cares have I abided,
Known on my keel many a care's hold,
And dire sea-surge, and there I oft spent
Narrow nightwatch nigh the ship's head
While she tossed close to cliffs. Coldly afflicted,
My feet were by frost benumbed.
Chill its chains are; chafing sighs
Hew my heart round and hunger begot
Mere-weary mood. Lest man know not
That he on dry land loveliest liveth,
List how I, care-wretched, on ice-cold sea,
Weathered the winter, wretched outcast
Deprived of my kinsmen;
Hung with hard ice-flakes, where hail-scur flew,
There I heard naught save the harsh sea
And ice-cold wave, at whiles the swan cries,
Did for my games the gannet's clamour,
Sea-fowls' loudness was for me laughter,
The mews' singing all my mead-drink.
Storms, on the stone-cliffs beaten, fell on the stern
In icy feathers; full oft the eagle screamed
With spray on his pinion.
                              Not any protector
May make merry man faring needy.
This he little believes, who aye in winsome life
Abides 'mid burghers some heavy business,

Wealthy and wine-flushed, how I weary oft
Must bide above brine.
Neareth nightshade, snoweth from north,
Frost froze the land, hail fell on earth then,
Corn of the coldest. Nathless there knocketh now
The heart's thought that I on high streams
The salt-wavy tumult traverse alone.
Moaneth alway my mind's lust
That I fare forth, that I afar hence
Seek out a foreign fastness.
For this there's no mood-lofty man over earth's midst,
Not though he be given his good, but will have in his youth greed;
Nor his deed to the daring, nor his king to the faithful
But shall have his sorrow for sea-fare
Whatever his lord will.
He hath not heart for harping, nor in ring-having
Nor winsomeness to wife, nor world's delight
Nor any whit else save the wave's slash,
Yet longing comes upon him to fare forth on the water.
Bosque taketh blossom, cometh beauty of berries,
Fields to fairness, land fares brisker,
All this admonisheth man eager of mood,
The heart turns to travel so that he then thinks
On flood-ways to be far departing.
Cuckoo calleth with gloomy crying,
He singeth summerward, bodeth sorrow,
The bitter heart's blood. Burgher knows not –
He the prosperous man – what some perform
Where wandering them widest draweth.
So that but now my heart burst from my breastlock,
My mood 'mid the mere-flood,
Over the whale's acre, would wander wide.
On earth's shelter cometh oft to me,
Eager and ready, the crying lone-flyer,
Whets for the whale-path the heart irresistibly,
O'er tracks of ocean; seeing that anyhow

My lord deems to me this dead life
On loan and on land, I believe not
That any earth-weal eternal standeth
Save there be somewhat calamitous
That, ere a man's tide go, turn it to twain.
Disease or oldness or sword-hate
Beats out the breath from doom-gripped body.
And for this, every earl whatever, for those speaking after –
Laud of the living, boasteth some last word,
That he will work ere he pass onward,
Frame on the fair earth 'gainst foes his malice,
Daring ado, . . .
So that all men shall honour him after
And his laud beyond them remain 'mid the English,
Aye, for ever, a lasting life's-blast,
Delight 'mid the doughty.

                    Days little durable,
And all arrogance of earthen riches,
There come now no kings nor Cæsars
Nor gold-giving lords like those gone.
Howe'er in mirth most magnified,
Whoe'er lived in life most lordliest,
Drear all this excellence, delights undurable!
Waneth the watch, but the world holdeth.
Tomb hideth trouble. The blade is layed low.
Earthly glory ageth and seareth.
No man at all going the earth's gait,
But age fares against him, his face paleth,
Grey-haired he groaneth, knows gone companions,
Lordly men, are to earth o'ergiven,
Nor may he then the flesh-cover, whose life ceaseth,
Nor eat the sweet nor feel the sorry,
Nor stir hand nor think in mid heart,
And though he strew the grave with gold,
His born brothers, their buried bodies
Be an unlikely treasure hoard.

The Garden

En robe de parade
                    – Samain

Like a skein of loose silk blown against a wall
She walks by the railing of a path in Kensington Gardens,
And she is dying piece-meal
    of a sort of emotional anæmia.

And round about there is a rabble
Of the filthy, sturdy, unkillable infants of the very poor.
They shall inherit the earth.

In her is the end of breeding.
Her boredom is exquisite and excessive.
She would like some one to speak to her,
And is almost afraid that I
    will commit that indiscretion.

A Pact

I make a pact with you, Walt Whitman –
I have detested you long enough.
I come to you as a grown child
Who has had a pig-headed father;
I am old enough now to make friends.
It was you that broke the new wood,
Now is a time for carving.
We have one sap and one root –
Let there be commerce between us.

The Temperaments

Nine adulteries, 12 liaisons, 64 fornications and something approaching a rape
  Rest nightly upon the soul of our delicate friend Florialis,
And yet the man is so quiet and reserved in demeanour
That he passes for both bloodless and sexless.
Bastidides, on the contrary, who both talks and writes of nothing save copulation,
Has become the father of twins,
But he accomplished this feat at some cost;
  He had to be four times cuckold.

In a Station of the Metro

    The apparition of these faces in the crowd;
    Petals on a wet, black bough.

Alba

  As cool as the pale wet leaves
                 of lily-of-the-valley
  She lay beside me in the dawn.

The River-Merchant's Wife: A Letter

While my hair was still cut straight across my forehead
I played about the front gate, pulling flowers.

You came by on bamboo stilts, playing horse,
You walked about my seat, playing with blue plums.
And we went on living in the village of Chokan:
Two small people, without dislike or suspicion.

At fourteen I married My Lord you.
I never laughed, being bashful.
Lowering my head, I looked at the wall.
Called to, a thousand times, I never looked back.

At fifteen I stopped scowling,
I desired my dust to be mingled with yours
Forever and forever and forever.
Why should I climb the look out?

At sixteen you departed,
You went into far Ku-to-yen, by the river of swirling eddies,
And you have been gone five months.
The monkeys make sorrowful noise overhead.

You dragged your feet when you went out.
By the gate now, the moss is grown, the different mosses,
Too deep to clear them away!
The leaves fall early this autumn, in wind.
The paired butterflies are already yellow with August
Over the grass in the West garden;
They hurt me. I grow older.
If you are coming down through the narrows of the river Kiang,
Please let me know beforehand,
And I will come out to meet you
                    As far as Cho-fu-Sa.

Near Perigord

A Perigord, pres del muralh
Tan que i puosch' om gitar ab malh.

You'd have men's hearts up from the dust
And tell their secrets, Messire Cino,
Right enough? Then read between the lines of Uc St Circ,
Solve me the riddle, for you know the tale.

Bertrans, En Bertrans, left a fine canzone:
'Maent, I love you, you have turned me out.
The voice at Montfort, Lady Agnes' hair,
Bel Miral's stature, the viscountess' throat,
Set all together, are not worthy of you . . .'
And all the while you sing out that canzone,
Think you that Maent lived at Montaignac,
One at Chalais, another at Malemort
Hard over Brive – for every lady a castle,
Each place strong.

       Oh, *is* it easy enough?
Tairiran held hall in Montaignac,
His brother-in-law was all there was of power
In Perigord, and this good union
Gobbled all the land, and held it later for some hundred years.
And our En Bertrans was in Altafort,
Hub of the wheel, the stirrer-up of strife,
As caught by Dante in the last wallow of hell –
The headless trunk 'that made its head a lamp',
For separation wrought out separation,
And he who set the strife between brother and brother
And had his way with the old English king,
Viced in such torture for the 'counterpass'.
How would you live, with neighbours set about you –

Poictiers and Brive, untaken Rochecouart,
Spread like the finger-tips of one frail hand;
And you on that great mountain of a palm –
Not a neat ledge, not Foix between its streams,
But one huge back half-covered up with pine,
Worked for and snatched from the string-purse of Born –
The four round towers, four brothers – mostly fools:
What could he do but play the desperate chess,
And stir old grudges?
  'Pawn your castles, lords!
Let the Jews pay.'
  And the great scene –
(That, maybe, never happened!)
  Beaten at last,
Before the hard old king:
  'Your son, ah, since he died
'My wit and worth are cobwebs brushed aside
'In the full flare of grief. Do what you will.'

Take the whole man, and ravel out the story.
He loved this lady in castle Montaignac?
The castle flanked him – he had need of it.
You read to-day, how long the overlords of Perigord,
The Talleyrands, have held the place; it was no transient fiction.
And Maent failed him? Or saw through the scheme?

And all his net-like thought of new alliance?
Chalais is high, a-level with the poplars.
Its lowest stones just meet the valley tips
Where the low Dronne is filled with water-lilies.
And Rochecouart can match it, stronger yet,
The very spur's end, built on sheerest cliff,
And Malemort keeps its close hold on Brive,
While Born, his own close purse, his rabbit warren,
His subterranean chamber with a dozen doors,
A-bristle with antennæ to feel roads,

To sniff the traffic into Perigord.
And that hard phalanx, that unbroken line,
The ten good miles from there to Maent's castle,
All of his flank – how could he do without her?
And all the road to Cahors, to Toulouse?
What would he do without her?

   'Papiol,
Go forthright singing – Anhes, Cembelins.
There is a throat; ah, there are two white hands;
There is a trellis full of early roses,
And all my heart is bound about with love.
Where am I come with compound flatteries –
What doors are open to fine compliment?'
And every one half jealous of Maent?
He wrote the catch to pit their jealousies
Against her; give her pride in them?

Take his own speech, make what you will of it –
And still the knot, the first knot, of Maent?

   Is it a love poem? Did he sing of war?
Is it an intrigue to run subtly out,
Born of a jongleur's tongue, freely to pass
Up and about and in and out the land,
Mark him a craftsman and a strategist?
(St Leider had done as much as Polhonac,
Singing a different stave, as closely hidden.)
Oh, there is precedent, legal tradition,
To sing one thing when your song means another,
'*Et albirar ab lor bordon –*'
Foix' count knew that. What is Sir Bertrans' singing?
Maent, Maent, and yet again Maent,
Or war and broken heaumes and politics?

II

End fact. Try fiction. Let us say we see
En Bertrans, a tower-room at Hautefort,
Sunset, the ribbon-like road lies, in red cross-light,
Southward toward Montaignac, and he bends at a table
Scribbling, swearing between his teeth; by his left hand
Lie little strips of parchment covered over,
Scratched and erased with *al* and *ochaisos*.
Testing his list of rhymes, a lean man? Bilious?
With a red straggling beard?
And the green cat's-eye lifts toward Montaignac.

Or take his 'magnet' singer setting out,
Dodging his way past Aubeterre, singing at Chalais
    In the vaulted hall,
Or, by a lichened tree at Rochecouart
Aimlessly watching a hawk above the valleys,
Waiting his turn in the mid-summer evening,
Thinking of Aelis, whom he loved heart and soul . . .
To find her half alone, Montfort away,
And a brown, placid, hated woman visiting her,
Spoiling his visit, with a year before the next one.
Little enough?
Or carry him forward. 'Go through all the courts,
My Magnet,' Bertrans had said.

We came to Ventadour
In the mid love court, he sings out the canzon,
No one hears save Arrimon Luc D'Esparo –
No one hears aught save the gracious sound of compliments.
Sir Arrimon counts on his fingers, Montfort,
Rochecouart, Chalais, the rest, the tactic,
Malemort, guesses beneath, sends word to Cœur-de-Lion:
The compact, de Born smoked out, trees felled
About his castle, cattle driven out!
Or no one sees it, and En Bertrans prospered?

And ten years after, or twenty, as you will,
Arnaut and Richard lodge beneath Chalus:
The dull round towers encroaching on the field,
The tents tight drawn, horses at tether
Further and out of reach, the purple night,
The crackling of small fires, the bannerets,
The lazy leopards on the largest banner,
Stray gleams on hanging mail, an armourer's torch-flare
Melting on steel.

    And in the quietest space
They probe old scandals, say de Born is dead;
And we've the gossip (skipped six hundred years).
Richard shall die to-morrow – leave him there
Talking of *trobar clus* with Daniel.
And the 'best craftsman' sings out his friend's song,
Envies its vigour . . . and deplores the technique,
Dispraises his own skill? – That's as you will.
And they discuss the dead man,
Plantagenet puts the riddle: 'Did he love her?'
And Arnaut parries: 'Did he love your sister?
True, he has praised her, but in some opinion
He wrote that praise only to show he had
The favour of your party; had been well received.'

'You knew the man.'
               '*You* knew the man.'
'I am an artist, you have tried both métiers.'
'You were born near him.'
                 'Do we know our friends?'
'Say that he saw the castles, say that he loved Maent!'
'Say that he loved her, does it solve the riddle?'

    End the discussion, Richard goes out next day
And gets a quarrel-bolt shot through his vizard,
Pardons the bowman, dies,

Ends our discussion. Arnaut ends
'In sacred odour' – (that's apocryphal!)
And we can leave the talk till Dante writes:
Surely I saw, and still before my eyes
Goes on that headless trunk, that bears for light
Its own head swinging, gripped by the dead hair,
And like a swinging lamp that says, 'Ah me!
I severed men, my head and heart
Ye see here severed, my life's counterpart.'

Or take En Bertrans?

III

Ed eran due in uno, ed uno in due;
– Inferno, XXVIII, 125

Bewildering spring, and by the Auvezere
Poppies and day's eyes in the green émail
Rose over us; and we knew all that stream,
And our two horses had traced out the valleys;
Knew the low flooded lands squared out with poplars,
In the young days when the deep sky befriended.
    And great wings beat above us in the twilight,
And the great wheels in heaven
Bore us together ... surging ... and apart ...
Believing we should meet with lips and hands,

    High, high and sure ... and then the counter-thrust:
'Why do you love me? Will you always love me?
But I am like the grass, I can not love you.'
Or, 'Love, and I love and love you,
And hate your mind, not *you*, your soul, your hands.'

    So to this last estrangement, Tairiran!

    There shut up in his castle, Tairiran's,
She who had nor ears nor tongue save in her hands,

Gone – ah, gone – untouched, unreachable!
She who could never live save through one person,
She who could never speak save to one person,
And all the rest of her a shifting change,
A broken bundle of mirrors . . . !

Hugh Selwyn Mauberley

LIFE AND CONTACTS

Vocat æstus in umbram
– Nemesianus Ec. IV.

E. P. ODE POUR L'ELECTION DE SON SEPULCHRE

I

For three years, out of key with his time,
He strove to resuscitate the dead art
Of poetry; to maintain 'the sublime'
In the old sense. Wrong from the start –

No, hardly, but seeing he had been born
In a half savage country, out of date;
Bent resolutely on wringing lilies from the acorn;
Capaneus; trout for factitious bait;

Ἴδμεν γάρ τοι πάνθ', ὅσ' ἐνὶ Τροίη
Caught in the unstopped ear;
Giving the rocks small lee-way
The chopped seas held him, therefore, that year.

His true Penelope was Flaubert,
He fished by obstinate isles;
Observed the elegance of Circe's hair
Rather than the mottoes on sun-dials.

Unaffected by 'the march of events',
He passed from men's memory in *l'an trentuniesme*
De son eage; the case presents
No adjunct to the Muses' diadem.

II

The age demanded an image
Of its accelerated grimace,
Something for the modern stage,
Not, at any rate, an Attic grace;

Not, not certainly, the obscure reveries
Of the inward gaze;
Better mendacities
Than the classics in paraphrase!

The 'age demanded' chiefly a mould in plaster,
Made with no loss of time,
A prose kinema, not, not assuredly, alabaster
Or the 'sculpture' of rhyme.

III

The tea-rose tea-gown, etc.
Supplants the mousseline of Cos,
The pianola 'replaces'
Sappho's barbitos.

Christ follows Dionysus,
Phallic and ambrosial
Made way for macerations;
Caliban casts out Ariel.

All things are a flowing,
Sage Heracleitus says;
But a tawdry cheapness
Shall outlast our days.

Even the Christian beauty
Defects – after Samothrace;
We see τό καλόν
Decreed in the market place.

Faun's flesh is not to us,
Nor the saint's vision.
We have the press for wafer;
Franchise for circumcision.

All men, in law, are equals.
Free of Pisistratus,
We choose a knave or an eunuch
To rule over us.

O bright Apollo,
τίν' ἄνδρα, τίν' ἥρωα, τίνα θεὸν,
What god, man, or hero
Shall I place a tin wreath upon!

IV

These fought in any case,
and some believing,

     pro domo, in any case ...

Some quick to arm,
some for adventure,
some from fear of weakness,
some from fear of censure,
some for love of slaughter, in imagination,
learning later ...
some in fear, learning love of slaughter;

Died some, pro patria,

     non 'dulce' non 'et decor' ...
walked eye-deep in hell

believing in old men's lies, then unbelieving
came home, home to a lie,
home to many deceits,
home to old lies and new infamy;
usury age-old and age-thick
and liars in public places.

Daring as never before, wastage as never before.
Young blood and high blood,
fair cheeks, and fine bodies;

fortitude as never before

frankness as never before,
disillusions as never told in the old days,
hysterias, trench confessions,
laughter out of dead bellies.

V

There died a myriad,
And of the best, among them,
For an old bitch gone in the teeth,
For a botched civilization,

Charm, smiling at the good mouth,
Quick eyes gone under earth's lid,

For two gross of broken statues,
For a few thousand battered books.

YEUX GLAUQUES

Gladstone was still respected,
When John Ruskin produced
'Kings' Treasuries'; Swinburne
And Rossetti still abused.

Fœtid Buchanan lifted up his voice
When that faun's head of hers
Became a pastime for
Painters and adulterers.

The Burne-Jones cartons
Have preserved her eyes;
Still, at the Tate, they teach
Cophetua to rhapsodize;

Thin like brook-water,
With a vacant gaze.
The English Rubaiyat was still-born
In those days.

The thin, clear gaze, the same
Still darts out faun-like from the half-ruin'd face,
Questing and passive ...
'Ah, poor Jenny's case' ...

Bewildered that a world
Shows no surprise
At her last maquero's
Adulteries.

'SIENA MI FE'; DISFECEMI MAREMMA'

Among the pickled fœtuses and bottled bones,
Engaged in perfecting the catalogue,
I found the last scion of the
Senatorial families of Strasbourg, Monsieur Verog.

For two hours he talked of Gallifet;
Of Dowson; of the Rhymers' Club;
Told me how Johnson (Lionel) died
By falling from a high stool in a pub ...

But showed no trace of alcohol
At the autopsy, privately performed –
Tissue preserved – the pure mind
Arose toward Newman as the whiskey warmed.

Dowson found harlots cheaper than hotels;
Headlam for uplift; Image impartially imbued
With raptures for Bacchus, Terpsichore and the Church.
So spoke the author of 'The Dorian Mood',

M. Verog, out of step with the decade,
Detached from his contemporaries,
Neglected by the young,
Because of these reveries.

BRENNBAUM

The sky-like limpid eyes,
The circular infant's face,
The stiffness from spats to collar
Never relaxing into grace;

The heavy memories of Horeb, Sinai and the forty years,
Showed only when the daylight fell
Level across the face
Of Brennbaum 'The Impeccable'.

MR NIXON

In the cream gilded cabin of his steam yacht
Mr Nixon advised me kindly, to advance with fewer
Dangers of delay. 'Consider
        'Carefully the reviewer.

'I was as poor as you are;
'When I began I got, of course,
'Advance on royalties, fifty at first,' said Mr Nixon,
'Follow me, and take a column,
'Even if you have to work free.

'Butter reviewers. From fifty to three hundred
'I rose in eighteen months;
'The hardest nut I had to crack
'Was Dr Dundas.

'I never mentioned a man but with the view
'Of selling my own works.
'The tip's a good one, as for literature
'It gives no man a sinecure.

'And no one knows, at sight, a masterpiece.
'And give up verse, my boy,
'There's nothing in it.'

             . . .

Likewise a friend of Blougram's once advised me:
Don't kick against the pricks,
Accept opinion. The 'Nineties' tried your game
And died, there's nothing in it.

X

Beneath the sagging roof
The stylist has taken shelter,
Unpaid, uncelebrated,
At last from the world's welter

Nature receives him;
With a placid and uneducated mistress
He exercises his talents
And the soil meets his distress.

The haven from sophistications and contentions
Leaks through its thatch;
He offers succulent cooking;
The door has a creaking latch.

XI

'Conservatrix of Milésien'
Habits of mind and feeling,
Possibly. But in Ealing
With the most bank-clerkly of Englishmen?

No, 'Milésian' is an exaggeration.
No instinct has survived in her
Older than those her grandmother
Told her would fit her station.

XII

'Daphne with her thighs in bark
Stretches toward me her leafy hands,' –
Subjectively. In the stuffed-satin drawing-room
I await The Lady Valentine's commands,

Knowing my coat has never been
Of precisely the fashion
To stimulate, in her,
A durable passion;

Doubtful, somewhat, of the value
Of well-gowned approbation
Of literary effort,
But never of The Lady Valentine's vocation:

Poetry, her border of ideas,
The edge, uncertain but a means of blending
With other strata
Where the lower and higher have ending;

A hook to catch the Lady Jane's attention,
A modulation toward the theatre,
Also, in the case of revolution,
A possible friend and comforter.

. . .

Conduct, on the other hand, the soul
'Which the highest cultures have nourished'
To Fleet St where
Dr Johnson flourished;

Beside this thoroughfare
The sale of half-hose has
Long since superseded the cultivation
Of Pierian roses.

ENVOI (1919)

Go, dumb-born book,
Tell her that sang me once that song of Lawes:
Hadst thou but song
As thou hast subjects known,
Then were there cause in thee that should condone
Even my faults that heavy upon me lie,
And build her glories their longevity.

Tell her that sheds
Such treasure in the air,
Recking naught else but that her graces give
Life to the moment,
I would bid them live
As roses might, in magic amber laid,
Red overwrought with orange and all made
One substance and one colour
Braving time.

Tell her that goes
With song upon her lips
But sings not out the song, nor knows
The maker of it, some other mouth,
May be as fair as hers,
Might, in new ages, gain her worshippers,

When our two dusts with Waller's shall be laid,
Siftings on siftings in oblivion,
Till change hath broken down
All things save Beauty alone.

Canto I

And then went down to the ship,
Set keel to breakers, forth on the godly sea, and
We set up mast and sail on that swart ship,
Bore sheep aboard her, and our bodies also
Heavy with weeping, and winds from sternward
Bore us out onward with bellying canvas,
Circe's this craft, the trim-coifed goddess.
Then sat we amidships, wind jamming the tiller,
Thus with stretched sail, we went over sea till day's end.
Sun to his slumber, shadows o'er all the ocean,
Came we then to the bounds of deepest water,
To the Kimmerian lands, and peopled cities
Covered with close-webbed mist, unpiercéd ever
With glitter of sun - rays
Nor with stars stretched, nor looking back from heaven
Swartest night stretched over wretched men there.
The ocean flowing backward, came we then to the place
Aforesaid by Circe.
Here did they rites, Perimedes and Eurylochus,
And drawing sword from my hip
I dug the ell-square pitkin;
Poured we libations unto each the dead,
First mead and then sweet wine, water mixed with white flour.
Then prayed I many a prayer to the sickly death's-heads;
As set in Ithaca, sterile bulls of the best

For sacrifice, heaping the pyre with goods,
A sheep to Tiresias only, black and a bell-sheep.
Dark blood flowed in the fosse,
Souls out of Erebus, cadaverous dead, of brides,
Of youths and of the old who had borne much;
Souls stained with recent tears, girls tender,
Men many, mauled with bronze lance heads,
Battle spoil, bearing yet dreory arms,
These many crowded about me; with shouting,
Pallor upon me, cried to my men for more beasts;
Slaughtered the herds, sheep slain of bronze;
Poured ointment, cried to the gods,
To Pluto the strong, and praised Proserpine;
Unsheathed the narrow sword,
I sat to keep off the impetuous impotent dead,
Till I should hear Tiresias.
But first Elpenor came, our friend Elpenor,
Unburied, cast on the wide earth,
Limbs that we left in the house of Circe,
Unwept, unwrapped in sepulchre, since toils urged other.
Pitiful spirit. And I cried in hurried speech:
'Elpenor, how art thou come to this dark coast?
Cam'st thou afoot, outstripping seamen?'
          And he in heavy speech:
'Ill fate and abundant wine. I slept in Circe's ingle.
'Going down the long ladder unguarded,
'I fell against the buttress,
'Shattered the nape-nerve, the soul sought Avernus.
'But thou, O King, I bid remember me, unwept, unburied,
'Heap up mine arms, be tomb by sea-bord, and inscribed:
'*A man of no fortune, and with a name to come.*
'And set my oar up, that I swung mid fellows.'
And Anticlea came, whom I beat off, and then Tiresias Theban,
Holding his golden wand, knew me, and spoke first:
'A second time? why? man of ill star,
'Facing the sunless dead and this joyless region?

332

'Stand from the fosse, leave me my bloody bever
'For soothsay.'
　　　And I stepped back,
And he strong with the blood, said then: 'Odysseus
'Shalt return through spiteful Neptune, over dark seas,
'Lose all companions.' And then Anticlea came.
Lie quiet Divus. I mean, that is Andreas Divus,
In officina Wecheli, 1538, out of Homer.
And he sailed, by Sirens and thence outward and away
And unto Circe
　　　Venerandam,
In the Cretain's phrase, with the golden crown, Aphrodite,
Cypri munimenta sortita est, mirthful, orichalchi, with golden
Girdles and breast bands, thou with dark eyelids
Bearing the golden bough of Argicida. So that:

Canto
LI

Shines
in the mind of heaven　　God
who made it
more than the sun
in our eye.
Fifth element; mud; said Napoleon
With usury has no man a good house
made of stone, no paradise on his church wall
With usury the stone cutter is kept from his stone
the weaver is kept from his loom by usura
Wool does not come into market
the peasant does not eat his own grain
The girl's needle goes blunt in her hand
The looms are hushed one after another

ten thousand after ten thousand
Duccio was not by usura
Nor was 'La Calunnia' painted.
Neither Ambrogio Praedis nor Angelico
had their skill by usura
Nor St Trophime its cloisters;
Nor St Hilaire its proportion.
Usury rusts the man and his chisel
It destroys the craftsman; destroying craft
Azure is caught with cancer. Emerald comes to no Memling
Usury kills the child in the womb
And breaks short the young man's courting
Usury brings age into youth; it lies between the bride
and the bridegroom
Usury is against Nature's increase.
Whores for Eleusis;
Under usury no stone is cut smooth
Peasant has no gain from his sheep herd
        Blue dun; number 2 in most rivers
for dark days; when it is cold
A starling's wing will give you the colour
or duck widgeon; if you take feather from under the wing
Let the body be of blue fox fur, or a water rat's
or grey squirrel's. Take this with a portion of mohair
and a cock's hackle for legs.
12th of March to 2nd of April
Hen pheasant's feather does for a fly,
green tail, the wings flat on the body
Dark fur from a hare's ear for a body
a green shaded partridge feather
        grizzled yellow cock's hackle
green wax; harl from a peacock's tail
bright lower body; about the size of pin
the head should be. can be fished from seven a.m.
till eleven; at which time the brown marsh fly comes on.
As long as the brown continues, no fish will take Granham

That hath the light of the doer; as it were
a form cleaving to it.
Deo similis quodam modo
his intellectus adeptus
Grass; nowhere out of place. Thus speaking in Konigsberg
Zwischen die Volkern erzielt wird
a modus vivendi.
circling in eddying air; in a hurry;
the 12: close eyed in the oily wind
these were the regents; and a sour song from the folds
    of his belly
sang Geryone: I am the help of the aged;
I pay men to talk peace;
Mistress of many tongues; merchant of chalcedony
I am Geryon twin with usura,
You who have lived in a stage set.
A thousand were dead in his folds;
in the eel-fishers basket
Time was of the League of Cambrai:

H. D. 1886–1961

From *The Walls Do Not Fall*

I

An incident here and there,
and rails gone (for guns)
from your (and my) old town square:

mist and mist-grey, no colour,
still the Luxor bee, chick and hare
pursue unalterable purpose

in green, rose-red, lapis;
they continue to prophesy
from the stone papyrus:

there, as here, ruin opens
the tomb, the temple; enter,
there as here, there are no doors:

the shrine lies open to the sky,
the rain falls, here, there
sand drifts; eternity endures:

ruin everywhere, yet as the fallen roof
leaves the sealed room
open to the air,

so, through our desolation,
thoughts stir, inspiration stalks us
through gloom:

unaware, Spirit announces the Presence;
shivering overtakes us,
as of old, Samuel:

trembling at a known street-corner,
we know not nor are known;
the Pythian pronounces – we pass on

to another cellar, to another sliced wall
where poor utensils show
like rare objects in a museum;

Pompeii has nothing to teach us,
we know crack of volcanic fissure,
slow flow of terrible lava,

pressure on heart, lungs, the brain
about to burst its brittle case
(what the skull can endure!):

over us, Apocryphal fire,
under us, the earth sway, dip of a floor,
slope of a pavement

where men roll, drunk
with a new bewilderment,
sorcery, bedevilment:

the bone-frame was made for
no such shock knit within terror,
yet the skeleton stood up to it:

the flesh? it was melted away,
the heart burnt out, dead ember,
tendons, muscles shattered, outer husk dismembered,

yet the frame held:
we pass the flame: we wonder
what saved us? what for?

2

Evil was active in the land,
Good was impoverished and sad;

Ill promised adventure,
Good was smug and fat;

Dev-ill was after us,
tricked up like Jehovah;

Good was the tasteless pod,
stripped from the manna-beans, pulse, lentils:

they were angry when we were so hungry
for the nourishment, God;

they snatched off our amulets,
charms are not, they said, grace;

but gods always face two-ways,
so let us search the old highways

for the true-rune, the right-spell,
recover old values;

nor listen if they shout out,
your beauty, Isis, Aset or Astarte,

is a harlot; you are retrogressive,
zealot, hankering after old flesh-pots;

your heart, moreover,
is a dead canker,

they continue, and
your rhythm is the devil's hymn,

your stylus is dipped in corrosive sublimate,
how can you scratch out

indelible ink of the palimpsest
of past misadventure?

3

Let us, however, recover the Sceptre,
the rod of power:

it is crowned with the lily-head
or the lily-bud:

it is Caduceus; among the dying
it bears healing:

or evoking the dead,
it brings life to the living.

4

There is a spell, for instance,
in every sea-shell:

continuous, the sea thrust
is powerless against coral,

bone, stone, marble
hewn from within by that craftsman,

the shell-fish:
oyster, clam, mollusc

is master-mason planning
the stone marvel:

yet that flabby, amorphous hermit
within, like the planet

senses the finite,
it limits its orbit

of being, its house,
temple, fane, shrine:

it unlocks the portals
at stated intervals:

prompted by hunger,
it opens to the tide-flow:

but infinity? no,
of nothing-too-much:

I sense my own limit,
my shell-jaws snap shut

at invasion of the limitless,
ocean-weight; infinite water

can not crack me, egg in egg-shell;
closed in, complete, immortal

full-circle, I know the pull
of the tide, the lull

as well as the moon;
the octopus-darkness

is powerless against
her cold immortality;

so I in my own way know
that the whale

can not digest me:
be firm in your own small, static, limited

orbit and the shark-jaws
of outer circumstance

will spit you forth:
be indigestible, hard, ungiving.

so that, living within,
you beget, self-out-of-self,

selfless,
that pearl-of-great-price.

Robinson Jeffers 1887 – 1962

Shine, Perishing Republic

While this America settles in the mould of its vulgarity, heavily
    thickening to empire,
And protest, only a bubble in the molten mass, pops and sighs out,
    and the mass hardens,

I sadly smiling remember that the flower fades to make fruit, the
    fruit rots to make earth.
Out of the mother; and through the spring exultances, ripeness and
    decadence; and home to the mother.

You making haste haste on decay: not blameworthy; life is good, be
    it stubbornly long or suddenly
A mortal splendor: meteors are not needed less than mountains:
    shine, perishing republic.

But for my children, I would have them keep their distance from the
    thickening center; corruption
Never has been compulsory, when the cities lie at the monster's feet
    there are left the mountains.

And boys, be in nothing so moderate as in love of man, a clever
    servant, insufferable master.
There is the trap that catches noblest spirits, that caught – they say –
    God, when he walked on earth.

Hurt Hawks

The broken pillar of the wing jags from the clotted shoulder,
The wing trails like a banner in defeat,
No more to use the sky forever but live with famine
And pain a few days: cat nor coyote
Will shorten the week of waiting for death, there is game without
    talons.
He stands under the oak-bush and waits
The lame feet of salvation; at night he remembers freedom
And flies in a dream, the dawns ruin it.
He is strong and pain is worse to the strong, incapacity is worse.
The curs of the day come and torment him
At distance, no one but death the redeemer will humble that
    head,
The intrepid readiness, the terrible eyes.
The wild God of the world is sometimes merciful to those
That ask mercy, not often to the arrogant.
You do not know him, you communal people, or you have forgotten
    him;
Intemperate and savage, the hawk remembers him;
Beautiful and wild, the hawks, and men that are dying, remember
    him.

II

I'd sooner, except the penalties, kill a man than a hawk; but the great
    redtail
Had nothing left but unable misery
From the bone too shattered for mending, the wing that trailed under
    his talons when he moved.
We had fed him six weeks, I gave him freedom,
He wandered over the foreland hill and returned in the evening,
    asking for death,
Not like a beggar, still eyed with the old

Implacable arrogance. I gave him the lead gift in the twilight. What
    fell was relaxed,
Owl-downy, soft feminine feathers; but what
Soared: the fierce rush: the night-herons by the flooded river cried
    fear at its rising
Before it was quite unsheathed from reality.

Marianne Moore 1887 – 1972

Poetry

I, too, dislike it: there are things that are important beyond all this
    fiddle.
  Reading it, however, with a perfect contempt for it, one discovers in
  it after all, a place for the genuine.
     Hands that can grasp, eyes
     that can dilate, hair that can rise
       if it must, these things are important not because a

high-sounding interpretation can be put upon them but because they
    are
  useful. When they become so derivative as to become unintelligible,
  the same thing may be said for all of us, that we
    do not admire what
    we cannot understand: the bat
      holding on upside down or in quest of something to

eat, elephants pushing, a wild horse taking a roll, a tireless wolf under
  a tree, the immovable critic twitching his skin like a horse that feels
  a flea, the base-
  ball fan, the statistician –
    nor is it valid
      to discriminate against 'business documents and

school-books'; all these phenomena are important. One must make a
    distinction
  however: when dragged into prominence by half poets, the result is
    not poetry,

nor till the poets among us can be
  'literalists of
   the imagination' – above
    insolence and triviality and can present

for inspection, 'imaginary gardens with real toads in them', shall we
  have
  it. In the meantime, if you demand on the one hand,
  the raw material of poetry in
   all its rawness and
   that which is on the other hand
    genuine, you are interested in poetry.

Critics and Connoisseurs

There is a great amount of poetry in unconscious
  fastidiousness. Certain Ming
   products, imperial floor coverings of coach-
  wheel yellow, are well enough in their way but I have seen
                                  something
    that I like better – a
     mere childish attempt to make an imperfectly ballasted
      animal stand up,
     similar determination to make a pup
      eat his meat from the plate.

I remember a swan under the willows in Oxford,
  with flamingo-colored, maple-
   leaflike feet. It reconnoitered like a battle-
  ship. Disbelief and conscious fastidiousness were
    ingredients in its
     disinclination to move. Finally its hardihood was
      not proof against its
     proclivity to more fully appraise such bits
      of food as the stream

bore counter to it; it made away with what I gave it
   to eat. I have seen this swan and
     I have seen you; I have seen ambition without
understanding in a variety of forms. Happening to stand
     by an ant-hill, I have
        seen a fastidious ant carrying a stick north, south,
          east, west, till it turned on
       itself, struck out from the flower bed into the lawn,
       and returned to the point

from which it had started. Then abandoning the stick as
   useless and overtaxing its
   jaws with a particle of whitewash – pill-like but
heavy – it again went through the same course of procedure.
              What is
     there in being able
         to say that one has dominated the stream in an attitude
                    of self-defense;
    in proving that one has had the experience
     of carrying a stick?

Spenser's Ireland

    has not altered; –
      a place as kind as it is green,
       the greenest place I've never seen.
    Every name is a tune.
    Denunciations do not affect
       the culprit; nor blows, but it
   is torture to him to not be spoken to.
    They're natural –
        the coat, like Venus'
    mantle lined with stars,
    buttoned close at the neck – the sleeves new from disuse.

If in Ireland
   they play the harp backward at need,
   and gather at midday the seed
of the fern, eluding
their 'giants all covered with iron,' might
     there be fern seed for unlearn-
ing obduracy and for reinstating
the enchantment?
        Hindered characters
seldom have mothers
in Irish stories, but they all have grandmothers.

It was Irish;
   a match not a marriage was made
   when my great great grandmother'd said
with native genius for
disunion, 'Although your suitor be
     perfection, one objection
is enough; he is not
Irish.' Outwitting
       the fairies, befriending the furies,
whoever again
and again says, 'I'll never give in,' never sees

that you're not free
   until you've been made captive by
   supreme belief – credulity
you say? When large dainty
fingers tremblingly divide the wings
     of the fly for mid-July
with a needle and wrap it with peacock tail,
or tie wool and
      buzzard's wing, their pride,
like the enchanter's
is in care, not madness. Concurring hands divide

flax for damask
  that when bleached by Irish weather
  has the silvered chamois-leather
water-tightness of a
skin. Twisted torcs and gold new-moon-shaped
      lunulae aren't jewelry
like the purple-coral fuchsia-tree's. Eire –
the guillemot
          so neat and the hen
of the heath and the
linnet spinet-sweet – bespeak relentlessness? Then

they are to me
  like enchanted Earl Gerald who
  changed himself into a stag, to
a great green-eyed cat of
the mountain. Discommodity makes
      them invisible; they've dis-
appeared. The Irish say your trouble is their
trouble and your
          joy their joy? I wish
I could believe it;
I am troubled, I'm dissatisfied, I'm Irish.

Tom Fool at Jamaica

Look at Jonah embarking from Joppa, deterred by
the whale; hard going for a statesman whom nothing could detain,
  although one who would not rather die than repent.
  Be infallible at your peril, for your system will fail,
and select as a model the schoolboy in Spain
  who at the age of six, portrayed a mule and jockey
    who had pulled up for a snail.

'There is submerged magnificence, as Victor Hugo
said.' *Sentir avec ardeur*; that's it; magnetized by feeling.
   Tom Fool 'makes an effort and makes it oftener
      than the rest' – out on April first, a day of some significance
in the ambiguous sense – the smiling
   Master Atkinson's choice, with that mark of a champion, the extra
      spurt when needed. Yes, yes. 'Chance

   is a regrettable impurity'; like Tom Fool's
left white hind foot – an unconformity; though judging by results, a
   kind of cottontail to give him confidence.
      Up in the cupola comparing speeds, Fred Capossela keeps his
                                                                head.
'It's tough,' he said; 'but I get 'em; and why shouldn't I?
   I'm relaxed, I'm confident, and I *don't bet*.' Sensational. He does not
      bet on his animated

   valentines – his pink and black-striped, sashed or dotted silks.
Tom Fool is 'a handy horse', with a chiseled foot. You've the beat
   of a dancer to a measure or harmonious rush
      of a porpoise at the prow where the racers all win easily –
like centaurs' legs in tune, as when kettledrums compete;
   nose rigid and suede nostrils spread, a light left hand on the rein, till
      well – this is a rhapsody.

   Of course, speaking of champions, there was Fats Waller
with the feather touch, giraffe eyes, and that hand alighting in
   Ain't Misbehavin'! Ozzie Smith and Eubie Blake
      ennoble the atmosphere; you recall the Lippizan school;
the time Ted Atkinson charged by on Tiger Skin –
   no pursuers in sight – cat-loping along. And you may have seen a
                                                                monkey
      on a greyhound. 'But Tom Fool . . .

When I Buy Pictures

or what is closer to the truth,

when I look at that of which I may regard myself as the imaginary
     possessor,

I fix upon what would give me pleasure in my average moments:

the satire upon curiosity in which no more is discernible

than the intensity of the mood;

or quite the opposite – the old thing, the mediaeval decorated hat-box,

in which there are hounds with waists diminishing like the waist of
     the hour-glass,

and deer and birds and seated people;

it may be no more than a square of parquetry; the literal biography
     perhaps,

in letters standing well apart upon a parchment-like expanse;

an artichoke in six varieties of blue; the snipe-legged hieroglyphic in
     three parts;

the silver fence protecting Adam's grave, or Michael taking Adam by
     the wrist.

Too stern an intellectual emphasis upon this quality or that detracts
     from one's enjoyment.

It must not wish to disarm anything; nor may the approved triumph
     easily be honored –

that which is great because something else is small.

It comes to this: of whatever sort it is,

it must be 'lit with piercing glances into the life of things';

it must acknowledge the spiritual forces which have made it.

T. S. Eliot 1888 – 1965

The Love Song of J. Alfred Prufrock

S'io credessi che mia risposta fosse
a persona che mai tornasse al mondo,
questa fiamma staria senza più scosse.
Ma per ciò che giammai di questo fondo
non tornò vivo alcun, s'i'odo il vero,
senza tema d'infamia ti rispondo.

Let us go then, you and I,
When the evening is spread out against the sky
Like a patient etherised upon a table;
Let us go, through certain half-deserted streets,
The muttering retreats
Of restless nights in one-night cheap hotels
And sawdust restaurants with oyster-shells:
Streets that follow like a tedious argument
Of insidious intent
To lead you to an overwhelming question . . .
Oh, do not ask, 'What is it?'
Let us go and make our visit.

In the room the women come and go
Talking of Michelangelo.

The yellow fog that rubs its back upon the window-panes,
The yellow smoke that rubs its muzzle on the window-panes,
Licked its tongue into the corners of the evening,
Lingered upon the pools that stand in drains,
Let fall upon its back the soot that falls from chimneys,
Slipped by the terrace, made a sudden leap,
And seeing that it was a soft October night,
Curled once about the house, and fell asleep.

And indeed there will be time
For the yellow smoke that slides along the street
Rubbing its back upon the window-panes;
There will be time, there will be time
To prepare a face to meet the faces that you meet;
There will be time to murder and create,
And time for all the works and days of hands
That lift and drop a question on your plate;
Time for you and time for me,
And time yet for a hundred indecisions,
And for a hundred visions and revisions,
Before the taking of a toast and tea.

In the room the women come and go
Talking of Michelangelo.

And indeed there will be time
To wonder, 'Do I dare?' and, 'Do I dare?'
Time to turn back and descend the stair,
With a bald spot in the middle of my hair –
(They will say: 'How his hair is growing thin!')
My morning coat, my collar mounting firmly to the chin,
My necktie rich and modest, but asserted by a simple pin –
(They will say: 'But how his arms and legs are thin!')
Do I dare
Disturb the universe?
In a minute there is time
For decisions and revisions which a minute will reverse.

For I have known them all already, known them all –
Have known the evenings, mornings, afternoons,
I have measured out my life with coffee spoons;
I know the voices dying with a dying fall
Beneath the music from a farther room.
    So how should I presume?

And I have known the eyes already, known them all –
The eyes that fix you in a formulated phrase,
And when I am formulated, sprawling on a pin,
When I am pinned and wriggling on the wall,
Then how should I begin
To spit out all the butt-ends of my days and ways?
  And how should I presume?

And I have known the arms already, known them all –
Arms that are braceleted and white and bare
(But in the lamplight, downed with light brown hair!)
Is it perfume from a dress
That makes me so digress?
Arms that lie along a table, or wrap about a shawl.
  And should I then presume?
  And how should I begin?

      . . .

Shall I say, I have gone at dusk through narrow streets
And watched the smoke that rises from the pipes
Of lonely men in shirt-sleeves, leaning out of windows? . . .

I should have been a pair of ragged claws
Scuttling across the floors of silent seas.

      . . .

And the afternoon, the evening, sleeps so peacefully!
Smoothed by long fingers,
Asleep . . . tired . . . or it malingers,
Stretched on the floor, here beside you and me.
Should I, after tea and cakes and ices,
Have the strength to force the moment to its crisis?
But though I have wept and fasted, wept and prayed,
 Though I have seen my head (grown slightly bald) brought in upon a
    platter,
I am no prophet – and here's no great matter;

I have seen the moment of my greatness flicker,
And I have seen the eternal Footman hold my coat, and snicker,
And in short, I was afraid.

And would it have been worth it, after all,
After the cups, the marmalade, the tea,
Among the porcelain, among some talk of you and me,
Would it have been worth while,
To have bitten off the matter with a smile,
To have squeezed the universe into a ball
To roll it towards some overwhelming question,
To say: 'I am Lazarus, come from the dead,
Come back to tell you all, I shall tell you all' –
If one, settling a pillow by her head,
    Should say: 'That is not what I meant at all.
    That is not it, at all.'

And would it have been worth it, after all,
Would it have been worth while,
After the sunsets and the dooryards and the sprinkled streets,
After the novels, after the teacups, after the skirts that trail along the
    floor –
And this, and so much more? –
It is impossible to say just what I mean!
But as if a magic lantern threw the nerves in patterns on a screen:
Would it have been worth while
If one, settling a pillow or throwing off a shawl,
And turning toward the window, should say:
    'That is not it at all,
    That is not what I meant, at all.'

. . .

No! I am not Prince Hamlet, nor was meant to be;
Am an attendant lord, one that will do
To swell a progress, start a scene or two,
Advise the prince; no doubt, an easy tool,

Deferential, glad to be of use,
Politic, cautious, and meticulous;
Full of high sentence, but a bit obtuse;
At times, indeed, almost ridiculous –
Almost, at times, the Fool.

I grow old . . . I grow old . . .
I shall wear the bottoms of my trousers rolled.

Shall I part my hair behind? Do I dare to eat a peach?
I shall wear white flannel trousers, and walk upon the beach.
I have heard the mermaids singing, each to each.

I do not think that they will sing to me.

I have seen them riding seaward on the waves
Combing the white hair of the waves blown back
When the wind blows the water white and black.

We have lingered in the chambers of the sea
By sea-girls wreathed with seaweed red and brown
Till human voices wake us, and we drown.

Whispers of Immortality

Webster was much possessed by death
And saw the skull beneath the skin;
And breastless creatures under ground
Leaned backward with a lipless grin.

Daffodil bulbs instead of balls
Stared from the sockets of the eyes!
He knew that thought clings round dead limbs
Tightening its lusts and luxuries.

Donne, I suppose, was such another
Who found no substitute for sense,
To seize and clutch and penetrate;
Expert beyond experience,

He knew the anguish of the marrow
The ague of the skeleton;
No contact possible to flesh
Allayed the fever of the bone.

. . .

Grishkin is nice: her Russian eye
Is underlined for emphasis;
Uncorseted, her friendly bust
Gives promise of pneumatic bliss.

The couched Brazilian jaguar
Compels the scampering marmoset
With subtle effluence of cat;
Grishkin has a maisonnette;

The sleek Brazilian jaguar
Does not in its aboreal gloom
Distil so rank a feline smell
As Grishkin in a drawing-room.

And even the Abstract Entities
Circumambulate her charm;
But our lot crawls between dry ribs
To keep our metaphysics warm.

Mr Eliot's Sunday Morning Service

Look, look, master, here comes two religious caterpillars.
– The Jew of Malta.

Polyphiloprogenitive
The sapient sutlers of the Lord
Drift across the window-pane.
In the beginning was the Word.

In the beginning was the Word.
Superfetation of τὸ ἕν,
And at the mensual turn of time
Produced enervate Origen.

A painter of the Umbrian school
Designed upon a gesso ground
The nimbus of the Baptized God.
The wilderness is cracked and browned

But through the water pale and thin
Still shine the unoffending feet
And there above the painter set
The father and the Paraclete.

. . .

The sable presbyters approach
The avenue of penitence;
The young are red and pustular
Clutching piaculative pence.

Under the penitential gates
Sustained by staring Seraphim
Where the souls of the devout
Burn invisible and dim.

Along the garden-wall the bees
With hairy bellies pass between
The staminate and pistilate,
Blest office of the epicene.

Sweeney shifts from ham to ham
Stirring the water in his bath.
The masters of the subtle schools
Are controversial, polymath.

John Crowe Ransom 1888 – 1974

Here Lies a Lady

Here lies a lady of beauty and high degree.
Of chills and fever she died, of fever and chills,
The delight of her husband, her aunt, an infant of three,
And of medicos marveling sweetly on her ills.

For either she burned, and her confident eyes would blaze,
And her fingers fly in a manner to puzzle their heads –
What was she making? Why, nothing; she sat in a maze
Of old scraps of laces, snipped into curious shreds –

Or this would pass, and the light of her fire decline
Till she lay discouraged and cold, like a stalk white and blown,
And would not open her eyes, to kisses, to wine;
The sixth of these states was her last; the cold settled down.

Sweet ladies, long may ye bloom, and toughly I hope ye may thole,
But was she not lucky? In flowers and lace and mourning,
In love and great honor we bade God rest her soul
After six little spaces of chill, and six of burning.

Janet Waking

Beautifully Janet slept
Till it was deeply morning. She woke then
And thought about her dainty-feathered hen,
To see how it had kept.

One kiss she gave her mother,
Only a small one gave she to her daddy
Who would have kissed each curl of his shining baby;
No kiss at all for her brother.

'Old Chucky, old Chucky!' she cried,
Running across the world upon the grass
To Chucky's house, and listening. But alas,
Her Chucky had died.

It was a transmogrifying bee
Came droning down on Chucky's old bald head
And sat and put the poison. It scarcely bled,
But how exceedingly

And purply did the knot
Swell with the venom and communicate
Its rigor! Now the poor comb stood up straight
But Chucky did not.

So there was Janet
Kneeling on the wet grass, crying her brown hen
(Translated far beyond the daughters of men)
To rise and walk upon it.

And weeping fast as she had breath
Janet implored us, 'Wake her from her sleep!'
And would not be instructed in how deep
Was the forgetful kingdom of death.

Antique Harvesters

(SCENE: OF THE MISSISSIPPI THE BANK SINISTER, AND
OF THE OHIO THE BANK SINISTER.)

Tawny are the leaves turned but they still hold,
And it is harvest; what shall this land produce?
A meager hill of kernels, a runnel of juice;
Declension looks from our land, it is old.
Therefore let us assemble, dry, grey, spare,
And mild as yellow air.

'I hear the croak of a raven's funeral wing.'
The young men would be joying in the song
Of passionate birds; their memories are not long.
What is it thus rehearsed in sable? 'Nothing.'
Trust not but the old endure, and shall be older
Than the scornful beholder.

We pluck the spindling ears and gather the corn.
One spot has special yield? 'On this spot stood
Heroes and drenched it with their only blood.'
And talk meets talk, as echoes from the horn
Of the hunter – echoes are the old men's arts,
Ample are the chambers of their hearts.

Here come the hunters, keepers of a rite;
The horn, the hounds, the lank mares coursing by
Straddled with archetypes of chivalry;
And the fox, lovely ritualist, in flight
Offering his unearthly ghost to quarry;
And the fields, themselves to harry.

Resume, harvesters. The treasure is full bronze
Which you will garner for the Lady, and the moon
Could tinge it no yellower than does this noon;

But grey will quench it shortly – the field, men, stones.
Pluck fast, dreamers; prove as you amble slowly
Not less than men, not wholly.

Bare the arm, dainty youths, bend the knees
Under bronze burdens. And by an autumn tone
As by a grey, as by a green, you will have known
Your famous Lady's image; for so have these;
And if one say that easily will your hands
More prosper in other lands,

Angry as wasp-music be your cry then:
'Forsake the Proud Lady, of the heart of fire,
The look of snow, to the praise of a dwindled choir,
Song of degenerate specters that were men?
The sons of the fathers shall keep her, worthy of
What these have done in love.'

True, it is said of our Lady, she ageth.
But see, if you peep shrewdly, she hath not stooped;
Take no thought of her servitors that have drooped,
For we are nothing; and if one talk of death –
Why, the ribs of the earth subsist frail as a breath
If but God wearieth.

Conrad Aiken 1889 – 1973

From *Preludes for Memnon*

II

Two coffees in the Español, the last
Bright drops of golden Barsac in a goblet,
Fig paste and candied nuts . . . Hardy is dead,
And James and Conrad dead, and Shakspere dead,
And old Moore ripens for an obscene grave,
And Yeats for an arid one; and I, and you –
What winding sheet for us, what boards and bricks,
What mummeries, candles, prayers, and pious frauds?
You shall be lapped in Syrian scarlet, woman,
And wear your pearls, and your bright bracelets, too,
Your agate ring, and round your neck shall hang
Your dark blue lapis with its specks of gold.
And I, beside you – ah! but will that be?
For there are dark streams in this dark world, lady,
Gulf Streams and Arctic currents of the soul;
And I may be, before our consummation
Beds us together, cheek by jowl, in earth,
Swept to another shore, where my white bones
Will lie unhonored, or defiled by gulls.

What dignity can death bestow on us,
Who kiss beneath a streetlamp, or hold hands
Half hidden in a taxi, or replete
With coffee, figs and Barsac make our way
To a dark bedroom in a wormworn house?
The aspidistra guards the door; we enter,
Per aspidistra – then – *ad astra* – is it? –

And lock ourselves securely in our gloom
And loose ourselves from terror ... Here's my hand,
The white scar on my thumb, and here's my mouth
To stop your murmur; speechless let us lie,
And think of Hardy, Shakspere, Yeats and James;
Comfort our panic hearts with magic names;
Stare at the ceiling, where the taxi lamps
Make ghosts of light; and see, beyond this bed,
That other bed in which we will not move;
And, whether joined or separate, will not love.

XLII

Keep in the heart the journal nature keeps;
Mark down the limp nasturtium leaf with frost;
See that the hawthorn bough is ice-embossed,
And that the snail, in season, has his grief;
Design the winter on the window pane;
Admit pale sun through cobwebs left from autumn;
Remember summer when the flies are stilled;
Remember spring, when the cold spider sleeps.

Such diary, too, set down as this: the heart
Beat twice or thrice this day for no good reason;
For friends and sweethearts dead before their season;
For wisdom come too late, and come to naught.
Put down 'the hand that shakes', 'the eye that glazes';
The 'step that falters betwixt thence and hence';
Observe that hips and haws burn brightest red
When the North Pole and sun are most apart.

Note that the moon is here, as cold as ever,
With ages on her face, and ice and snow;
Such as the freezing mind alone can know,
When loves and hates are only twigs that shiver.
Add in a postscript that the rain is over,

The wind from southwest backing to the south,
Disasters all forgotten, hurts forgiven;
And that the North Star, altered, shines forever.

Then say: I was a part of nature's plan;
Knew her cold heart, for I was consciousness;
Came first to hate her, and at last to bless;
Believed in her; doubted; believed again.
My love the lichen had such roots as I, –
The snowflake was my father; I return,
After this interval of faith and question,
To nature's heart, in pain, as I began.

LVI

Rimbaud and Verlaine, precious pair of poets,
Genius in both (but what is genius?) playing
Chess on a marble table at an inn
With chestnut blossom falling in blond beer
And on their hair and between knight and bishop –
Sunlight squared between them on the chess-board
Cirrus in heaven, and a squeal of music
Blown from the leathern door of Ste Sulpice –

Discussing, between moves, iamb and spondee
Anacoluthon and the open vowel
God the great peacock with his angel peacocks
And his dependent peacocks the bright stars:
Disputing too of fate as Plato loved it,
Or Sophocles, who hated and admired,
Or Socrates, who loved and was amused:

Verlaine puts down his pawn upon a leaf
And closes his long eyes, which are dishonest,
And says 'Rimbaud, there is one thing to do:
We must take rhetoric, and wring its neck! . . .'
Rimbaud considers gravely, moves his Queen;
And then removes himself to Timbuctoo.

And Verlaine dead, – with all his jades and mauves;
And Rimbaud dead in Marseilles with a vision,
His leg cut off, as once before his heart;
And all reported by a later lackey,
Whose virtue is his tardiness in time.

Let us describe the evening as it is: –
The stars disposed in heaven as they are:
Verlaine and Shakspere rotting, where they rot,
Rimbaud remembered, and too soon forgot;

Order in all things, logic in the dark;
Arrangement in the atom and the spark;
Time in the heart and sequence in the brain –

Such as destroyed Rimbaud and fooled Verlaine.
And let us then take godhead by the neck –

And strangle it, and with it, rhetoric.

Edna St Vincent Millay 1892 — 1950

'What lips my lips have kissed, and where, and why'

What lips my lips have kissed, and where, and why,
I have forgotten, and what arms have lain
Under my head till morning; but the rain
Is full of ghosts tonight, that tap and sigh
Upon the glass and listen for reply;
And in my heart there stirs a quiet pain
For unremembered lads that not again
Will turn to me at midnight with a cry.
Thus in the winter stands the lonely tree,
Nor knows what birds have vanished one by one,
Yet knows its boughs more silent than before:
I cannot say what loves have come and gone;
I only know that summer sang in me
A little while, that in me sings no more.

'Hearing your words, and not a word among them'

Hearing your words, and not a word among them
Tuned to my liking, on a salty day
When inland woods were pushed by winds that flung them
Hissing to leeward like a ton of spray,
I thought how off Matinicus the tide
Came pounding in, came running through the Gut,
While from the Rock the warning whistle cried,

And children whimpered, and the doors blew shut;
There in the autumn when the men go forth,
With slapping skirts the island women stand
In gardens stripped and scattered, peering north,
With dahlia tubers dripping from the hand:
The wind of their endurance, driving south,
Flattened your words against your speaking mouth.

Archibald MacLeish 1892 – 1982

Ars Poetica

A poem should be palpable and mute
As a globed fruit,

Dumb
As old medallions to the thumb,

Silent as the sleeve-worn stone
Of casement ledges where the moss has grown –

A poem should be wordless
As the flight of birds.

*

A poem should be motionless in time
As the moon climbs,

Leaving, as the moon releases
Twig by twig the night-entangled trees,

Leaving, as the moon behind the winter leaves,
Memory by memory the mind –

A poem should be motionless in time
As the moon climbs.

*

A poem should be equal to:
Not true.

For all the history of grief
An empty doorway and a maple leaf.

For love
The leaning grasses and two lights above the sea –

A poem should not mean
But be.

The End of the World ; a sonnet

Quite unexpectedly as Vasserot
The armless ambidextrian was lighting
A match between his great and second toe
And Ralph the lion was engaged in biting
The neck of Madame Sossman while the drum
Pointed, and Teeny was about to cough
In waltz-time swinging Jocko by the thumb –
Quite unexpectedly the top blew off:

And there, there overhead, there, there, hung over
Those thousands of white faces, those dazed eyes,
There in the starless dark the poise, the hover,
There with vast wings across the canceled skies,
There in the sudden blackness the black pall
Of nothing, nothing, nothing – nothing at all.

E. E. Cummings 1894 – 1962

'in Just –'

in Just-
spring   when the world is mud-
luscious the little
lame balloonman

whistles   far   and wee

and eddieandbill come
running from marbles and
piracies and it's
spring

when the world is puddle-wonderful

the queer
old balloonman whistles
far   and   wee
and bettyandisbel come dancing

from hop-scotch and jump-rope and

it's
spring
and
  the
    goat-footed

balloonMan   whistles
far
and
wee

'Buffalo Bill's'

Buffalo Bill's
defunct
       who used to
       ride a watersmooth-silver
                    stallion
and break onetwothreefourfive pigeonsjustlikethat
                            Jesus
he was a handsome man
             and what i want to know is
how do you like your blueeyed boy
Mister Death

Poem, or Beauty Hurts Mr Vinal

take it from me kiddo
believe me
my country, 'tis of

you, land of the Cluett
Shirt Boston Garter and Spearmint
Girl With The Wrigley Eyes (of you
land of the Arrow Ide
and Earl &
Wilson
Collars) of you i
sing: land of Abraham Lincoln and Lydia E. Pinkham,
land above all of Just Add Hot Water And Serve –
from every B. V. D.

let freedom ring

amen. i do however protest, anent the un
-spontaneous and otherwise scented merde which
greets one (Everywhere Why) as divine poesy per
that and this radically defunct periodical. i would

suggest that certain ideas gestures
rhymes, like Gillette Razor Blades
having been used and reused
to the mystical moment of dullness emphatically are
Not To Be Resharpened. (Case in point

if we are to believe these gently O sweetly
melancholy trillers amid the thrillers
these crepuscular violinists among my and your
skyscrapers – Helen & Cleopatra were Just Too Lovely,
The Snail's On The Thorn enter Morn and God's
In His andsoforth

do you get me?) according
to such supposedly indigenous
throstles Art is O World O Life
a formula: example, Turn Your Shirttails Into
Drawers and If It Isn't An Eastman It Isn't A
Kodak therefore my friends let
us now sing each and all fortissimo A-
mer
i

ca, I
love,
You. And there're a
hun-dred-mil-lion-oth-ers, like
all of you successfully if
delicately gelded (or spaded)
gentlemen (and ladies) – pretty

littleliverpill-
hearted-Nujolneeding-There's-A-Reason
americans (who tensetendoned and with
upward vacant eyes, painfully
perpetually crouched, quivering, upon the
sternly allotted sandpile
– how silently
emit a tiny violetflavoured nuisance: Odor?

ono.
comes out like a ribbon lies flat on the brush

'she being Brand'

she being Brand

-new;and you
now consequently a
little stiff i was
careful of her and(having

thoroughly oiled the universal
joint tested my gas felt of
her radiator made sure her springs were O.

K.)i went right to it flooded-the-carburetor cranked her

up,slipped the
clutch(and then somehow got into reverse she
kicked what
the hell)next
minute i was back in neutral tried and

again slo-wly;bare,ly nudg.   ing(my

lev-er Right-
oh and her gears being in
A 1 shape passed
from low through
second-in-to-high like
greasedlightning)just as we turned the corner of Divinity

avenue i touched the accelerator and give

her the juice,good

                (it
was the first ride and believe i we was
happy to see how nice she acted right up to
the last minute coming back down by the Public
Gardens i slammed on
the

internalexpanding
&
externalcontracting
brakes Bothatonce and

brought allofher tremB
-ling
to a:dead.

stand-
;Still)

'my sweet old etcetera'

my sweet old etcetera
aunt lucy during the recent

war could and what
is more did tell you just
what everybody was fighting

for,
my sister

isabel created hundreds
(and
hundreds)of socks not to
mention shirts fleaproof earwarmers

etcetera wristers etcetera, my
mother hoped that

i would die etcetera
bravely of course my father used
to become hoarse talking about how it was
a privilege and if only he
could meanwhile my

self etcetetera lay quietly
in the deep mud et

cetera
(dreaming,
et
    cetera, of
Your smile
eyes knees and of your Etcetera)

'this little bride & groom are'

this little bride & groom are
standing) in a kind
of crown he dressed
in black candy she

veiled with candy white
carrying a bouquet of
pretend flowers this
candy crown with this candy

little bride & little
groom in it kind of stands on
a thin ring which stands on a much
less thin very much more

big & kinder of ring & which
kinder of stands on a
much more than very much
biggest & thickest & kindest

of ring & all one two three rings
are cake & everything is protected by
cellophane against anything (because
nothing really exists

'anyone lived in a pretty how town'

anyone lived in a pretty how town
(with up so floating many bells down)
spring summer autumn winter
he sang his didn't he danced his did.

Women and men(both little and small)
cared for anyone not at all
they sowed their isn't they reaped their same
sun moon stars rain

children guessed(but only a few
and down they forgot as up they grew
autumn winter spring summer)
that noone loved him more by more

when by now and tree by leaf
she laughed his joy she cried his grief
bird by snow and stir by still
anyone's any was all to her

someones married their everyones
laughed their cryings and did their dance
(sleep wake hope and then)they
said their nevers they slept their dream

stars rain sun moon
(and only the snow can begin to explain
how children are apt to forget to remember
with up so floating many bells down)

one day anyone died i guess
(and noone stooped to kiss his face)
busy folk buried them side by side
little by little and was by was

all by all and deep by deep
and more by more they dream their sleep
noone and anyone earth by april
wish by spirit and if by yes.

Women and men(both dong and ding)
summer autumn winter spring
reaped their sowing and went their came
sun moon stars rain

'my father moved through dooms of love'

my father moved through dooms of love
through sames of am through haves of give,
singing each morning out of each night
my father moved through depths of height

this motionless forgetful where
turned at his glance to shining here;
that if(so timid air is firm)
under his eyes would stir and squirm

newly as from unburied which
floats the first who,his april touch
drove sleeping selves to swarm their fates
woke dreamers to their ghostly roots

and should some why completely weep
my father's fingers brought her sleep:
vainly no smallest voice might cry
for he could feel the mountains grow.

Lifting the valleys of the sea
my father moved through griefs of joy;
praising a forehead called the moon
singing desire into begin

joy was his song and joy so pure
a heart of star by him could steer
and pure so now and now so yes
the wrists of twilight would rejoice

keen as midsummer's keen beyond
conceiving mind of sun will stand,
so strictly(over utmost him
so hugely)stood my father's dream

his flesh was flesh his blood was blood:
no hungry man but wished him food;
no cripple wouldn't creep one mile
uphill to only see him smile.

Scorning the pomp of must and shall
my father moved through dooms of feel;
his anger was as right as rain
his pity was as green as grain

septembering arms of year extend
less humbly wealth to foe and friend
than he to foolish and to wise
offered immeasurable is

proudly and(by octobering flame
beckoned)as earth will downward climb,
so naked for immortal work
his shoulders marched against the dark

his sorrow was as true as bread:
no liar looked him in the head;
if every friend became his foe
he'd laugh and build a world with snow.

My father moved through theys of we,
singing each new leaf out of each tree
(and every child was sure that spring
danced when she heard my father sing)

then let men kill which cannot share,
let blood and flesh be mud and mire,
scheming imagine,passion willed,
freedom a drug that's bought and sold

giving to steal and cruel kind,
a heart to fear,to doubt a mind,
to differ a disease of same,
conform the pinnacle of am

though dull were all we taste as bright,
bitter all utterly things sweet,
maggoty minus and dumb death
all we inherit,all bequeath

and nothing quite so least as truth
– i say though hate were why men breathe –
because my father lived his soul
love is the whole and more than all

'ygUDuh'

ygUDuh

    ydoan
    yunnuhstan

    ydoan o
    yunnuhstan dem
    yguduh ged

> yunnuhstan dem doidee
> yguduh ged riduh
> ydoan o nudn
LISN bud LISN

> > dem
> > gud
> > am
> >
> > lidl yelluh bas
> > tuds weer goin

duhSIVILEYEzum

'plato told'

plato told

him:he couldn't
believe it(jesus

told him;he
wouldn't believe

it)lao

tsze
certainly told
him,and general
(yes

mam)
sherman;
and even
(believe it
or

not)you
told him:i told
him;we told him
(he didn't believe it,no

sir)it took
a nipponized bit of
the old sixth

avenue
el;in the top of his head:to tell

him

'i thank You God for most this amazing'

i thank You God for most this amazing
day:for the leaping greenly spirits of trees
and a blue true dream of sky;and for everything
which is natural which is infinite which is yes

(i who have died am alive again today,
and this is the sun's birthday; this is the birth
day of life and of love and wings:and of the gay
great happening illimitably earth)

how should tasting touching hearing seeing
breathing any -- lifted from the no
of all nothing -- human merely being
doubt unimaginable You?

(now the ears of my ears awake and
now the eyes of my eyes are opened)

'the little horse is newlY'

the little horse is newlY

Born)he knows nothing,and feels
everything;all around whom is

perfectly a strange
ness Of sun
light and of fragrance and of

Singing)is ev
erywhere(a welcom
ing dream:is amazing)
a worlD.and in

this world lies:smoothbeautifuL
ly folded;a(brea
thing and a gro

Wing)silence, who;
is:somE

oNe.

Hart Crane 1899–1932

Voyages

I

Above the fresh ruffles of the surf
Bright striped urchins flay each other with sand.
They have contrived a conquest for shell shucks,
And their fingers crumble fragments of baked weed
Gaily digging and scattering.

And in answer to their treble interjections
The sun beats lightning on the waves,
The waves fold thunder on the sand;
And could they hear me I would tell them:

O brilliant kids, frisk with your dog,
Fondle your shells and sticks, bleached
By time and the elements; but there is a line
You must not cross nor ever trust beyond it
Spry cordage of your bodies to caresses
Too lichen-faithful from too wide a breast.
The bottom of the sea is cruel.

II

– And yet this great wink of eternity,
Of rimless floods, unfettered leewardings,
Samite sheeted and processioned where
Her undinal vast belly moonward bends,
Laughing the wrapt inflections of our love;

Take this Sea, whose diapason knells
On scrolls of silver snowy sentences,
The sceptred terror of whose sessions rends
As her demeanors motion well or ill,
All but the pieties of lovers' hands.

And onward, as bells off San Salvador
Salute the crocus lustres of the stars,
In these poinsettia meadows of her tides, –
Adagios of islands, O my Prodigal,
Complete the dark confessions her veins spell.

Mark how her turning shoulders wind the hours,
And hasten while her penniless rich palms
Pass superscription of bent foam and wave, –
Hasten, while they are true, – sleep, death, desire,
Close round one instant in one floating flower.

Bind us in time, O Seasons clear, and awe.
O minstrel galleons of Carib fire,
Bequeath us to no earthly shore until
Is answered in the vortex of our grave
The seal's wide spindrift gaze toward paradise.

III

Infinite consanguinity it bears –
This tendered theme of you that light
Retrieves from sea plains where the sky
Resigns a breast that every wave enthrones;
While ribboned water lanes I wind
Are laved and scattered with no stroke
Wide from your side, whereto this hour
The sea lifts, also, reliquary hands.

And so, admitted through black swollen gates
That must arrest all distance otherwise, –

Past whirling pillars and lithe pediments,
Light wrestling there incessantly with light,
Star kissing star through wave on wave unto
Your body rocking!
                and where death, if shed,
Presumes no carnage, but this single change, –
Upon the steep floor flung from dawn to dawn
The silken skilled transmemberment of song;

Permit me voyage, love, into your hands . . .

IV

Whose counted smile of hours and days, suppose
I know as spectrum of the sea and pledge
Vastly now parting gulf on gulf of wings
Whose circles bridge, I know, (from palms to the severe
Chilled albatross's white immutability)
No stream of greater love advancing now
Than, singing, this mortality alone
Through clay aflow immortally to you.

All fragrance irrefragibly, and claim
Madly meeting logically in this hour
And region that is ours to wreathe again,
Portending eyes and lips and making told
The chancel port and portion of our June –

Shall they not stem and close in our own steps
Bright staves of flowers and quills to-day as I
Must first be lost in fatal tides to tell?

In signature of the incarnate word
The harbor shoulders to resign in mingling
Mutual blood, transpiring as foreknown

And widening noon within your breast for gathering
All bright insinuations that my years have caught
For islands where must lead inviolably
Blue latitudes and levels of your eyes, –

In this expectant, still exclaim receive
The secret oar and petals of all love.

V

Meticulous, past midnight in clear rime,
Infrangible and lonely, smooth as though cast
Together in one merciless white blade –
The bay estuaries fleck the hard sky limits.

– As if too brittle or too clear to touch!
The cables of our sleep so swiftly filed,
Already hang, shred ends from remembered stars.
One frozen trackless smile . . . What words
Can strangle this deaf moonlight? For we

Are overtaken. Now no cry, no sword
Can fasten or deflect this tidal wedge,
Slow tyranny of moonlight, moonlight loved
And changed . . . 'There's

Nothing like this in the world,' you say,
Knowing I cannot touch your hand and look
Too, into that godless cleft of sky
Where nothing turns but dead sands flashing.

'– And never to quite understand!' No,
In all the argosy of your bright hair I dreamed
Nothing so flagless as this piracy.

But now
Draw in your head, alone and too tall here.
Your eyes already in the slant of drifting foam;
Your breath sealed by the ghosts I do not know:
Draw in your head and sleep the long way home.

VI

Where icy and bright dungeons lift
Of swimmers their lost morning eyes,
And ocean rivers, churning, shift
Green borders under stranger skies,

Steadily as a shell secretes
Its beating leagues of monotone,
Or as many waters trough the sun's
Red kelson past the cape's wet stone;

O rivers mingling toward the sky
And harbor of the phœnix' breast –
My eyes pressed black against the prow,
– Thy derelict and blinded guest

Waiting, afire, what name, unspoke,
I cannot claim: let thy waves rear
More savage than the death of kings,
Some splintered garland for the seer.

Beyond siroccos harvesting
The solstice thunders, crept away,
Like a cliff swinging or a sail
Flung into April's inmost day –

Creation's blithe and petalled word
To the lounged goddess when she rose
Conceding dialogue with eyes
That smile unsearchable repose –

Still fervid covenant, Belle Isle,
– Unfolded floating dais before
Which rainbows twine continual hair –
Belle Isle, white echo of the oar!

The imaged Word, it is, that holds
Hushed willows anchored in its glow.
It is the unbetrayable reply
Whose accent no farewell can know.

From *The Bridge*

PROEM: TO BROOKLYN BRIDGE

How many dawns, chill from his rippling rest
The seagull's wings shall dip and pivot him,
Shedding white rings of tumult, building high
Over the chained bay waters Liberty –

Then, with inviolate curve, forsake our eyes
As apparitional as sails that cross
Some page of figures to be filed away;
– Till elevators drop us from our day . . .

I think of cinemas, panoramic sleights
With multitudes bent toward some flashing scene
Never disclosed, but hastened to again,
Foretold to other eyes on the same screen;

And Thee, across the harbor, silver-paced
As though the sun took step of thee, yet left
Some motion ever unspent in thy stride, –
Implicitly thy freedom staying thee!

Out of some subway scuttle, cell or loft
A bedlamite speeds to thy parapets,
Tilting there momently, shrill shirt ballooning,
A jest falls from the speechless caravan.

Down Wall, from girder into street noon leaks,
A rip-tooth of the sky's acetylene;
All afternoon the cloud-flown derricks turn ...
Thy cables breathe the North Atlantic still.

And obscure as that heaven of the Jews,
Thy guerdon ... Accolade thou dost bestow
Of anonymity time cannot raise:
Vibrant reprieve and pardon thou dost show.

O harp and altar, of the fury fused,
(How could mere toil align thy choiring strings!)
Terrific threshold of the prophet's pledge,
Prayer of pariah, and the lover's cry, –

Again the traffic lights that skim thy swift
Unfractioned idiom, immaculate sigh of stars,
Beading thy path – condense eternity:
And we have seen night lifted in thine arms.

Under thy shadow by the piers I waited;
Only in darkness is thy shadow clear.
The City's fiery parcels all undone,
Already snow submerges an iron year ...

O Sleepless as the river under thee,
Vaulting the sea, the prairies' dreaming sod,
Unto us lowliest sometime sweep, descend
And of the curveship lend a myth to God.

THE RIVER

Stick your patent name on a signboard
brother – all over – going west – young man
Tintex – Japalac – Certain-teed Overalls ads
and land sakes! under the new playbill ripped
in the guaranteed corner – see Bert Williams what?
Minstrels when you steal a chicken just
save me the wing for if it isn't
Erie it ain't for miles around a
Mazda – and the telegraphic night coming on Thomas

*... and past
the din and
slogans of
the year –*

a Ediford – and whistling down the tracks
a headlight rushing with the sound – can you
imagine – while an EXPRESS makes time like
SCIENCE – COMMERCE and the HOLYGHOST
RADIO ROARS IN EVERY HOME WE HAVE THE NORTHPOLE
WALLSTREET AND VIRGINBIRTH WITHOUT STONES OR
WIRES OR EVEN RUNNing brooks connecting ears
and no more sermons windows flashing roar
Breathtaking – as you like it ... eh?

　　　So the 20th Century – so
whizzed the Limited – roared by and left
three men, still hungry on the tracks, ploddingly
watching the tail lights wizen and converge, slip-
ping gimleted and neatly out of sight.

*

393

The last bear, shot drinking in the Dakotas
Loped under wires that span the mountain stream.
Keen instruments, strung to a vast precision
Bind town to town and dream to ticking dream.   to those
But some men take their liquor slow – and count   whose
– Though they'll confess no rosary nor clue –   addresses are
The river's minute by the far brook's year.   never near
Under a world of whistles, wires and steam
Caboose-like they go ruminating through
Ohio, Indiana – blind baggage –
To Cheyenne tagging . . . Maybe Kalamazoo.

Time's rendings, time's blendings they construe
As final reckonings of fire and snow;
Strange bird-wit, like the elemental gist
Of unwalled winds they offer, singing low
My Old Kentucky Home and *Casey Jones*,
Some Sunny Day. I heard a road-gang chanting so.
And afterwards, who had a colt's eyes – one said,
'Jesus! Oh I remember watermelon days!' And sped
High in a cloud of merriment, recalled
'– And when my Aunt Sally Simpson smiled,' he drawled –
'It was almost Louisiana, long ago.'

'There's no place like Booneville though, Buddy,'
One said, excising a last burr from his vest,
'– For early trouting.' Then peering in the can,
'– But I kept on the tracks.' Possessed, resigned,
He trod the fire down pensively and grinned,
Spreading dry shingles of a beard . . .

                              Behind
My father's cannery works I used to see
Rail-squatters ranged in nomad raillery,
The ancient men – wifeless or runaway
Hobo-trekkers that forever search

An empire wilderness of freight and rails.
Each seemed a child, like me, on a loose perch,
Holding to childhood like some termless play.
John, Jake or Charley, hopping the slow freight
– Memphis to Tallahassee – riding the rods,
Blind fists of nothing, humpty-dumpty clods.

Yet they touch something like a key perhaps.
From pole to pole across the hills, the states
– They know a body under the wide rain;   but who have
Youngsters with eyes like fjords, old reprobates   touched her,
With racetrack jargon, – dotting immensity   knowing her
They lurk across her, knowing her yonder breast   without name
Snow-silvered, sumac-stained or smoky blue –
Is past the valley-sleepers, south or west.
– As I have trod the rumorous midnights, too,

And past the circuit of the lamp's thin flame
(O Nights that brought me to her body bare!)
Have dreamed beyond the print that bound her name.
Trains sounding the long blizzards out – I heard
Wail into distances I knew were hers.
Papooses crying on the wind's long mane
Screamed redskin dynasties that fled the brain,
– Dead echoes! But I knew her body there,
Time like a serpent down her shoulder, dark,
And space, an eaglet's wing, laid on her hair.

Under the Ozarks, domed by Iron Mountain,
The old gods of the rain lie wrapped in pools
Where eyeless fish curvet a sunken fountain   nor the
And re-descend with corn from querulous crows.   myths of her
Such pilferings make up their timeless eatage,   fathers . . .
Propitiate them for their timber torn
By iron, iron – always the iron dealt cleavage!
They doze now, below axe and powder horn.

And Pullman breakfasters glide glistening steel
From tunnel into field – iron strides the dew –
Straddles the hill, a dance of wheel on wheel.
You have a half-hour's wait at Siskiyou,
Or stay the night and take the next train through.
Southward, near Cairo passing, you can see
The Ohio merging, – borne down Tennessee;
And if it's summer and the sun's in dusk
Maybe the breeze will lift the River's musk
– As though the waters breathed that you might know
Memphis Johnny, Steamboat Bill, Missouri Joe.
Oh, lean from the window, if the train slows down,
As though you touched hands with some ancient clown,
– A little while gaze absently below
And hum *Deep River* with them while they go.

Yes, turn again and sniff once more – look see,
O Sheriff, Brakeman and Authority –
Hitch up your pants and crunch another quid,
For you, too, feed the River timelessly.
And few evade full measure of their fate;
Always they smile out eerily what they seem.
I could believe he joked at heaven's gate –
Dan Midland – jolted from the cold brake-beam.

Down, down – born pioneers in time's despite,
Grimed tributaries to an ancient flow –
They win no frontier by their wayward plight,
But drift in stillness, as from Jordan's brow.

You will not hear it as the sea; even stone
Is not more hushed by gravity . . . But slow,
As loth to take more tribute – sliding prone
Like one whose eyes were buried long ago

The River, spreading, flows – and spends your dream.
What are you, lost within this tideless spell?
You are your father's father, and the stream –
A liquid theme that floating niggers swell.

Damp tonnage and alluvial march of days –
Nights turbid, vascular with silted shale
And roots surrendered down of moraine clays:
The Mississippi drinks the farthest dale.

O quarrying passion, undertowed sunlight!
The basalt surface drags a jungle grace
Ochreous and lynx-barred in lengthening might;
Patience! and you shall reach the biding place!

Over De Soto's bones the freighted floors
Throb past the City storied of three thrones.
Down two more turns the Mississippi pours
(Anon tall ironsides up from salt lagoons)

And flows within itself, heaps itself free.
All fades but one thin skyline 'round . . . Ahead
No embrace opens but the stinging sea;
The River lifts itself from its long bed,

Poised wholly on its dream, a mustard glow
Tortured with history, its one will – flow!
– The Passion spreads in wide tongues, choked and slow,
Meeting the Gulf, hosannas silently below.

Ernest Hemingway 1899–1961

Oklahoma

All of the Indians are dead
(a good Indian is a dead Indian)
Or riding in motor cars –
(the oil lands, you know, they're all rich)
Smoke smarts my eyes,
Cottonwood twigs and buffalo dung
Smoke grey in the tepee –
(or is it my myopic trachoma)

The prairies are long,
The moon rises
Ponies
Drag at their pickets.
The grass has gone brown in the summer –
(or is it the hay crop failing)

Pull an arrow out:
If you break it
The wound closes.
Salt is good too
And wood ashes.
Pounding it throbs in the night –
(or is it the gonorrhea)

The Ernest Liberal's Lament

I know monks masturbate at night
That pet cats screw
That some girls bite
And yet
What can I do
To set things right?

Allen Tate 1899 –

Ode to the Confederate Dead

Row after row with strict impunity
The headstones yield their names to the element,
The wind whirrs without recollection;
In the riven troughs the splayed leaves
Pile up, of nature the casual sacrament
To the seasonal eternity of death;
Then driven by the fierce scrutiny
Of heaven to their election in the vast breath,
They sough the rumour of mortality.

Autumn is desolation in the plot
Of a thousand acres where these memories grow
From the inexhaustible bodies that are not
Dead, but feed the grass row after rich row.
Think of the autumns that have come and gone! –
Ambitious November with the humors of the year,
With a particular zeal for every slab,
Staining the uncomfortable angels that rot
On the slabs, a wing chipped here, an arm there:
The brute curiosity of an angel's stare
Turns you, like them, to stone,
Transforms the heaving air
Till plunged to a heavier world below
You shift your sea-space blindly
Heaving, turning like the blind crab.

Dazed by the wind, only the wind
The leaves flying, plunge

You know who have waited by the wall
The twilight certainty of an animal,
Those midnight restitutions of the blood
You know – the immitigable pines, the smoky frieze
Of the sky, the sudden call: you know the rage,
The cold pool left by the mounting flood,
Of muted Zeno and Parmenides.
You who have waited for the angry resolution
Of those desires that should be yours tomorrow,
You know the unimportant shrift of death
And praise the vision
And praise the arrogant circumstance
Of those who fall
Rank upon rank, hurried beyond decision –
Here by the sagging gate, stopped by the wall.

Seeing, seeing only the leaves
Flying, plunge and expire

Turn your eyes to the immoderate past,
Turn to the inscrutable infantry rising
Demons out of the earth – they will not last.
Stonewall, Stonewall, and the sunken fields of hemp,
Shiloh, Antietam, Malvern Hill, Bull Run.
Lost in that orient of the thick-and-fast
You will curse the setting sun.

Cursing only the leaves crying
Like an old man in a storm

You hear the shout, the crazy hemlocks point
With troubled fingers to the silence which
Smothers you, a mummy, in time.

                              The hound bitch
Toothless and dying, in a musty cellar
Hears the wind only.

                    Now that the salt of their blood
Stiffens the saltier oblivion of the sea,
Seals the malignant purity of the flood,
What shall we who count our days and bow
Our heads with a commemorial woe
In the ribboned coats of grim felicity,
What shall we say of the bones, unclean,
Whose verdurous anonymity will grow?
The ragged arms, the ragged heads and eyes
Lost in these acres of the insane green?
The gray lean spiders come, they come and go;
In a tangle of willows without light
The singular screech-owl's tight
Invisible lyric seeds the mind
With the furious murmur of their chivalry.

   We shall say only the leaves
   Flying, plunge and expire

We shall say only the leaves whispering
In the improbable mist of nightfall
That flies on multiple wing;
Night is the beginning and the end
And in between the ends of distraction
Waits mute speculation, the patient curse
That stones the eyes, or like the jaguar leaps
For his own image in a jungle pool, his victim.

What shall we say who have knowledge
Carried to the heart? Shall we take the act
To the grave? Shall we, more hopeful, set up the grave
In the house? The ravenous grave?

                                        Leave now
The shut gate and the decomposing wall:
The gentle serpent, green in the mulberry bush,
Riots with his tongue through the hush –
Sentinel of the grave who counts us all!

Kenneth Fearing 1902–61

Dirge

1-2-3 was the number he played but today the number came 3-2-1;
Bought his Carbide at 30 and it went to 29; had the favorite at Bowie
    but the track was slow –

O executive type, would you like to drive a floating-power, knee-
    action, silk-upholstered six? Wed a Hollywood star? Shoot the
    course in 58? Draw to the ace, king, jack?
O fellow with a will who won't take no, watch out for three cigarettes
    on the same, single match; O democratic voter born in August
    under Mars, beware of liquidated rails –

Denouement to denouement, he took a personal pride in the certain,
    certain way he lived his own, private life,
But nevertheless, they shut off his gas; nevertheless, the bank fore-
    closed; nevertheless, the landlord called; nevertheless, the radio
    broke,

And twelve o'clock arrived just once too often,
Just the same he wore one gray tweed suit, bought one straw hat,
    drank one straight Scotch, walked one short step, took one long
    look, drew one deep breath,
Just one too many,

And wow he died as wow he lived,
Going whop to the office and blooie home to sleep and biff got
    married and bam had children and oof got fired,
Zowie did he live and zowie did he die,

With who the hell are you at the corner of his casket, and where the
hell're we going on the right-hand silver knob, and who the hell
cares walking second from the end with an American Beauty
wreath from why the hell not,

Very much missed by the circulation staff of the New York Evening
Post; deeply, deeply mourned by the B.M.T.

Wham, Mr Roosevelt; pow, Sears Roebuck; awk, big dipper; bop,
summer rain;
Bong, Mr, bong, Mr, bong, Mr, bong.

Langston Hughes 1902–67

Brass Spittoons

Clean the spittoons, boy.
   Detroit,
   Chicago,
   Atlantic City,
   Palm Beach.
Clean the spittoons.
The steam in hotel kitchens,
And the smoke in hotel lobbies,
And the slime in hotel spittoons:
Part of my life.
   Hey, boy!
   A nickel,
   A dime,
   A dollar,
Two dollars a day.
   Hey, boy!
   A nickel,
   A dime,
   A dollar,
   Two dollars
Buy shoes for the baby.
House rent to pay.
Gin on Saturday,
Church on Sunday.
   My God!
Babies and gin and church
And women and Sunday
All mixed with dimes and

Dollars and clean spittoons
And house rent to pay.
  Hey, boy!
A bright bowl of brass is beautiful to the Lord.
Bright polished brass like the cymbals
Of King David's dancers,
Like the wine cups of Solomon.
  Hey, boy!
A clean spittoon on the altar of the Lord.
A clean bright spittoon all newly-polished –
At least I can offer that.
  Com'mere, boy!

Theme for English B

The instructor said,

  Go home and write
  a page tonight.
  And let that page come out of you –
  Then, it will be true.

I wonder if it's that simple?
I am twenty-two, colored, born in Winston-Salem.
I went to school there, then Durham, then here
to this college on the hill above Harlem.
I am the only colored student in my class.
The steps from the hill lead down into Harlem,
through a park, then I cross St Nicholas,
Eighth Avenue, Seventh, and I come to the Y,
the Harlem Branch Y, where I take the elevator
up to my room, sit down, and write this page:

It's not easy to know what is true for you or me
at twenty-two, my age. But I guess I'm what
I feel and see and hear, Harlem, I hear you:
hear you, hear me – we two – you, me, talk on this page.
(I hear New York, too.) Me – who?

Well, I like to eat, sleep, drink, and be in love.
I like to work, read, learn, and understand life.
I like a pipe for a Christmas present,
or records – Bessie, bop, or Bach.
I guess being colored doesn't make me *not* like
the same things other folks like who are other races.
So will my page be colored that I write?

Being me, it will not be white.
But it will be
a part of you, instructor.
You are white –
yet a part of me, as I am a part of you.
That's American.
Sometimes perhaps you don't want to be a part of me.
Nor do I often want to be a part of you.
But we are, that's true!
As I learn from you,
I guess you learn from me –
although you're older – and white –
and somewhat more free.

This is my page for English B.

Ogden Nash 1902—71

You Bet Travel is Broadening

Doctors tell me that some people wonder who they are, they don't
    know if they are Peter Pumpkin-eater or Priam,
But I know who I am.
My identity is no mystery to unravel,
Because I know who I am, especially when I travel.
I am he who lies either over or under the inevitable snores,
I am he who the air conditioning is in conflict with whose pores,
I am he whom the dear little old ladies who have left their pocketbooks
    on the bureau at home invariably approach,
And he whom the argumentative tippler oozes in beside though there
    are thirty empty seats in the coach.
I am he who finds himself reading comics to somebody else's children
    while the harassed mother attends to the youngest's needs,
Ending up with candy bar on the lapel of whose previously fautlless
    tweeds.
I am he in the car full of students celebrating victory with instruments
    saxophonic and ukulelean,
And he who, speaking only English, is turned to for aid by the non-
    English-speaking alien.
I am he who, finding himself the occupant of one Pullman space that
    has been sold twice, next finds himself playing Santa,
Because it was sold the second time to an elderly invalid, so there is no
    question about who is going to sit in the washroom from
    Philadelphia to Atlanta.
I guess I am he who if he had his own private car
Would be jockeyed into sharing the master bedroom with a man with
    a five-cent cigar.

Very Like a Whale

One thing that literature would be greatly the better for

Would be a more restricted employment by authors of simile and metaphor.

Authors of all races, be they Greeks, Romans, Teutons or Celts,

Can't seem just to say that anything is the thing it is but have to go out of their way to say that it is like something else.

What does it mean when we are told

That the Assyrian came down like a wolf on the fold?

In the first place, George Gordon Byron had had enough experience

To know that it probably wasn't just one Assyrian, it was a lot of Assyrians.

However, as too many arguments are apt to induce apoplexy and thus hinder longevity,

We'll let it pass as one Assyrian for the sake of brevity.

Now then, this particular Assyrian, the one whose cohorts were gleaming in purple and gold,

Just what does the poet mean when he says he came down like a wolf on the fold?

In heaven and earth more than is dreamed of in our philosophy there are a great many things,

But I don't imagine that among them there is a wolf with purple and gold cohorts or purple and gold anythings.

No, no, Lord Byron, before I'll believe that this Assyrian was actually like a wolf I must have some kind of proof;

Did he run on all fours and did he have a hairy tail and a big red mouth and big white teeth and did he say Woof woof woof?

Frankly I think it very unlikely, and all you were entitled to say, at the very most,

Was that the Assyrian cohorts came down like a lot of Assyrian cohorts about to destroy the Hebrew host.

But that wasn't fancy enough for Lord Byron, oh dear me no, he had to invent a lot of figures of speech and then interpolate them.

With the result that whenever you mention Old Testament soldiers
    to people they say Oh yes, they're the ones that a lot of wolves
    dressed up in gold and purple ate them.

That's the kind of thing that's being done all the time by poets, from
    Homer to Tennyson;

They're always comparing ladies to lilies and veal to venison,

And they always say things like that the snow is a white blanket after
    a winter storm.

Oh it is, is it, all right then, you sleep under a six-inch blanket of snow
    and I'll sleep under a half-inch blanket of unpoetical blanket
    material and we'll see which one keeps warm,

And after that maybe you'll begin to comprehend dimly

What I mean by too much metaphor and simile.

Countee Cullen 1903–46

Heritage

(FOR HAROLD JACKMAN)

What is Africa to me:
Copper sun or scarlet sea,
Jungle star or jungle track,
Strong bronzed men, or regal black
Women from whose loins I sprang
When the birds of Eden sang?
One three centuries removed
From the scenes his fathers loved,
Spicy grove, cinnamon tree,
What is Africa to me?

So I lie, who all day long
Want no sound except the song
Sung by wild barbaric birds
Goading massive jungle herds,
Juggernauts of flesh that pass
Trampling tall defiant grass
Where young forest lovers lie,
Plighting troth beneath the sky.
So I lie, who always hear,
Though I cram against my ear
Both my thumbs, and keep them there,
Great drums throbbing through the air.
So I lie, whose fount of pride,
Dear distress, and joy allied,
Is my somber flesh and skin,
With the dark blood dammed within

Like great pulsing tides of wine
That, I fear, must burst the fine
Channels of the chafing net
Where they surge and foam and fret.

Africa? A book one thumbs
Listlessly, till slumber comes.
Unremembered are her bats
Circling through the night, her cats
Crouching in the river reeds,
Stalking gentle flesh that feeds
By the river brink; no more
Does the bugle-throated roar
Cry that monarch claws have leapt
From the scabbards where they slept.
Silver snakes that once a year
Doff the lovely coats you wear,
Seek no covert in your fear
Lest a mortal eye should see;
What's your nakedness to me?
Here no leprous flowers rear
Fierce corollas in the air;
Here no bodies sleek and wet,
Dripping mingled rain and sweat,
Tread the savage measures of
Jungle boys and girls in love.
What is last year's snow to me,
Last year's anything? The tree
Budding yearly must forget
How its past arose or set —
Bough and blossom, flower, fruit,
Even what shy bird with mute
Wonder at her travail there,
Meekly labored in its hair.
One three centuries removed
From the scenes his fathers loved,

Spicy grove, cinnamon tree,
What is Africa to me?

So I lie, who find no peace
Night or day, no slight release
From the unremittent beat
Made by cruel padded feet
Walking through my body's street.
Up and down they go, and back,
Treading out a jungle track.
So I lie, who never quite
Safely sleep from rain at night –
I can never rest at all
When the rain begins to fall;
Like a soul gone mad with pain
I must match its weird refrain;
Ever must I twist and squirm,
Writhing like a baited worm,
While its primal measures drip
Through my body, crying, 'Strip!
Doff this new exuberance.
Come and dance the Lover's Dance!'
In an old remembered way
Rain works on me night and day.

Quaint, outlandish heathen gods
Black men fashion out of rods,
Clay, and brittle bits of stone,
In a likeness like their own,
My conversion came high-priced;
I belong to Jesus Christ,
Preacher of humility;
Heathen gods are naught to me.

Father, Son, and Holy Ghost,
So I make an idle boast;

Jesus of the twice-turned cheek,
Lamb of God, although I speak
With my mouth thus, in my heart
Do I play a double part.
Ever at Thy glowing altar
Must my heart grow sick and falter,
Wishing He I served were black,
Thinking then it would not lack
Precedent of pain to guide it,
Let who would or might deride it;
Surely then this flesh would know
Yours had borne a kindred woe.
Lord, I fashion dark gods, too,
Daring even to give You
Dark despairing features where,
Crowned with dark rebellious hair,
Patience wavers just so much as
Mortal grief compels, while touches
Quick and hot, of anger, rise
To smitten cheek and weary eyes.
Lord, forgive me if my need
Sometimes shapes a human creed.
All day long and all night through,
One thing only must I do:
Quench my pride and cool my blood,
Lest I perish in the flood.
Lest a hidden ember set
Timber that I thought was wet
Burning like the dryest flax,
Melting like the merest wax,
Lest the grave restore its dead.
Nor yet has my heart or head
In the least way realized
They and I are civilized.

Louis Zukofsky 1904–78

'Tall and singularly dark you pass among the breakers'

Tall and singularly dark you pass among the breakers –
Companionship as of another world bordering on this;
To the intelligence fastened by the senses you are lost
In a world of sunlight where nothing is amiss:

For nothing but the sun is there and peace vital with the sun,
The heaviest changes shift through no feature more than a smile,
Currents spread, and are gone, and as the high waves appear,
You dive, in the calming are as lost awhile.

How in that while intelligence escapes from sense
And fear with hurled human might darkens upon bliss!
Till as again you stand above the waters,
Fear turns to sleep as one who dreamt of falling, an abyss!

Catullus viii

Miserable Catullus, stop being foolish
And admit it's over,
The sun shone on you those days
When your girl had you
When you gave it to her
            like nobody else ever will.
Everywhere together then, always at it
And you liked it and she can't say
                        she didn't

Yes, those days glowed.
Now she doesn't want it: why
          should you, washed out
Want to. Don't trail her,
Don't eat yourself up alive,
Show some spunk, stand up
                and take it.
So long, girl. Catullus
             can take it.
He won't bother you, he won't
            be bothered:
But you'll be, nights.
What do you want to live for?
Whom will you see?
Who'll say you're pretty?
Who'll give it to you now?
Whose name will you have?
Kiss what guy? bite whose
                   lips?
Come on Catullus, you can
            take it.

Richard Eberhart 1904–

The Fury of Aerial Bombardment

You would think the fury of aerial bombardment
Would rouse God to relent; the infinite spaces
Are still silent. He looks on shock-pried faces.
History, even, does not know what is meant.

You would feel that after so many centuries
God would give man to repent; yet he can kill
As Cain could, but with multitudinous will,
No farther advanced than in his ancient furies.

Was man made stupid to see his own stupidity?
Is God by definition indifferent, beyond us all?
Is the eternal truth man's fighting soul
Wherein the Beast ravens in its own avidity?

Of Van Wettering I speak, and Averill,
Names on a list, whose faces I do not recall
But they are gone to early death, who late in school
Distinguished the belt feed lever from the belt holding pawl.

'If I could only live at the pitch that is near madness'

If I could only live at the pitch that is near madness
When everything is as it was in my childhood
Violent, vivid, and of infinite possibility:
That the sun and the moon broke over my head.

Then I cast time out of the trees and fields,
Then I stood immaculate in the Ego;
Then I eyed the world with all delight,
Reality was the perfection of my sight.

And time has big handles on the hands,
Fields and trees a way of being themselves.
I saw battalions of the race of mankind
Standing stolid, demanding a moral answer.

I gave the moral answer and I died
And into a realm of complexity came
Where nothing is possible but necessity
And the truth wailing there like a red babe.

Kenneth Rexroth 1905 –

The Bad Old Days

The summer of nineteen eighteen
I read *The Jungle* and *The
Research Magnificent*. That fall
My father died and my aunt
Took me to Chicago to live.
The first thing I did was to take
A streetcar to the stockyards.
In the winter afternoon,
Gritty and fetid, I walked
Through the filthy snow, through the
Squalid streets, looking shyly
Into the people's faces,
Those who were home in the daytime.
Debauched and exhausted faces,
Starved and looted brains, faces
Like the faces in the senile
And insane wards of charity
Hospitals. Predatory
Faces of little children.
Then as the soiled twilight darkened,
Under the green gas lamps, and the
Sputtering purple arc lamps,
The faces of the men coming
Home from work, some still alive with
The last pulse of hope or courage,
Some sly and bitter, some smart and
Silly, most of them, already
Broken and empty, no life,

Only blinding tiredness, worse
Than any tired animal.
The sour smells of a thousand
Suppers of fried potatoes and
Fried cabbage bled into the street.
I was giddy and sick, and out
Of my misery I felt rising
A terrible anger and out
Of the anger, an absolute vow.
Today the evil is clean
And prosperous, but it is
Everywhere, you don't have to
Take a streetcar to find it,
And it is the same evil.
And the misery, and the
Anger, and the vow are the same.

Robert Penn Warren 1905 –

From *Promises*
VIII FOUNDING FATHERS, NINETEENTH-CENTURY STYLE, SOUTHEAST U.S.A.

They were human, they suffered, wore long black coat and gold
    watch chain.
They stare from daguerreotype with severe reprehension,
Or from genuine oil, and you'd never guess any pain
In those merciless eyes that now remark our own time's sad declension.

Some composed declarations, remembering Jefferson's language.
Knew pose of the patriot, left hand in crook of the spine or
With finger to table, while right invokes the Lord's just rage.
There was always a grandpa, or cousin at least, who had been, of
    course, a real Signer.

Some were given to study, read Greek in the forest, and these
Longed for an epic to do their own deeds right honor:
Were Nestor by pigpen, in some tavern brawl played Achilles.
In the ring of Sam Houston they found, when he died, one word
    engraved: *Honor.*

Their children were broadcast, like millet seed flung in a wind-flare.
Wives died, were dropped like old shirts in some corner of country.
Said, 'Mister,' in bed, the child-bride; hadn't known what to find
    there;
Wept all the next morning for shame; took pleasure in silk; wore the
    keys to the pantry.

'Will die in these ditches if need be,' wrote Bowie, at the Alamo.
And did, he whose left foot, soft-catting, came forward, and breath
    hissed:
Head back, gray eyes narrow, thumb flat along knife-blade, blade low.
'Great gentleman,' said Henry Clay, 'and a patriot.' Portrait by
    Benjamin West.

Or take those, the nameless, of whom no portraits remain,
No locket or seal ring, though somewhere, broken and rusted,
In attic or earth, the long Decherd, stock rotten, has lain;
Or the mold-yellow Bible, God's Word, in which, in their strength,
    they had also trusted.

Some wrestled the angel, and took a fall by the corncrib.
Fought the brute, stomp-and-gouge, but knew they were doomed in
    that glory.
All night, in sweat, groaned; fell at last with spit red and a cracked rib.
How sweet were the tears! Thus gentled they roved the dark land
    with their old story.

Some prospered, had black men and lands, and silver on table,
But remembered the owl call, the smell of burnt bear fat on dusk-air.
Loved family and friends, and stood it as long as able,
'But money and women, too much in ruination, am Arkansas-
    bound.' So went there.

One of mine was a land shark, or so the book with scant praise
Denominates him, 'a man large and shapeless,
Like a sack of potatoes set on a saddle,' and says,
'Little learning but shrewd, not well trusted.' Rides thus out of
    history, neck fat and napeless.

One saw Shiloh and such, got cranky, would fiddle all night.
The boys nagged for Texas. 'God damn it, there's nothing, God
    damn it,

In Texas,' but took wagons, went, and to prove he was right,
Stayed a year and a day, 'hell, nothing in Texas,' had proved it, came
    back to black vomit,

And died, and they died, and are dead, and now their voices
Come thin, like last cricket in frost-dark, in grass lost,
With nothing to tell us for our complexity of choices,
But beg us only one word to justify their own old life-cost.

So let us bend ear to them in this hour of lateness,
And what they are trying to say, try to understand,
And try to forgive them their defects, even their greatness,
For we are their children in the light of humanness, and under the
    shadow of God's closing hand.

Theodore Roethke 1908–63

Dolor

I have known the inexorable sadness of pencils,
Neat in their boxes, dolor of pad and paper-weight,
All the misery of manila folders and mucilage,
Desolation in immaculate public places,
Lonely reception room, lavatory, switchboard,
The unalterable pathos of basin and pitcher,
Ritual of multigraph, paper-clip, comma,
Endless duplication of lives and objects.
And I have seen dust from the walls of institutions,
Finer than flour, alive, more dangerous than silica,
Sift, almost invisible, through long afternoons of tedium,
Dropping a fine film on nails and delicate eyebrows,
Glazing the pale hair, the duplicate gray standard faces.

The Waking

I wake to sleep, and take my waking slow.
I feel my fate in what I cannot fear.
I learn by going where I have to go.

We think by feeling. What is there to know?
I hear my being dance from ear to ear.
I wake to sleep, and take my waking slow.

Of those so close beside me, which are you?
God bless the Ground! I shall walk softly there,
And learn by going where I have to go.

Light takes the Tree; but who can tell us how?
The lowly worm climbs up a winding stair;
I wake to sleep, and take my waking slow.

Great Nature has another thing to do
To you and me; so take the lively air,
And, lovely, learn by going where to go.

This shaking keeps me steady. I should know.
What falls away is always. And is near.
I wake to sleep, and take my waking slow.
I learn by going where I have to go.

Meditation at Oyster River

I

Over the low, barnacled, elephant-colored rocks,
Come the first tide-ripples, moving, almost without sound, toward
    me,
Running along the narrow furrows of the shore, the rows of dead
    clam shells;
Then a runnel behind me, creeping closer,
Alive with tiny striped fish, and young crabs climbing in and out of
    the water.

No sound from the bay. No violence.
Even the gulls quiet on the far rocks,
Silent, in the deepening light,
Their cat-mewing over,
Their child-whimpering.

At last one long undulant ripple,
Blue-black from where I am sitting,

Makes almost a wave over a barrier of small stones,
Slapping lightly against a sunken log.
I dabble my toes in the brackish foam sliding forward,
Then retire to a rock higher up on the cliff-side.
The wind slackens, light as a moth fanning a stone:
A twilight wind, light as a child's breath
Turning not a leaf, not a ripple.
The dew revives on the beach-grass;
The salt-soaked wood of a fire crackles;
A fish raven turns on its perch (a dead tree in the rivermouth),
Its wings catching a last glint of the reflected sunlight.

2

The self persists like a dying star,
In sleep, afraid. Death's face rises afresh,
Among the shy beasts, the deer at the salt-lick,
The doe with its sloped shoulders loping across the highway,
The young snake, poised in green leaves, waiting for its fly,
The hummingbird, whirring from quince-blossom to morning-
     glory –
With these I would be.
And with water: the waves coming forward, without cessation,
The waves, altered by sand-bars, beds of kelp, miscellaneous drift-
     wood,
Topped by cross-winds, tugged at by sinuous undercurrents
The tide rustling in, sliding between the ridges of stone,
The tongues of water, creeping in, quietly.

3

In this hour,
In this first heaven of knowing,
The flesh takes on the pure poise of the spirit,
Acquires, for a time, the sandpiper's insouciance,
The hummingbird's surety, the kingfisher's cunning –
I shift on my rock, and I think:
Of the first trembling of a Michigan brook in April,

Over a lip of stone, the tiny rivulet;
And that wrist-thick cascade tumbling from a cleft rock,
Its spray holding a double rain-bow in early morning,
Small enough to be taken in, embraced, by two arms, –
Or the Tittebawasee, in the time between winter and spring,
When the ice melts along the edges in early afternoon.
And the midchannel begins cracking and heaving from the pressure
    beneath,
The ice piling high against the iron-bound spiles,
Gleaming, freezing hard again, creaking at midnight –
And I long for the blast of dynamite,
The sudden sucking roar as the culvert loosens its debris of branches
    and sticks,
Welter of tin cans, pails, old bird nests, a child's shoe riding a log,
As the piled ice breaks away from the battered spiles,
And the whole river begins to move forward, its bridges shaking.

4

Now, in this waning of light,
I rock with the motion of morning;
In the cradle of all that is,
I'm lulled into half-sleep.
By the lapping of water,
Cries of the sandpiper.
Water's my will, and my way,
And the spirit runs, intermittently,
In and out of the small waves,
Runs with the intrepid shorebirds –
How graceful the small before danger!

In the first of the moon,
All's a scattering,
A shining.

Charles Olson 1910-70

I, *Maximus of Gloucester, to You*

> Off-shore, by islands hidden in the blood
> jewels & miracles, I, Maximus
> a metal hot from boiling water, tell you
> what is a lance, who obeys the figures of
> the present dance

1

the thing you're after
may lie around the bend
of the nest (second, time slain, the bird! the bird!

And there! (strong) thrust, the mast! flight
                   (of the bird
                    o kylix, o
                    Antony of Padua
                    sweep low, o bless

the roofs, the old ones, the gentle steep ones
on whose ridge-poles the gulls sit, from which they depart,

                          And the flake-racks
of my city!

2

love is form, and cannot be without
important substance (the weight
say, 58 carats each one of us, perforce
our goldsmith's scale

feather to feather added
(and what is mineral, what
is curling hair, the string
you carry in your nervous beak, these

make bulk, these, in the end, are
the sum
(o my lady of good voyage
in whose arm, whose left arm rests
no boy but a carefully carved wood, a painted face, a schooner!
a delicate mast, as bow-sprit for

                    forwarding

3

the underpart is, though stemmed, uncertain
is, as sex is, as moneys are, facts!
fact, to be dealt with, as the sea is, the demand
that they be played by, that they only can be, that they must
be played by, said he, coldly, the
ear!

By ear, he sd.
But that which matters, that which insists, that which will last,
that! o my people, where shall you find it, how, where, where shall
        you listen
when all is become billboards, when, all, even silence, is spray-gunned?

when even our bird, my roofs,
cannot be heard

when even you, when sound itself is neoned in?

when, on the hill, over the water
where she who used to sing,
when the water glowed,
black, gold, the tide
outward, at evening

when bells came like boats
over the oil-slicks, milkweed
hulls

And a man slumped,
attentionless,
against pink shingles

o sea city)

4
one loves only form,
and form only comes
into existence when
the thing is born

       born of yourself, born
       of hay and cotton struts,
       of street-pickings, wharves, weeds
       you carry in, my bird

              of a bone of a fish
              of a straw, or will
              of a color, of a bell
              of yourself, torn

5

love is not easy
but how shall you know,
New England, now
that pejorocracy is here, how
that street-cars, o Oregon, twitter
in the afternoon, offend
a black-gold loin?

how shall you strike,
o swordsman, the blue-red back
when, last night, your aim
was mu-sick, mu-sick, mu-sick
And not the cribbage game?

                            (o Gloucester-man,
                            weave
                            your birds and fingers
                            new, your roof-tops,
                            clean shit upon racks
                            sunned on
                            American
                            braid
                            with others like you, such
                            extricable surface
                            as faun and oral,
                            satyr lesbos vase

                            o kill kill kill kill kill
                            those
                            who advertise you
                            out)

6

in! in! the bow-sprit, bird, the beak
in, the bend is, in, goes in, the form
that which you make, what holds, which is
the law of object, strut after strut, what you are, what you must be,
    what
the force can throw up, can, right now hereinafter erect,
the mast, the mast, the tender
mast!

The nest, I say, to you, I Maximus, say
under the hand, as I see it, over the waters
from this place where I am, where I hear,
can still hear

from where I carry you a feather
as though, sharp, I picked up,
in the afternoon delivered you
a jewel,
            it flashing more than a wing,
than any old romantic thing,
than memory, than place,
than anything other than that which you carry

than that which is,
call it a nest, around the head of, call it
the next second

than that which you
can do!

Elizabeth Bishop 1911-

The Prodigal

The brown enormous odor he lived by
was too close, with its breathing and thick hair,
for him to judge. The floor was rotten; the sty
was plastered halfway up with glass-smooth dung.
Light-lashed, self-righteous, above moving snouts,
the pigs' eyes followed him, a cheerful stare –
even to the sow that always ate her young –
till, sickening, he leaned to scratch her head.
But sometimes mornings after drinking bouts
(he hid the pints behind a two-by-four),
the sunrise glazed the barnyard mud with red;
the burning puddles seemed to reassure.
And then he thought he almost might endure
his exile yet another year or more.

But evenings the first star came to warn.
The farmer whom he worked for came at dark
to shut the cows and horses in the barn
beneath their overhanging clouds of hay,
with pitchforks, faint forked lightnings, catching light,
safe and companionable as in the Ark.
The pigs stuck out their little feet and snored.
The lantern – like the sun, going away –
laid on the mud a pacing aureole.
Carrying a bucket along a slimy board,
he felt the bats' uncertain staggering flight,
his shuddering insights, beyond his control,
touching him. But it took him a long time
finally to make his mind up to go home.

First Death in Nova Scotia

In the cold, cold parlor
my mother laid out Arthur
beneath the chromographs:
Edward, Prince of Wales,
with Princess Alexandra,
and King George with Queen Mary.
Below them on the table
stood a stuffed loon
shot and stuffed by Uncle
Arthur, Arthur's father.

Since Uncle Arthur fired
a bullet into him,
he hadn't said a word.
He kept his own counsel
on his white, frozen lake,
the marble-topped table.
His breast was deep and white,
cold and caressable;
his eyes were red glass,
much to be desired.

'Come,' said my mother,
'Come and say goodbye
to your little cousin Arthur.'
I was lifted up and given
one lily of the valley
to put in Arthur's hand.
Arthur's coffin was
a little frosted cake,
and the red-eyed loon eyed it
from his white, frozen lake.

Arthur was very small.
He was all white, like a doll
that hadn't been painted yet.
Jack Frost had started to paint him
the way he always painted
the Maple Leaf (Forever).
He had just begun on his hair,
a few red strokes, and then
Jack Frost had dropped the brush
and left him white, forever.

The gracious royal couples
were warm in red and ermine;
their feet were well wrapped up
in the ladies' ermine trains.
They invited Arthur to be
the smallest page at court.
But how could Arthur go,
clutching his tiny lily,
with his eyes shut up so tight
and the roads deep in snow?

Delmore Schwartz 1913–66

The Heavy Bear Who Goes With Me

'the withness of the body'

The heavy bear who goes with me,
A manifold honey to smear his face,
Clumsy and lumbering here and there,
The central ton of every place,
The hungry beating brutish one
In love with candy, anger, and sleep,
Crazy factotum, dishevelling all,
Climbs the building, kicks the football,
Boxes his brother in the hate-ridden city.

Breathing at my side, that heavy animal,
That heavy bear who sleeps with me,
Howls in his sleep for a world of sugar,
A sweetness intimate as the water's clasp,
Howls in his sleep because the tight-rope
Trembles and shows the darkness beneath.
– The strutting show-off is terrified,
Dressed in his dress-suit, bulging his pants,
Trembles to think that his quivering meat
Must finally wince to nothing at all.

That inescapable animal walks with me,
Has followed me since the black womb held,
Moves where I move, distorting my gesture,
A caricature, a swollen shadow,
A stupid clown of the spirit's motive,

Perplexes and affronts with his own darkness,
The secret life of belly and bone,
Opaque, too near, my private, yet unknown,
Stretches to embrace the very dear
With whom I would walk without him near,
Touches her grossly, although a word
Would bare my heart and make me clear,
Stumbles, flounders, and strives to be fed
Dragging me with him in his mouthing care,
Amid the hundred million of his kind,
The scrimmage of appetite everywhere.

Karl Shapiro 1913–

Buick

As a sloop with a sweep of immaculate wing on her delicate spine
And a keel as steel as a root that holds in the sea as she leans,
Leaning and laughing, my warm-hearted beauty, you ride, you ride,
You tack on the curves with parabola speed and a kiss of goodbye,
Like a thoroughbred sloop, my new high-spirited spirit, my kiss.

As my foot suggests that you leap in the air with your hips of a girl,
My finger that praises your wheel and announces your voices of song,
Flouncing your skirts, you blueness of joy, you flirt of politeness,
You leap, you intelligence, essence of wheelness with silvery nose,
And your platinum clocks of excitement stir like the hairs of a fern.

But how alien you are from the booming belts of your birth and the
    smoke
Where you turned on the stinging lathes of Detroit and Lansing at
    night
And shrieked at the torch in your secret parts and the amorous tests,
But now with your eyes that enter the future of roads you forget;
You are all instinct with your phosphorous glow and your streaking
    hair.

And now when we stop it is not as the bird from the shell that I
    leave
Or the leathery pilot who steps from his bird with a sneer of delight,
And not as the ignorant beast do you squat and watch me depart,
But with exquisite breathing you smile, with satisfaction of love,
And I touch you again as you tick in the silence and settle in sleep.

Auto Wreck

Its quick soft silver bell beating, beating,
And down the dark one ruby flare
Pulsing out red light like an artery,
The ambulance at top speed floating down
Past beacons and illuminated clocks
Wings in a heavy curve, dips down,
And brakes speed, entering the crowd.
The doors leap open, emptying light;
Stretchers are laid out, the mangled lifted
And stowed into the little hospital.
Then the bell, breaking the hush, tolls once,
And the ambulance with its terrible cargo
Rocking, slightly rocking, moves away,
As the doors, an afterthought, are closed.

We are deranged, walking among the cops
Who sweep glass and are large and composed.
One is still making notes under the light.
One with a bucket douches ponds of blood
Into the street and gutter.
One hangs lanterns on the wrecks that cling,
Empty husks of locusts, to iron poles.

Our throats were tight as tourniquets,
Our feet were bound with splints, but now,
Like convalescents intimate and gauche,
We speak through sickly smiles and warn
With the stubborn saw of common sense,
The grim joke and the banal resolution.
The traffic moves around with care,
But we remain, touching a wound
That opens to our richest horror.
Already old, the question Who shall die?

Becomes unspoken Who is innocent?
For death in war is done by hands;
Suicide has cause and stillbirth, logic;
And cancer, simple as a flower, blooms.
But this invites the occult mind,
Cancels our physics with a sneer,
And spatters all we knew of denouement
Across the expedient and wicked stones.

Weldon Kees 1914–55

Relating to Robinson

Somewhere in Chelsea, early summer;
And, walking in the twilight toward the docks,
I thought I made out Robinson ahead of me.

From an uncurtained second-story room, a radio
Was playing *There's a Small Hotel*; a kite
Twisted above dark rooftops and slow drifting birds.
We were alone there, he and I,
Inhabiting the empty street.

Under a sign for Natural Bloom Cigars,
While lights clicked softly in the dusk from red to green,
He stopped and gazed into a window
Where a plaster Venus, modeling a truss,
Looked out at Eastbound traffic. (But Robinson,
I knew, was out of town: he summers at a place in Maine,
Sometimes on Fire Island, sometimes the Cape,
Leaves town in June and comes back after Labor Day.)
And yet, I almost called out, 'Robinson!'

There was no chance. Just as I passed,
Turning my head to search his face,
His own head turned with mine
And fixed me with dilated, terrifying eyes
That stopped my blood. His voice
Came at me like an echo in the dark.

'I thought I saw the whirlpool opening.
Kicked all night at a bolted door.
You must have followed me from Astor Place.
An empty paper floats down at the last.
And then a day as huge as yesterday in pairs
Unrolled its horror on my face
Until it blocked —' Running in sweat
To reach the docks, I turned back
For a second glance. I had no certainty,
There in the dark, that it was Robinson
Or someone else.

     The block was bare. The Venus,
Bathed in blue fluorescent light,
Stared toward the river. As I hurried West,
The lights across the bay were coming on.
The boats moved silently and the low whistles blew.

Randall Jarrell 1914–65

The Death of the Ball Turret Gunner

From my mother's sleep I fell into the State,
And I hunched in its belly till my wet fur froze.
Six miles from earth, loosed from its dream of life,
I woke to black flak and the nightmare fighters.
When I died they washed me out of the turret with a hose.

Thinking of the Lost World

This spoonful of chocolate tapioca
Tastes like – like peanut butter, like the vanilla
Extract Mama told me not to drink.
Swallowing the spoonful, I have already traveled
Through time to my childhood. It puzzles me
That age is like it.
                    Come back to that calm country
Through which the stream of my life first meandered,
My wife, our cat, and I sit here and see
Squirrels quarreling in the feeder, a mockingbird
Copying our chipmunk, as our end copies
Its beginning.
                    Back in Los Angeles, we missed
Los Angeles. The sunshine of the Land
Of Sunshine is a gray mist now, the atmosphere
Of some factory planet: when you stand and look
You see a block or two, and your eyes water.
The orange groves are all cut down ... My bow
Is lost, all my arrows are lost or broken,
My knife is sunk in the eucalyptus tree

Too far for even Pop to get it out,
And the tree's sawed down. It and the stair-sticks
And the planks of the tree house are all firewood
Burned long ago; its gray smoke smells of Vicks.

Twenty Years After, thirty-five years after,
Is as good as ever – better than ever,
Now that D'Artagnan is no longer old –
Except that it is unbelievable.
I say to my old self: 'I believe. Help thou
Mine unbelief.'
               I believe the dinosaur
Or pterodactyl's married the pink sphinx
And lives with those Indians in the undiscovered
Country between California and Arizona
That the mad girl told me she was princess of –
Looking at me with the eyes of a lion,
Big, golden, without human understanding,
As she threw paper-wads from the back seat
Of the car in which I drove her with her mother
From the jail in Waycross to the hospital
In Daytona. If I took my eyes from the road
And looked back into her eyes, the car would – I'd be –

Or if only I could find a crystal set
Sometimes, surely, I could still hear their chief
Reading to them from Dumas or *Amazing Stories*;
If I could find in some Museum of Cars
Mama's dark blue Buick, Lucky's electric,
Couldn't I be driven there? Hold out to them,
The paraffin half picked out, Tawny's dewclaw –
And have walk to me from among their wigwams
My tall brown aunt, to whisper to me: 'Dead?
They told you I was dead?'
                   As if you could die!
If I never saw you, never again

Wrote to you, even, after a few years,
How often you've visited me, having put on,
As a mermaid puts on her sealskin, another face
And voice, that don't fool me for a minute –
That are yours for good . . . All of them are gone
Except for me; and for me nothing is gone –
The chicken's body is still going round
And round in widening circles, a satellite
From which, as the sun sets, the scientist bends
A look of evil on the unsuspecting earth.
Mama and Pop and Dandeen are still there
In the Gay Twenties.
            The Gay Twenties! You say
The Gay Nineties . . . But it's all right: they *were* gay,
O so gay! A certain number of years after,
Any time is Gay, to the new ones who ask:
'Was that the first World War or the second?'
Moving between the first world and the second,
I hear a boy call, now that my beard's gray:
'Santa Claus! Hi, Santa Claus!' It *is* miraculous
To have the children call you Santa Claus.
I wave back. When my hand drops to the wheel,
It is brown and spotted, and its nails are ridged
Like Mama's. Where's my own hand? My smooth
White bitten-fingernailed one? I seem to see
A shape in tennis shoes and khaki riding-pants
Standing there empty-handed; I reach out to it
Empty-handed, my hand comes back empty,
And yet my emptiness is traded for its emptiness,
I have found that Lost World in the Lost and Found
Columns whose gray illegible advertisements
My soul has memorized world after world:
LOST – NOTHING. STRAYED FROM NOWHERE. NO
    REWARD.
I hold in my own hands, in happiness,
Nothing: the nothing for which there's no reward.

John Berryman 1914–72

From *The Dream Songs*

4 'FILLING HER COMPACT & DELICIOUS BODY'

Filling her compact & delicious body
with chicken páprika, she glanced at me
twice.
Fainting with interest, I hungered back
and only the fact of her husband & four other people
kept me from springing on her

or falling at her little feet and crying
'You are the hottest one for years of night
Henry's dazed eyes
have enjoyed, Brilliance.' I advanced upon
(despairing) my spumoni. – Sir Bones: is stuffed,
de world, wif feeding girls.

– Black hair, complexion Latin, jewelled eyes
downcast . . . The slob beside her   feasts . . . What wonders is
she sitting on, over there?
The restaurant buzzes. She might as well be on Mars.
Where did it all go wrong? There ought to be a law against Henry.
– Mr Bones: there is.

14 'LIFE, FRIENDS, IS BORING. WE MUST NOT SAY SO'

Life, friends, is boring. We must not say so.
After all, the sky flashes, the great sea yearns,

we ourselves flash and yearn,
and moreover my mother told me as a boy
(repeatedly) 'Ever to confess you're bored
means you have no

Inner Resources.' I conclude now I have no
inner resources, because I am heavy bored.
Peoples bore me,
literature bores me, especially great literature,
Henry bores me, with his plights & gripes
as bad as achilles,

who loves people and valiant art, which bores me.
And the tranquil hills, & gin, look like a drag
and somehow a dog
has taken itself & its tail considerably away
into mountains or sea or sky, leaving
behind: me, wag.

15 'LET US SUPPOSE, VALLEYS & SUCH AGO'

Let us suppose, valleys & such ago,
one pal unwinding from his labours in
one bar of Chicago,
and this did actual happen. This was so.
And many graces are slipped, & many a sin
even that laid man low

but this will be remembered & told over,
that she was heard at last, haughtful & greasy,
to bawl in that low bar:
'You can biff me, you can bang me, get it you'll never.
I may be only a Polack   broad but I don't lay easy.
Kiss my ass, that's what you are.'

Women is better, braver. In a foehn of loss
entire, which too they hotter understand,
having had it,
we struggle. Some hang heavy on the sauce,
some invest in the past, one hides in the land.
Henry was not his favourite.

29 'THERE SAT DOWN, ONCE, A THING ON HENRY'S HEART'

There sat down, once, a thing on Henry's heart
só heavy, if he had a hundred years
& more, & weeping, sleepless, in all them time
Henry could not make good.
Starts again always in Henry's ears
the little cough somewhere, an odour, a chime.

And there is another thing he has in mind
like a grave Sienese face a thousand years
would fail to blur the still profiled reproach of. Ghastly,
with open eyes, he attends, blind.
All the bells say: too late. This is not for tears;
thinking.

But never did Henry, as he thought he did,
end anyone and hacks her body up
And hide the pieces, where they may be found.
He knows: he went over everyone, & nobody's missing.
Often he reckons, in the dawn, them up.
Nobody is ever missing.

63 'BATS HAVE NO BANKERS AND THEY DO NOT DRINK'

Bats have no bankers and they do not drink
and cannot be arrested and pay no tax
and, in general, bats have it made.
Henry for joining the human race is *bats*,
known to be so, by few them who think,
out of the cave.

Instead of the cave! ah lovely-chilly, dark,
ur-moist his cousins hang in hundreds or swerve
with personal radar,
crisisless, kid. Instead of the cave? I serve,
inside, my blind term. Filthy four-foot lights
reflect on the whites of our eyes.

He then salutes for sixty years of it
just now a one of valor and insights,
a theatrical man,
O scholar & Legionnaire who as quickly might
have killed as cast you. *Olè*. Stormed with years
he tranquil commands and appears.

67 'I DON'T OPERATE OFTEN. WHEN I DO'

I don't operate often. When I do,
persons take note.
Nurses look amazed. They pale.
The patient is brought back to life, or so.
The reason I don't do this more (I quote)
is: I have a living to fail –

450

because of my wife & son – to keep from earning.
– Mr Bones, I sees that.
They for these operations thanks you, what?
not pays you. – Right.
You have seldom been so understanding.
Now there is further a difficulty with the light:

I am obliged to perform in complete darkness
operations of great delicacy
on my self.
– Mr Bones, you terrifies me.
No wonder they don't pay you. Will you die?
– My
　　　　　　friend, I succeeded. Later.

380 FROM THE FRENCH HOSPITAL IN NEW YORK, 901

Wordsworth, thou form almost divine, cried Henry,
'the egotistical sublime' said Keats,
oh ho, you lovely man!
make from the rafters some mere sign to me
whether when after this raving heart which beats
& which to beat began

Long so years since　stops　I may (ah) expect
a fresh version of living or if I stop
wholly.
Oblongs attend my convalescence, wreckt
and now again, by many full propt up,
not irreversible Henry.

Punctured Henry wondered would he die
forever, all his fine body forever lost

and his very useful mind?
Hopeless & violent the man will lie,
on decades' questing, whose crazed hopes have crossed
to wind up here blind.

Olympus

In my serpentine researches
I came on a book review in *Poetry*
which began, with sublime assurance,
a comprehensive air of majesty,

'The art of poetry
is amply distinguished from the manufacture of verse
by the animating presence in the poetry
of a fresh idiom: language

so twisted & posed in a form
that it not only expresses the matter in hand
but adds to the stock of available reality.'
I was never altogether the same man after *that*.

I found this new Law-giver all unknown
except in the back numbers of a Cambridge quarterly
Hound & Horn, just defunct.
I haunted on Sixth Avenue until

at 15¢ apiece or 25
I had all 28 numbers
& had fired my followers at Philolexian & Boar's Head
with the merits of this prophet.

My girls suffered during this month or so,
so did my seminars & lectures &
my poetry even. To be a *critic*, ah,
how deeper & more scientific.

I wrote & printed an essay on Yeats's plays
re-deploying all of Blackmur's key terms
& even his sentence-structure wherever I could.
When he answered by hand from Boston my nervous invitation

to come & be honoured at our annual Poetry Reading,
it must have been ten minutes before I could open the envelope.
I got *him* to review Tate's book of essays
& *Mark* to review *The Double Agent*. Olympus!

I have travelled in some high company since
but never so dizzily.
I have had some rare girls since but never one so philosophical
as that same Spring (my last Spring there) Jean Bennett.

Robert Lowell 1917–77

Ford Madox Ford

1873–1939

The lobbed ball plops, then dribbles to the cup . . .
(a birdie Fordie!) But it nearly killed
the ministers. Lloyd George was holding up
the flag. He gabbled, 'Hop-toad, hop-toad, hop-toad!
Hueffer has used a niblick on the green;
it's filthy art, Sir, filthy art!'
You answered, 'What is art to me and thee?
Will a blacksmith teach a midwife how to bear?'
That cut the puffing statesman down to size,
Ford. You said, 'Otherwise,
I would have been general of a division.' Ah Ford!
Was it war, the sport of kings, that your *Good Soldier*,
the best French novel in the language, taught
those Georgian Whig magnificoes at Oxford,
at Oxford decimated on the Somme?
Ford, five times black-balled for promotion,
then mustard gassed voiceless some seven miles
behind the lines at Nancy or Belleau Wood:
you emerged in your 'worn uniform,
gilt dragons on the revers of the tunic,'
a Jonah – O divorced, divorced
from the whale-fat of post-war London! Boomed,
cut, plucked and booted! In Provence, New York . . .
marrying, blowing . . . nearly dying
at Boulder, when the altitude
pressed the world on your heart,
and your audience, almost football-size,

shrank to a dozen, while you stood
mumbling, with fish-blue eyes,
and mouth pushed out
fish-fashion, as if you gagged for air . . .
Sandman! Your face, a childish O. The sun
is pernod-yellow and it gilds the heirs
of all the ages there on Washington
and Stuyvesant, your Lilliputian squares,
where writing turned your pockets inside out.
But master, mammoth mumbler, tell me why
the bales of your left-over novels buy
less than a bandage for your gouty foot.
Wheel-horse, O unforgetting elephant,
I hear you huffing at your old Brevoort,
Timon and Falstaff, while you heap the board
for publishers. Fiction! I'm selling short
your lies that made the great your equals. Ford,
you were a kind man and you died in want.

Sailing Home From Rapallo

(FEBRUARY 1954)

Your nurse could only speak Italian,
but after twenty minutes I could imagine your final week,
and tears ran down my cheeks . . .

When I embarked from Italy with my Mother's body,
the whole shoreline of the *Golfo di Genova*
was breaking into fiery flower.
The crazy yellow and azure sea-sleds
blasting like jack hammers across
the *spumante*-bubbling wake of our liner,

recalled the clashing colors of my Ford.
Mother travelled first-class in the hold,
her *Risorgimento* black and gold casket
was like Napoleon's at the *Invalides* . . .

While the passengers were tanning
on the Mediterranean in deck-chairs,
our family cemetery in Dunbarton
lay under the White Mountains
in the sub-zero weather.
The graveyard's soil was changing to stone –
so many of its deaths had been midwinter.
Dour and dark against the blinding snowdrifts,
its black brook and fir trunks were as smooth as masts.
A fence of iron spear-hafts
black-bordered its mostly Colonial grave-slates.
The only 'unhistoric' soul to come here
was Father, now buried beneath his recent
unweathered, pink-veined slice of marble.
Even the Latin of his Lowell motto:
Occasionem cognosce,
seemed too businesslike and pushing here,
where the burning cold illuminated
the hewn inscriptions of Mother's relatives:
twenty or thirty Winslows and Starks.
Frost had given their names a diamond edge . . .

In the grandiloquent lettering on Mother's coffin,
Lowell had been misspelled *LOVEL.*
The corpse
was wrapped like *panetone* in Italian tinfoil.

Waking in the Blue

The night attendant, a B.U. sophomore,
rouses from the mare's-nest of his drowsy head
propped on *The Meaning of Meaning*.
He catwalks down our corridor.
Azure day
makes my agonized blue window bleaker.
Crows maunder on the petrified fairway.
Absence! My heart grows tense
as though a harpoon were sparring for the kill.
(This is the house for the 'mentally ill'.)

What use is my sense of humor?
I grin at 'Stanley', now sunk in his sixties,
once a Harvard all-American fullback,
(if such were possible!)
still hoarding the build of a boy in his twenties,
as he soaks, a ramrod
with the muscle of a seal
in his long tub,
vaguely urinous from the Victorian plumbing.
A kingly granite profile in a crimson golf-cap,
worn all day, all night,
he thinks only of his figure,
of slimming on sherbert and ginger ale –
more cut off from words than a seal.

This is the way day breaks in Bowditch Hall at McLean's;
the hooded night lights bring out 'Bobbie',
Porcellian '29,
a replica of Louis XVI
without the wig –
redolent and roly-poly as a sperm whale,

as he swashbuckles about in his birthday suit
and horses at chairs.

These victorious figures of bravado ossified young.

In between the limits of day,
hours and hours go by under the crew haircuts
and slightly too little nonsensical bachelor twinkle
of the Roman Catholic attendants.
(There are no Mayflower
screwballs in the Catholic Church.)

After a hearty New England breakfast,
I weigh two hundred pounds
this morning. Cock of the walk,
I strut in my turtle-necked French sailor's jersey
before the metal shaving mirrors,
and see the shaky future grow familiar
in the pinched, indigenous faces
of these thoroughbred mental cases,
twice my age and half my weight.
We are all old-timers,
each of us holds a locked razor.

Memories of West Street and Lepke

Only teaching on Tuesdays, book-worming
in pajamas fresh from the washer each morning,
I hog a whole house on Boston's
'hardly passionate Marlborough Street',
where even the man
scavenging filth in the back alley trash cans,
has two children, a beach wagon, a helpmate,

and is 'a young Republican'.
I have a nine months' daughter,
young enough to be my granddaughter.
Like the sun she rises in her flame-flamingo infants' wear.

These are the tranquillized *Fifties*,
and I am forty. Ought I to regret my seedtime?
I was a fire-breathing Catholic C.O.,
and made my manic statement,
telling off the state and president, and then
sat waiting sentence in the bull pen
beside a negro boy with curlicues
of marijuana in his hair.

Given a year,
I walked on the roof of the West Street Jail, a short
enclosure like my school soccer court,
and saw the Hudson River once a day
through sooty clothesline entanglements
and bleaching khaki tenements.
Strolling, I yammered metaphysics with Abramowitz,
a jaundice-yellow ('it's really tan')
and fly-weight pacifist,
so vegetarian,
he wore rope shoes and preferred fallen fruit.
He tried to convert Bioff and Brown,
the Hollywood pimps, to his diet.
Hairy, muscular, suburban,
wearing chocolate double-breasted suits,
they blew their tops and beat him black and blue.

I was so out of things, I'd never heard
of the Jehovah's Witnesses.
'Are you a C.O.?' I asked a fellow jailbird.
'No,' he answered, 'I'm a J.W.'

He taught me the hospital 'tuck',
and pointed out the T-shirted back
of *Murder Incorporated's* Czar Lepke,
there piling towels on a rack,
or dawdling off to his little segregated cell full
of things forbidden the common man:
a portable radio, a dresser, two toy American
flags tied together with a ribbon of Easter palm.
Flabby, bald, lobotomized,
he drifted in a sheepish calm,
where no agonizing reappraisal
jarred his concentration on the electric chair –
hanging like an oasis in his air
of lost connections . . .

Skunk Hour

(FOR ELIZABETH BISHOP)

Nautilus Island's hermit
heiress still lives through winter in her Spartan cottage;
her sheep still graze above the sea.
Her son's a bishop. Her farmer
is first selectman in our village,
she's in her dotage.

Thirsting for
the hierarchic privacy
of Queen Victoria's century,
she buys up all
the eyesores facing her shore,
and lets them fall.

The season's ill –
we've lost our summer millionaire,
who seemed to leap from an L. L. Bean
catalogue. His nine-knot yawl
was auctioned off to lobstermen.
A red fox stain covers Blue Hill.

And now our fairy
decorator brightens his shop for fall,
his fishnet's filled with orange cork,
orange, his cobbler's bench and awl,
there is no money in his work,
he'd rather marry.

One dark night,
my Tudor Ford climbed the hill's skull,
I watched for love-cars. Lights turned down,
they lay together, hull to hull,
where the graveyard shelves on the town . . .
My mind's not right.

A car radio bleats,
'Love, O careless Love . . .' I hear
my ill-spirit sob in each blood cell,
as if my hand were at its throat . . .
I myself am hell,
nobody's here –

only skunks, that search
in the moonlight for a bite to eat.
They march on their soles up Main Street:
white stripes, moonstruck eyes' red fire
under the chalk-dry and spar spire
of the Trinitarian Church.

I stand on top
of our back steps and breathe the rich air —
a mother skunk with her column of kittens swills the garbage pail.
She jabs her wedge head in a cup
of sour cream, drops her ostrich tail,
and will not scare.

For the Union Dead

Relinquunt Omnia Servare Rem Publicam.

The old South Boston Aquarium stands
in a Sahara of snow now. Its broken windows are boarded.
The bronze weathervane cod has lost half its scales.
The airy tanks are dry.

Once my nose crawled like a snail on the glass;
my hand tingled
to burst the bubbles
drifting from the noses of the cowed, compliant fish.

My hand draws back. I often sigh still
for the dark downward and vegetating kingdom
of the fish and reptile. One morning last March,
I pressed against the new barbed and galvanized

fence on the Boston Common. Behind their cage,
yellow dinosaur steamshovels were grunting
as they cropped up tons of mush and grass
to gouge their underworld garage.

Parking spaces luxuriate like civic
sandpiles in the heart of Boston.
A girdle of orange, Puritan-pumpkin colored girders
braces the tingling Statehouse,

shaking over the excavations, as it faces Colonel Shaw
and his bell-cheeked Negro infantry
on St Gaudens' shaking Civil War relief,
propped by a plank splint against the garage's earthquake.

Two months after marching through Boston,
half the regiment was dead;
at the dedication,
William James could almost hear the bronze Negroes breathe.

Their monument sticks like a fishbone
in the city's throat.
Its Colonel is as lean
as a compass-needle.

He has an angry wrenlike vigilance,
a greyhound's gentle tautness;
he seems to wince at pleasure,
and suffocate for privacy.

He is out of bounds now. He rejoices in man's lovely,
peculiar power to choose life and die –
when he leads his black soldiers to death,
he cannot bend his back.

On a thousand small town New England greens,
the old white churches hold their air
of sparse, sincere rebellion; frayed flags
quilt the graveyards of the Grand Army of the Republic.

The stone statues of the abstract Union Soldier
grow slimmer and younger each year –
wasp-wasted, they doze over muskets
and muse through their sideburns . . .

Shaw's father wanted no monument
except the ditch,
where his son's body was thrown
and lost with his 'niggers'.

The ditch is nearer.
There are no statues for the last war here;
on Boylston Street, a commercial photograph
shows Hiroshima boiling

over a Mosler Safe, the 'Rock of Ages'
that survived the blast. Space is nearer.
When I crouch to my television set,
the drained faces of Negro school-children rise like balloons.

Colonel Shaw
is riding on his bubble,
he waits
for the blessèd break.

The Aquarium is gone. Everywhere,
giant finned cars nose forward like fish;
a savage servility
slides by on grease.

T. S. Eliot

Caught between two streams of traffic, in the gloom
of Memorial Hall and Harvard's war-dead . . . And he:
'Don't you loathe to be compared with your relatives?
I do. I've just found two of mine reviewed by Poe.
He wiped the floor with them . . . and I was *delighted*.'
Then on with warden's pace across the Yard,

talking of Pound, 'It's balls to say he only
pretends to be Ezra . . . He's better though. This year,
he no longer wants to rebuild the Temple at Jerusalem.
Yes, he's better. "*You* speak," he said, when he'd talked two hours.
By then I had absolutely nothing to *say*.'
Ah Tom, one muse, one music, had one your luck –
lost in the dark night of the brilliant talkers,
humor and honor from the everlasting dross!

Ezra Pound

Horizontal on a deckchair in the ward
of the criminal mad . . . A man without shoestrings clawing
the Social Credit broadside from your table, you saying,
'. . . here with a black suit and black briefcase; in the brief,
an abomination, Possum's *hommage* to Milton.'
Then sprung; Rapallo, and the decade gone;
and three years later, Eliot dead, you saying,
'Who's left alive to understand my jokes?
My old Brother in the arts . . . besides, he was a smash of a poet.'
You showed me your blotched, bent hands, saying, 'Worms.
When I talked that nonsense about Jews on the Rome
wireless, Olga knew it was shit, and still loved me.'
And I, 'Who else has been in Purgatory?'
You, 'I began with a swelled head and end with swelled feet.'

Gwendolyn Brooks 1917–

The Lovers of the Poor

           arrive. The Ladies from the Ladies' Betterment
  League
Arrive in the afternoon, the late light slanting
In diluted gold bars across the boulevard brag
Of proud, seamed faces with mercy and murder hinting
Here, there, interrupting, all deep and debonair,
The pink paint on the innocence of fear;
Walk in a gingerly manner up the hall.
Cutting with knives served by their softest care,
Served by their love, so barbarously fair.
Whose mothers taught: You'd better not be cruel!
You had better not throw stones upon the wrens!
Herein they kiss and coddle and assault
Anew and dearly in the innocence
With which they baffle nature. Who are full,
Sleek, tender-clad, fit, fiftyish, a-glow, all
Sweetly abortive, hinting at fat fruit,
Judge it high time that fiftyish fingers felt
Beneath the lovelier planes of enterprise.
To resurrect. To moisten with milky chill.
To be a random hitching-post or plush.
To be, for wet eyes, random and handy hem.
              Their guild is giving money to the poor.
The worthy poor. The very very worthy
And beautiful poor. Perhaps just not too swarthy?
Perhaps just not too dirty nor too dim
Nor – passionate. In truth, what they could wish
Is – something less than derelict or dull.
Not staunch enough to stab, though, gaze for gaze!

God shield them sharply from the beggar-bold!
The noxious needy ones whose battle's bald
Nonetheless for being voiceless, hits one down.
            But it's all so bad! and entirely too much for them.
The stench; the urine, cabbage, and dead beans,
Dead porridges of assorted dusty grains,
The old smoke, *heavy* diapers, and, they're told,
Something called chitterlings. The darkness. Drawn
Darkness, or dirty light. The soil that stirs.
The soil that looks the soil of centuries.
And for that matter the general oldness. Old
Wood. Old marble. Old tile. Old old old.
Not homekind Oldness! Not Lake Forest, Glencoe.
Nothing so sturdy, nothing is majestic,
There is no quiet drama, no rubbed glaze, no
Unkillable infirmity of such
A tasteful turn as lately they have left,
Glencoe, Lake Forest, and to which their cars
Must presently restore them. When they're done
With dullards and distortions of this fistic
Patience of the poor and put-upon.
            They've never seen such a make-do-ness as
Newspaper rugs before! In this, this 'flat',
Their hostess is gathering up the oozed, the rich
Rugs of the morning (tattered! the bespattered . . .)
Readies to spread clean rugs for afternoon.
Here is a scene for you. The Ladies look,
In horror, behind a substantial citizeness
Whose trains clank out across her swollen heart.
Who, arms akimbo, almost fills a door.
All tumbling children, quilts dragged to the floor
And tortured thereover, potato peelings, soft-
Eyed kitten, hunched-up, haggard, to-be-hurt.
            Their League is allotting largesse to the Lost.
But to put their clean, their pretty money, to put
Their money collected from delicate rose-fingers

Tipped with their hundred flawless rose-nails seems . . .
　　　　　They own Spode, Lowestoft, candelabra,
Mantels, and hostess gowns, and sunburst clocks,
Turtle soup, Chippendale, red satin 'hangings',
Aubussons and Hattie Carnegie. They Winter
In Palm Beach; cross the Water in June, attend,
When suitable, the nice Art Institute;
Buy the right books in the best bindings; saunter
On Michigan, Easter mornings, in sun or wind.
Oh Squalor! This sick four-story hulk, this fibre
With fissures everywhere! Why, what are bringings
Of loathe-love largesse? What shall peril hungers
So old old, what shall flatter the desolate?
Tin can, blocked fire escape and chitterling
And swaggering seeking youth and the puzzled wreckage
Of the middle passage, and urine and stale shames
And, again, the porridges of the underslung
And children children children. Heavens! That
Was a rat, surely, off there, in the shadows? Long
And long-tailed? Gray? The Ladies from the Ladies'
Betterment League agree it will be better
To achieve the outer air that rights and steadies,
To hie to a house that does not holler, to ring
Bells elsetime, better presently to cater
To no more Possibilities, to get
Away. Perhaps the money can be posted.
Perhaps they two may choose another Slum!
Some serious sooty half-unhappy home! –
Where loathe-love likelier may be invested.
　　　　　Keeping their scented bodies in the center
Of the hall as they walk down the hysterical hall,
They allow their lovely skirts to graze no wall,
Are off at what they manage of a canter,
And, resuming all the clues of what they were,
Try to avoid inhaling the laden air.

Robert Duncan 1919–

Often I Am Permitted to Return to a Meadow

as if it were a scene made-up by the mind,
that is not mine, but is a made place,

that is mine, it is so near to the heart,
an eternal pasture folded in all thought
so that there is a hall therein

that is a made place, created by light
wherefrom the shadows that are forms fall.

Wherefrom fall all architectures I am
I say are likenesses of the First Beloved
whose flowers are flames lit to the Lady.

She it is Queen Under The Hill
whose hosts are a disturbance of words within words
that is a field folded.

It is only a dream of the grass blowing
east against the source of the sun
in an hour before the sun's going down

whose secret we see in a children's game
of ring a round of roses told.

Often I am permitted to return to a meadow
as if it were a given property of the mind
that certain bounds hold against chaos,

that is a place of first permission,
everlasting omen of what is.

Poetry, a Natural Thing

Neither our vices nor our virtues
further the poem. 'They came up
and died
just like they do every year
on the rocks.'

The poem
feeds upon thought, feeling, impulse,
to breed itself,
a spiritual urgency at the dark ladders leaping.

This beauty is an inner persistence
toward the source
striving against (within) down-rushet of the river,
a call we heard and answer
in the lateness of the world
primordial bellowings
from which the youngest world might spring,

salmon not in the well where the
hazelnut falls
but at the falls battling, inarticulate,
blindly making it.

This is one picture apt for the mind.

A second: a moose painted by Stubbs,
where last year's extravagant antlers
   lie on the ground.
The forlorn moosey-faced poem wears
   new antler-buds,
    the same,

'a little heavy, a little contrived',

his only beauty to be
   all moose.

Lawrence Ferlinghetti 1919–

From *A Coney Island of the Mind*

I

In Goya's greatest scenes we seem to see
                    the people of the world
  exactly at the moment when
    they first attained the title of
              'suffering humanity'
   They writhe upon the page
         in a veritable rage
              of adversity
   Heaped up
     groaning with babies and bayonets
                under cement skies
   in an abstract landscape of blasted trees
    bent statues bats wings and beaks
       slippery gibbets
   cadavers and carnivorous cocks
  and all the final hollering monsters
    of the
       'imagination of disaster'
  they are so bloody real
           it is as if they really still existed
And they do
    Only the landscape is changed

They still are ranged along the roads
    plagued by legionnaires
         false windmills and demented roosters

They are the same people
                      only further from home
   on freeways fifty lanes wide
                      on a concrete continent
                            spaced with bland billboards
                illustrating imbecile illusions of happiness

The scene shows fewer tumbrils
               but more maimed citizens
                      in painted cars
   and they have strange license plates
and engines
         that devour America

15

   Constantly risking absurdity
                    and death
       whenever he performs
                 above the heads
                      of his audience
the poet like an acrobat
             climbs on rime
                 to a high wire of his own making
and balancing on eyebeams
               above a sea of faces
     paces his way
             to the other side of day
   performing entrechats
               and sleight-of-foot tricks
and other high theatrics
             and all without mistaking
         any thing
            for what it may not be

For he's the super realist
                              who must perforce perceive
              taut truth
                       before the taking of each stance or step
  in his supposed advance
                              toward that still higher perch
 where Beauty stands and waits
                         with gravity
                                 to start her death-defying leap
      And he
            a little charleychaplin man
                              who may or may not catch
              her fair eternal form
                              spreadeagled in the empty air
              of existence

Reed Whittemore 1919–

Clamming

I go digging for clams once every two or three years
Just to keep my hand in (I usually cut it),
And I'm sure that whenever I do so I tell the
    same story
Of how, at the age of four, I was trapped by the tide
As I clammed a sandbar. It's no story at all,
But I tell it and tell it. It serves my small lust
To be thought of as someone who's lived.
I've a war too to fall back on, and some years of flying,
As well as a high quota of drunken parties,
A wife and children; but somehow the clamming thing
Gives me an image of me that soothes my psyche
Like none of the louder events: me helpless,
Alone with my sandpail,
As fate in the form of soupy Long Island Sound
Comes stalking me.

I've a son now at that age.
He's spoiled. He's been sickly.
He's handsome and bright, affectionate and demanding.
I think of the tides when I look at him.
I'd have him alone and sea-girt, poor little boy.

The self, what a brute it is. It wants, wants.
It will not let go of its even most fictional grandeur,
But must grope, grope down in the muck of its past
For some little squirting life and bring it up tenderly
To the lo and behold of death, that it may weep
And pass on the weeping, keep the thing going.

                    Son, when you clam,
Watch out for the tides and take care of yourself,
Yet no great care,
Lest you care too much and talk of the caring
And bore your best friends and inhibit your children and sicken
At last into opera on somebody's sandbar. Son, when you clam,
Clam.

Our Ruins

Our ruins are not ambitious yet, mostly.
Except for a couple of Williamsburgs they age
In the grass and thistle of waste country
Where nobody who would rebuild or tear down comes to rage
At what is unsafe, un-American, unsightly.

The small silent mills are the solemnest – squat, square,
With a thickness of wall and an air of social stability
That the fishermen in their hook-and-fly hats from the city
Take to be clear
Evidence that the Greeks or Romans have been here.

But in death the square-eyed farms have their dignity too,
Where the myth of the fixed point, the still center
In all this surge and wash, this flux and flow
Has been gelded again and again, over and over,
As each agrarian buries his deathless hoe.

And now, as the country's thoroughfares widen and stiffen,
Soft little cultures with country store, gas pump, crossway,
Depot (long-closed), and a weedy, rusted siding
Display some of the virtues of long-term decay
Without the agrarians even moving away.

Antiquity doesn't matter. In but a decade
An empty house can gain centuries, and old mills
Can lure the bright trout and slim pike for miles and miles
To swim in the depths by their old walls by falls
Or lurk in their rotten wheelways, savoring the shade.

Charles Bukowski 1920–

don't come round but if you do . . .

yeah sure, I'll be in unless I'm out
don't knock if the lights are out
or you hear voices or then
I might be reading Proust
if someone slips Proust under my door
or one of his bones for my stew,
and I can't loan money or
the phone
or what's left of my car
though you can have yesterday's newspaper
an old shirt or a bologna sandwich
or sleep on the couch
if you don't scream at night
and you can talk about yourself
that's only normal;
hard times are upon us all
only I am not trying to raise a family
to send through Harvard
or buy hunting land,
I am not aiming high
I am only trying to keep myself alive
just a little longer,
so if you sometimes knock
and I don't answer
and there isn't a woman in here
maybe I have broken my jaw
and am looking for wire
or I am chasing the butterflies in

my wallpaper,
I mean if I don't answer
I don't answer, and the reason is
that I am not yet ready to kill you
or love you, or even accept you,
it means I don't want to talk
I am busy, I am mad, I am glad
or maybe I'm stringing up a rope;
so even if the lights are on
and you hear sound
like breathing or praying or singing
a radio or the roll of dice
or typing –
go away, it is not the day
the night, the hour;
it is not the ignorance of impoliteness,
I wish to hurt nothing, not even a bug
but sometimes I gather evidence of a kind
that takes some sorting,
and your blue eyes, be they blue
and your hair, if you have some
or your mind – they cannot enter
until the rope is cut or knotted
or until I have shaven into
new mirrors, until the wound is
stopped or opened
                    forever.

Men's Crapper

take this one:
first before he shits he wipes with
easy grace the
lid of the seat, he really *shines* the damn
thing
then he spreads toilet paper over the seat,
quite neatly, even
dangling a gob of it where his powerful genitals will
hang, and then he lowers with
dignity and manliness
his shorts and pants
and
   sits and
      shits
almost without *passion*
scuffling an old dirty newspaper
between his feet and reading about yesterday's basketball
game –
this you see here is a Man: worldly, and no crabs for this
baby, and an easy
a real easy
shit, and he will wipe his ass
while conversing with the man who is washing his hands
at the nearest sink,
and if you are standing nearby
his little mouse eyes will fall upon yours without a
quiver, and then –
the shorts up, the pants up, the hook of belt, the flush of
toilet,
the washing of the hands
and then he stands before the mirror
surveying the glory of himself
combing his hair carefully in neat and

delicate swoops, finishing,
then putting that
face
close to the mirror
and looking in and upon himself, then
satisfied
he leaves
first making sure to give you the elbow
or the ponderous nightmare insult of his empty
eyes, and then with
the twirling of his dumbstruck egotistical buttocks
he leaves the men's room,
and I am left with facetowels like flowers
mirrors like the sea
and I am left with the sickest of hopes
that someday the real human being will arrive
so that there will be something to save
let alone
shit
out.

the catch

crud, he said,
hauling it out of the water,
what is it?

a Hollow-Back June Whale, I said.

no, said a guy standing by us on the pier,
it's a Billow-Wind Sand-Groper.

a guy walking by said,
it's a Fandango Escadrille without stripes.

we took the hook out and the thing stood up and
farted. it was grey and covered with hair
and fat and it stank like old socks.

it began to walk down the pier and we followed it.
it ate a hot dog and bun right out of the hands of
a little girl. then it leaped on the merry-go-round
and rode a pinto. it fell off near the end and
rolled in the sawdust.

we picked it up.

grop, it said, grop.

then it walked back out on the pier.
a large crowd followed us as we walked along.

it's a publicity stunt, said somebody,
it's a man in a rubber suit.

then as it was walking along it began to breathe
very heavily. it fell on its
back and began to thrash.

somebody poured a cup of beer over its head.

grop, it went, grop.

then it was dead.

we rolled it to the edge of the pier and pushed it
back into the water. we watched it sink and vanish.

it was a Hollow-Back June Whale, I said.

no, said the other guy, it was a Billow-Wind Sand-Groper.

no, said the other expert, it was a Fandango Escadrille
without stripes.

then we all went our way on a mid-afternoon in August.

Howard Nemerov 1920–

Make Love Not War

Lovers everywhere are bringing babies into the world.
Lovers with stars in their eyes are turning the stars
Into babies, lovers reading the instructions in comic books
Are turning out babies according to the instructions; this
Progression is said by demographers to be geometric and
Accelerating the rate of its acceleration. Lovers abed
Read up the demographers' reports, and accordingly produce
Babies with contact lenses and babies diapered in the flags
Of new and underdeveloped nations. Some experts contend
That bayonets are being put into the hands of babies
Not old enough to understand their use. And in the U.S.,
Treasury officials have expressed their grave concern about
The unauthorized entry of stateless babies without
Passports and knowing no English: these 'wetbacks',
As they are called from the circumstance of their swimming
Into this country, are to be reported to the proper
Authority wherever they occur and put through channels
For deportation to Abysmo the equatorial paradise
Believed to be their country of origin – 'where',
According to one of our usually unformed sorcerers,
'The bounteous foison of untilled Nature alone
Will rain upon the heads of these homeless, unhappy
And helpless beings apples, melons, honey, nuts, and gum
Sufficient to preserve them in their prelapsarian state
Under the benign stare of Our Lord Et Cetera forevermore.'

Meanwhile I forgot to tell you, back at the ranch,
The lovers are growing older, becoming more responsible.
Beginning with the mortal courtship of the Emerald Goddess

By Doctor Wasp – both of them twelve feet high
And insatiable; he wins her love by scientific means
And she has him immolated in a specially designed mole –
They have now settled down in an L-shaped ranch-type home
Where they are running a baby ranch and bringing up
Powerful babies able to defend their Way of Life
To the death if necessary. Of such breeding pairs
The average he owns seven and a half pair of pants,
While she generally has three girdles and a stove.
They keep a small pump-action repeater in the closet,
And it will not go off in the last act of this epic.

To sum up, it was for all the world as if one had said
Increase! Be fruitful! Multiply! Divide!
Be as the sands of the sea, the stars in the firmament,
The moral law within, the number of molecules
In the unabridged dictionary. BVD. Amen. Ahen.

                                                    AUM.
(Or, roughly, the peace that passeth understanding.)

Richard Wilbur 1921–

Still, Citizen Sparrow

Still, citizen sparrow, this vulture which you call
Unnatural, let him but lumber again to air
Over the rotten office, let him bear
The carrion ballast up, and at the tall

Tip of the sky lie cruising. Then you'll see
That no more beautiful bird is in heaven's height,
No wider more placid wings, no watchfuller flight;
He shoulders nature there, the frightfully free,

The naked-headed one. Pardon him, you
Who dart in the orchard aisles, for it is he
Devours death, mocks mutability,
Has heart to make an end, keeps nature new.

Thinking of Noah, childheart, try to forget
How for so many bedlam hours his saw
Soured the song of birds with its wheezy gnaw,
And the slam of his hammer all the day beset

The people's ears. Forget that he could bear
To see the towns like coral under the keel,
And the fields so dismal deep. Try rather to feel
How high and weary it was, on the waters where

He rocked his only world, and everyone's.
Forgive the hero, you who would have died
Gladly with all you knew; he rode that tide
To Ararat; all men are Noah's sons.

Love Calls Us to the Things of This World

   The eyes open to a cry of pulleys,
And spirited from sleep, the astounded soul
Hangs for a moment bodiless and simple
As false dawn.
              Outside the open window
The morning air is all awash with angels.

Some are in bed-sheets, some are in blouses,
Some are in smocks: but truly there they are.
Now they are rising together in calm swells
Of halcyon feeling, filling whatever they wear
With the deep joy of their impersonal breathing;

Now they are flying in place, conveying
The terrible speed of their omnipresence, moving
And staying like white water; and now of a sudden
They swoon down into so rapt a quiet
That nobody seems to be there.
                    The soul shrinks

From all that it is about to remember,
From the punctual rape of every blessèd day,
And cries,
         'Oh, let there be nothing on earth but laundry,
Nothing but rosy hands in the rising steam
And clear dances done in the sight of heaven.'

   Yet, as the sun acknowledges
With a warm look the world's hunks and colors,
The soul descends once more in bitter love
To accept the waking body, saying now
In a changed voice as the man yawns and rises,

'Bring them down from their ruddy gallows;
Let there be clean linen for the backs of thieves;
Let lovers go fresh and sweet to be undone,
And the heaviest nuns walk in a pure floating
Of dark habits,

     keeping their difficult balance.'

Pangloss's Song: A Comic-Opera Lyric

I

Dear boy, you will not hear me speak
 With sorrow or with rancor
Of what has paled my rosy cheek
 And blasted it with canker;
'Twas Love, great Love, that did the deed
 Through Nature's gentle laws,
And how should ill effects proceed
 From so divine a cause?

Sweet honey comes from bees that sting,
 As you are well aware;
To one adept in reasoning,
 Whatever pains disease may bring
Are but the tangy seasoning
 To Love's delicious fare.

II

Columbus and his men, they say,
 Conveyed the virus hither
Whereby my features rot away
 And vital powers wither;
Yet had they not traversed the seas
 And come infected back,
Why, think of all the luxuries
 That modern life would lack!

All bitter things conduce to sweet,
   As this example shows;
Without the little spirochete
   We'd have no chocolate to eat,
Nor would tobacco's fragrance greet
   The European nose.

III

Each nation guards its native land
   With cannon and with sentry,
Inspectors look for contraband
   At every port of entry,
Yet nothing can prevent the spread
   Of Love's divine disease;
It rounds the world from bed to bed
   As pretty as you please.

Men worship Venus everywhere,
   As plainly may be seen;
The decorations which I bear
   Are nobler than the Croix de Guerre,
And gained in service of our fair
   And universal Queen.

On the Marginal Way

FOR J.C.P.

Another cove of shale,
But the beach here is rubbled with strange rock
   That is sleek, fluent, and taffy-pale.
I stare, reminded with a little shock
How, by a shore in Spain, George Borrow saw
A hundred women basking in the raw.

They must have looked like this,
That catch of bodies on the sand, that strew
   Of rondure, crease, and orifice,
Lap, flank, and knee – a too abundant view
Which, though he'd had the lenses of a fly,
Could not have waked desire in Borrow's eye.

—

   Has the light altered now?
The rocks flush rose and have the melting shape
   Of bodies fallen anyhow.
It is a Géricault of blood and rape,
Some desert town despoiled, some caravan
Pillaged, its people murdered to a man,

   And those who murdered them
Galloping off, a rumpling line of dust
   Like the wave's white, withdrawing hem.
But now the vision of a colder lust
Clears, as the wind goes chill and all is greyed
By a swift cloud that drags a carrion shade.

   If these are bodies still,
Theirs is a death too dead to look asleep,
   Like that of Auschwitz' final kill,
Poor slaty flesh abandoned in a heap
And then, like sea-rocks buried by a wave,
Bulldozed at last into a common grave.

   It is not tricks of sense
But the time's fright within me which distracts
   Least fancies into violence
And makes my thought take cover in the facts,
As now it does, remembering how the bed
Of layered rock two miles above my head

Hove ages up and broke
Soundless asunder, when the shrinking skin
  Of Earth, blacked out by steam and smoke,
Gave passage to the muddled fire within,
Its crannies flooding with a sweat of quartz,
And lathered magmas out of deep retorts

  Welled up, as here, to fill
With tumbled rockmeal, stone-fume, lithic spray,
  The dike's brief chasm and the sill.
Weathered until the sixth and human day
By sanding winds and water, scuffed and brayed
By the slow glacier's heel, these forms were made

  That now recline and burn
Comely as Eve and Adam, near a sea
  Transfigured by the sun's return.
And now three girls lie golden in the lee
Of a great arm or thigh, and are as young
As the bright boulders that they lie among.

  Though, high above the shore
On someone's porch, spread wings of newsprint flap
  The tidings of some dirty war,
It is a perfect day: the waters clap
Their hands and kindle, and the gull in flight
Loses himself at moments, white in white,

  And like a breaking thought
Joy for a moment floods into the mind,
  Blurting that all things shall be brought
To the full state and stature of their kind,
By what has found the manhood of this stone.
May that vast motive wash and wash our own.

Alan Dugan 1923–

Love Song: I and Thou

Nothing is plumb, level or square:
   the studs are bowed, the joists
are shaky by nature, no piece fits
   any other piece without a gap
or pinch, and bent nails
   dance all over the surfacing
like maggots. By Christ
   I am no carpenter. I built
the roof for myself, the walls
   for myself, the floors
for myself, and got
   hung up in it myself. I
danced with a purple thumb
   at this house-warming, drunk
with my prime whiskey: rage.
   Oh I spat rage's nails
into the frame-up of my work:
   it held. It settled plumb,
level, solid, square and true
   for that great moment. Then
it screamed and went on through,
   skewing as wrong the other way.
God damned it. This is hell,
   but I planned it, I sawed it,
I nailed it, and I
   will live in it until it kills me.
I can nail my left palm
   to the left-hand cross-piece but

ALAN DUGAN

I can't do everything myself.
    I need a hand to nail the right,
a help, a love, a you, a wife.

Fabrication of Ancestors

FOR OLD BILLY DUGAN, SHOT IN THE ASS
IN THE CIVIL WAR, MY FATHER SAID.

The old wound in my ass
has opened up again, but I
am past the prodigies
of youth's campaigns, and weep
where I used to laugh
in war's red humors, half
in love with silly-assed pains
and half not feeling them.
I have to sit up with
an indoor unsittable itch
before I go down late
and weeping to the storm-
cellar on a dirty night
and go to bed with the worms.
So pull the dirt up over me
and make a family joke
for Old Billy Blue Balls,
the oldest private in the world
with two ass-holes and no
place more to go to for a laugh
except the last one. Say:
The North won the Civil War
without much help from me
although I wear a proof
of the war's obscenity.

493

Anthony Hecht 1923–

Japan

It was a miniature country once
To my imagination; Home of the Short,
And also the academy of stunts
    Where acrobats are taught
  The famous secrets of the trade:
  To cycle in the big parade
While spinning plates upon their parasols,
Or somersaults that do not touch the ground,
    Or tossing seven balls
In Most Celestial Order round and round.

A child's quick sense of the ingenious stamped
All their invention: toys I used to get
At Christmastime, or the peculiar, cramped
    Look of their alphabet.
  Fragile and easily destroyed,
  Those little boats of celluloid
Driven by camphor round the bathroom sink,
And delicate the folded paper prize
    Which, dropped into a drink
Of water, grew up right before your eyes.

Now when we reached them it was with a sense
Sharpened for treachery compounding in their brains
Like mating weasels; our Intelligence
    Said: The Black Dragon reigns
  Secretly under yellow skin,
  Deeper than dyes of atabrine
And deadlier. The War Department said:

Remember you are Americans; forsake
    The wounded and the dead
At your own cost; remember Pearl and Wake.

And yet they bowed us in with ceremony,
Told us what brands of Sake were the best,
Explained their agriculture in a phony
    Dialect of the West,
  Meant vaguely to be understood
  As a shy sign of brotherhood
In the old human bondage to the facts
Of day-to-day existence. And like ants,
    Signalling tiny pacts
With their antennae, they would wave their hands.

At last we came to see them not as glib
Walkers of tightropes, worshippers of carp,
Nor yet a species out of Adam's rib
    Meant to preserve its warp
  In Cain's own image. They had learned
  That their tough eye-born goddess burned
Adoring fingers. They were very poor.
The holy mountain was not moved to speak.
    Wind at the paper door
Offered them snow out of its hollow peak.

Human endeavor clumsily betrays
Humanity. Their excrement served in this;
    For, planting rice in water, they would raise
      Schistosomiasis
  Japonica, that enters through
  The pores into the avenue
And orbit of the blood, where it may foil
The heart and kill, or settle in the brain.
    This fruit of their nightsoil
Thrives in the skull, where it is called insane.

Now the quaint early image of Japan
That was so charming to me as a child
Seems like a bright design upon a fan,
    Of water rushing wild
  On rocks that can be folded up,
  A river which the wrist can stop
With a neat flip, revealing merely sticks
And silk of what had been a fan before,
    And like such winning tricks,
It shall be buried in excelsior.

Kenneth Koch 1925–

Mending Sump

'Hiram, I think the sump is backing up.
The bathroom floor boards for above two weeks
Have seemed soaked through. A little bird, I think
Has wandered in the pipes, and all's gone wrong.'
'Something there is that doesn't hump a sump,'
He said; and through his head she saw a cloud
That seemed to twinkle. 'Hiram, well,' she said,
'Smith is come home! I saw his face just now
While looking through your head. He's come to die
Or else to laugh, for hay is dried-up grass
When you're alone.' He rose, and sniffed the air.
'We'd better leave him in the sump,' he said.

You Were Wearing

You were wearing your Edgar Allan Poe printed cotton blouse.
In each divided up square of the blouse was a picture of Edgar Allan
    Poe.
Your hair was blonde and you were cute. You asked me, 'Do most
    boys think that most girls are bad?'
I smelled the mould of your seaside resort hotel bedroom on your
    hair held in place by a John Greenleaf Whittier clip.
'No,' I said, 'it's girls who think that boys are bad.' Then we read
    Snowbound together
And ran around in an attic, so that a little of the blue enamel was
    scraped off my George Washington, Father of His Country,
    shoes.

Mother was walking in the living room, her Strauss Waltzes comb in her hair.

We waited for a time and then joined her, only to be served tea in cups painted with pictures of Herman Melville

As well as with illustrations from his book *Moby Dick* and from his novella, *Benito Cereno*.

Father came in wearing his Dick Tracy necktie: 'How about a drink, everyone?'

I said, 'Let's go outside a while.' Then we went onto the porch and sat on the Abraham Lincoln swing.

You sat on the eyes, mouth, and beard part, and I sat on the knees.

In the yard across the street we saw a snowman holding a garbage can lid smashed into the likeness of the mad English king, George the Third.

Frank O'Hara 1926–66

To the Film Industry in Crisis

Not you, lean quarterlies and swarthy periodicals
with your studious incursions toward the pomposity of ants,
nor you, experimental theatre in which Emotive Fruition
is wedding Poetic Insight perpetually, nor you,
promenading Grand Opera, obvious as an ear (though you
are close to my heart), but you, Motion Picture Industry,
it's you I love!

In time of crisis, we must all decide again and again whom we love.
And give credit where it's due: not to my starched nurse, who taught
    me
how to be bad and not bad rather than good (and has lately availed
herself of this information), not to the Catholic Church
which is at best an oversolemn introduction to cosmic entertainment,
not to the American Legion, which hates everybody, but to you,
glorious Silver Screen, tragic Technicolor, amorous Cinemascope,
stretching Vistavision and startling Stereophonic Sound, with all
your heavenly dimensions and reverberations and iconoclasms! To
Richard Barthelmess as the 'tol'able' boy barefoot and in pants,
Jeanette MacDonald of the flaming hair and lips and long, long neck.
Sue Carroll as she sits for eternity on the damaged fender of a car
and smiles, Ginger Rogers with her pageboy bob like a sausage
on her shuffling shoulders, peach-melba-voiced Fred Astaire of the
    feet,
Eric von Stroheim, the seducer of mountain-climbers' gasping
    spouses,
the Tarzans, each and every one of you (I cannot bring myself to
    prefer

Johnny Weissmuller to Lex Barker, I cannot!), Mae West in a furry
    sled,
her bordello radiance and bland remarks, Rudolph Valentino of the
    moon,
its crushing passions, and moonlike, too, the gentle Norma Shearer,
Miriam Hopkins dropping her champagne glass off Joel McCrea's
    yacht
and crying into the dappled sea, Clark Gable rescuing Gene Tierney
from Russia and Allan Jones rescuing Kitty Carlisle from Harpo Marx,
Cornel Wilde coughing blood on the piano keys while Merle
    Oberon berates,
Marilyn Monroe in her little spike heels reeling through Niagara
    Falls,
Joseph Cotten puzzling and Orson Welles puzzled and Dolores del
    Rio
eating orchids for lunch and breaking mirrors, Gloria Swanson
    reclining,
and Jean Harlow reclining and wiggling, and Alice Faye reclining
and wiggling and singing, Myrna Loy being calm and wise, William
    Powell
in his stunning urbanity, Elizabeth Taylor blossoming, yes, to you

and to all you others, the great, the near-great, the featured, the extras
who pass quickly and return in dreams saying your one or two lines,
    my love!
Long may you illumine space with your marvellous appearances,
    delays
and enunciations, and may the money of the world glitteringly cover
    you
as you rest after a long day under the kleig lights with your faces
in packs for our edification, the way the clouds come often at night
but the heavens operate on the star system. It is a divine precedent
you perpetuate! Roll on, reels of celluloid, as the great earth rolls on!

Paul Blackburn 1926–71

Sunflower Rock

'C'mon, get out,
    y gotta get out,' sez Milly,
      'stop sleeping'n get out, I call the cop.'
The old man
crumples up his check and drops it onto the sawdust floor.

'Mary,' he says, and staggers to his feet and
begins to come on to Mary behind the counter. She
wipes the glass counter and does not meet his eyes,
says, 'You'll get out now.'

He does, stiffening his body and pushing it back
off the counter with his arms, reels
        lightly toward the door:
            'See ya tomorrow, Mary,' and
                something else low.
                    'You'll get out,' she says.
                        He does.

Milly the waitress is full of plump wrath and righteousness
finding the unpaid, crumpled bill on the floor: 'He
comes in, eats, he goes ta sleep,
don't even pay his bill!' Milly
lays the crumpled paper on the counter.
        I suppose there's a place to put it.

'Hey, he's all right, he
just thinks it's a flophouse!' Aunt
Ella joins in, having emerged from the kitchen
            where she is these nights,
                        wipes her hands on her apron
                                    and grins .

                        'Sunstroke!' it's Max,
                        a customer at the front table,
                        'He wuz
                        hit in that head widda sunflower!'
                        makes the finger-gesture
                        to his own head.

He sports a new pair of those half-sized aluminium crutches
crippled open on the chair beside him.

The circles grow from the stone.
Woodie, black dog with a curly tail,
circles back of the counter, out front again.
The Mrs circles up from the ovens to find out
what the shouting's about . Mary
circles back of the register for someone who does pay .
Aunt Ella circles back to the kitchen,
another order's in .

Struck in the head with a sunflower,
the old man's circle has taken him out the door
            into the rain.
                        Outside,
                                    the night is full of March rain,
                                    That was the joke,
some joke . and the evening traffic uptown .

Soon,
we step into it ourself, stop
to buy a half-pint at the corner
for the cold night, for the pocket.
Already wet, we turned our back to the northwind,
feel the whiskey burn .

A. R. Ammons 1926–

Coon Song

I got one good look
    in the raccoon's eyes
        when he fell from the tree
came to his feet
    and perfectly still
        seized the baying hounds
in his dull fierce stare,
    in that recognition all
        decision lost,
choice irrelevant, before the
    battle fell
        and the unwinding
of his little knot of time began:

        Dostoevsky would think
it important if the coon
    could choose to
        be back up the tree:
or if he could choose to be
    wagging by a swamp pond,
        dabbling at scuttling
crawdads: the coon may have
    dreamed in fact of curling
        into the holed-out gall
of a fallen oak some squirrel
    had once brought
        high into the air
clean leaves to: but

reality can go to hell
is what the coon's eyes said to me:
        and said how simple
            the solution to my
problem is: it needs only
        not to be: I thought the raccoon
            felt no anger,
saw none; cared nothing for cowardice,
        bravery; was in fact
            bored at
knowing what would ensue:
        the unwinding, the whirling growls,
            exposed tenders,
the wet teeth – a problem to be
        solved, the taut-coiled vigor
            of the hunt
ready to snap loose:

        you want to know what happened,
you want to hear me describe it,
        to placate the hound's-mouth
            slobbering in your own heart:
I will not tell you: actually the coon
        possessing secret knowledge
            pawed dust on the dogs
and they disappeared, yapping into
        nothingness, and the coon went
            down to the pond
and washed his face and hands and beheld
        the world: maybe he didn't:
            I am no slave that I
should entertain you, say what you want
        to hear, let you wallow in
            your silt: one two three four five:
one two three four five six seven eight nine ten:

(all this time I've been
        counting spaces
while you were thinking of something else)
        mess in your own sloppy silt:
                the hounds disappeared
yelping (the way you would at extinction)
        into – the order
        breaks up here – immortality:
I know that's where you think the brave
        little victims should go:
                I do not care what
you think: I do not care what you think:
        I do not care what you
                think: one two three four five
six seven eight nine ten: here we go
        round the here-we-go-round, the
                here-we-go-round, the here-we-
go-round: coon will end in disorder at the
        teeth of hounds: the situation
                will get him:
spheres roll, cubes stay put: now there
        one two three four five
        are two philosophies:
here we go round the mouth-wet of hounds:

                what I choose
                is youse:
                baby

Corsons Inlet

I went for a walk over the dunes again this morning
to the sea,
then turned right along
   the surf
              rounded a naked headland
              and returned

  along the inlet shore:

it was muggy sunny, the wind from the sea steady and high,
crisp in the running sand,
    some breakthroughs of sun
  but after a bit

continuous overcast:

the walk liberating, I was released from forms,
from the perpendiculars,
    straight lines, blocks, boxes, binds
of thought
into the hues, shadings, rises, flowing bends and blends
        of sight:

                I allow myself eddies of meaning:
yield to a direction of significance
running
like a stream through the geography of my work:
  you can find
in my sayings
              swerves of action
              like the inlet's cutting edge:
      there are dunes of motion,
organizations of grass, white sandy paths of remembrance
in the overall wandering of mirroring mind:

but Overall is beyond me: is the sum of these events
I cannot draw, the ledger I cannot keep, the accounting
beyond the account:

in nature there are few sharp lines: there are areas of
primrose
    more or less dispersed;
disorderly orders of bayberry; between the rows
of dunes,
irregular swamps of reeds,
though not reeds alone, but grass, bayberry, yarrow, all . . .
predominantly reeds:

I have reached no conclusions, have erected no boundaries,
shutting out and shutting in, separating inside
    from outside: I have
    drawn no lines:
    as

manifold events of sand
change the dune's shape that will not be the same shape
tomorrow,

so I am willing to go along, to accept
the becoming
thought, to stake off no beginnings or ends, establish
       no walls:

by transitions the land falls from grassy dunes to creek
to undercreek: but there are no lines, though
    change in that transition is clear
    as any sharpness: but 'sharpness' spread out,
allowed to occur over a wider range
than mental lines can keep:

the moon was full last night: today, low tide was low:
black shoals of mussels exposed to the risk
of air
and, earlier, of sun,
waved in and out with the waterline, waterline inexact,
caught always in the event of change:
    a young mottled gull stood free on the shoals
      and ate
to vomiting: another gull, squawking possession, cracked a crab,
picked out the entrails, swallowed the soft-shelled legs, a ruddy
turnstone running in to snatch leftover bits:

risk is full: every living thing in
siege: the demand is life, to keep life: the small
white blacklegged egret, how beautiful, quietly stalks and spears
        the shallows, darts to shore
                to stab – what? I couldn't
   see against the black mudflats – a frightened
   fiddler crab?

        the news to my left over the dunes and
reeds and bayberry clumps was
        fall: thousands of tree swallows
        gathering for flight:
        an order held
        in constant change: a congregation
rich with entropy: nevertheless, separable, noticeable
        as one event,
                not chaos: preparations for
flight from winter,
cheet, cheet, cheet, cheet, wings rifling the green clumps,
beaks
at the bayberries:
  a perception full of wind, flight, curve,
  sound:

the possibility of rule as the sum of rulelessness:
the 'field' of action
with moving, incalculable center;

in the smaller view, order tight with shape:
blue tiny flowers on a leafless weed: carapace of crab:
snail shell:
       pulsations of order
       in the bellies of minnows: orders swallowed,
broken down, transferred through membranes
to strengthen larger orders: but in the large view, no
lines or changeless shapes: the working in and out, together
       and against, of millions of events: this,
              so that I make
              no form of
              formlessness:

orders as summaries, as outcomes of actions override
or in some way result, not predictably (seeing me gain
the top of a dune,
the swallows
could take flight – some other fields of bayberry
       could enter fall
       berryless) and there is serenity:

       no arranged terror: no forcing of image, plan,
or thought:
no propaganda, no humbling of reality to precept:

terror pervades but is not arranged, all possibilities
of escape open: no route shut, except in
   the sudden loss of all routes:

       I see narrow orders, limited tightness, but will
not run to that easy victory:
       still around the looser, wider forces work:
       I will try

to fasten into order enlarging grasps of disorder, widening
scope, but enjoying the freedom that
Scope eludes my grasp, that there is no finality of vision,
that I have perceived nothing completely,
    that tomorrow a new walk is a new walk.

Robert Bly 1926–

The Executive's Death

Merchants have multiplied more than the stars of heaven.
Half the population are like the long grasshoppers
That sleep in the bushes in the cool of the day:
The sound of their wings is heard at noon, muffled, near the earth.
The crane handler dies, the taxi driver dies, slumped over
In his taxi. Meanwhile, high in the air, executives
Walk on cool floors, and suddenly fall:
Dying, they dream they are lost in a snowstorm in mountains,
On which they crashed, carried at night by great machines.
As he lies on the wintry slope, cut off and dying,
A pine stump talks to him of Goethe and Jesus.
Commuters arrive in Hartford at dusk like moles
Or hares flying from a fire behind them,
And the dusk in Hartford is full of their sighs;
Their trains come through the air like a dark music,
Like the sound of horns, the sound of thousands of small wings.

Waking from Sleep

Inside the veins there are navies setting forth,
Tiny explosions at the water lines,
And seagulls weaving in the wind of the salty blood.

It is the morning. The country has slept the whole winter.
Window seats were covered with fur skins, the yard was full
Of stiff dogs, and hands that clumsily held heavy books.

Now we wake, and rise from bed, and eat breakfast! –
Shouts rise from the harbor of the blood,
Mist, and masts rising, the knock of wooden tackle in the sunlight.

Now we sing, and do tiny dances on the kitchen floor.
Our whole body is like a harbor at dawn;
We know that our master has left us for the day.

Robert Creeley 1926–

The Operation

By Saturday I said you would be better on Sunday.
The insistence was a part of a reconciliation.

Your eyes bulged, the grey
light hung on you, you were hideous.

My involvement is just an old
habitual relationship.

Cruel, cruel to describe
what there is no reason to describe.

The Whip

I spent a night turning in bed,
my love was a feather, a flat

sleeping thing. She was
very white

and quiet, and above us on
the roof, there was another woman I

also loved, had
addressed myself to in

a fit she
returned. That

encompasses it. But now I was
lonely, I yelled,

but what is that? Ugh,
she said, beside me, she put

her hand on
my back, for which act

I think to say this
wrongly.

The Rain

All night the sound had
come back again,
and again falls
this quiet, persistent rain.

What am I to myself
that must be remembered,
insisted upon
so often? Is it

that never the ease,
even the hardness,
of rain falling
will have for me

something other than this,
something not so insistent –
am I to be locked in this
final uneasiness.

Love, if you love me,
lie next to me.
Be for me, like rain,
the getting out

of the tiredness, the fatuousness, the semi-
lust of intentional indifference.
Be wet
with a decent happiness.

Something

I approach with such
a careful tremor, always
I feel the finally foolish

question of how it is,
then, supposed to be felt,
and by whom. I remember

once in a rented room on
27th street, the woman I loved
then, literally, after we

had made love on the large
bed sitting across from
a basin with two faucets, she

had to pee but was nervous,
embarrassed I suppose I
would watch her who had but

a moment ago been completely
open to me, naked, on
the same bed. Squatting, her

head reflected in the mirror,
the hair dark there, the
full of her face, the shoulders,

sat spread-legged, turned on
one faucet and shyly pissed. What
love might learn from such a sight.

'I Keep to Myself Such Measures . . . '

I keep to myself such
measures as I care for,
daily the rocks
accumulate position.

There is nothing
but what thinking makes
it less tangible. The mind,
fast as it goes, loses

pace, puts in place of it
like rocks simple markers,
for a way only to
hopefully come back to

where it cannot. All
forgets. My mind sinks.
I hold in both hands such weight
it is my only description.

The World

I wanted so ably
to reassure you, I wanted
the man you took to be me,

to comfort you, and got
up, and went to the window,
pushed back, as you asked me to,

the curtain, to see
the outline of the trees
in the night outside.

The light, love,
the light we felt then,
greyly, was it, that

came in, on us, not
merely my hands or yours,
or a wetness so comfortable,

but in the dark then
as you slept, the grey
figure came so close

and leaned over,
between us, as you
slept, restless, and

my own face had to
see it, and be seen by it,
the man it was, your

grey lost tired bewildered
brother, unused, untaken –
hated by love, and dead,

but not dead, for an
instant, saw me, myself
the intruder, as he was not.

I tried to say, it is
all right, she is
happy, you are no longer

needed. I said,
he is dead, and he
went as you shifted

and woke, at first afraid,
then knew by my own knowing
what had happened –

and the light then
of the sun coming
for another morning
in the world.

Allen Ginsberg 1926–

From *Howl*

FOR CARL SOLOMON

I

I saw the best minds of my generation destroyed by madness,
    starving hysterical naked,

dragging themselves through the negro streets at dawn looking for
    an angry fix,

angelheaded hipsters burning for the ancient heavenly connection
    to the starry dynamo in the machinery of night,

who poverty and tatters and hollow-eyed and high sat up smoking
    in the supernatural darkness of cold-water flats floating across
    the tops of cities contemplating jazz,

who bared their brains to Heaven under the El and saw Moham-
    medan angels staggering on tenement roofs illuminated,

who passed through universities with radiant cool eyes hallucinating
    Arkansas and Blake-light tragedy among the scholars of war,

who were expelled from the academies for crazy & publishing
    obscene odes on the windows of the skull,

who cowered in unshaven rooms in underwear, burning their money
    in wastebaskets and listening to the Terror through the wall,

who got busted in their pubic beards returning through Laredo
    with a belt of marijuana for New York,

who ate fire in paint hotels or drank turpentine in Paradise Alley,
    death, or purgatoried their torsos night after night

with dreams, with drugs, with waking nightmares, alcohol and
    cock and endless balls,

incomparable blind streets of shuddering cloud and lightning in the
    mind leaping toward poles of Canada & Paterson, illuminating
    all the motionless world of Time between,

Peyote solidities of halls, backyard green tree cemetery dawns, wine
    drunkenness over the rooftops, storefront boroughs of teahead
    joyride neon blinking traffic light, sun and moon and tree
    vibrations in the roaring winter dusks of Brooklyn, ashcan
    rantings and kind king light of mind,

who chained themselves to subways for the endless ride from Battery
    to holy Bronx on benzedrine until the noise of wheels and
    children brought them down shuddering mouth-wracked and
    battered bleak of brain all drained of brilliance in the drear light
    of Zoo,

who sank all night in submarine light of Bickford's floated out and
    sat through the stale beer afternoon in desolate Fugazzi's, listening
    to the crack of doom on the hydrogen jukebox,

who talked continuously seventy hours from park to pad to bar to
    Bellevue to museum to the Brooklyn Bridge,

a lost battalion of platonic conversationalists jumping down the
    stoops off fire escapes off windowsills off Empire State out of
    the moon,

yacketayakking screaming vomiting whispering facts and memories
    and anecdotes and eyeball kicks and shocks of hospitals and
    jails and wars,

whole intellects disgorged in total recall for seven days and nights
    with brilliant eyes, meat for the Synagogue cast on the pavement,

who vanished into nowhere Zen New Jersey leaving a trail of
    ambiguous picture postcards of Atlantic City Hall,

suffering Eastern sweats and Tangerian bone-grindings and migraines
    of China under junk-withdrawal in Newark's bleak furnished
    room,

who wandered around and around at midnight in the railroad
    yard wondering where to go, and went, leaving no broken
    hearts,

who lit cigarettes in boxcars boxcars boxcars racketing through snow
    toward lonesome farms in grandfather night,

who studied Plotinus Poe St John of the Cross telepathy and bop
    kaballa because the cosmos instinctively vibrated at their feet in
    Kansas,

who loned it through the streets of Idaho seeking visionary indian
    angels who were visionary indian angels,

who thought they were only mad when Baltimore gleamed in
    supernatural ecstasy,

who jumped in limousines with the Chinaman of Oklahoma on the
    impulse of winter midnight streetlight smalltown rain,

who lounged hungry and lonesome through Houston seeking jazz
    or sex or soup, and followed the brilliant Spaniard to converse
    about America and Eternity, a hopeless task, and so took ship to
    Africa,

who disappeared into the volcanoes of Mexico leaving behind
    nothing but the shadow of dungarees and the lava and ash of
    poetry scattered in fireplace Chicago,

who reappeared on the West Coast investigating the F.B.I. in beards
    and shorts with big pacifist eyes sexy in their dark skin passing
    out incomprehensible leaflets,

who burned cigarette holes in their arms protesting the narcotic
    tobacco haze of Capitalism,

who distributed Supercommunist pamphlets in Union Square
    weeping and undressing while the sirens of Los Alamos wailed
    them down, and wailed down Wall, and the Staten Island ferry
    also wailed,

who broke down crying in white gymnasiums naked and trembling
    before the machinery of other skeletons,

who bit detectives in the neck and shrieked with delight in policecars
    for committing no crime but their own wild cooking pederasty
    and intoxication,

who howled on their knees in the subway and were dragged off the
    roof waving genitals and manuscripts,

who let themselves be fucked in the ass by saintly motorcyclists, and
    screamed with joy,

who blew and were blown by those human seraphim, the sailors,
    caresses of Atlantic and Caribbean love,

who balled in the morning in the evenings in rosegardens and the
    grass of public parks and cemeteries scattering their semen freely
    to whomever come who may,

who hiccupped endlessly trying to giggle but wound up with a sob
behind a partition in a Turkish Bath when the blonde & naked
angel came to pierce them with a sword,

who lost their loveboys to the three old shrews of fate the one eyed
shrew of the heterosexual dollar the one eyed shrew that winks
out of the womb and the one eyed shrew that does nothing but
sit on her ass and snip the intellectual golden threads of the
craftsman's loom,

who copulated ecstatic and insatiate with a bottle of beer a sweetheart
a package of cigarettes a candle and fell off the bed, and con-
tinued along the floor and down the hall and ended fainting on
the wall with a vision of ultimate cunt and come eluding the
last gyzym of consciousness,

who sweetened the snatches of a million girls trembling in the
sunset, and were red eyed in the morning but prepared to
sweeten the snatch of the sunrise, flashing buttocks under barns
and naked in the lake,

who went out whoring through Colorado in myriad stolen night-
cars, N.C., secret hero of these poems, cocksman and Adonis of
Denver – joy to the memory of his innumerable lays of girls in
empty lots & diner backyards, moviehouses' rickety rows, on
mountaintops in caves or with gaunt waitresses in familiar road-
side lonely petticoat upliftings & especially secret gas-station
solipisisms of johns, & hometown alleys too,

who faded out in vast sordid movies, were shifted in dreams, woke
on a sudden Manhattan, and picked themselves up out of base-
ments hungover with heartless Tokay and horrors of Third
Avenue iron dreams & stumbled to unemployment offices,

who walked all night with their shoes full of blood on the snowbank
docks waiting for a door in the East River to open to a room full
of steamheat and opium,

who created great suicidal dramas on the apartment cliff-banks of
the Hudson under the wartime blue floodlight of the moon
& their heads shall be crowned with laurel in oblivion,

who ate the lamb stew of the imagination or digested the crab at
the muddy bottom of the rivers of Bowery,

who wept at the romance of the streets with their pushcarts full of onions and bad music,

who sat in boxes breathing in the darkness under the bridge, and rose up to build harpsichords in their lofts,

who coughed on the sixth floor of Harlem crowned with flame under the tubercular sky surrounded by orange crates of theology,

who scribbled all night rocking and rolling over lofty incantations which in the yellow morning were stanzas of gibberish,

who cooked rotten animals lung heart feet tail borsht & tortillas dreaming of the pure vegetable kingdom,

who plunged themselves under meat trucks looking for an egg,

who threw their watches off the roof to cast their ballot for Eternity outside of Time, & alarm clocks fell on their heads every day for the next decade,

who cut their wrists three times successively unsuccessfully, gave up and were forced to open antique stores where they thought they were growing old and cried,

who were burned alive in their innocent flannel suits on Madison Avenue amid blasts of leaden verse & the tanked-up clatter of the iron regiments of fashion & the nitroglycerine shrieks of the fairies of advertising & the mustard gas of sinister intelligent editors, or were run down by the drunken taxicabs of Absolute Reality,

who jumped off the Brooklyn Bridge this actually happened and walked away unknown and forgotten into the ghostly daze of Chinatown soup alleyways & firetrucks, not even one free beer,

who sang out of their windows in despair, fell out of the subway window, jumped in the filthy Passaic, leaped on negroes, cried all over the street, danced on broken wineglasses barefoot smashed phonograph records of nostalgic European 1930's German jazz finished the whiskey and threw up groaning into the bloody toilet, moans in their ears and the blast of colossal steamwhistles,

who barreled down the highways of the past journeying to each other's hotrod-Golgotha jail-solitude watch or Birmingham jazz incarnation,

who drove crosscountry seventytwo hours to find out if I had a
   vision or you had a vision or he had a vision to find out Eternity,

who journeyed to Denver, who died in Denver, who came back to
   Denver & waited in vain, who watched over Denver & brooded
   & loned in Denver and finally went away to find out the Time,
   & now Denver is lonesome for her heroes,

who fell on their knees in hopeless cathedrals praying for each
   other's salvation and light and breasts, until the soul illuminated
   its hair for a second,

who crashed through their minds in jail waiting for impossible
   criminals with golden heads and the charm of reality in their
   hearts who sang sweet blues to Alcatraz,

who retired to Mexico to cultivate a habit, or Rocky Mount to
   tender Buddha or Tangiers to boys or Southern Pacific to the
   black locomotive or Harvard to Narcissus to Woodlawn to the
   daisychain or grave,

who demanded sanity trials accusing the radio of hypnotism & were
   left with their insanity & their hands & a hung jury,

who threw potato salad at CCNY lecturers on Dadaism and sub-
   sequently presented themselves on the granite steps of the
   madhouse with shaven heads and harlequin speech of suicide,
   demanding instantaneous lobotomy,

and who were given instead the concrete void of insulin metrasol
   electricity hydrotherapy psychotherapy occupational therapy
   pingpong & amnesia,

who in humorless protest overturned only one symbolic pingpong
   table, resting briefly in catatonia,

returning years later truly bald except for a wig of blood, and tears
   and fingers, to the visible madman doom of the wards of the
   madtowns of the East,

Pilgrim State's Rockland's and Greystone's foetid halls, bickering
   with the echoes of the soul, rocking and rolling in the midnight
   solitude-bench dolmen-realms of love, dream of life a nightmare,
   bodies turned to stone as heavy as the moon,

with mother finally ******, and the last fantastic book flung out
   of the tenement window, and the last door closed at 4 AM

and the last telephone slammed at the wall in reply and the last furnished room emptied down to the last piece of mental furniture, a yellow paper rose twisted on a wire hanger in the closet, and even that imaginary, nothing but a hopeful little bit of hallucination –

ah, Carl, while you are not safe I am not safe, and now you're really in the total animal soup of time –

and who therefore ran through the icy streets obsessed with a sudden flash of the alchemy of the use of the ellipse the catalog the meter & the vibrating plane,

who dreamt and made incarnate gaps in Time & Space through images juxtaposed, and trapped the archangel of the soul between 2 visual images and joined the elemental verbs and set the noun and dash of consciousness together jumping with sensation of Pater Omnipotens Aeterna Deus

to recreate the syntax and measure of poor human prose and stand before you speechless and intelligent and shaking with shame, rejected yet confessing out the soul to conform to the rhythm of thought in his naked and endless head,

the madman bum and angel beat in Time, unknown, yet putting down here what might be left to say in time come after death,

and rose reincarnate in the ghostly clothes of jazz in the goldhorn shadow of the band and blew the suffering of America's naked mind for love into an eli eli lamma lamma sabacthani saxophone cry that shivered the cities down to the last radio

with the absolute heart of the poem of life butchered out of their own bodies good to eat a thousand years.

A Supermarket in California

What thoughts I have of you tonight, Walt Whitman, for I walked down the sidestreets under the trees with a headache self-conscious looking at the full moon.

In my hungry fatigue, and shopping for images, I went into the neon fruit supermarket, dreaming of your enumerations!

What peaches and what penumbras! Whole families shopping at night! Aisles full of husbands! Wives in the avocados, babies in the tomatoes! – and you, Garcia Lorca, what were you doing down by the watermelons?

I saw you, Walt Whitman, childless, lonely old grubber, poking among the meats in the refrigerator and eyeing the grocery boys.

I heard you asking questions of each: Who killed the pork chops? What price bananas? Are you my Angel?

I wandered in and out of the brilliant stacks of cans following you, and followed in my imagination by the store detective.

We strode down the open corridors together in our solitary fancy tasting artichokes, possessing every frozen delicacy, and never passing the cashier.

Where are we going, Walt Whitman? The doors close in an hour. Which way does your beard point tonight?

(I touch your book and dream of our odyssey in the supermarket and feel absurd.)

Will we walk all night through solitary streets? The trees add shade to shade, lights out in the houses, we'll both be lonely.

Will we stroll dreaming of the lost America of love past blue automobiles in driveways, home to our silent cottage?

Ah, dear father, graybeard, lonely old courage-teacher, what America did you have when Charon quit poling his ferry and you got out on a smoking bank and stood watching the boat disappear on the black waters of Lethe?

America

America I've given you all and now I'm nothing.
America two dollars and twentyseven cents January 17, 1956.
I can't stand my own mind.
America when will we end the human war?
Go fuck yourself with your atom bomb.
I don't feel good don't bother me.
I won't write my poem till I'm in my right mind.
America when will you be angelic?
When will you take off your clothes?
When will you look at yourself through the grave?
When will you be worthy of your million Trotskyites?
America why are your libraries full of tears?
America when will you send your eggs to India?
I'm sick of your insane demands.
When can I go into the supermarket and buy what I need with my
    good looks?
America after all it is you and I who are perfect not the next world.
Your machinery is too much for me.
You made me want to be a saint.
There must be some other way to settle this argument.
Burroughs is in Tangiers I don't think he'll come back it's sinister.
Are you being sinister or is this some form of practical joke?
I'm trying to come to the point.
I refuse to give up my obsession.
America stop pushing I know what I'm doing.
America the plum blossoms are falling.
I haven't read the newspapers for months, everyday somebody goes
    on trial for murder.
America I feel sentimental about the Wobblies.
America I used to be a communist when I was a kid I'm not sorry.
I smoke marijuana every chance I get.
I sit in my house for days on end and stare at the roses in the closet.
When I go to Chinatown I get drunk and never get laid.

My mind is made up there's going to be trouble.
You should have seen me reading Marx,
My psychoanalyst thinks I'm perfectly right.
I won't say the Lord's Prayer.
I have mystical visions and cosmic vibrations.
America I still haven't told you what you did to Uncle Max after
    he came over from Russia.

I'm addressing you.
Are you going to let your emotional life be run by Time Magazine?
I'm obsessed by Time Magazine.
I read it every week.
Its cover stares at me every time I slink past the corner candystore.
I read it in the basement of the Berkeley Public Library.
It's always telling me about responsibility. Businessmen are serious.
    Movie producers are serious. Everybody's serious but me.
It occurs to me that I am America.
I am talking to myself again.

Asia is rising against me.
I haven't got a chinaman's chance.
I'd better consider my national resources.
My national resources consist of two joints of marijuana millions of
    genitals an unpublishable private literature that goes 1400 miles
    an hour and twentyfive-thousand mental institutions.
I say nothing about my prisons nor the millions of underprivileged
    who live in my flowerpots under the light of five hundred
    suns.

I have abolished the whorehouses of France, Tangiers is the next to
    go.
My ambition is to be President despite the fact that I'm a Catholic.

America how can I write a holy litany in your silly mood?
I will continue like Henry Ford my strophes are as individual as his
    automobiles more so they're all different sexes.

America I will sell your strophes $2500 apiece $500 down on your
    old strophe
America free Tom Mooney
America save the Spanish Loyalists
America Sacco & Vanzetti must not die
America I am the Scottsboro boys.
America when I was seven momma took me to Communist Cell
    meetings they sold us garbanzos a handful per ticket a ticket
    costs a nickel and the speeches were free everybody was angelic
    and sentimental about the workers it was all so sincere you have
    no idea what a good thing the party was in 1835 Scott Nearing
    was a grand old man a real mensch Mother Bloor made me cry I
    once saw Israel Amter plain. Everybody must have been a spy.
America you don't really want to go to war.
America it's them bad Russians.
Them Russians them Russians and them Chinamen. And them
    Russians.
The Russia wants to eat us alive. The Russia's power mad. She wants
    to take our cars from out our garages.
Her wants to grab Chicago. Her needs a Red Readers' Digest. Her
    wants our auto plants in Siberia. Him big bureaucracy running
    our fillingstations.
That no good. Ugh. Him make Indians learn read. Him need big
    black niggers. Hah. Her make us all work sixteen hours a day.
    Help.
America this is quite serious.
America this is the impression I get from looking in the television set.
America is this correct?
I'd better get right down to the job.
It's true I don't want to join the Army or turn lathes in precision
    parts factories, I'm nearsighted and psychopathic anyway.
America I'm putting my queer shoulder to the wheel.

My Sad Self

TO FRANK O'HARA

Sometimes when my eyes are red
I go up on top of the RCA Building
    and gaze at my world, Manhattan –
        my buildings, streets I've done feats in,
          lofts, beds, coldwater flats
– on Fifth Ave below which I also bear in mind,
    its ant cars, little yellow taxis, men
    walking the size of specks of wool –
Panorama of the bridges, sunrise over Brooklyn machine,
    sun go down over New Jersey where I was born
    & Paterson where I played with ants –
my later loves on 15th Street,
    my greater loves of Lower East Side,
        my once fabulous amours in the Bronx
                faraway –
paths crossing in these hidden streets,
    my history summed up, my absences
    and ecstasies in Harlem –
– sun shining down on all I own
    in one eyeblink to the horizon
    in my last eternity –
          matter is water.

Sad,
  I take the elevator and go
      down, pondering,
and walk on the pavements staring into all man's
                plateglass, faces,
      questioning after who loves,
    and stop, bemused
      in front of an automobile shopwindow
    standing lost in calm thought,

traffic moving up & down 5th Avenue blocks
behind me
waiting for a moment when . . .

Time to go home & cook supper & listen to
the romantic war news on the radio

. . . all movement stops
& I walk in the timeless sadness of existence,
tenderness flowing thru the buildings,
my fingertips touching reality's face,
my own face streaked with tears in the mirror
of some window – at dusk –
where I have no desire –
for bonbons – or to own the dresses or Japanese
lampshades of intellection –

Confused by the spectacle around me,
Man struggling up the street
with packages, newspapers,
ties, beautiful suits
toward his desire
Man, woman, streaming over the pavements
red lights clocking hurried watches &
movements at the curb –

And all these streets leading
so crosswise, honking, lengthily,
by avenues
stalked by high buildings or crusted into slums
thru such halting traffic
screaming cars and engines
so painfully to this
countryside, this graveyard
this stillness
on deathbed or mountain

once seen
                never regained or desired
                        in the mind to come
    where all Manhattan that I've seen must disappear.

Death to Van Gogh's Ear!

Poet is Priest
Money has reckoned the soul of America
Congress broken thru to the precipice of Eternity
the President built a War machine which will vomit and rear up
    Russia out of Kansas
The American Century betrayed by a mad Senate which no longer
    sleeps with its wife
Franco has murdered Lorca the fairy son of Whitman
just as Mayakovsky committed suicide to avoid Russia
Hart Crane distinguished Platonist committed suicide to cave in the
    wrong America
just as millions of tons of human wheat were burned in secret caverns
    under the White House
while India starved and screamed and ate mad dogs full of rain
and mountains of eggs were reduced to white powder in the halls of
    Congress
no godfearing man will walk there again because of the stink of the
    rotten eggs of America
and the Indians of Chiapas continue to gnaw their vitaminless tortillas
aborigines of Australia perhaps gibber in the eggless wilderness
and I rarely have an egg for breakfast tho my work requires infinite
    eggs to come to birth in Eternity
eggs should be eaten or given to their mothers
and the grief of the countless chickens of America is expressed in the
    screaming of her comedians over the radio
Detroit has built a million automobiles of rubber trees and phantoms

but I walk, I walk, and the Orient walks with me, and all Africa
 walks

and sooner or later North America will walk

for as we have driven the Chinese Angel from our door he will drive
 us from the Golden Door of the future

we have not cherished pity on Tanganyika

Einstein alive was mocked for his heavenly politics

Bertrand Russell driven from New York for getting laid

and the immortal Chaplin has been driven from our shores with the
 rose in his teeth

a secret conspiracy by Catholic Church in the lavatories of Congress
 has denied contraceptives to the unceasing masses of India.

Nobody publishes a word that is not the cowardly robot ravings of a
 depraved mentality

the day of the publication of the true literature of the American body
 will be day of Revolution

the revolution of the sexy lamb

the only bloodless revolution that gives away corn

poor Genet will illuminate the harvesters of Ohio

Marijuana is a benevolent narcotic but J. Edgar Hoover prefers his
 deathly scotch

And the heroin of Lao-Tze & the Sixth Patriarch is punished by the
 electric chair

but the poor sick junkies have nowhere to lay their heads

fiends in our government have invented a cold-turkey cure for
 addiction as obsolete as the Defense Early Warning Radar
 System.

I am the defense early warning radar system

I see nothing but bombs

I am not interested in preventing Asia from being Asia

and the governments of Russia and Asia will rise and fall but Asia and
 Russia will not fall

the government of America also will fall but how can America fall

I doubt if anyone will ever fall anymore except governments

fortunately all the governments will fall

the only ones which won't fall are the good ones

and the good ones don't yet exist
But they have to begin existing they exist in my poems
they exist in the death of the Russian and American governments
they exist in the death of Hart Crane & Mayakovsky
Now is the time for prophecy without death as a consequence
the universe will ultimately disappear
Hollywood will rot on the windmills of Eternity
Hollywood whose movies stick in the throat of God
Yes Hollywood will get what it deserves
Time
Seepage or nerve-gas over the radio
History will make this poem prophetic and its awful silliness a hideous
     spiritual music
I have the moan of doves and the feather of ecstasy
Man cannot long endure the hunger of the cannibal abstract
War is abstract
the world will be destroyed
but I will die only for poetry, that will save the world
Monument to Sacco & Vanzetti not yet financed to ennoble Boston
natives of Kenya tormented by idiot con-men from England
South Africa in the grip of the white fool
Vachel Lindsay Secretary of the Interior
Poe Secretary of Imagination
Pound Secty. Economics
and Kra belongs to Kra, and Pukti to Pukti
crossfertilization of Blok and Artaud
Van Gogh's Ear on the currency
no more propaganda for monsters
and poets should stay out of politics or become monsters
I have become monsterous with politics
the Russian poet undoubtedly monsterous in his secret notebook
Tibet should be left alone
These are obvious prophecies
America will be destroyed
Russian poets will struggle with Russia
Whitman warned against this 'fabled Damned of nations'

Where was Theodore Roosevelt when he sent out ultimatums from his castle in Camden

Where was the House of Representatives when Crane read aloud from his prophetic books

What was Wall Street scheming when Lindsay announced the doom of Money

Were they listening to my ravings in the locker rooms of Bickfords Employment Offices?

Did they bend their ears to the moans of my soul when I struggled with market research statistics in the Forum at Rome?

No they were fighting in fiery offices, on carpets of heartfailure, screaming and bargaining with Destiny

fighting the Skeleton with sabres, muskets, buck teeth, indigestion, bombs of larceny, whoredom, rockets, pederasty,

back to the wall to build up their wives and apartments, lawns, suburbs, fairydoms,

Puerto Ricans crowded for massacre on 114th St for the sake of an imitation Chinese-Moderne refrigerator

Elephants of mercy murdered for the sake of an Elizabethan birdcage

millions of agitated fanatics in the bughouse for the sake of the screaming soprano of industry

Money-chant of soapers – toothpaste apes in television sets – deodorizers on hypnotic chairs –

petroleum mongers in Texas – jet plane streaks among the clouds –

sky writers liars in the face of Divinity – fanged butchers of hats and shoes, all Owners! Owners! Owners! with obsession on property and vanishing Selfhood!

and their long editorials on the fence of the screaming negro attacked by ants crawled out of the front page!

Machinery of a mass electrical dream! A war-creating Whore of Babylon bellowing over Capitols and Academies!

Money! Money! Money! shrieking mad celestial money of illusion! Money made of nothing, starvation, suicide! Money of failure! Money of death!

Money against Eternity! and eternity's strong mills grind out vast paper of Illusion!

Death News

Visit to W.C.W. circa 1957, poets Kerouac Corso Orlovsky on sofa in living room inquired wise words, stricken Williams pointed thru window curtained on Main Street, 'There's a lot of bastards out there!'

Walking at night on asphalt campus
road by the German Instructor with Glasses
W.C. Williams is dead he said in accent
under the trees in Benares; I stopped and asked
Williams is Dead? Enthusiastic and wide-eyed
under the Big Dipper. Stood on the Porch
of the International House Annex bungalow
insects buzzing round the electric light
reading the Medical obituary in *Time*.
'out among the sparrows behind the shutters'
Williams is in the Big Dipper. He isn't dead
as the many pages of words arranged thrill
with his intonations the mouths of meek kids
becoming subtle even in Bengal. Thus
there's a life moving out of his pages; Blake
also 'alive' thru his experienced machines.
Were his last words anything Black out there
in the carpeted bedroom of the gabled wood house
in Rutherford? Wonder what he said,
or was there anything left in realms of speech
after the stroke & brain-thrill doom entered
his thoughts? If I pray to his soul in Bardo Thodol
he may hear the unexpected vibration of foreign mercy.
Quietly unknown for three weeks; now I saw Passaic
and Ganges one, consenting his devotion,
because he walked on the steeley bank & prayed
to a Goddess in the river, that he only invented,
another Ganga-Ma. Riding on the old
rusty Holland submarine on the ground floor
Paterson Museum instead of a celestial crockodile.

Mourn O Ye Angels of the Left Wing! that the poet
of the streets is a skeleton under the pavement now
and there's no other old soul so kind and meek
and feminine jawed and him-eyed can see you
What you wanted to be among the bastards out there.

Uptown

Yellow-lit Budweiser signs over oaken bars,
'I've seen everything' – the bartender handing me change of $10,
I stared at him amiably eyes thru an obvious Adamic beard –
with Montana musicians homeless in Manhattan, teen age
curly hair themselves – we sat at the antique booth & gossiped,
Madame Grady's literary salon a curious value in New York –
'If I had my way I'd cut off your hair and send you to Vietnam' –
'Bless you then' I replied to a hatted thin citizen hurrying to the
    barroom door
upon wet dark Amsterdam Avenue decades later –
'And if I couldn't do that I'd cut your throat' he snarled farewell
and 'Bless you sir' I added as he went to his fate in the rain dapper
    Irishman.

A Vow

I will haunt these States
    with beard bald head
      eyes staring out plane window,
        hair hanging in Greyhound bus midnight
leaning over taxicab seat to admonish
      an angry cursing driver
        hand lifted to calm
          his outraged vehicle
that I pass with the Green Light of common law.

Common Sense, Common law, common tenderness
              & common tranquillity
our means in America to control the money munching
          war machine, bright lit industry
everywhere digesting forests & excreting soft pyramids
     of newsprint, Redwood and Ponderosa patriarchs
      silent in Meditation murdered & regurgitated as smoke,
       sawdust, screaming ceilings of Soap Opera,
        thick dead Lifes, slick Advertisements
              for Gubernatorial big guns
          burping Napalm on palm rice tropic greenery.

Dynamite in forests,
     boughs fly slow motion
         thunder down ravine,
      Helicopters roar over National Park, Mekong Swamp,
       Dynamite fire blasts thru Model Villages,
Violence screams at Police, Mayors get mad over radio,
     Drop the Bomb on Niggers!
            drop Fire on the gook China
               Frankenstein Dragon
          waving its tail over Bayonne's domed Aluminum
                        oil reservoir!

I'll haunt these States all year
         gazing bleakly out train windows, blue airfield
           red TV network on evening plains,
      decoding radar Provincial editorial paper message,
        deciphering Iron Pipe laborers' curses as
          clanging hammers they raise steamshovel claws
        over Puerto Rican agony lawyers' screams in slums.

James Merrill 1926 –

The Broken Home

Crossing the street,
I saw the parents and the child
At their window, gleaming like fruit
With evening's mild gold leaf.

In a room on the floor below,
Sunless, cooler – a brimming
Saucer of wax, marbly and dim –
I have lit what's left of my life.

I have thrown out yesterday's milk
And opened a book of maxims.
The flame quickens. The word stirs.

Tell me, tongue of fire,
That you and I are as real
At least as the people upstairs.

My father, who had flown in World War I,
Might have continued to invest his life
In cloud banks well above Wall Street and wife.
But the race was run below, and the point was to win.

Too late now, I make out in his blue gaze
(Through the smoked glass of being thirty-six)
The soul eclipsed by twin black pupils, sex
And business; time was money in those days.

Each thirteenth year he married. When he died
There were already several chilled wives
In sable orbit – rings, cars, permanent waves.
We'd felt him warming up for a green bride.
He could afford it. He was 'in his prime'
At three score ten. But money was not time.

When my parents were younger this was a popular act:
A veiled woman would leap from an electric, wine-dark car
To the steps of no matter what – the Senate or the Ritz Bar –
And bodily, at newsreel speed, attack

No matter whom – Al Smith or José Maria Sert
Or Clemenceau – veins standing out on her throat
As she yelled *War mongerer! Pig! Give us the vote!*,
And would have to be hauled away in her hobble skirt.

What had the man done? Oh, made history.
Her business (he had implied) was giving birth,
Tending the house, mending the socks.

Always that same old story –
Father Time and Mother Earth,
A marriage on the rocks.

One afternoon, red, satyr-thighed
Michael, the Irish setter, head
Passionately lowered, led
The child I was to a shut door. Inside,

Blinds beat sun from the bed.
The green-gold room throbbed like a bruise.
Under a sheet, clad in taboos
Lay whom we sought, her hair undone, outspread,

And of a blackness found, if ever now, in old
Engravings where the acid bit.
I must have needed to touch it
Or the whiteness – was she dead?
Her eyes flew open, startled strange and cold.
The dog slumped to the floor. She reached for me. I fled.

Tonight they have stepped out onto the gravel.
The party is over. It's the fall
Of 1931. They love each other still.

She: Charlie, I can't stand the pace.
He: Come on, honey – why, you'll bury us all!

A lead soldier guards my windowsill:
Khaki rifle, uniform, and face.
Something in me grows heavy, silvery, pliable.

How intensely people used to feel!
Like metal poured at the close of a proletarian novel,
Refined and glowing from the crucible,
I see those two hearts, I'm afraid,
Still. Cool here in the graveyard of good and evil,
They are even so to be honored and obeyed.

... Obeyed, at least, inversely. Thus
I rarely buy a newspaper, or vote.
To do so, I have learned, is to invite
The tread of a stone guest within my house.

Shooting this rusted bolt, though, against him,
I trust I am no less time's child than some
Who on the heath impersonate Poor Tom
Or on the barricades risk life and limb.

Nor do I try to keep a garden, only
An avocado in a glass of water –
Roots pallid, gemmed with air. And later,

When the small gilt leaves have grown
Fleshy and green, I let them die, yes, yes,
And start another. I am earth's no less.

A child, a red dog roam the corridors,
Still, of the broken home. No sound. The brilliant
Rag runners halt before wide-open doors.
My old room! Its wallpaper – cream, medallioned
With pink and brown – brings back the first nightmares,
Long summer colds, and Emma, sepia-faced,
Perspiring over broth carried upstairs
Aswim with golden fats I could not taste.

The real house became a boarding-school.
Under the ballroom ceiling's allegory
Someone at last may actually be allowed
To learn something; or, from my window, cool
With the unstiflement of the entire story,
Watch a red setter stretch and sink in cloud.

W. D. Snodgrass 1926 –

From *Heart's Needle*

8

I thumped on you the best I could
    which was no use;
you would not tolerate your food
until the sweet, fresh milk was soured
    with lemon juice.

That puffed you up like a fine yeast.
   The first June in your yard
like some squat Nero at a feast
you sat and chewed on white, sweet clover.
    That is over.

When you were old enough to walk
    we went to feed
the rabbits in the park milkweed;
saw the paired monkeys, under lock,
  consume each other's salt.

Going home we watched the slow
stars follow us down Heaven's vault.
You said, let's catch one that comes low,
    pull off its skin
   and cook it for our dinner.

  As absentee bread-winner,
I seldom got you such cuisine;
we ate in local restaurants
or bought what lunches we could pack
    in a brown sack

with stale, dry bread to toss for ducks
   on the green-scummed lagoons,
crackers for porcupine and fox,
life-savers for the footpad coons
     to scour and rinse,

snatch after in their muddy pail
   and stare into their paws.
When I moved next door to the jail
    I learned to fry
omelettes and griddlecakes so I

could set you supper at my table.
As I built back from helplessness,
    when I grew able,
the only possible answer was
   you had to come here less.

This Hallowe'en you come one week.
    You masquerade
   as a vermilion, sleek,
fat, crosseyed fox in the parade
or, where grim jackolanterns leer,

go with your bag from door to door
foraging for treats. How queer:
    when you take off your mask
my neighbors must forget and ask
    whose child you are.

Of course you lose your appetite,
    whine and won't touch your plate;
     as local law
I set your place on an orange crate
in your own room for days. At night

you lie asleep there on the bed
    and grate your jaw.
Assuredly your father's crimes
    are visited
on you. You visit me sometimes.

The time's up. Now our pumpkin sees
  me bringing your suitcase.
    He holds his grin;
the forehead shrivels, sinking in.
You break this year's first crust of snow

off the runningboard to eat.
  We manage, though for days
I crave sweets when you leave and know
they rot my teeth. Indeed our sweet
    foods leave us cavities.

John Ashbery 1927 --

'How Much Longer Will I Be Able to Inhabit the Divine Sepulcher ...'

How much longer will I be able to inhabit the divine sepulcher
Of life, my great love? Do dolphins plunge bottomward
To find the light? Or is it rock
That is searched? Unrelentingly? Huh. And if some day

Men with orange shovels come to break open the rock
Which encases me, what about the light that comes in then?
What about the smell of the light?
What about the moss?

In pilgrim times he wounded me
Since then I only lie
My bed of light is a furnace choking me
With hell (and sometimes I hear salt water dripping).

I mean it – because I'm one of the few
To have held my breath under the house. I'll trade
One red sucker for two blue ones. I'm
Named Tom. The

Light bounces off mossy rocks down to me
In this glen (the neat villa! which
When he'd had he would not had he of
And jests under the smarting of privet

Which on hot spring nights perfumes the empty rooms
With the smell of sperm flushed down toilets
On hot summer afternoons within sight of the sea.
If you knew why then professor) reads

To his friends: Drink to me only with
And the reader is carried away
By a great shadow under the sea.
Behind the steering wheel

The boy took out his own forehead.
His girlfriend's head was a green bag
Of narcissus stems. 'OK you win
But meet me anyway at Cohen's Drug Store

In 22 minutes.' What a marvel is ancient man!
Under the tulip roots he has figured out a way to be a religious animal
And would be a mathematician. But where in unsuitable heaven
Can he get the heat that will make him grow?

For he needs something or will forever remain a dwarf,
Though a perfect one, and possessing a normal-sized brain
But he has got to be released by giants from things.
And as the plant grows older it realizes it will never be a tree,

Will probably always be haunted by a bee
And cultivates stupid impressions
So as not to become part of the dirt. The dirt
Is mounting like a sea. And we say goodbye

Shaking hands in front of the crashing of the waves
That give our words lonesomeness, and make these flabby hands seem
    ours –
Hands that are always writing things
On mirrors for people to see later –

Do you want them to water
Plant, tear listlessly among the exchangeable ivy –
Carrying food to mouth, touching genitals –
But no doubt you have understood

It all now and I am a fool. It remains
For me to get better, and to understand you so
like a chair-sized man. Boots
Were heard on the floor above. In the garden the sunlight was still
    purple

But what buzzed in it had changed slightly
But not forever . . . but casting its shadow
On sticks, and looking around for an opening in the air, was quite as
    if it had never refused to exist differently. Guys
In the yard handled the belt he had made

Stars
Painted the garage roof crimson and black
He is not a man
Who can read these signs . . . his bones were stays . . .

And even refused to live
In a world and refunded the hiss
Of all that exists terribly near us
Like you, my love, and light.

For what is obedience but the air around us
To the house? For which the federal men came
In a minute after the sidewalk
Had taken you home? ('Latin . . . blossom . . .')

After which you led me to water
And bade me drink, which I did, owing to your kindness.
You would not let me out for two days and three nights,
Bringing me books bound in wild thyme and scented wild grasses

As if reading had any interest for me, you ...
Now you are laughing.
Darkness interrupts my story.
Turn on the light.

Meanwhile what am I going to do?
I am growing up again, in school, the crisis will be very soon.
And you twist the darkness in your fingers, you
Who are slightly older ...

Who are you, anyway?
And it is the color of sand,
The darkness, as it sifts through your hand
Because what does anything mean,

The ivy and the sand? That boat
Pulled up on the shore? Am I wonder,
Strategically, and in the light
Of the long sepulcher that hid death and hides me?

W. S. Merwin 1927 –

The Child

Sometimes it is inconceivable that I should be the age I am
Almost always it is at a dry point in the afternoon
I cannot remember what
I am waiting for and in my astonishment I
Can hear the blood crawling over the plains
Hurrying on to arrive before dark
I try to remember my faults to make sure
One after the other but it is never
Satisfactory the list is never complete

At times night occurs to me so that I think I have been
Struck from behind I remain perfectly
Still feigning death listening for the
Assailant perhaps at last
I even sleep a little for later I have moved
I open my eyes the lanternfish have gone home in darkness
On all sides the silence is unharmed
I remember but I feel no bruise

Then there are the stories and after a while I think something
Else must connect them besides just this me
I regard myself starting the search turning
Corners in remembered metropoli
I pass skins withering in gardens that I see now
Are not familiar
And I have lost even the thread I thought I had

If I could be consistent even in destitution
The world would be revealed

While I can try to repeat what I believe
Creatures spirits not this posture
I do not believe in knowledge as we know it
But I forget

This silence coming at intervals out of the shell of names
It must be all one person really coming at
Different hours for the same thing
If I could learn the word for yes it could teach me questions
I would see that it was itself every time and I would
Remember to say take it up like a hand
And go with it this is at last
Yourself

The child that will lead you

James Wright 1927 –

A Blessing

Just off the highway to Rochester, Minnesota,
Twilight bounds softly forth on the grass.
And the eyes of those two Indian ponies
Darken with kindness.
They have come gladly out of the willows
To welcome my friend and me.
We step over the barbed wire into the pasture
Where they have been grazing all day, alone.
They ripple tensely, they can hardly contain their happiness
That we have come.
They bow shyly as wet swans. They love each other.
There is no loneliness like theirs.
At home once more,
They begin munching the young tufts of spring in the darkness.
I would like to hold the slenderer one in my arms,
For she has walked over to me
And nuzzled my left hand.
She is black and white,
Her mane falls wild on her forehead,
And the light breeze moves me to caress her long ear
That is delicate as the skin over a girl's wrist.
Suddenly I realize
That if I stepped out of my body I would break
Into blossom.

Anne Sexton 1928–74

Unknown Girl in the Maternity Ward

Child, the current of your breath is six days long.
You lie, a small knuckle on my white bed;
lie, fisted like a snail, so small and strong
at my breast. Your lips are animals; you are fed
with love. At first hunger is not wrong.
The nurses nod their caps; you are shepherded
down starch halls with the other unnested throng
in wheeling baskets. You tip like a cup; your head
moving to my touch. You sense the way we belong
But this is an institution bed.
You will not know me very long.

The doctors are enamel. They want to know
the facts. They guess about the man who left me,
some pendulum soul, going the way men go
and leave you full of child. But our case history
stays blank. All I did was let you grow.
Now we are here for all the ward to see.
They thought I was strange, although
I never spoke a word. I burst empty
of you, letting you learn how the air is so.
The doctors chart the riddle they ask of me
and I turn my head away. I do not know.

Yours is the only face I recognize.
Bone at my bone, you drink my answers in.
Six times a day I prize
your need, the animals of your lips, your skin

growing warm and plump. I see your eyes
lifting their tents. They are blue stones, they begin
to outgrow their moss. You blink in surprise
and I wonder what you can see, my funny kin,
as you trouble my silence. I am a shelter of lies
Should I learn to speak again, or hopeless in
such sanity will I touch some face I recognize?

Down the hall the baskets start back. My arms
fit you like a sleeve, they hold
catkins of your willows, the wild bee farms
of your nerves, each muscle and fold
of your first days. Your old man's face disarms
the nurses. But the doctors return to scold
me. I speak. It is you my silence harms.
I should have known; I should have told
them something to write down. My voice alarms
my throat. 'Name of father – none.' I hold
you and name you bastard in my arms.

And now that's that. There is nothing more
that I can say or lose.
Others have traded life before
and could not speak. I tighten to refuse
your owling eyes, my fragile visitor.
I touch your cheeks, like flowers. You bruise
against me. We unlearn. I am a shore
rocking you off. You break from me. I choose
your only way, my small inheritor
and hand you off, trembling the selves we lose.
Go child, who is my sin and nothing more.

All My Pretty Ones

> All my pretty ones?
> Did you say all? O hell-kite! All?
> What! all my pretty chickens and their dam
> At one fell swoop? . . .
> I cannot but remember such things were,
> That were most precious to me.
>
>   *– Macbeth*

Father, this year's jinx rides us apart
where you followed our mother to her cold slumber,
a second shock boiling its stone to your heart,
leaving me here to shuffle and disencumber
you from the residence you could not afford:
a gold key, your half of a woollen mill,
twenty suits from Dunne's, an English Ford,
the love and legal verbiage of another will,
boxes of pictures of people I do not know.
I touch their cardboard faces. They must go.

But the eyes, as thick as wood in this album,
hold me. I stop here, where a small boy
waits in a ruffled dress for someone to come . . .
for this soldier who holds his bugle like a toy
or for this velvet lady who cannot smile.
Is this your father's father, this commodore
in a mailman suit? My father, time meanwhile
has made it unimportant who you are looking for.
I'll never know what these faces are all about.
I lock them into their book and throw them out.

This is the yellow scrapbook that you began
the year I was born; as crackling now and wrinkly
as tobacco leaves: clippings where Hoover outran
the Democrats, wriggling his dry finger at me

and Prohibition; news where the *Hindenburg* went
down and recent years where you went flush
on war. This year, solvent but sick, you meant
to marry that pretty widow in a one-month rush.
But before you had that second chance, I cried
on your fat shoulder. Three days later you died.

These are the snapshots of marriage, stopped in places.
Side by side at the rail toward Nassau now;
here, with the winner's cup at the speedboat races,
here, in tails at the Cotillion, you take a bow,
here, by our kennel of dogs with their pink eyes,
running like show-bred pigs in their chain-link pen;
here, at the horseshow where my sister wins a prize;
and here, standing like a duke among groups of men.
Now I fold you down, my drunkard, my navigator,
my first lost keeper, to love or look at later.

I hold a five-year diary that my mother kept
for three years, telling all she does not say
of your alcoholic tendency. You overslept,
she writes. My God, father, each Christmas Day
with your blood, will I drink down your glass
of wine? The diary of your hurly-burly years
goes to my shelf to wait for my age to pass.
Only in this hoarded span will love persevere.
Whether you are pretty or not, I outlive you,
bend down my strange face to yours and forgive you.

Edward Dorn 1929 –

From *Slinger, Book 1*

The curtain might rise anywhere on a single speaker.

I met in Mesilla
The Cautious Gunslinger
of impeccable personal smoothness
and slender leather encased hands
folded casually
to make his knock.
He would show you his map.

There is your domain.
Is it the domicile it looks to be
or simply a retinal block
of seats in,
he will flip the phrase
the theater of impatience.

   If it is where you are,
the footstep in the flat above
in a foreign land
or any shimmer the city
sends you
the prompt sounds
of a metropolitan nearness
he will unroll the map of locations.

His knock resounds
inside its own smile, where?
I ask him is my heart.
Not this pump he answers
artificial already and bound
touching me
with his leathern finger
as the Queen of Hearts burns
from his gauntlet into my eyes.

   Flageolets of fire
he says there will be.
      This is for your sadly missing heart
the girl you left
in Juarez, the blank
political days press her now
in the narrow adobe
confines of the river town
her dress is torn
by the misadventure of
         her gothic search

The mission bells are ringing
in Kansas.
Have you left something out:
Negative, says my Gunslinger,
no *thing* is omitted.

Time is more fundamental than space.
It is, indeed, the most pervasive
of all the categories
in other words
theres plenty of it.
And it stretches things themselves
until they blend into one,
so if youve seen one thing
youve seen them all.

I held the reins of his horse
while he went into the desert
to pee. *Yes*, he reflected
when he returned, that's less.

How long, he asked
have you been in this territory.

Years I said. Years.
Then you will know where we can have
a cold drink before sunset and then a bed
will be my desire
if you can find one for me
I have no wish to continue
my debate with men,
my mare lathers with tedium
her hooves are dry
Look they are covered with the alkali
of the enormous space
between here and formerly.
Need I repeat, we have come
without sleep from Nuevo Laredo.
And why do you have such a horse
Gunslinger? I asked. Don't move
he replied
the sun rests deliberately
on the rim of the sierra.

And where will you now I asked.
Five days northeast of here
depending of course on whether one's horse
is of iron or flesh
there is a city called Boston
and in that city there is a hotel
whose second floor has been let
to an inscrutable Texan named Hughes

Howard? I asked
The very same.
And what do you mean by inscrutable,
     oh Gunslinger?
I mean to say that He
has not been seen since 1833.

But when you have found him my Gunslinger
what will you do, oh what will you do?
You would not know
that the souls of old Texans
are in jeopardy in a way not common
to other men, my singular friend.

You would not know
of the long plains night
where they carry on
and arrange their genetic duels
with men of other states –
so there is a longhorn bull half mad
half deity
who awaits an account from me
back of the sun you nearly disturbed
just then.
Lets have that drink . . .

Gregory Corso 1930 –

Marriage

Should I get married? Should I be good?
Astound the girl next door with my velvet suit and faustus hood?
Don't take her to movies but to cemeteries
tell all about werewolf bathtubs and forked clarinets
then desire her and kiss her and all the preliminaries
and she going just so far and I understanding why
not getting angry saying You must feel! It's beautiful to feel!
Instead take her in my arms lean against an old crooked tombstone
and woo her the entire night the constellations in the sky –

When she introduces me to her parents
back straightened, hair finally combed, strangled by a tie,
should I sit knees together on their 3rd degree sofa
and not ask Where's the bathroom?
How else to feel other than I am,
often thinking Flash Gordon soap –
O how terrible it must be for a young man
seated before a family and the family thinking
We never saw him before! He wants our Mary Lou!
After tea and homemade cookies they ask What do you do for a
      living?

Should I tell them? Would they like me then?
Say All right get married, we're losing a daughter
but we're gaining a son –
And should I then ask Where's the bathroom?

O God, and the wedding! All her family and her friends
and only a handful of mine all scroungy and bearded

just wait to get at the drinks and food –
And the priest! he looking at me as if I masturbated
asking me Do you take this woman for your lawful wedded wife?
And I trembling what to say say Pie Glue!
I kiss the bride all those corny men slapping me on the back
She's all yours, boy! Ha-ha-ha!
And in their eyes you could see some obscene honeymoon going on –

Then all that absurd rice and clanky cans and shoes
Niagara Falls! Hordes of us! Husbands! Wives! Flowers! Chocolates!

All streaming into cozy hotels
All going to do the same thing tonight
The indifferent clerk he knowing what was going to happen
The lobby zombies they knowing what
The whistling elevator man he knowing
The winking bellboy knowing
Everybody knowing! I'd be almost inclined not to do anything!
Stay up all night! Stare that hotel clerk in the eye!
Screaming: I deny honeymoon! I deny honeymoon!
running rampant into those almost climactic suites
yelling Radio belly! Cat shovel!
O I'd live in Niagara forever! in a dark cave beneath the Falls
I'd sit there the Mad Honeymooner
devising ways to break marriages, a scourge of bigamy
a saint of divorce –

But I should get married I should be good
How nice it'd be to come home to her
and sit by the fireplace and she in the kitchen
aproned young and lovely wanting my baby
and so happy about me she burns the roast beef
and comes crying to me and I get up from my big papa chair
saying Christmas teeth! Radiant brains! Apple deaf!
God what a husband I'd make! Yes, I should get married!
So much to do! like sneaking into Mr Jones' house late at night

and cover his golf clubs with 1920 Norwegian books
Like hanging a picture of Rimbaud on the lawnmower
like pasting Tannu Tuva postage stamps all over the picket fence
like when Mrs Kindhead comes to collect for the Community Chest
grab her and tell her There are unfavorable omens in the sky!
And when the mayor comes to get my vote tell him
When are you going to stop people killing whales!
And when the milkman comes leave him a note in the bottle
Penguin dust, bring me penguin dust, I want penguin dust –

Yet if I should get married and it's Connecticut and snow
and she gives birth to a child and I am sleepless, worn,
up for nights, head bowed against a quiet window, the past behind
  me,
finding myself in the most common of situations a trembling man
knowledged with responsibility not twig-smear nor Roman coin
  soup –
O what would that be like!
Surely I'd give it for a nipple a rubber Tacitus
For a rattle a bag of broken Bach records
Tack Della Francesca all over its crib
Sew the Greek alphabet on its bib
And build for its playpen a roofless Parthenon

No, I doubt I'd be that kind of father
not rural not snow no quiet window
but hot smelly tight New York City
seven flights up roaches and rats in the walls
a fat Reichian wife screeching over potatoes Get a job!
And five nose running brats in love with Batman
And the neighbors all toothless and dry haired
like those hag masses of the 18th century
all wanting to come in and watch TV
The landlord wants his rent
Grocery store Blue Cross Gas & Electric Knights of Columbus
Impossible to lie back and dream Telephone snow, ghost parking –

No! I should not get married I should never get married!
But – imagine If I were married to a beautiful sophisticated woman
tall and pale wearing an elegant black dress and long black gloves
holding a cigarette holder in one hand and a highball in the other
and we lived high up in a penthouse with a huge window
from which we could see all of New York and ever farther on clearer
    days
No, can't imagine myself married to that pleasant prison dream –

O but what about love? I forget love
not that I am incapable of love
it's just that I see love as odd as wearing shoes –
I never wanted to marry a girl who was like my mother
And Ingrid Bergman was always impossible
And there's maybe a girl now but she's already married
And I don't like men and –
but there's got to be somebody!
Because what if I'm 60 years old and not married,
all alone in a furnished room with pee stains on my underwear
and everybody else is married! All the universe married but me!

Ah, yet well I know that were a woman possible as I am possible
then marriage would be possible –
Like SHE in her lonely alien gaud waiting her Egyptian lover
so I wait – bereft of 2,000 years and the bath of life.

Gary Snyder 1930 –

A Walk

Sunday the only day we don't work:
Mules farting around the meadow,
                    Murphy fishing.
The tent flaps in the warm
Early sun: I've eaten breakfast and I'll
                    take a walk
To Benson Lake. Packed a lunch,
Goodbye. Hopping on creekbed boulders
Up the rock throat three miles
                    Piute Creek –
In steep gorge glacier-slick rattlesnake country
Jump, land by a pool, trout skitter,
The clear sky. Deer tracks.
Bad place by a falls, boulders big as houses,
Lunch tied to belt,
I stemmed up a crack and almost fell
But rolled out safe on a ledge
                    and ambled on.
Quail chicks freeze underfoot, color of stone
Then run cheep! away, hen quail fussing.
Craggy west end of Benson Lake – after edging
Past dark creek pools on a long white slope –
Lookt down in the ice-black lake
                    lined with cliff
From far above: deep shimmering trout.
A lone duck in a gunsightpass
                    steep side hill
Through slide-aspen and talus, to the east end,

Down to grass, wading a wide smooth stream
Into camp. At last.
                    By the rusty three-year-
Ago left-behind cookstove
Of the old trail crew,
Stoppt and swam and ate my lunch.

Things to Do Around a Lookout

Wrap up in a blanket in cold weather and just read.
Practise writing Chinese characters with a brush
Paint pictures of the mountains
Put out salt for deer
Bake coffee cake and biscuit in the iron oven,
Hours off hunting twisty firewood, packing it all back up and
    chopping.
Rice out for the ptarmigan and the conies
Mark well sunrise and sunset – drink lapsang soochong.
Rolling smokes
The Flower book and the Bird book and the Star book
Old Readers Digests left behind
Bullshitting on the radio with a distant pinnacle,
    like you, hid in clouds;
Drawing little sexy sketches of bare girls.
Reading maps, checking on the weather, airing out
    musty Forest Service sleeping bags and blankets
Oil the saws, sharpen axes,
Learn the names of all the peaks you see
    and which is highest
Learn by heart the drainages between.
Go find a shallow pool of snowmelt on a good day,
    bathe in the lukewarm water.
Take off in foggy weather and go climbing all alone

The Rock book, – strata, dip, and strike
Get ready for the snow, get ready
To go down.

The Hudsonian Curlew

FOR DRUM AND DIANA

The end of a desert track – turnaround –
    parked the truck and walked over dunes.
a cobbly point   hooks in the shallow bay;

       the Mandala of Birds.

pelican, seagulls, and terns,
       one curlew
       far at the end –
they fly up as they see us
          and settle back down.
tern keep coming
       – skies of wide seas –
frigate birds keep swooping

pelicans sit nearest the foam;

tern bathing and fluttering
       in frothy wave-lapping
          between the round stones.

      we
gather driftwood for firewood
for camping
get four shells to serve up steamed snail

*

in the top of the cardón cactus
two vultures
look, yawn, hunch, preen.
out on the point   the seabirds
squabble and settle, meet and leave;
        speak.

two sides of a border.
the margins.   tidewater.   zones.
up in the void,   under the surface,
two worlds   touch
and greet

★

Three shotgun shots as it gets dark;
two birds.
    'how come three shots?'
' one went down on the water
and started to swim.
I didn't want another thing like that duck.'

the bill curved in, and the long neck limp –
a grandmother plumage of cinnamon and brown.
the beak not so long – bars on the head;
    by the eye.
    Hudsonian Curlew

    and those tern most likely
    'Royal Tern'
    with forked tail,
    that heavy orange bill.

★

The down
i pluck from the
neck of the curlew
eddies and whirls at my knees
in the twilight wind
from sea.
kneeling in sand

warm in the hand.

*

'*Do you want to do it right? I'll tell you.*'
he tells me.
at the edge of the water on the stones.
a transverse cut just below the sternum
the forefinger and middle finger
                    forced in and up, following the
                    curve of the rib cage.
then fingers arched, drawn slowly down and back,
forcing all the insides up and out,
toward the palm and heel of the hand.
firm organs, well-placed, hot.
save the liver;
finally scouring back, toward the vent, the last of the
                    large intestine.

the insides string out, begin to wave, in the lapping
                    waters of the bay.
the bird has no feathers, head, or feet;
                    he is empty inside.
the rich body muscle that he moved by, the wing-beating
                    muscle
anchored to the blade-like high breast bone,
is what you eat.

*

The black iron frying pan on the coals.
two birds singed in flame.
bacon, onion, and garlic
browning, then steaming with a lid
put the livers in,
half a bird apiece and bulghour
passed about the fire on metal plates.
dense firm flesh,
dark and rich,
            gathered news of skies and seas.

                    *

at dawn
looking out from the dunes
no birds at all but
three curlew

                ker-lew!

                ker-lew!

pacing   and glancing   around.

Sylvia Plath 1932 – 63

Lady Lazarus

I have done it again.
One year in every ten
I manage it –

A sort of walking miracle, my skin
Bright as a Nazi lampshade,
My right foot

A paperweight,
My face a featureless, fine
Jew linen.

Peel off the napkin
O my enemy.
Do I terrify? –

The nose, the eye pits, the full set of teeth?
The sour breath
Will vanish in a day.

Soon, soon the flesh
The grave cave ate will be
At home on me

And I a smiling woman.
I am only thirty.
And like the cat I have nine times to die.

This is Number Three.
What a trash
To annihilate each decade.

What a million filaments.
The peanut-crunching crowd
Shoves in to see

Them unwrap me hand and foot –
The big strip tease.
Gentleman, ladies,

These are my hands,
My knees.
I may be skin and bone,

Nevertheless, I am the same, identical woman.
The first time it happened I was ten.
It was an accident.

The second time I meant
To last it out and not come back at all.
I rocked shut

As a seashell.
They had to call and call
And pick the worms off me like sticky pearls.

Dying
Is an art, like everything else.
I do it exceptionally well.

I do it so it feels like hell.
I do it so it feels real.
I guess you could say I've a call.

It's easy enough to do it in a cell.
It's easy enough to do it and stay put.
It's the theatrical

Comeback in broad day
To the same place, the same face, the same brute
Amused shout:

'A miracle!'
That knocks me out.
There is a charge

For the eyeing of my scars, there is a charge
For the hearing of my heart –
It really goes.

And there is a charge, a very large charge,
For a word or a touch
Or a bit of blood

Or a piece of my hair or my clothes.
So, so, Herr Doktor.
So, Herr Enemy.

I am your opus,
I am your valuable,
The pure gold baby

That melts to a shriek.
I turn and burn.
Do not think I underestimate your great concern.

Ash, ash –
You poke and stir.
Flesh, bone, there is nothing there –

A cake of soap,
A wedding ring,
A gold filling.

Herr God, Herr Lucifer,
Beware
Beware.

Out of the ash
I rise with my red hair
And I eat men like air.

Daddy

You do not do, you do not do
Any more, black shoe
In which I have lived like a foot
For thirty years, poor and white,
Barely daring to breathe or Achoo.

Daddy, I have had to kill you.
You died before I had time –
Marble-heavy, a bag full of God,
Ghastly statue with one grey toe
Big as a Frisco seal

And a head in the freakish Atlantic
Where it pours bean green over blue
In the waters off beautiful Nauset.
I used to pray to recover you.
Ach, du.

In the German tongue, in the Polish town
Scraped flat by the roller
Of wars, wars, wars.
But the name of the town is common.
My Polack friend

Says there are a dozen or two.
So I never could tell where you
Put your foot, your root,
I never could talk to you.
The tongue stuck in my jaw.

It stuck in a barb wire snare.
Ich, ich, ich, ich,
I could hardly speak.
I thought every German was you.
And the language obscene

An engine, an engine
Chuffing me off like a Jew.
A Jew to Dachau, Auschwitz, Belsen.
I began to talk like a Jew.
I think I may well be a Jew.

The snows of the Tyrol, the clear beer of Vienna
Are not very pure or true.
With my gypsy ancestress and my weird luck
And my Taroc pack and my Taroc pack
I may be a bit of a Jew.

I have always been scared of *you*,
With your Luftwaffe, your gobbledygoo.
And your neat moustache
And your Aryan eye, bright blue.
Panzer-man, panzer-man, O You –

Not God but a swastika
So black no sky could squeak through.
Every woman adores a Fascist,
The boot in the face, the brute
Brute heart of a brute like you.

You stand at the blackboard, daddy,
In the picture I have of you,
A cleft in your chin instead of your foot
But no less a devil for that, no not
Any less the black man who

Bit my pretty red heart in two.
I was ten when they buried you.
At twenty I tried to die
And get back, back, back to you.
I thought even the bones would do.

But they pulled me out of the sack,
And they stuck me together with glue.
And then I knew what to do.
I made a model of you,
A man in black with a Meinkampf look

And a love of the rack and the screw.
And I said I do, I do.
So daddy, I'm finally through.
The black telephone's off at the root,
The voices just can't worm through.

If I've killed one man, I've killed two –
The vampire who said he was you
And drank my blood for a year,
Seven years, if you want to know.
Daddy, you can lie back now.

There's a stake in your fat black heart
And the villagers never liked you.
They are dancing and stamping on you.
They always *knew* it was you.
Daddy, daddy, you bastard, I'm through.

The Applicant

First, are you our sort of a person?
Do you wear
A glass eye, false teeth or a crutch,
A brace or a hook,
Rubber breasts or a rubber crotch,

Stitches to show something's missing? No, no? Then
How can we give you a thing?
Stop crying.
Open your hand.
Empty? Empty. Here is a hand

To fill it and willing
To bring teacups and roll away headaches
And do whatever you tell it.
Will you marry it?
It is guaranteed

To thumb shut your eyes at the end
And dissolve of sorrow.
We make new stock from the salt.
I notice you are stark naked.
How about this suit –

Black and stiff, but not a bad fit.
Will you marry it?
It is waterproof, shatterproof, proof
Against fire and bombs through the roof.
Believe me, they'll bury you in it.

Now your head, excuse me, is empty.
I have the ticket for that.
Come here, sweetie, out of the closet.
Well, what do you think of *that*?
Naked as paper to start

But in twenty-five years she'll be silver,
In fifty, gold.
A living doll, everywhere you look.
It can sew, it can cook,
It can talk, talk, talk.

It works, there is nothing wrong with it.
You have a hole, it's a poultice.
You have an eye, it's an image.
My boy, it's your last resort.
Will you marry it, marry it, marry it.

The Arrival of the Bee Box

I ordered this, this clean wood box
Square as a chair and almost too heavy to lift.
I would say it was the coffin of a midget
Or a square baby
Were there not such a din in it.

The box is locked, it is dangerous.
I have to live with it overnight
And I can't keep away from it.
There are no windows, so I can't see what is in there.
There is only a little grid, no exit.

I put my eye to the grid.
It is dark, dark,
With the swarmy feeling of African hands
Minute and shrunk for export,
Black on black, angrily clambering.

How can I let them out?
It is the noise that appals me most of all,
The unintelligible syllables.
It is like a Roman mob,
Small, taken one by one, but my god, together!

I lay my ear to furious Latin.
I am not a Caesar.
I have simply ordered a box of maniacs.
They can be sent back.
They can die, I need feed them nothing, I am the owner.

I wonder how hungry they are.
I wonder if they would forget me
If I just undid the locks and stood back and turned into a tree.
There is the laburnum, its blond colonnades,
And the petticoats of the cherry.

They might ignore me immediately
In my moon suit and funeral veil.
I am no source of honey
So why should they turn on me?
Tomorrow I will be sweet God, I will set them free.

The box is only temporary.

Etheridge Knight 1933–

Hard Rock Returns to Prison from the Hospital for the Criminal Insane

Hard Rock was 'known not to take no shit
From nobody', and he had the scars to prove it:
Split purple lips, lumped ears, welts above
His yellow eyes, and one long scar that cut
Across his temple and plowed through a thick
Canopy of kinky hair.

The WORD was that Hard Rock wasn't a mean nigger
Anymore, that the doctors had bored a hole in his head,
Cut out part of his brain, and shot electricity
Through the rest. When they brought Hard Rock back,
Handcuffed and chained, he was turned loose,
Like a freshly gelded stallion, to try his new status.
And we all waited and watched, like indians at a corral,
To see if the WORD was true.

As we waited we wrapped ourselves in the cloak
Of his exploits: 'Man, the last time, it took eight
Screws to put him in the Hole.' 'Yeah, remember when he
Smacked the captain with his dinner tray?' 'He set
The record for time in the Hole – 67 straight days!'
'Ol Hard Rock! man, that's one crazy nigger.'
And then the jewel of a myth that Hard Rock had once bit
A screw on the thumb and poisoned him with syphilitic spit.

The testing came, to see if Hard Rock was really tame.
A hillbilly called him a black son of a bitch

And didn't lose his teeth, a screw who knew Hard Rock
From before shook him down and barked in his face.
And Hard Rock did *nothing*. Just grinned and looked silly,
His eyes empty like knot holes in a fence.

And even after we discovered that it took Hard Rock
Exactly 3 minutes to tell you his first name,
We told ourselves that he had just wised up,
Was being cool; but we could not fool ourselves for long,
And we turned away, our eyes on the ground. Crushed.
He had been our Destroyer, the doer of things
We dreamed of doing but could not bring ourselves to do,
The fears of years, like a biting whip,
Had cut grooves too deeply across our backs.

Imamu Amiri Baraka (LeRoi Jones)
1934–

Evil Nigger Waits for Lightnin'

Alone, at night, with all the world
not watching, around me,
who for the understanding
intended, the love
withheld,
would be lost in the blackness
of self-nights
howling like something
or scurrying behind iceboxes
like something
would be them things
in my conscious
ness, or waddlegirls
full of invisible demands
they are children the world will tell you
only children, lost dreams, that you should love
if you can, from the tower of Headlust, you they moan
should always adore them, lost feeling, should love and
take yrself through any change to understand their blankness.

Alone at night the world disappears breathing over my head weeping
it is lost or unappreciated. It says I do not love it. And sends its
dopey messengers to touch me right. The world, the world says, is
full of love can you find it, can you enter, and remain, grow strong
with it beautiful
thing
in the rain, the world,

these sent things whisper
mice, fucked ladies, whisps of cloud
still visible four oclock in the nighttime
for the expanding or retracting dying or just coming
thing
we will always
be.

The Astronomers,
The Philosophers,
The Crowd, of them,
Things, These dangerous feelers, for understanding,
now that I am alone so much I can manage to
hear another thing
singing through my face
describing the arc
and the constant
return . . .

    way out now,
    describing its own voice
    its
    reason

Richard Emil Braun 1934–

Goose

Trailing her father, bearing his hand axe,
    the girl thought she had never
  guessed what earthly majesty
      was before

then, as he strode unconcernedly
    holding a vicious gander
  by the horny mitts and let
      the big wings

batter his knees. She was also surprised
    to feel a liberating
  satisfaction in the coming
      bloodshed, and

that notwithstanding all the times she had
    been beleaguered and
  had fled, today she did not fear
      the barnyard hubub.

Yet, as her father's clever stroke fell, as
    the pronged head skipped sideways
  and the neck plumes stiffened with blood
      from the cleft,

she was angry; and, when the headless goose
    ran to the brook and was
  carried off into the woods alive,
      she rejoiced,

and subsequently frequented those woods
    and avoided her father.
  When the goose began to mend she
    brought him small

hominy, which was welcome though she had
    to press the kernels one
  by one into the pink neck that
    throbbed into

her palm; when haemorrhage occurred she would
    not spare handkerchiefs,
  and stanching the spot she felt a thrill
    of sympathy.

But for the most part there was steady progress,
    and growing vigor was
  accompanied by restlessness,
    and one cool day

the blind thing was batted out of existence
    by a motorcycle.
  She had no time for tears. She ran
    upstairs to miss

her father's barytone commiseration,
    then out onto the fields,
  and, holding an old red pinwheel,
    ran ran ran ran.

Robert Mezey 1935–

My Mother

My mother writes from Trenton,
a comedian to the bone
but underneath, serious
and all heart. 'Honey,' she says,
'be a mensch and Mary too,
its no good to worry, you
are doing the best you can
your Dad and everyone
thinks you turned out very well
as long as you pay your bills
nobody can say a word
you can tell them to drop dead
so save a dollar it can't
hurt – remember Frank you went
to highschool with? he still lives
with his wife's mother, his wife
works while he writes his books and
did he ever sell a one
the four kids run around naked
36 and he's never had,
you'll forgive my expression
even a pot to piss in
or a window to throw it,
such a smart boy he couldnt
read the footprints on the wall
honey you think you know all
the answers you dont, please try
to put some money away
believe me it wouldn't hurt

artist shmartist life's too short
for that kind of, forgive me,
horseshit, I know what you want
better than you, all that counts
is to make a good living
and the best of everything,
as Sholem Aleichem said
he was a great writer did
you ever read his books dear,
you should make what he makes a year
anyway he says some place
Poverty is no disgrace
but its no honor either
that's what I say,
     love,
      Mother'

Sonia Sanchez 1935–

TCB

wite/motha/fucka
wite/motha/fucka
wite/motha/fucka

whitey.

wite/motha/fucker
wite/motha/fucker
wite/motha/fucker

ofay.

wite/mutha/fucka
wite/mutha/fucka
wite/mutha/fucka

devil.

wite/mutha/fucker
wite/mutha/fucker
wite/mutha/fucker

pig.

wite/mother/fucker
wite/mother/fucker
wite/mother/fucker

cracker.

wite/muther/fucka
wite/muther/fucka
wite/muther/fucka

honky.

now.   that it's all sed.
let's get to work.

Right on: white america

this country might have
been a pio
   neer land
once.
 but. there ain't
no mo
   indians   blowing
custer's mind
    with a different
image of america.
       this country
might have
   needed shoot/
outs/ daily/
   once.
      but. there ain't
no mo real/ white/   allamerican
         bad/guys.
just.
  u & me.
    blk/ and un/armed.
this country might have
been a pion
   eer land. once.
       and it still is.
check out
   the falling
gun/shells   on our blk/tomorrows.

Diane Wakoski 1937–

The Father of My Country

All fathers in Western civilization must have
a military origin. The
ruler,
governor,
yes,
he is
was the
general at one time or other.
And George Washington
won the hearts
of his country – the rough military man
with awkward
sincere
drawing-room manners.

My father;
have you ever heard me speak of him? I seldom
do. But I had a father,
and he had military origins – or my origins from
him
are military,
militant. That is, I remember him only in uniform. But of the navy,
30 years a chief petty officer,
Always away from home.

It is rough/hard for me to
speak now.
I'm not used to talking
about him.

Not used to
naming his objects/
objects
that never surrounded me.

A woodpecker with fresh bloody crest
knocks
at my mouth. Father, for the first
time I say
your name. Name rolled in thick Polish parchment scrolls,
name of Roman candle drippings when I sit at my table
alone, each night,
name of naval uniforms and name of
telegrams, name of
coming home from your aircraft carrier,
name of shiny shoes,
name of Hawaiian dolls, name
of mess spoons, name of greasy machinery, and name of
stencilled names.
Is it your blood I carry in a test tube,
my arm,
to let fall, crack, and spill on the sidewalk
in front of the men
I know,
I love,
I know, and
want? So you left my house when I was under two,
being replaced by other machinery, and
I didn't believe you left me.

      This scene: the trunk yielding treasures of
      a green fountain pen, heart-shaped mirror,
      amber beads, old letters with brown ink, and
      the gopher snake stretched across the palm tree
      in the front yard with woody trunk like monkey skins,
      and a sunset through the skinny persimmon trees. You

came walking, not even a telegram or post card from
Tahiti. Love, love, through my heart like ink in
the thickest nubbed pen, black and flowing into words.
You came to me, and I at least six. Six doilies
of lace, six battleship cannon, six old beerbottles,
six thick steaks, six love letters, six clocks running
backwards, six watermelons, and six baby teeth, a six
cornered hat on six men's heads, six lovers at once
or one lover at sixes and sevens; how I confuse
all this with my
dream
walking the tightrope bridge
with gold knots
over
the mouth of an anemone / tissue spiral lips
and holding on so that the ropes burned
as if my wrists had been tied

If George Washington
had not
been the Father
of my Country,
it is doubtful that I would ever have
found
a father. Father in my mouth, on my lips, in my
tongue, out of all my womanly fire,
Father I have left in my steel filing cabinet as a name on my birth
certificate, Father, I have left in the teeth pulled out at
dentists' offices and thrown into their garbage cans,
Father living in my wide cheekbones and short feet,
Father in my Polish tantrums and my American speech, Father, not a
holy name, not a name I cherish but the name I bear, the name
that makes me one of a kind in any phone book because
you changed it, and nobody
but us
has it,

Father who makes me dream in the dead of night of the falling cherry
blossoms, Father who makes me know all men will leave me
if I love them,
Father who made me a maverick,
a writer
a namer,
name/father, sun/father, moon/father, bloody mars/father,

other children said, 'My father is a doctor,'
or
'My father gave me this camera,'
or
'My father took me to
the movies,'
or
'My father and I went swimming,'
but
my father is coming in a letter
once a month
for a while,
and my father
sometimes came in a telegram
but
mostly
my father came to me
in sleep, my father because I dreamed in one night that I dug through
the ash heap in back of the pepper tree and found a diamond shaped
like a dog and my father called the dog and it came leaping over to
him and he walked away out of the yard down the road with the dog
jumping and yipping at his heels,

my father was not in the telephone book
in my city;
my father was not sleeping with my mother
at home;

my father did not care if I studied the
piano;
my father did not care what
I did;
and I thought my father was handsome and I loved him and I
wondered
why
he left me alone so much,
so many years
in fact, but
my father
made me what I am
a lonely woman
without a purpose, just as I was
a lonely child
without any father. I walked with words, words, and names,
names. Father was not
one of my words.
Father was not
one of my names. But now I say, George you have become my father,
in his 20th century naval uniform. George Washington, I need your
love; George, I want to call you Father, Father, my Father,
Father of my country,
that is
me. And I say the name to chant it. To sing it. To lace it around me
like weaving cloth. Like a happy child on that shining afternoon in
the palmtree sunset with her mother's trunk yielding treasures,
I cry and
cry,
Father,
Father,
Father,
have you really come home?

Haki R. Mahubuti (Don L. Lee)
1942–

But He Was Cool
or: He Even Stopped for Green Lights

super-cool
ultrablack
a tan/purple
had a beautiful shade.

he had a double-natural
that wd put the sisters to shame.
his dashikis were tailor made
& his beads were imported sea shells
    (from some blk/country i never heard of)
he was triple-hip.

his tikis were hand carved
out of ivory
& came express from the motherland.
he would greet u in swahili
& say good-by in yoruba.
woooooooooooooo-jim he bes so cool & ill tel li gent
                  cool-cool is so cool he was un-cooled by other
                      niggers' cool
                  cool-cool ultracool was bop-cool/ice box cool so
                      cool cold cool
                  his wine didn't have to be cooled, him was air
                      conditioned cool

cool-cool/real cool made me cool – now ain't that
cool
cool-cool so cool him nick-named refrigerator

cool-cool so cool
he didn't know,
after detroit, newark, chicago &c.,
we had to hip
cool-cool/ super-cool/ real cool
that
to be black
is
to be
very-hot.

Nikki Giovanni 1943–

Nikki-Rosa

childhood remembrances are always a drag
if you're Black
you always remember things like living in Woodlawn
with no inside toilet
and if you become famous or something
they never talk about how happy you were to have your mother
all to yourself and
how good the water felt when you got your bath from one of those
big tubs that folk in chicago barbecue in
and somehow when you talk about home
it never gets across how much you
understood their feelings
as the whole family attended meetings about Hollydale
and even though you remember
your biographers never understand
your father's pain as he sells his stock
and another dream goes
and though you're poor it isn't poverty that
concerns you
and though they fought a lot
it isn't your father's drinking that makes any difference
but only that everybody is together and you
and your sister have happy birthdays and very good christmasses
and I really hope no white person ever has cause to write about me
because they never understand Black love is Black wealth and they'll
probably talk about my hard childhood and never understand that
all the while I was quite happy

Woman Poem

you see, my whole life
is tied up
to unhappiness
its father cooking breakfast
and me getting fat as a hog
or having no food
at all and father proving
his incompetence
again
i wish i knew how it would feel
to be free

its having a job
they won't let you work
or no work at all
castrating me
(yes it happens to women too)

its a sex object if you're pretty
and no love
or love and no sex if you're fat
get back fat black woman be a mother
grandmother strong thing but not woman

gameswoman romantic woman love needer
man seeker dick eater sweat getter
fuck needing love seeking woman

its a hole in your shoe
and buying lil sis a dress
and her saying you shouldn't
when you know
all too well – that you shouldn't

but smiles are only something we give
to properly dressed social workers
not each other
only smiles of i know
your game sister
which isn't really
a smile

joy is finding a pregnant roach
and squashing it
not finding someone to hold
let go get off get back don't turn
me on you black dog
how dare you care
about me
you ain't got no good sense
cause i ain't shit you must be lower
than that to care

its a filthy house
with yesterday's watermelon
and monday's tears
cause true ladies don't
know how to clean

its intellectual devastation
of everybody
to avoid emotional committment
'yeah honey i would've married
him but he didn't have no degree'

its knock-kneed mini skirted
wig wearing died blond mamma's scar
born dead my scorn your whore

rough heeled broken nailed powdered
face me
whose whole life is tied
up to unhappiness
cause its the only
for real thing

know

James Tate 1943–

The Blue Booby

The blue booby lives
on the bare rocks
of Galápagos
and fears nothing.
It is a simple life:
they live on fish,
and there are few predators.
Also, the males do not
make fools of themselves
chasing after the young
ladies. Rather,
they gather the blue
objects of the world
and construct from them

a nest – an occasional
Gaulois package,
a string of beads,
a piece of cloth from
a sailor's suit. This
replaces the need for
dazzling plumage;
in fact, in the past
fifty million years
the male has grown
considerably duller,
nor can he sing well.
The female, though,

asks little of him –
the blue satisfies her
completely, has
a magical effect
on her. When she returns
from her day of
gossip and shopping,
she sees he has found her
a new shred of blue foil:
for this she rewards him
with her dark body,
the stars turn slowly
in the blue foil beside them
like the eyes of a mild savior.

Selected Bibliography of Poetry and Criticism

CONRAD AIKEN

Earth Triumphant (1914); *The Jig of Forslin: A Symphony* (1916); *Turns and Movies* (1916); *Nocturnes of Remembered Spring* (1917); *The Charnel Rose* (1918); *The House of Dust: A Symphony* (1920); *Punch: The Immortal Liar* (1921); *Priapus and the Pool* (1922); *The Pilgrimage of Festus* (1923); *Selected Poems* (1929, rev. 1935); *Preludes for Memnon* (1931); *The Coming Forth by Day of Osiris Jones* (1931); *Landscape West of Eden* (1934); *Time in the Rock* (1936); *And in the Human Heart* (1940); *Brownstone Eclogues* (1942); *The Soldier* (1944); *The Kid* (1947); *The Divine Pilgrim* (1949); *Skylight One* (1949); *Collected Poems* (1953, rev. 1970); *A Letter from Li Po* (1955); *The Fluteplayer* (1956); *Selected Poems* (1961); *The Morning Song of Lord Zero* (1963); *A Seizure of Limericks* (1964); *Cats and Bats and Things with Wings* (1965); *The Clerk's Journal* (1971).

Criticism:
Reuel Denney, *Conrad Aiken* (1964); F. J. Hoffman, *Conrad Aiken* (1962); Jay Martin, *Conrad Aiken: A Life of His Art* (1962); Houston Peterson, *Melody of Chaos* (1931).

A. R. AMMONS

Ommateum (1955); *Expressions of Sea Level* (1964); *Corsons Inlet* (1965); *Tape for the Turn of Year* (1965); *Northfield Poems* (1966); *Selected Poems* (1968); *Uplands* (1970); *Briefings* (1971); *Collected Poems, 1951–1971* (1972); *Sphere: The Form of a Motion* (1974); *Diversifications* (1975); *Selected Poems: 1951–1977* (1977); *The Snow Poems* (1977).

JOHN ASHBERY

Turandot and Other Poems (1953); *Some Trees* (1956); *The Poems* (1960); *The Tennis Court Oath* (1962); *Rivers and Mountains* (1966); *Selected Poems* (1967); *Fragment* (1969); *The Double Dream of Spring* (1970); *Three Poems* (1972); *Self Portrait in a Convex Mirror* (1975); *The Vermont Journal* (1975); *Houseboat Days* (1977).

IMAMU AMIRI BARAKA (LeRoi Jones)

Preface to A Twenty Volume Suicide Note (1962); *The Dead Lecturer* (1965); *Black Art* (1966); *Black Magic: Poetry 1961–1967* (1967); *It's Nation Time* (1970); *Spirit Reach* (1972).

Criticism:
K. W. Benston, *Baraka: The Renegade and the Mask* (1976); Theodore R. Hudson, *From LeRoi Jones to Amiri Baraka, The Literary Works* (1973).

JOEL BARLOW

The Vision of Columbus (1787); *The Hasty-Pudding* (1796); *The Columbiad* (1807).

Criticism:
A. L. Ford, *Joel Barlow* (1972); Leon Howard, *The Vision of Joel Barlow* (1937); J. L. Woodress, *A Yankee Odyssey: The Life of Joel Barlow* (1958).

JOHN BERRYMAN

Poems (1942); *The Dispossessed* (1948); *Homage to Mistress Bradstreet* (1956); *His Thought Made Pockets & the Plane Buckt* (1958); *77 Dream Songs* (1964); *Berryman's Sonnets* (1967); *Short Poems* (1967); *His Toy, His Dream, His Rest* (1968); *The Dream Songs* (1969); *Love & Fame* (1970); *Delusions, Etc.* (1972); *Selected Poems* (1972); *Henry's Fate and other Poems* (1977).

Criticism:
J. Connarroe, *John Berryman* (1977); William J. Martz, *John Berryman* (1969).

ELIZABETH BISHOP

North and South (1946); *Poems: North and South – A Cold Spring* (1955); *Questions of Travel* (1965); *Selected Poems* (1967); *The Ballad of the Burglar of Babylon* (1968); *The Complete Poems* (1969); *Geography III* (1978).

Criticism:
Ann Stevenson, *Elizabeth Bishop* (1966).

PAUL BLACKBURN

Brooklyn-Manhattan Transit (1960); The Nets (1961); *Sing-Song* (1966);
The Dissolving Fabric (1966); *The Reardon Poems* (1967); *The Cities*
(1967); *In, On, or About the Premises* (1968); *Early Selected γ Mas:
Collected Poems, 1949–1961* (1972); *Halfway Down the Coast* (1975).

ROBERT BLY

Silence in the Snowy Fields (1962, rev. 1967); *The Light Around the
Body* (1967); *The Morning Glory* (1969); *Teeth-Mother Naked at Last*
(1970); *The Shadow-Mothers* (1970); *Jumping out of Bed* (1972); *Sleepers
Joining Hands* (1972); *Point Reyes Poems* (1974); *This Body is made of
Camphor and Gopherwood* (1977).

Criticism:
I. Friberg, *Moving Inward: A Study of Robert Bly's Poetry* (1977).

ANNE BRADSTREET

*The Tenth Muse Lately Sprung up in America: Or Severall Poems, Compiled
with Great Variety of Wit and Learning, Full of Delight* (1650); *Several
Poems Compiled with Great Variety of Wit and Learning, Full of Delight*
(1678).

Standard Editions:
J. H. Ellis, ed., *The Works of Anne Bradstreet in Prose and Verse* (1867);
F. E. Hopkins, ed., *The Poems of Mrs Anne Bradstreet (1612–1672)
Together with Her Prose Remains* (1897).

Criticism:
J. K. Piercy, *Anne Bradstreet* (1965); A. Stanford, *Anne Bradstreet: The
Worldly Puritan* (1975); E. W. White, *Anne Bradstreet: 'The Tenth
Muse'* (1972).

RICHARD EMIL BRAUN

Companions to Your Doom (1961); *Children Passing* (1962); *Bad Land*
(1971); *The Foreclosure* (1972).

GWENDOLYN BROOKS

A Street in Bronzeville (1945); *Annie Allen* (1949); *Bronzeville Boys and
Girls* (1956); *Selected Poems* (1963); *In the Mecca* (1968); *Riot* (1970);

Family Pictures (1971); *The World of Gwendolyn Brooks* (1971); *Aloneness* (1972); *The Tiger Who Wore White Gloves* (1974).

WILLIAM CULLEN BRYANT

Poems (1821); *Poems* (1832); *Poems* (1836); *The Fountain and Other Poems* (1842); *Poems* (1854); *Thirty Poems* (1864); *Poems* (1871); *Poems* (1875, 3 vols).

Criticism:
W. A. Bradley, *William Cullen Bryant* (1905); A. F. McLean, Jr, *William Cullen Bryant* (1964).

CHARLES BUKOWSKI

Flower, Fist and Bestial Wail (1959); *Longshot Pomes for Broke Players* (1961); *Run with the Hunted* (1962); *It Catches My Heart in Its Hands* (1963); *Cold Dogs in the Courtyard* (1965); *Crucifix in a Deathhand* (1965); *At Terror Street and Agony Way* (1968); *Poems Written Before Jumping Out of an 8-Storey Window* (1968); *Days Run Away Like Wild Horses Over the Hills* (1969); *Fire Station* (1970); *Mockingbird Wish Me Luck* (1972); *Burning in Water, Drowning in Flame* (1974); *Love is a Dog from Hell: Poems 1974–1977* (1977).

Criticism:
Sanford Dorbin, *A Bibliography of Charles Bukowski* (1969).

GREGORY CORSO

The Vestal Lady on Brattle (1955); *Gasoline* (1958); *Bomb* (1958); *The Happy Birthday of Death* (1960); *Long Live Man* (1962); *Selected Poems* (1962); *The Mutation of the Spirit* (1964); *There Is Yet Time to Run Back Through Life and Expiate All That's Been Sadly Done* (1965); *Elegiac Feelings American* (1970).

HART CRANE

White Buildings (1926); *The Bridge* (1930); *Collected Poems* (1933); *Seven Lyrics* (1966); *The Complete Poems and Selected Letters and Prose* (1966); *Ten Unpublished Poems* (1972).

Criticism:
R. W. Butterfield, *The Broken Arc: A Study of Hart Crane* (1969); Samuel Hazo, *Hart Crane: An Introduction and Interpretation* (1963),

Smithereened Apart: A Critique of Hart Crane (1977); Gary Lane, *A Concordance to the Poems of Hart Crane* (1972); R. W. B. Lewis, *The Poetry of Hart Crane: A Critical Study* (1967); Herbert A. Leibowitz, *Hart Crane: An Introduction to the Poetry* (1968); Robert L. Perry, *The Shared Vision of Waldo Frank and Hart Crane* (1966); Vincent Quinn, *Hart Crane* (1963); Joseph Schwartz and Robert C. Schweik, eds., *Hart Crane: A Descriptive Bibliography* (1972); Monroe K. Spears, *Hart Crane* (1965); R. P. Sugg, *Hart Crane's 'The Bridge'* (1977).

STEPHEN CRANE

The Black Riders (1895); *War Is Kind* (1899).

Criticism:
J. Berryman, *Stephen Crane* (1975); D. G. Hoffman, *The Poetry of Stephen Crane* (1957); R. W. Stallman, *Stephen Crane: A Biography* (1968).

ROBERT CREELEY

Le Fou (1952); *The Immoral Proposition* (1953); *The Kind of Act of* (1953); *All That Is Lovely in Men* (1955); *If You* (1956); *The Whip* (1957); *A Form of Women* (1959); *For Love: Poems 1950–1960* (1962); *Poems 1950–1965* (1966); *Words: Poems* (1967); *The Finger* (1968, rev. 1970); *The Charm: Early and Uncollected Poems* (1968); *5 Numbers* (1969); *Divisions and Other Early Poems* (1969); *Pieces* (1969); *As Now It Would Be Snow* (1970); *St Martin's* (1971); *Gold Diggers* (1972); *A Day Book* (1972); *Thirty Things* (1974); *Selected Poems* (1976); *Away* (1976); *Hello* (1978).

Criticism:
Mary Novik, *Robert Creeley: An Inventory* (1973).

COUNTEE CULLEN

Color (1925); *Copper Sun* (1927); *The Black Christ* (1929); *The Medea* (1935); *On These I Stand* (1947).

Criticism:
Blanche E. Ferguson, *Countee Cullen and the Negro Renaissance* (1966); Margaret Perry, *A Bio-Bibliography of Countee Cullen* (1971).

E. E. CUMMINGS

Tulips and Chimneys (1923); *&* (1925); *is 5* (1926); *CIOPW* (1931);
ViVa (1931); *no thanks* (1935); *One Over Twenty* (1936); *Collected
Poems* (1938); *50 Poems* (1940); *I × I* (1944); *XAIPE: 71 Poems*
(1950); *Poems, 1923–1954* (1954); *95 Poems* (1958); *100 Selected Poems*
(1959); *73 Poems* (1963); *Complete Poems* (1973).

Criticism:
S. V. Baum, ed., *EΣTI: eec: E. E. Cummings and The Critics* (1962);
Norman Friedman, *E. E. Cummings: The Art of His Poetry* (1960),
E. E. Cummings: The Growth of a Writer (1964), (ed.), *E. E. Cummings:
A Collection of Critical Essays* (1972); G. Lane, *I Am: A Study of E. E.
Cummings' Poems* (1976); Barry A. Marks, *E. E. Cummings* (1964);
Eve Triem, *E. E. Cummings* (1969); Robert E. Wegner, *The Poetry
and Prose of E. E. Cummings* (1965).

EMILY DICKINSON

Poems (1890); *Poems* (1891); *Poems* (1896); *The Single Hound* (1914);
Complete Poems (1924); *Further Poems* (1929); *Poems of Emily Dickinson*
(1930); *Unpublished Poems* (1935); *Bolts of Melody* (1945); *Poems of
Emily Dickinson* (3 vols, 1955); *Complete Poems* (1960).

Criticism:
Charles R. Anderson, *Emily Dickinson's Poetry: Stairway of Surprise*
(1960); Millicent Todd Bingham, *Ancestors' Brocades: The Literary
Discovery of Emily Dickinson* (1945); Willis J. Buckingham, ed.,
Emily Dickinson, an Annotated Bibliography (1970); Jack L. Capps,
Emily Dickinson's Reading, 1836–1886 (1966); Richard Chase, *Emily
Dickinson* (1951); Denis Donoghue, *Emily Dickinson* (1969); Ralph W.
Franklin, *The Editing of Emily Dickinson* (1967); Albert J. Gelpi,
Emily Dickinson: The Mind of the Poet (1965); Clark Griffith, *The
Long Shadow: Emily Dickinson's Tragic Poetry* (1964); Stanford P.
Rosenbaum, ed., *A Concordance to the Poems of Emily Dickinson* (1964);
R. B. Sewall, ed., *Emily Dickinson: A Collection of Critical Essays*
(1963); W. R. Sherwood, *Circumference and Circumstance: Stages in the
Mind and Art of Emily Dickinson* (1968); R. Weisbuch, *Emily Dickinson's
Poetry* (1975).

H.D. (HILDA DOOLITTLE)

Sea Garden (1916); *Hymen* (1921); *Heliodora and Other Poems* (1924); *Collected Poems* (1925); *Red Roses for Bronze* (1931); *The Walls Do Not Fall* (1944); *Tribute to Angels* (1945); *The Flowering of the Rod* (1946); *By Avon River* (1949); *Selected Poems* (1957); *Helen in Egypt* (1961); *Hermetic Definition* (1972); *Trilogy* (1973).

Criticism:
Vincent Quinn, *H.D.* (1967); Thomas B. Swann, *The Classical World of H.D.* (1962).

EDWARD DORN

The Newly Fallen (1961); *From Gloucester Out* (1964); *Hands Up!* (1964); *Idaho Out* (1965); *Geography* (1966); *The North Atlantic Turbine* (1967); *Gunslinger, Part I* (1968); *Gunslinger, Part II* (1969); *24 Love Songs* (1969); *Songs, Set Two: A Short Count* (1970); *The Cycle* (1971); *Gunslinger III* (1972); *Recollections of Gran Apacheria* (1974); *Collected Poems* (1975); *Slinger* (1975).

ALAN DUGAN

Poems (1961); *Poems 2* (1963); *Poems 3* (1967); *Collected Poems* (1969); *Poems 4* (1974).

ROBERT DUNCAN

Heavenly City, Earthly City (1947); *Poems 1948–1949* (1949); *Medieval Scenes* (1950); *Song of the Borderguard* (1952); *Caesar's Gate* (1955); *Letters: Poems 1953–1956* (1958); *Selected Poems 1942–1950* (1959); *The Opening of the Field* (1960); *Roots and Branches* (1964); *Wine* (1964); *A Book of Remembrances* (1966); *Fragments of a Disordered Devotion* (1966); *Passages, 22–27* (1966); *The Years as Catches, First Poems 1939–41* (1966); *Bending the Bow* (1968); *The First Decade: Selected Poems, vol. 1* (1968); *Derivations: Selected Poems, 1950–1956* (1968); *Tribunals: Passages 31–55* (1970); *Dante* (1974); *A Seventeenth-Century Suite* (1974).

RICHARD EBERHART

A Bravery of Earth (1930); *Reading the Spirit* (1936); *Song and Idea* (1940); *Poems, New and Selected* (1944); *Burr Oaks* (1947); *Brotherhood of Men* (1949); *An Herb Basket* (1950); *Selected Poems* (1951); *Under-cliff: Poems 1946–1953*; (1953) *Great Praises* (1957); *Collected Poems 1930–1960* (1960); *The Quarry* (1964); *Selected Poems 1930–1965* (1965); *Thirty One Sonnets* (1967); *Shifts of Being* (1968); *Fields of Grace* (1972); *Collected Poems, 1930–1976* (1976).

Criticism:
Bernard F. Engle, *Richard Eberhart* (1970); Ralph J. Mills, Jr, *Richard Eberhart* (1966); Joel H. Roache, *Richard Eberhart: The Progress of an American Poet* (1971).

T. S. ELIOT

Prufrock and Other Observations (1917); *Poems* (1919); *Ara Vos Prec* (1920); *The Waste Land* (1922); *Poems 1909–1925* (1925); *Ash-Wednesday* (1930); *Collected Poems, 1909–1935* (1936); *Old Possum's Book of Practical Cats* (1939); *The Waste Land and Other Poems* (1940); *East Coker* (1940); *Burnt Norton* (1941); *The Dry Salvages* (1941); *Little Gidding* (1942); *Four Quartets* (1943); *Poems Written in Early Youth* (1950); *The Complete Poems and Plays* (1952); *Collected Poems 1909–1962* (1963); *The Waste Land* [Facsimile of MS] (1971).

Criticism:
M. C. Bradbrook, *T. S. Eliot* (1951); N. Braybrooke, *T. S. Eliot* (1967), (ed), *T. S. Eliot: A Symposium for His Seventieth Birthday* (1958); D. Daiches and others, eds, The Waste Land by *T. S. Eliot: Critical Analysis* (1971); E. Drew, *T. S. Eliot: The Design of His Poetry* (1949); N. Frye, *T. S. Eliot* (1963); H. Gardner, *The Art of T. S. Eliot* (1950); Hugh Kenner, *The Invisible Poet* (1959), (ed.) *T. S. Eliot: A Collection of Critical Essays* (1962); R. Kirk, *Eliot and His Age* (1972); R. E. Knoll, ed., *Storm over the Waste Land* (1964); R. March and T. Tambimuttu, eds, *T. S. Eliot* (1949); J. Martin, ed., *Twentieth-Century Interpretations of* The Waste Land (1968); M. Martin, *A Half-Century of Eliot Criticism: An Annotated Bibliography* (1972); F. O. Matthiessen, *The Achievement of T. S. Eliot* (1947); D. E. S. Maxwell, *The Poetry of T. S. Eliot* (1952); D. B. Morris, *The Poetry of Gerard Manley Hopkins and T. S. Eliot in the Light of the Donne Tradition* (1953); Sydney Musgrove, *T. S. Eliot and Walt Whitman* (1952); Grover Smith, *T. S. Eliot's Poetry and Plays: A Study in Sources and Meaning* (1956); S. Spender, *Eliot* (1975); A. Tate, ed., *T. S. Eliot: The Man and His Work* (1966); D. A. Traversi, *T. S. Eliot: The Longer*

Poems (1976); L. Unger, *T. S. Eliot* (1961), *T. S. Eliot: Monuments and Patterns* (1965), (ed.) *T. S. Eliot: A Selected Critique* (1948); G. Williamson, *A Reader's Guide to T. S. Eliot* (1965).

RALPH WALDO EMERSON

Poems (1847); *Selected Poems* (1876); *The Works of Ralph Waldo Emerson* (1890).

Criticism:

J. Benton, *Emerson as a Poet* (1975); Sherman Paul, *Emerson's Angle of Vision: Man and Nature in American Experience* (1952); S. E. Whicher, *Freedom and Fate: An Inner Life of Ralph Waldo Emerson* (1953).

KENNETH FEARING

Poems (1935); *Dead Reckoning: A Book of Poetry* (1938); *Collected Poems of Kenneth Fearing* (1940); *Afternoon of a Pawnbroker* (1943); *Stranger at Coney Island* (1948); *New and Selected Poems* (1956).

LAWRENCE FERLINGHETTI

Pictures of the Gone World (1955); *A Coney Island of the Mind* (1958); *Tentative Description of a Dinner Given to Promote the Impeachment of President Eisenhower* (1958); *One Thousand Fearful Words for Fidel Castro* (1961); *Starting from San Francisco* (1961); *Where Is Vietnam?* (1965); *An Eye of the World: Selected Poems* (1967); *After the Cries of the Birds* (1967); *Moscow in the Wilderness, Segovia in the Snow* (1967); *The Secret Meaning of Things* (1969); *Tyrannus Nix?* (1969); *Open Eye, Open Heart* (1973).

PHILIP FRENEAU

The Poems of Philip Freneau (1786); *Poems Written and Published During the American Revolutionary War, and Now Republished from the Original Manuscripts* (1809); *A Collection of Poems, on American Affairs, and a Variety of Other Subjects, Chiefly Moral and Political* (1815).

Criticism:

Nelson F. Adkins, *Philip Freneau and the Cosmic Enigma* (1949); Jacob Axelrod, *Philip Freneau: Champion of Democracy* (1967); M. W. Bowden, *Philip Freneau* (1976); P. Marsh, *The Works of Philip Freneau: A Critical Study* (1968).

ROBERT FROST

A Boy's Will (1913); *North of Boston* (1914); *Mountain Interval* (1916); *New Hampshire* (1923); *Selected Poems* (1923, rev. 1928 and 1934); *West-Running Brook* (1928); *Collected Poems* (1930); *A Further Range* (1936); *Selected Poems* (1936); *Collected Poems* (1939); *A Witness Tree* (1942); *A Masque of Reason* (1945); *Poems* (1946); *A Masque of Mercy* (1947); *A Sermon* (1947); *Steeple Bush* (1947); *Complete Poems* (1949); *Aforesaid* (1954); *In the Clearing* (1962); *The Poetry of Robert Frost* (1969).

Criticism:
Reuben Brower, *The Poetry of Robert Frost: Constellations of Intention* (1963); W. B. S. Clymer, *Robert Frost: A Bilbiography* (1972); Reginald L. Cook, *The Dimensions of Robert Frost* (1958); James M. Cox, ed., *Robert Frost: A Collection of Critical Essays* (1962); John R. Doyle, Jr, *The Poetry of Robert Frost: An Analysis* (1962); Philip L. Gerber, *Robert Frost* (1966); Robert A. Greenberg and James G. Hepburn, eds, *Robert Frost: An Introduction* (1961); Elizabeth Isaacs, *An Introduction to Robert Frost* (1962); Elizabeth Jennings, *Robert Frost* (1964); John F. Lynen, *The Pastoral Art of Robert Frost* (1964); George W. Nitchie, *Human Values in the Poetry of Robert Frost* (1960); W. R. Poirier, *Robert Frost* (1977); Radcliffe Squires, *The Major Themes of Robert Frost* (1963); Lawrance R. Thompson, *Fire and Ice: The Art and Thought of Robert Frost* (1942), *Robert Frost* (1964); Richard Thornton, ed., *The Recognition of Robert Frost* (1970).

ALLEN GINSBERG

Howl (1956); *Empty Mirror: Early Poems* (1961); *Kaddish and Other Poems, 1958–1960* (1961); *Reality Sandwiches* (1963); *Wichita Vortex Sutra* (1966); *T.V. Baby Poems* (1967); *Ankor-Wat* (1968); *Planet News 1961–1967* (1968); *Airplane Dreams* (1969); *The Fall of America* (1972); *The Gates of Wrath* (1973); *Iron Horse* (1974); *Mind Breaths, 1972–1977* (1977).

Criticism:
G. Dowden and L. McGilvery, eds, *A Bibliography of the Works of Allen Ginsberg* (1971); Jane Kramer, *Allen Ginsberg in America* (1968); T. F. Merrill, *Allen Ginsberg* (1969); Eric Mottram, *Allen Ginsberg in the 6os* (1972).

NIKKI GIOVANNI

Black Judgment (1968); *Black Feeling, Black Talk* (1968); *Black Feeling, Black Talk, Black Judgment* (1970); *Re:Creation* (1970); *Spin a Soft Black Song* (1971); *My House* (1972); *Ego Tripping and Other Poems for Young Readers* (1974).

FRANCIS BRET HARTE

The Lost Galleon and Other Tales (1867); *Plain Language from Truthful James* (1870); *Poems* (1871); *East and West Poems* (1871); *The Complete Poetical Works* (1889); *Some Later Verses* (1898).

Criticism:
R. O'Connor, *Bret Harte: A Biography* (1966); G. R. Stewart, *Bret Harte: Argonaut and Exile* (1931).

ANTHONY HECHT

A Summoning of Stones (1954); *The Seven Deadly Sins* (1958); *Jiggery-Pokery: A Compendium of Double Dactyls* (with J. Hollander *et al.*) (1967); *The Hard Hours* (1967); *Aesopic* (1968); *Millions of Strange Shadows* (1977).

ERNEST HEMINGWAY

Three Stories and Ten Poems (1923); *Collected Poems* (n.d., pirated edition).

Criticism:
C. H. Baker, *The Writer as Artist* (1952), *Ernest Hemingway: A Life Story* (1969); S. Baker, *Ernest Hemingway: An Introduction and Appreciation* (1967); C. A. Fenton, *The Apprenticeship of Ernest Hemingway: The Early Years* (1954).

OLIVER WENDELL HOLMES

Poems (1836); *Poems* (1849); *Songs of Many Seasons, 1862–1874* (1875); *The Iron Gate and Other Poems* (1880); *The Writings of Oliver Wendell Holmes* (1891, 13 vols); *The Poetical Works of Oliver Wendell Holmes* (rev. 1975).

Criticism:
W. L. Schroeder, *Oliver Wendell Holmes: An Appreciation* (1909);
M. R. Small, *Oliver Wendell Holmes* (1963).

JULIA WARD HOWE

Passion Flowers (1854); *Words for the Hour* (1857); *Later Lyrics* (1868);
From Sunset Ridge: Poems Old and New (1898).

Criticism:
John J. MacIntyre, *The Composer of the* Battle Hymn of the Republic
(1916); L. E. Richards and M. H. Elliot, *Julia Ward Howe 1819–1910*
(1915).

LANGSTON HUGHES

The Weary Blues (1926); *Fine Clothes to the Jew* (1927); *Dear Lovely
Death* (1931); *The Negro Mother* (1931); *The Dream Keeper and Other
Poems* (1932); *Scottsboro Limited* (1932); *A New Song* (1938); *Shakespeare
in Harlem* (1942); *Jim Crow's Last Stand* (1943); *Lament for Dark Peoples*
(1944); *Fields of Wonder* (1947); *One Way Ticket* (1949); *Montage of a
Dream Deferred* (1951); *Selected Poems* (1959); *Ask Your Mama* (1961);
The Panther and the Lash (1967); *Black Misery* (1969); *Don't You Turn
Back: Poems* (1969).

Criticism:
R. K. Barksdale, *Langston Hughes* (1977); Donald C. Dickinson,
A Bio-Bibliography of Langston Hughes, 1902–1967 (1967); James
Emmanuel, *Langston Hughes* (1967); Therman B. O'Daniel, ed.,
Langston Hughes, Black Genius: A Critical Evaluation (1972).

RANDALL JARRELL

The Rage for the Lost Penny (1940); *Blood for a Stranger* (1942); *Little
Friend, Little Friend* (1945); *Losses* (1948); *The Seven-League Crutches*
(1951); *Selected Poems* (1955); *The Woman at the Washington Zoo*
(1960); *Selected Poems* (1964); *The Lost World* (1965); *Complete Poems*
(1969); *Jerome: The Biography of a Poem* (1971).

Criticism:
Suzanne Ferguson, *The Poetry of Randall Jarrell* (1971); Robert Lowell

and others, eds., *Randall Jarrell, 1914–1965* (1967); M. L. Rosenthal, *Randall Jarrell* (1972).

ROBINSON JEFFERS

Flagons and Apples (1912); *Californians* (1916); *Tamar and Other Poems* (1924); *Roan Stallion* (1925); *The Woman at Point Sur* (1927); *Poems* (1928); *Cawdor and Other Poems* (1928); *Dear Judas and Other Poems* (1929); *Descent to the Dead: Poems Written in Ireland and Great Britain* (1931); *Thurso's Landing* (1932); *Give Your Heart to the Hawks and Other Poems* (1933); *Solstice and Other Poems* (1935); *Such Counsels You Gave to Me and Other Poems* (1937); *Poems Known and Unknown* (1938); *Selected Poetry* (1938); *Be Angry at the Sun* (1941); *The Double Axe and Other Poems* (1948); *Hungerfield and Other Poems* (1954); *The Beginning and the End* (1963); *Selected Poems* (1965).

Criticism:
Sydney S. Alberts, *A Bibliography of the Works of Robinson Jeffers* (1933); Brother Antoninus, *Robinson Jeffers: Fragments of an Older Fury* (1970); Arthur B. Coffin, *Robinson Jeffers: Poet of Inhumanism* (1971); J. Shebl, *In this Wild Water: the Suppressed Poems of Robinson Jeffers* (1976); Radcliffe Squires, *The Loyalties of Robinson Jeffers* (1966); Alex A. Verdamis, *The Critical Reputation of Robinson Jeffers* (1972).

WELDON KEES

The Last Man (1943); *The Fall of the Magicians* (1947); *Poems 1947–1954* (1954); *Collected Poems* (1962); *Collected Poems* (rev. 1975).

FRANCIS SCOTT KEY

Poems (1857).

Criticism:
Edward S. Delaplaine, *Francis Scott Key: Life and Times* (1937); Rupert Sargeant Holland, *Freedom's Flag: The Story of Francis Scott Key* (1943).

ETHERIDGE KNIGHT

Poems from Prison (1968); *Belly Song* (1972).

KENNETH KOCH

Poems (1953); *Ko: or, A Season on Earth* (1959); *Permanently* (1961); *Thank You and Other Poems* (1962); *Poems from 1952 and 1953* (1968); *When the Sun Tries to Go On* (1969); *Sleeping with Women* (1969); *The Pleasures of Peace and Other Poems* (1969); *The Red Robins* (1975); *The Duplications* (1977).

HAKI R. MAHUBUTI (DON L. LEE)

Think Black (1967); *Black Pride* (1968); *Back Again, Home* (1968); *One-Sided Shoot-Out* (1968); *For Black People (and Negroes too)* (1968); *Don't Cry, Scream* (1969); *We Walk the Way of the New World* (1970); *Directionscore: Selected and New Poems* (1971); *Book of Life* (1973); *From Plan to Planet* (1973).

VACHEL LINDSAY

The Tramp's Excuse and Other Poems (1909); *General William Booth Enters into Heaven and Other Poems* (1913); *The Congo and Other Poems* (1914); *The Chinese Nightingale and Other Poems* (1917); *The Golden Whales of California and Other Rhymes in the American Language* (1920); *The Daniel Jazz and Other Poems* (1920); *Going-to-the-Sun* (1923); *The Candle in the Cabin: A Weaving Together of Script and Singing* (1926); *Going-to-the-Stars* (1926); *Johnny Appleseed* (1928); *Every Soul is a Circus* (1929); *Selected Poems* (1931, rev. 1963).

Criticism:
M. Harris, *City of Discontent: An Interpretive Biography of Vacel Lindsay* (1952); Ann Massa, *Vachel Lindsay: Field Worker for the American Dream* (1970); E. L. Masters, *Vachel Lindsay: A Poet in America* (1935); George Scouffas, *Vachel Lindsay: A Study in Retreat and Repudiation* (1951).

HENRY WADSWORTH LONGFELLOW

Voices of the Night (1839); *Ballads and Other Poems* (1942); *The Belfry of Bruges and Other Poems* (1846); *The Seaside and the Fireside* (1850); *The Courtship of Miles Standish and Other Poems* (1858); *Tales of a Wayside Inn* (1863); *Dante, the Divine Comedy* (1865–7, translation); *Flower-de-Luce* (1967); *Aftermath* (1873); *The Masque of Pandora and Other Poems* (1875); *Kiramos and Other Poems* (1878); *Ultima Thule* (1880); *In the Harbor* (1882).

Criticism:
Newton Arvin, *Longfellow: His Life and Work* (1963); E. L. Hirsch, *Henry Wadsworth Longfellow* (1964).

AMY LOWELL

A Dome of Many-Coloured Glass (1912); *Sword Blades and Poppy Seeds* (1914); *Men, Women and Ghosts* (1916); *Can Grande's Castle* (1918); *Pictures of the Floating World* (1919); *Legends* (1921); *Fir-Flower Tablets* (1921); *A Critical Fable* (1922); *What's O'Clock* (1925); *East Wind* (1926); *Ballads for Sale* (1927); *Selected Poems* (1928); *The Complete Poetical Works of Amy Lowell* (1955).

Criticism:
S. Foster Damon, *Amy Lowell: A Chronicle* (1935); F. C. Flint, *Amy Lowell* (1969); H. Gregory, *Amy Lowell: Portrait of a Poet in Her Time* (1958).

JAMES RUSSELL LOWELL

A Year's Life and Other Poems (1841); *Poems* (1844); *A Fable for Critics* (1848); *The Biglow Papers* (1848); *The Ode Recited at the Harvard Commemoration* (1865); *The Biglow Papers, Second Series* (1867); *Under the Willows* (1868); *The Cathedral* (1870); *Three Memorial Poems* (1877); *Heartsease and Rue* (1888); *Uncollected Poems* (1950); *Uncollected Poems* (1976).

Criticism:
M. B. Dubermann, *James Russell Lowell* (1966); C. McGlinchee, *James Russell Lowell* (1967); E. C. Wagenknecht, *James Russell Lowell: Portrait of a Many-Sided Man* (1971).

ROBERT LOWELL

The Land of Unlikeness (1944); *Lord Weary's Castle* (1946, rev. 1947); *Poems, 1938–1949* (1950); *The Mills of the Kavanaughs* (1951); *Life Studies* (1959); *Imitations* (1961); *For the Union Dead* (1964); *Selected Poems* (1965); *Near the Ocean* (1967); *The Voyage and Other Versions of Poems by Baudelaire* (1968); *Notebook, 1967–68* (1969, rev. 1970); *The Dolphin* (1973); *For Lizzie and Harriet* (1973); *History* (1973); *Selected Poems* (1976); *Day by Day* (1977).

Criticism:
Philip Cooper, *The Autobiographical Myth of Robert Lowell* (1970);
Patrick Cosgrave, *The Public Poetry of Robert Lowell* (1972); J. M.
Edelstein, ed., *Robert Lowell: A Checklist* (1972); Robert J. Fein,
Robert Lowell (1971); Jay Martin, *Robert Lowell* (1970); Jerome Mazzaro,
The Achievement of Robert Lowell (1960), *The Poetic Themes of Robert
Lowell* (1965); T. Parkinson, ed., *Lowell: A Collection of Critical
Essays* (1968); Hugh Staples, *Robert Lowell: The First Twenty Years*
(1962); S. Yenser, *Circle to Circle: The Poetry of Robert Lowell* (1975).

ARCHIBALD MACLEISH

Songs for a Summer's Day (1915); *Tower of Ivory* (1917); *The Happy
Marriage* (1924); *Streets in the Moon* (1926); *The Hamlet of A. MacLeish*
(1928); *New Found Land* (1930); *Conquistador* (1932); *Before March*
(1932); *Poems 1924–1933* (1933); *Frescoes for Mr Rockefeller's City*
(1933); *Public Speech* (1936); *Land of the Free* (1938); *America Was
Promises* (1939); *Act five* (1948); *Collected Poems* (1952, rev. 1963);
Songs for Eve (1954); *The Wild Old Wicked Man and Other Poems*
(1967); *The Human Season: Selected Poems, 1926–1972* (1972); *New and
Collected Poems 1917–1976* (1976).

Criticism:
Signi Falk, *Archibald MacLeish* (1965); G. Smith, *Archibald MacLeish*
(1971).

DON MARQUIS

Dreams and Dust: Poems (1915); *Noah an' Jonah an' Cap'n John Smith*
(1921); *Poems and Portraits* (1922); *The Awakening* (1924); *Sonnets to a
Red-haired Lady* (1927); *Love Sonnets of a Caveman* (1928); *Archy and
Mehitabel* (1931); *Archy's Life of Mehitabel* (1933); *Archy Does His
Part* (1935).

EDGAR LEE MASTERS

The Book of Verses (1898); *The Blood of the Prophets* (1905); *Spoon
River Anthology* (1915); *Songs and Satires* (1916); *Toward the Gulf*
(1918); *Starved Rock* (1919); *Domesday Book* (1920); *The New Spoon
River* (1924); *Selected Poems* (1925); *The Fate of the Jury: An Epilogue
to 'Domesday Book'* (1929); *Lichee Nuts* (1930); *The Serpent in the*

Wilderness (1933); *Invisible Landscapes* (1935); *The Golden Fleece of California* (1936); *Poems of People* (1936); *The New World* (1937); *More People* (1939); *Illinois Poems* (1941); *The Sangamon* (1942).

Criticism:
Kimball Flaccus, *The Vermont Background of Edgar Lee Masters* (1955); Lois Teal Hartley, *Edgar Lee Masters: A Study* (1950).

HERMAN MELVILLE

Battle-Pieces and Aspects of the War (1866); *Clarel: A Poem and Pilgrimage in the Holy Land* (1876); *John Marr and Other Sailors* (1888); *Timoleon* (1891); *Collected Poems* (1947).

Criticism:
N. Arvin, *Herman Melville* (1950); W. Braswell, *Melville's Religious Thought: An Essay in Interpretation* (1943); R. Chase, *Herman Melville: A Critical Study* (1949); L. Mumford, *Herman Melville: A Study of His Life and Vision* (1962); W. E. Sedgwick, *Herman Melville: The Tragedy of Mind* (1944).

JAMES MERRILL

The Black Swan (1946); *First Poems* (1951); *Short Stories* (1954); *The Country of a Thousand Years of Peace* (1959, rev. 1970); *Selected Poems* (1961); *Water Street* (1962); *Nights and Days* (1966); *The Thousand and Second Night* (1966); *The Fire Screen* (1969); *Braving the Elements* (1972); *The Yellow Pages* (1974); *Divine Comedies* (1976).

W. S. MERWIN

A Mask for Janus (1952); *The Dancing Bears* (1954); *Green with Beasts* (1956); *The Drunk in the Furnace* (1960); *The Moving Target* (1963); *The Lice* (1967); *Three Poems* (1968); *Animae* (1969); *The Carrier of Ladders* (1970); *The Miner's Pale Children* (1971); *The First Four Books of Poems* (1975); *The Compass Flowers* (1977).

ROBERT MEZEY

The Lovemaker (1961); *White Blossoms* (1965); *The Mercy of Sorrow* (1966); *Door Standing Open: New and Selected Poems* (1970); *Book of Dying* (1970).

EDNA ST VINCENT MILLAY

Renascence and Other Poems (1917); *A Few Figs from Thistles* (1920); *Second April* (1921); *The Harp-Weaver and Other Poems* (1923); *The Buck in the Snow* (1928); *Fatal Interview* (1931); *Wine from These Grapes* (1934); *Conversation at Midnight* (1937); *Huntsman, What Quarry?* (1939); *Make Bright the Arrows* (1940); *Collected Sonnets* (1941); *Collected Lyrics* (1943); *Mine the Harvest* (1954); *Collected Poems* (1956).

Criticism:
Elizabeth Atkins, *Edna St Vincent Millay and Her Times* (1936); Norman A. Britten, *Edna St Vincent Millay* (1967); Jean Gould, *The Poet and Her Book: The Life and Work of Edna St Vincent Millay* (1969); James Gray, *Edna St Vincent Millay* (1967); Karl Yost, *A Bibliography of the Works of Edna St Vincent Millay* (1937).

MARIANNE MOORE

Poems (1921); *Observations* (1924); *Selected Poems* (1935); *The Pangolin* (1936); *What Are Years?* (1941); *Nevertheless* (1944); *Collected Poems* (1951); *Like a Bulwark* (1956); *O To Be a Dragon* (1959); *The Arctic Ox* (1964); *Tell Me, Tell Me* (1966); *Complete Poems* (1967).

Criticism:
Bernard F. Engle, *Marianne Moore* (1963); Jean Garrigue, *Marianne Moore* (1965); P. W. Hadas, *Marianne Moore: Poet of Affection* (1977); Donald Hall, *Marianne Moore: The Cage and the Animal* (1970); George W. Nitchie, *Marianne Moore: An Introduction to the Poetry* (1969); Eugene P. Sheehy and Kenneth A. Lohf, *The Achievement of Marianne Moore* (1958); Charles Tomlinson, ed., *Marianne Moore: A Collection of Critical Essays* (1969).

OGDEN NASH

Freewheeling (1931); *Hard Lines* (1931); *The Primrose Path* (1935); *I'm a Stranger Here Myself* (1938); *The Face is Familiar* (1940); *Many Long Years Ago* (1945); *Versus* (1949); *Family Reunion* (1950); *Parents Keep Out* (1951); *The Private Dining Room* (1953); *You Can't Get There From Here* (1957); *Verses From 1929 On* (1959), (English ed. *Collected Verse from 1929*, 1961); *Marriage Lines* (1964); *There's Always Another Windmill* (1968); *I Wouldn't Have Missed It: Selected Poems* (1975).

HOWARD NEMEROV

The Image and the Law (1947); *Guide to the Ruins* (1950); *The Salt Garden* (1955); *Mirrors and Windows* (1958); *New and Selected Poems* (1960); *Endor* (1961); *The Next Room of the Dream: Poems and Two Plays* (1962); *The Blue Swallows* (1967); *The Winter Lightning: Selected Poems* (1968); *Gnomes and Occasions* (1972); *The Western Approaches: Poems* (1975); *Collected Poems* (1977).

Criticism:
Julia A. Bartholomay, *The Shield of Perseus: The Vision and Imagination of Howard Nemerov* (1971); Bowie Duncan, *The Critical Reception of Howard Nemerov* (1971); Peter Meinke, *Howard Nemerov* (1968).

FRANK O'HARA

A City Winter, and Other Poems (1952); *Meditations in an Emergency* (1957); *Odes* (1960); *Lunch Poems* (1964); *Love Poems (Tentative Title)* (1965); *In Memory of My Feelings* (1967); *Collected Poems* (1971); *Selected Poems* (1974); *Poems Retrieved* (1975); *Early Writing* (1977).

CHARLES OLSON

To Corrado Cagli (1947); *Y and X* (1950); *Letter for Melville* (1951); *This* (1952); *In Cold Hell, in Thicket* (1953); *The Maximus Poems 1–10* (1953); *The Maximus Poems 11–22* (1956); *O'Ryan 2 4 6 8 10* (1958); *The Maximus Poems* (1960); *The Distances* (1960); *Maximus from Dogtown I* (1961); *Proprioception* (1965); *O'Ryan 1 2 3 4 5 6 7 8 9 10* (1965); *Selected Writings* (1967); *The Maximus Poems IV, V, VI* (1968); *Archaeologist of Morning* (1970); *Maximus Volume III* (1975).

Criticism:
G. Butterick and A. Glover, eds, *A Bibliography of Works by Charles Oslon* (1967); Anne Charters, *Olson/Melville: A Study in Affinity* (1968); Ed Dorn, *What I See in* The Maximus Poems (1960).

SYLVIA PLATH

The Colossus (1962); *Ariel* (1965); *Crossing the Water* (1971); *Winter Trees* (1971).

Criticism:
Eileen Aird, *Sylvia Plath* (1973); E. Butscher, *Sylvia Plath: Method and Madness* (1975); D. Holbrook, *Sylvia Plath: Poetry and Existence* (1976);

I. Melander, *The Poetry of Sylvia Plath: A Study of Themes* (1972); Charles Newman, ed., *The Art of Sylvia Plath* (1970); Nancy H. Steiner, *A Closer Look at Ariel: A Memory of SP* (1972).

EDGAR ALLAN POE

Tamerlane and Other Poems (1827); *Al Aaraaf, Tamerlane and Minor Poems* (1829); *Poems* (1831); *The Raven and Other Poems* (1845).

Criticism:
K. Campbell, *The Mind of Poe and Other Studies* (1932); L. N. Chase, *Poe and his Poetry* (1976); E. H. Davidson, *Poe: A Critical Study* (1957); T. S. Eliot, *From Poe to Valéry* (1948); J. P. Fruit, *The Mind and Art of Poe's Poetry* (1975); P. F. Quinn, *The French Face of Edgar Allan Poe* (1957).

EZRA POUND

A Lume Spento (1908); *A Quinzaine for This Yule* (1908); *Personae* (1909); *Exultations* (1909); *Provença: Poems Selected from Personae, Exulatations and Canzoniere* (1910); *Canzoni* (1911); *Ripostes* (1912); *Lustra* (1916); *Quia Pauper Amavi* (1919); *Umbra: The Early Poems* (1920); *Hugh Selwyn Mauberley* (1920); *Poems, 1918–1921* (1921); *A Draft of XVI Cantos* (1925); *Personae: Collected Poems* (1926, rev. 1949); *Selected Poems* (1928); *A Draft of The Cantos 17–27* (1928); *A Draft of XXX Cantos* (1930); *Homage to Sextus Propertius* (1934); *Eleven New Cantos: XXXI–XLI* (1934); *The Fifth Decad of Cantos* (1937); *Cantos LII–LXXI* (1940); *The Cantos* (1948, 1965, 1971); *The Pisan Cantos* (1948); *Selected Poems* (1949, rev. 1957); *Seventy Cantos* (1950); *Section: Rock-Drill: 86–95 de los cantares* (1955); *Thrones: 96–109 de los cantares* (1959); *A Lume Spento and Other Early Poems* (1965); *Selected Cantos* (1967); *Drafts and Fragments of Cantos CX to CXVII* (1969); *The Cantos of Ezra Pound* (1975).

Criticism:
Walter Baumann, *The Rose in the Steel Dust: An Examination of the Cantos of Ezra Pound* (1967); Christine Brooke-Rose, *A ZBC of Ezra Pound* (1971); Donald Davie, *Ezra Pound: Poet as Sculptor* (1964), *Pound* (1975); George Dekker, *Sailing After Knowledge: The Cantos of Ezra Pound* (1963); N. Christophe de Nagy, *The Poetry of Ezra Pound: The Pre-Imagist Stage* (1960, rev. 1968); John H. Edwards and William

W. Vasse, Jr, eds, *Annotated Index to the Cantos of Ezra Pound* (to Canto 84) (1957); T. S. Eliot, *Ezra Pound: His Metric and Poetry* (1917); Clark Emery, *Ideas into Action: A Study of Pound's Cantos* (1958); John Epsey, *Ezra Pound's* Mauberley (1955); G. S. Fraser, *Ezra Pound* (1961); Donald Gallup, *A Bibliography of Ezra Pound* (1964); K. L. Goodwin, *The Influence of Ezra Pound* (1966); Eva Hesse, ed., *New Approaches to Ezra Pound* (1969); C. D. Heymann, *Ezra Pound* (1976); Eric Homberger, *Ezra Pound: The Critical Heritage* (1972); Thomas H. Jackson, *The Early Poetry of Ezra Pound* (1968); Hugh Kenner, *The Poetry of Ezra Pound* (1951), *The Pound Era* (1972); Gary Lane, *A Concordance to the Poems of Ezra Pound* (1972); Lewis Leary, *Motive and Method in the Cantos of Ezra Pound* (1954); William Van O'Connor, *Ezra Pound* (1963), (ed., with Edward Stone) *A Case Book on Ezra Pound* (1959); Daniel D. Pearlman, *The Barb of Time: On the Unity of Pound's Cantos* (1969); M. L. Rosenthal, *A Primer of Ezra Pound* (1960); Peter Russell, ed., *An Examination of Ezra Pound* (1950); K. K. Ruthven, *A Guide to Ezra Pound's* Personae (1969); J. P. Sullivan, *Ezra Pound and Sextus Propertius: A Study in Creative Translation* (1964), *Ezra Pound: A Collection of Critical Essays* (1963); J. J. Wilhelm, *The Later Cantos of Ezra Pound* (1977); Hugh Witemeyer, *The Poetry of Ezra Pound: Forms and Renewal, 1908–1920* (1969).

JOHN CROWE RANSOM

Poems About God (1919); *Chills and Fever* (1924); *Grace After Meat* (1924); *Two Gentlemen in Bonds* (1927); *Selected Poems* (1945, rev. 1963); *Poems and Essays* (1955).

Criticism:
Robert Buffington, *But What I Wear Is Flesh* (1967); Karl F. Knight, *The Poetry of John Crowe Ransom: A Study of Diction, Metaphor, and Symbol* (1971); Thornton H. Parsons, *John Crowe Ransom* (1969); John L. Stewart, *John Crowe Ransom* (1962); Thomas H. Young, ed., *John Crowe Ransom: Critical Essays and a Bibliography* (1968).

KENNETH REXROTH

In What Hour (1941); *The Phoenix and the Tortoise* (1944); *The Signature of All Things* (1949); *The Art of Worldly Wisdom* (1949); *The Dragon and the Unicorn* (1952); *In Defense of the Earth* (1956); *The Homestead Called Damascus* (1963); *Natural Numbers: New and Selected Poems*

(1963); *Complete Collected Shorter Poems* (1966); *Collected Longer Poems* (1968); *The Heart's Garden, the Garden's Heart* (1968); *Sky Sea Birds Trees Earth* (1972); *New Poems* (1974).

Criticism:
Morgan Gibson, *Kenneth Rexroth* (1972).

EDWIN ARLINGTON ROBINSON

The Torrent and the Night Before (1896); *The Children of the Night* (1897); *Captain Craig* (1902); *The Town down the River* (1910); *The Man Against the Sky* (1916); *Merlin* (1917); *Lancelot* (1920); *The Three Taverns* (1920); *Avon's Harvest* (1921); *Collected Poems* (1921); *Roman Bartholow* (1923); *The Man Who Died Twice* (1924); *Dionysus in Doubt* (1925); *Tristram* (1927); *Collected Poems* (5 vols, 1927); *Sonnets: 1889–1927* (1928); *Cavender's House* (1929); *Collected Poems* (1929); *The Glory of the Nightingales* (1930); *Selected Poems* (1931); *Matthias at the Door* (1931); *Nicodemus* (1932); *Talifer* (1933); *Amaranth* (1934); *King Jasper* (1935); *Collected Poems* (1937).

Criticism:
Wallace L. Anderson, *Edwin Arlington Robinson: A Critical Introduction* (1967); Ellsworth Barnard, *Edwin Alrington Robinson: A Critical Study* (1952), (ed.), *Edwin Arlington Robinson: Centenary Essays* (1969); Richard Cary, ed., *An Appreciation of Edwin Arlington Robinson* (1969); Charles Cestre, *An Introduction to Edwin Arlington Robinson* (1930); Louis O. Coxe, *Edwin Arlington Robinson* (1962), *Edwin Arlington Robinson: The Life of Poetry* (1968); Hoyt C. Franchere, *Edwin Arlington Robinson* (1968); Edwin S. Fussell, *Edwin Arlington Robinson: The Literary Background of a Traditional Poet* (1954); Charles B. Hogan, *A Bibliography of Edwin Arlington Robinson* (1936); Francis Murphy, ed., *Edwin Arlington Robinson: A Collection of Critical Essays* (1970); Emery Neff, *Edwin Arlington Robinson* (1948); W. R. Robinson, *Edwin Arlington Robinson: A Poetry of the Act* (1967); William White, *Edwin Arlington Robinson: A Supplementary Bibliography, 1936–1970* (1971); Yvor Winters, *Edwin Arlington Robinson* (1946).

THEODORE ROETHKE

Open House (1941); *The Lost Son* (1948); *Praise to the End!* (1951); *The Waking: Poems 1933–1953* (1953); *Words for the Wind: The*

Collected Verse (1957); *I Am! Says the Lamb* (1961); *Party at the Zoo* (1963); *The Far Field* (1964); *Sequence, Sometimes Metaphysical* (1964); *Collected Poems* (1966).

Criticism:
J. La Belle, *The Echoing Wood of Theodore Roethke* (1976); Gary Lane, *A Concordance to the Poems of Theodore Roethke* (1972); Karl Malkoff, *Theodore Roethke: An Introduction to the Poetry* (1966); Ralph J. Mills, Jr, *Theodore Roethke* (1963); Arnold Stein, ed., *Theodore Roethke: Essays on the Poetry* (1965); R. Sullivan, *Theodore Roethke* (1976).

SONIA SANCHEZ

Homecoming (1968); *We a BaddDDD People* (1970); *It's a New Day: Poems for Young Brothas and Sistuhs* (1971); *Adventures of Small Head, Square Head and Fat Head* (1973); *A Blues Book for Magical Black Women* (1973); *Love Poems* (1974).

CARL SANDBURG

In Reckless Ecstasy (1904); *Chicago Poems* (1916); *Cornhuskers* (1918); *Smoke and Steel* (1920); *Slabs of the Sunburnt West* (1922); *Selected Poems* (1926); *Good Morning, America* (1928); *The People, Yes* (1936); *Complete Poems* (1950, rev. 1970); *Wind Song* (1960).

Criticism:
Gay Wilson Allen, *Carl Sandburg* (1972); Richard Crowder, *Carl Sandburg* (1963); Harry Golden, *Carl Sandburg* (1961); Lucas Longo, *Carl Sandburg: Poet and Historian* (1972); Thomas S. Shaw, *Carl Sandburg: A Bibliography* (1948).

DELMORE SCHWARTZ

In Dreams Begin Responsibilities (1938); *Genesis I* (1943); *Vaudeville for a Princess* (1950); *Selected Poems: Summer Knowledge* (1959).

Criticism:
R. McDougall, *Delmore Schwartz* (1974).

ANNE SEXTON

To Bedlam and Part Way Back (1960); *All My Pretty Ones* (1962); *Selected Poems* (1964); *Live or Die* (1966); *Love Poems* (1969); *Trans-*

formations (1971); *The Book of Folly* (1973); *O Ye Tongues* (1973); *The Death Notebooks* (1974); *The Awful Rowing Towards God* (1975); *45 Mercy Street* (1976).

KARL SHAPIRO

Poems (1935); *Person, Place and Thing* (1942); *The Place of Love* (1943); *V-Letter* (1944); *Essay on Rime* (1945); *Trial of a Poet* (1957); *Poems, 1940–1953* (1953); *Poems of a Jew* (1958); *The Bourgeois Poet* (1964); *Selected Poems* (1968); *White Haired Lover* (1968); *Adult Bookstore* (1976); *Collected Poems 1940–1978* (1978).

Criticism:
William White, *Karl Shapiro: A Bibliography* (1960).

W. D. SNODGRASS

Heart's Needle (1959); *After Experience* ... (1968); *Remains: Poems* (1970); *Six Troubadour Poems* (1978).

Criticism:
William White, *W. D. Snodgrass: A Bibliography* (1960).

GARY SNYDER

Riprap (1959); *Myths and Texts* (1960); *Riprap and Cold Mountain Poems* (1965); *Six Sections from Mountains and Rivers without End* (1965); *A Range of Poems* (collected poems) (1966); *The Back Country* (1967); *Earth House Hold* (1969); *Six Sections from Mountains and Rivers Without End Plus One* (1970); *Regarding Wave* (1970); *Manzanita* (1972); *The Fudo Trilogy* (1974); *Turtle Island* (1974).

Criticism:
D. Kherdian, *Gary Snyder: A Biographical Sketch and Descriptive Checklist* (1965); Howard McCord, *Some Notes to Gary Snyder's* Myths and Texts (1971); R. Steuding, *Gary Snyder* (1976).

WALLACE STEVENS

Harmonium (1923); *Ideas of Order* (1935); *Owl's Clover* (1936); *The Man with the Blue Guitar* (1937); *Transport to Summer* (1947); *The Auroras of Autumn* (1950); *Selected Poems* (1953); *Collected Poems*

(1954); *Opus Posthumous* (1957); *The Palm at the End of the Mind* (1971).

Criticism:

James Baird, *The Dome and the Rock: Structure in the Poetry of Wallace Stevens* (1968); Michel Benamou, *Wallace Stevens and the Symbolist Imagination* (1972); Richard Blessing, *Wallace Stevens, Whole Harmonium* (1970); Marie Borroff, ed., *Wallace Stevens: A Collection of Critical Essays* (1963); Ashley Brown and Robert Haller, eds, *The Achievement of Wallace Stevens* (1962); Merle E. Brown, *Wallace Stevens: The Poem as Act* (1971); William Burney, *Wallace Stevens* (1968); Robert Buttel, *Wallace Stevens: The Making of* Harmonium (1967); Frank Doggett, *Stevens' Poetry of Thought* (1966); John J. Enck, *Wallace Stevens: Images and Judgments* (1964); Daniel Fuchs, *The Comic Spirit of Wallace Stevens* (1962); T. J. Hines, *The Later Poetry of Wallace Stevens* (1976); Frank Kermode, *Wallace Stevens* (1960); Edward Kessler, *Images of Wallace Stevens* (1972); Frank Lentricchia, *The Gaiety of Language: An Essay on the Radical Poetics of Wallace Stevens* (1968); Walton A. Litz, *Introspective Voyager: The Poetic Development of Wallace Stevens* (1972); Samuel French Morse, *Wallace Stevens: Life as Poetry* (1970), *A Wallace Stevens Checklist and Bibliography of Stevens Criticism* (1963); Eugene P. Nassar, *Wallace Stevens: An Anatomy of Figuration* (1965); William Van O'Connor, *The Shaping Spirit: A Study of Wallace Stevens* (1950); Roy H. Pearce and J. H. Miller, eds, *The Act of the Mind: Essays on the Poetry of Wallace Stevens* (1965); Joseph N. Riddell, *The Clairvoyant Eye: The Poetry and Poetics of Wallace Stevens* (1965); Herbert J. Stern, *Wallace Stevens: Art of Uncertainty* (1966); Helen H. Vendler, *On Extended Wings: Wallace Stevens' Longer Poems* (1969); Thomas F. Walsh, *A Concordance to the Poetry of Wallace Stevens* (1963); Henry Wells, *Introduction to Wallace Stevens* (1964); S. B. Weston, *Wallace Stevens: An Introduction to the Poetry* (1977).

GEORGE A. STRONG

The Song of Milkanwatha (1856); *Songs of the Pacific* (1889).

ALLEN TATE

Mr Pope and Other Poems (1928); *Poems, 1928–1931* (1932); *The Mediterranean and Other Poems* (1936); *Selected Poems* (1937); *The Winter Sea* (1944); *Poems, 1920–1945* (1947); *Poems, 1922–1947* (1948); *Two*

Conceits for the Eye to Sing, If Possible (1950); *Poems* (1960); *Poems* (1961); *The Swimmers and Other Selected Poems* (1970); *Collected Poems 1919–1976* (1977).

Criticism:
Willard Burdett Arnold, *The Social Ideas of Allen Tate* (1955); Ferman Bishop, *Allen Tate* (1967); George Hemphill, *Allen Tate* (1964); R. K. Meiners, *The Last Alternatives* (1963); Radcliffe Squires, *Allen Tate: A Literary Biography* (1971), (ed.), *Allen Tate and His Work: Critical Evaluations* (1972).

JAMES TATE

Cages (1967); *The Destination* (1967); *The Lost Pilot* (1967); *The Torches* (1968); *Notes of Woe* (1968); *Mystics in Chicago* (1968); *Camping in the Valley* (1968); *Row with Your Hair* (1969); *Is There Anything* (1969); *Shepherds of the Mist* (1969); *The Oblivion Ha-Ha* (1970); *Amnesia People* (1970); *Deaf Girl Playing* (1970); *Hints to Pilgrims* (1971); *Absences* (1972); *Viper Jazz* (1976).

EDWARD TAYLOR

Preparatory Meditations before my Approach to the Lords Supper (1939); *Gods Determinations touching his Elect: and The Elects Combat in their Conversion, and Coming up to God in Christ together with the Comfortable Effects thereof* (1739).

Standard Editions:
T. H. Johnson, ed., *The Poetical Works of Edward Taylor* (1939); D. E. Stanford, ed., *The Poems of Edward Taylor* (1960).

Criticism:
N. S. Grabo, *Edward Taylor* (1961).

HENRY DAVID THOREAU

Poems of Nature (1895); *Collected Poems* (1964).

Criticism:
J. B. Atkinson, *Henry Thoreau: The Cosmic Yankee* (1927); R. L. Cook, *Passage to Walden* (1949); Walter Harding, ed., *Thoreau: A Century of Criticism* (1954); J. W. Krutch, *Henry David Thoreau* (1948); Sherman

Paul, *The Shores of America: Thoreau's Inward Exploration* (1958); Ethel Seybold, *Thoreau: The Quest and the Classics* (1951); Mark Van Doren, *Henry David Thoreau: A Critical Study* (1961).

FREDERICK GODDARD TUCKERMAN

Poems (1860); *Poems* (1864); *Poems* (1867); *The Cricket* (1950, posthumous).

JONES VERY

Essays and Poems (1839).

Criticism:
E. Gittleman, *Jones Very: The Effective Years 1833–1840* (1967).

DIANE WAKOSKI

Coins and Coffins (1961); *Discrepancies and Apparitions* (1966); *The George Washington Poems* (1967); *Greed: Parts I and II* (1968); *The Diamond Merchant* (1968); *Inside the Blood Factory* (1968); *Some Poems for the Buddha's Birthday* (1969); *The Magellanic Clouds* (1969); *Greed: Parts III and IV* (1969); *The Moon Has a Complicated Geography* (1969); *Black Dream Ditty for Billy 'The Kid' M Seen in Dr Generosity's Bar Recruiting for Hell's Angels and Black Mafia* (1970); *Greed: Parts V–VII* (1971); *The Motorcycle Betrayal Poems* (1971); *Smudging* (1972); *Dancing on the Grave of a Son of a Bitch* (1973); *Greed: Parts VIII, IX and XI* (1973); *Trilogy* (1974); *Waiting for the King of Spain* (1976).

Criticism:
R. Gemmet and P. Gerber, eds, *A Terrible War: A Conversation with Diane Wakoski* (1970).

ROBERT PENN WARREN

Thirty-Six Poems (1936); *Eleven Poems on the Same Theme* (1942); *Selected Poems, 1923–1943* (1944); *Brother to Dragons* (1953); *Promises: Poems, 1954–1956* (1957); *You, Emperors and Others: Poems 1957–1960* (1960); *Selected Poems: New and Old, 1923–66* (1966); *Incarnations* (1968); *Audubon: A Vision* (1969); *Selected Poems 1923–1975* (1977).

Criticism:
Charles H. Bohner, *Robert Penn Warren* (1964); Leonard Casper, *Robert Penn Warren: The Dark and Bloody Ground* (1960); John Longley,

ed., *Robert Penn Warren* (1964); Victor Strandberg, *A Colder Fire* (1965); Paul West, *Robert Penn Warren* (1964).

WALT WHITMAN

Leaves of Grass (1855, rev. 1856, 1860, 1867, 1871, 1872, 1876, 1881, 1889, 1891); *Drum-Taps* (1865); *Passage to India* (1871).

Criticism:
Gay Wilson Allen, *A Reader's Guide to Walt Whitman* (1970), (ed.) *Walt Whitman Abroad* (1955), *A Walt Whitman Handbook* (1962); Roger Asselineau, *The Evolution of Walt Whitman: The Creation of a Book* (1962); Richard Chase, *Walt Whitman* (1961); Edwin H. Eby, *A Concordance of Walt Whitman's* Leaves of Grass *and Selected Prose Writings* (1949); Milton Hindus, ed., *Leaves of Grass One Hundred Years After* (1955); R. W. B. Lewis, ed., *The Presence of Walt Whitman* (1962); Edwin H. Miller, *Walt Whitman's Poetry: A Psychological Journey* (1968), (ed.) *A Century of Whitman Criticism* (1969); James E. Miller, Jr, *A Critical Guide to* Leaves of Grass (1957), *Walt Whitman* (1962); Sydney Musgrove, *T. S. Eliot and Walt Whitman* (1952); Roy H. Pearce, ed., *Walt Whitman: A Collection of Critical Essays* (1962); James T. Tanner, *Walt Whitman: A Supplementary Bibliography 1961–1967* (1968); Carolyn Wells, *A Concise Bibliography of the Works of Walt Whitman* (1922).

REED WHITTEMORE

Heroes and Heroines (1947); *An American Takes a Walk* (1956); *The Self-Made Man and Other Poems* (1959); *The Boy from Iowa* (1962); *The Fascination of the Abomination* (1963); *Poems New and Selected* (1967); *Fifty Poems Fifty* (1970); *The Mother's Breast and the Father's House* (1974).

JOHN GREENLEAF WHITTIER

Legends of New England in Prose and Verse (1831); *Poems Written During the Progress of the Abolition Question* (1837); *Lays of My Home and Other Poems* (1843); *Voices of Freedom* (1846); *Songs of Labor* (1850); *The Chapel of the Hermits* (1853); *The Panorama and Other Poems* (1856); *Home Ballads, Poems and Lyrics* (1860); *In War Time and Other Poems* (1864); *Snow-Bound* (1866); *The Tent on the Beach* (1867);

Among the Hills (1869); *Miriam and Other Poems* (1871); *Hazel-Blossoms* (1875); *The Vision of Echard* (1878); *St Gregory's Guest* (1886); *At Sundown* (1890).

Criticism:

R. Burton, *John Greenleaf Whittier* (1975); W. H. Hudson, *Whittier and his Poetry* (1976); Lewis G. Leary, *John Greenleaf Whittier* (1961); John P. Pickard, *John Greenleaf Whittier: An Introduction and Interpretation* (1961).

MICHAEL WIGGLESWORTH

The Day of Doom (1662); *Meat Out of the Eater* (1670).

Criticism:
Richard Crowder, *No Featherbed to Heaven: A Biography of Michael Wigglesworth 1631–1705* (1962); John W. Dean, *Sketch of the Life of the Rev. Michael Wigglesworth* (1863).

RICHARD WILBUR

The Beautiful Changes (1947); *Ceremony* (1950); *Things of This World* (1956); *Poems 1943–56* (1957); *Advice to a Prophet* (1961); *Poems of Richard Wilbur* (1963); *Walking to Sleep: New Poems and Translations* (1969); *Digging for China* (1970); *Opposites* (1973); *Seed Leaves* (1974); *The Mind Reader* (1976).

Criticism:

P. F. Cummins, *Richard Wilbur* (1971); John P. Field, *Richard Wilbur: A Bibliographical Checklist* (1971); Donald L. Hill, *Richard Wilbur* 1967).

WILLIAM CARLOS WILLIAMS

Poems (1909); *The Tempers* (1913); *Al Que Quiere!* (1917); *Sour Grapes* (1921); *Spring and All* (1923); *Collected Poems, 1921–1931* (1934); *An Early Martyr* (1935); *Adam and Eve and the City* (1936); *The Complete Collected Poems, 1906–1938* (1938); *Paterson, Book I* (1946); *Paterson, Book II* (1948); *The Clouds* (1948); *Selected Poems* (1949); *Paterson, Book III* (1949); *The Collected Later Poems* (1950, rev. 1963); *The Collected Earlier Poems* (1951); *Paterson, Book IV* (1951); *The Desert Music* (1954); *Journey to Love* (1955); *Paterson, Book V* (1958); *Pictures from Brueghel* (1962); *Paterson* (1963); *Imaginations* (1970).

Criticism:

James Breslin, *William Carlos Williams: An American Artist* (1970); John Malcolm Brinnin, *William Carlos Williams* (1963); Joel Conarroe, *William Carlos William's* Paterson: *Language and Landscape* (1970); Bram Dijkstra, *The Hieroglyphics of a New Speech: Cubism, Stieglitz, and the Early Poetry of William Carlos Williams* (1968); James Guimond, *The Art of William Carlos Williams: A Discovery and Possession of America* (1968); J. Hillis Miller, ed., *William Carlos Williams: A Collection of Critical Essays* (1966); Sherman Paul, *The Music of Survival* (1968); Walter Scott Peterson, *An Approach to* Paterson (1967); Benjamin Sankey, *A Companion to William Carlos Williams's* Paterson (1971); Linda W. Wagner, *The Poems of William Carlos Williams: A Critical Study* (1964); Emily Mitchell Wallace, *A Bibliography of William Carlos Williams* (1968); M. Weaver, *William Carlos Williams: The American Background* (1977); Thomas Whitaker, *William Carlos Williams* (1968); R. Whittemore, *William Carlos Williams: Poet from Jersey* (1975).

JAMES WRIGHT

The Green Wall (1957); *Saint Judas* (1959); *The Branch Will Not Break* (1963); *Shall We Gather at the River* (1968); *Collected Poems* (1971); *Salt Mines and Such: Poems* (1971); *I See the Wind* (1974); *Two Citizens* (1974); *To A Blossoming Pear Tree* (1977).

LOUIS ZUKOFSKY

55 Poems (1941); *Anew* (1946); *Some Time* (1956); *Barely and Widely* (1958); '*A*' *1–12* (1959); *Found Objects* (1964); *I's* (1963); *After I's* (1964); *IYYOB* (1965); *An Unearthing* (1965); *I Sent Thee Late* (1965); '*A*' *13–21* (1969); *Autobiography* (1970); *All: The Collected Shorter Poems 1923–1964* (1971); '*A*' *24* (1972); '*A*' *22 and 23* (1975).

General Works of Criticism

Allen, D. M., and Tallman, T., eds., *Poetics of the New American Poetry* (1970)

Allen, Gay Wilson, *American Prosody* (1935)

Alvarez, A., *The Shaping Spirit* (American ed.: *Stewards of Excellence*) (1958)

Bewley, Marius, *The Complex Fate* (1952)

Bigsby, C. W. E., ed., *The Black American Writer: Volume 2. Poetry and Drama* (1969)

Blackmur, R. P., *Language as Gesture* (1954)

Bode, Carl, *The Great Experiment in American Literature* (1961)

Bogan, Louise, *Achievement in American Poetry 1900–1950* (1951)

Bradbury, J. M., *The Fugitives: A Critical Account* (1958)

Brooks, Cleanth, *Modern Poetry and the Tradition* (1939)

Cambon, Glauco, *The Inclusive Flame: Studies in American Poetry* (1963)

Carroll, Paul, *The Poem in its Skin* (1968)

Ciardi, John, *Mid-Century American Poets* (1950)

Coffman, Stanley K., *Imagism, A Chapter for the History of Modern Poetry* (1951)

Cook, Bruce, *The Beat Generation* (1971)

Dembo, Lawrence S., *Conceptions of Reality in Modern American Poetry* (1966)

Deutsch, Babette, *Poetry in Our Time* (1952, rev. 1963)

Dodsworth, Martin, ed., *The Survival of Poetry: A Contemporary Survey by Donald Davie and Others* (1970)

Donoghue, Denis, *Connoisseurs of Chaos: Ideas of Order in Modern American Poetry* (1965)

Duberman, Martin, *Black Mountain: An Experiment in Community* (1972)

Ellmann, Richard, and Feidelson, Jr, Charles, eds, *The Modern Tradition: Backgrounds of Modern Literature* (1965)

Feidelson, Jr, Charles, *Symbolism and American Literature* (1953)

Frankenberg, Lloyd, *Pleasure Dome* (1949)

Fussell, Edwin, *Lucifer in Harness: American Meter, Metaphor and Diction* (1973)

Gayle, Jr, Addison, *The Black Aesthetic* (1971)

Gregory, Horace, and Zaturenska, Marya, *A History of American Poetry, 1900–1940* (1946)

Hamilton, Ian, ed., *The Modern Poet: Essays from* The Review (1968)

Howard, Richard, *Alone with America: The Art of Poetry in the United States since 1950* (1969)

Hughes, Glenn, *Imagism and the Imagists: A Study in Modern Poetry* (1941)

Hungerford, Edward B., ed., *Poets in Progress: Critical Prefaces to Ten Contemporary Americans* (1962)

Jarrell, Randall, *Poetry and the Age* (1953)

Jones, Peter, *Imagist Poetry* (1973)

Kherdian, David, ed., *Six San Francisco Poets* (1969)

Lee, Don L., *Dynamite Voices: Black Poets of the 1960s* (1971)

Lowell, Amy, *Tendencies in Modern American Poetry* (1927)

Ludwig, Richard M., ed., *Aspects of American Poetry* (1963)

Lutyens, David Bulwer, *The Creative Encounter* (1960)

Mazzaro, Jerome, ed., *Modern American Poetry: Essays in Criticism* (1970)

Meltzer, David, ed., *The San Francisco Poets* (1971)

Mills, Ralph J., Jr, *Contemporary American Poetry* (1965)

Nemerov, Howard, ed., *Poets on Poetry* (1966)

Norman, Charles, ed., *Poets on Poetry* (1962)

O'Connor, W. V., *Sense and Sensibility in Modern Poetry* (1948)

Ossman, David, *The Sullen Art: Interviews with Modern American Poets* (1963)

Ostroff, Anthony, ed., *The Contemporary Poet as Artist and Critic* (1964)

Paris Review, Writers at Work: The Paris Review *Interviews* (1950, First series; 1963, Second series; 1967, Third series)

Parkinson, Thomas, ed., *A Casebook on the Beat* (1961)

Pearce, Roy Harvey, *The Continuity of American Poetry* (1961)

Pound, Ezra, *Make it New* (1934), *Polite Essays* (1937)

Quinn, M. B., *The Metamorphic Tradition in Modern Poetry* (1955)

Raiziss, Sonia, *The Metaphysical Passion: Seven Modern American Poets and the Seventeenth-Century Tradition* (1952)

Rajan, B., *Modern American Poetry* (1950)

Rexroth, Kenneth, *American Poetry in the Twentieth Century* (1971)

Rosenthal, M. L., *The Modern Poets: A Critical Introduction* (1960), *The New Poets, American and British Poetry since World War II* (1967)

Schlauch, Margaret, *Modern British and American Poetry: Techniques and Ideologies* (1956)

Solt, Mary Ellen, ed., *Concrete Poetry: A World View* (1968)

Southworth, J. G., *Some Modern American Poets* (1950), *More Modern American Poets* (1954)

Spears, Monroe K., *Dionysus and the City: Modernism in Twentieth Century American Poetry* (1970)

Stepanchev, Stephen, *American Poetry Since 1945* (1965)

Tate, Allen, ed., *Six American Poets from Emily Dickinson to the Present* (1969)

Taupin, René, *L'Influence du symbolisme Français sur la poésie Américaine* (1929)

Turner, Darwin T., *Black American Literature: Poetry* (1969)

Waggoner, Hyatt H., *American Poets: From the Puritans to the Present* (1968)

Wagner, Jean, *Black Poets of the United States: Racial and Religious Feeling in Poetry from P. L. Dunbar to L. Hughes, 1890–1940* (1963)

Weatherhead, A. Kingsley, *The Edge of the Image: Marianne Moore, William Carlos Williams, and Some Other Poets* (1967)

Weirick, B., *From Whitman to Sandburg in American Poetry* (1924)

Wells, Henry W., *The American Way of Poetry* (1943)

Williams, Stanley T., *The Beginnings of American Poetry, 1620–1855* (1970)

Wilson, Edmund, *Axel's Castle* (1936)

Winters, Yvor, *In Defense of Reason* (including *Maule's Curse, Primitivism and Decadence,* and *The Anatomy of Nonsense*) (1947)

Acknowledgements

Thanks are due to the following poets, copyright owners, and publishers for permission to reprint poems and selections in this book:

EMILY DICKINSON – thirteen poems from *The Poems of Emily Dickinson*, ed. Thos. H. Johnson, copyright © 1951, 1955 by the President and Fellows of Harvard College, reprinted by permission of the publishers and the Trustees of Amherst College. 'After great pain, a formal feeling comes' from *The Complete Poems of Emily Dickinson*, ed. Thos. H. Johnson, copyright © 1929, 1957 by Mary L. Hampson, reprinted by permission of Little, Brown & Co.

EDGAR LEE MASTERS – from *Spoon River Anthology*, published by Macmillan Publishing Co. Inc., reprinted by permission of Mrs Edgar Lee Masters.

EDWIN ARLINGTON ROBINSON – 'Eros Turannos', copyright © 1916 by Edwin Arlington Robinson, renewed 1944 by Ruth Nivison, and 'Mr Flood's Party', copyright © 1921 by Edwin Arlington Robinson, renewed 1949 by Ruth Nivison, from *Collected Poems*, published by Macmillan Publishing Co. Inc., and reprinted with their permission. 'Reuben Bright' and 'Richard Cory' from *The Children of the Night* and 'Miniver Cheevey' copyright © 1907 Charles Scribner's Sons, from *The Town Down The River* are reprinted by permission of Charles Scribner's Sons.

ROBERT FROST – from *The Poetry of Robert Frost*, ed. Edward Connery Lathem, reprinted by permission of the Estate of Robert Frost and the publishers, Jonathan Cape Ltd.

DON MARQUIS – from *archy & mehitabel* reprinted by permission of Faber & Faber Ltd.

CARL SANDBURG – 'Limited' from *Chicago Poems*, copyright © 1916 by Holt, Rinehart & Winston Inc.; copyright © 1944 by Carl Sandburg. 'The Copperfaces, the Red Men' from *The People, Yes*, copyright © 1936 by Harcourt Brace Jovanovich, Inc.; copyright © 1964 by Carl Sandburg. Reprinted by permission of Harcourt Brace Jovanovich, Inc.

VACHEL LINDSAY – from *Collected Poems*, copyright © 1920 by Macmillan Publishing Co. Inc., renewed 1948 by Elizabeth C. Lindsay, reprinted by permission of the publishers.

ACKNOWLEDGEMENTS

WALLACE STEVENS – from *Collected Poems* reprinted by permission of the publishers Faber & Faber Ltd.

WILLIAM CARLOS WILLIAMS – New Directions Publishing Corp. for 'By the road to the contagious hospital', 'The Red Wheelbarrow', 'This Is Just to Say', 'Proletarian Portrait', 'To a Poor Old Woman', 'An Elegy for D. H. Lawrence', 'Paterson: Episode 17' from *Collected Earlier Poems*, copyright © 1938 by New Directions. 'Paterson: The Falls', 'The Dance', 'To Ford Madox Ford in Heaven' from *Collected Later Poems*, copyright © 1944 by William Carlos Williams. 'The Ivy Crown' from *Pictures From Brueghel and Other Poems*, copyright © 1955 by William Carlos Williams.

EZRA POUND – nine poems from *Collected Shorter Poems*, 'Canto I and 'Canto LI' from *The Cantos of Ezra Pound*, reprinted by permission of Faber & Faber Ltd.

H.D. – from H.D. (Hilda Doolittle) *Trilogy*, copyright © 1944 by Oxford University Press, copyright © 1973 by Norman Holmes Pearson. Reprinted by permission of New Directions Publishing Corp.

ROBINSON JEFFERS – 'Shine, Perishing Republic', copyright © 1925 and renewed 1953 by Robinson Jeffers, and 'Hurt Hawks', copyright © 1928 and renewed 1956 by Robinson Jeffers. Both reprinted from *Selected Poetry of Robinson Jeffers* by permission of Random House, Inc.

MARIANNE MOORE – from *The Complete Poems of Marianne Moore*, reprinted by permission of Faber & Faber Ltd.

T. S. ELIOT – from *Collected Poems 1909–1962*, reprinted by permission of Faber & Faber Ltd.

JOHN CROWE RANSOM – three poems from *Selected Poems* by permission of the proprietors, Alfred A. Knopf, Inc. and the publishers, Eyre Methuen Ltd.

CONRAD AIKEN – from *Collected Poems*, copyright © 1953, 1970 by Conrad Aiken, reprinted by permission of Oxford University Press, Inc.

EDNA ST VINCENT MILLAY – 'Sonnet xlii', copyright © 1923, 1951 by Edna St Vincent Millay and Norma Millay Ellis, 'Sonnet cv', copyright, 1931, 1958 by Edna St Vincent Millay and Norma Millay Ellis, both from *Collected Poems*, Harper & Row, Inc.

ARCHIBALD MACLEISH – from *Collected Poems 1917–1952* by Archibald MacLeish, reprinted by permission of Houghton Mifflin Co.

ACKNOWLEDGEMENTS

E. E. CUMMINGS – from *The Complete Poems of E. E. Cummings* reprinted by permission of MacGibbon & Kee Ltd.

HART CRANE – from *The Complete Poems, Selected Letters and Prose of Hart Crane*. Reprinted by permission of Liveright Publishing Corp., and Oxford University Press.

ERNEST HEMINGWAY – copyright © Mrs Ernest Hemingway. Reprinted with her permission.

ALLEN TATE – from *Poems*. Reprinted by permission of The Swallow Press Inc.

KENNETH FEARING – from *New and Selected Poems*, copyright © 1956 by Kenneth Fearing. Reprinted by permission of Indiana University Press.

LANGSTON HUGHES – 'Theme for English B' from *Montage of a Dream Deferred*, copyright © 1951 by Langston Hughes, published by Henry Holt. 'Brass Spittoons' from *Fine Clothes to the Jew*, copyright © 1927 by Langston Hughes, renewed, published by Alfred A. Knopf Inc. Both poems reprinted by permission of Harold Ober Associates Inc.

OGDEN NASH – 'You Bet Travel is Broadening' from *Versus* and 'Very Like a Whale' from *Many Long Years Ago* published by, and reprinted by permission of, J. M. Dent Ltd.

COUNTEE CULLEN – from *On These I Stand* by Countee Cullen, copyright © 1925 by Harper & Row, Inc.; renewed 1953 by Ida M. Cullen.

LOUIS ZUKOFSKY – from *All: The Collected Short Poems, 1923–1958* published by Jonathan Cape Ltd.

RICHARD EBERHART – from *Collected Poems 1930–1960* published by Chatto & Windus Ltd.

ROBERT PENN WARREN – VIII from *Promises* published by Random House Inc, copyright © 1955, 1957 by Robert Penn Warren. Reprinted by permission of William Morris Agency, Inc., on behalf of the author.

KENNETH REXROTH – from *In Defense of the Earth*. Reprinted by permission of Laurence Pollinger Ltd. on behalf of the proprietors New Directions Publishing Corp.

THEODORE ROETHKE – from *The Collected Poems of Theodore Roethke* published by, and permission of, Faber & Faber Ltd.

CHARLES OLSON – from *The Maximus Poems* published by Cape

639

Goliard Press. Reprinted by permission of Jonathan Cape Ltd. on behalf of the Estate of Charles Oslon.

DELMORE SCHWARTZ – from *Selected Poems: Summer Knowledge*, copyright © 1938 by New Directions Publishing Corp. Reprinted by permission of New Directions Publishing Corp.

KARL SHAPIRO – from *Person, Place and Thing*, reprinted by permission of Laurence Pollinger Ltd on behalf of Random House Inc.

WELDON KEES – from *The Collected Poems of Weldon Kees*, reprinted by permission of the University of Nebraska Press.

RANDALL JARRELL – 'Thinking of the Lost World' from *The Lost World* by Randall Jarrell, published by Eyre Spottiswoode Ltd. 'Death of the Ball Turret Gunner' from *The Complete Poems*, reprinted by permission of Faber & Faber Ltd.

JOHN BERRYMAN – six poems from *77 Dream Songs*, 'From the French Hospital in New York, 901' from *His Toy, His Dream, His Rest*, 'Olympus' from *Love and Fame*. Reprinted by permission of Faber & Faber Ltd.

ROBERT LOWELL – five poems from *Life Studies*, 'For the Union Dead' from *For the Union Dead*, 'T. S. Eliot', 'Ezra Pound' from *History*. Reprinted by permission of Faber & Faber Ltd.

GWENDOLYN BROOKS – from *The World of Gwendolyn Brooks* copyright © 1960 by Gwendolyn Brooks. Reprinted by permission of Harper & Row Inc.

ROBERT DUNCAN – from *The Opening of the Field* published by Jonathan Cape Ltd.

LAWRENCE FERLINGHETTI – from *A Coney Island of the Mind*, copyright © 1958 by Lawrence Ferlinghetti. Reprinted by permission of New Directions Publishing Corp.

REED WHITTEMORE – 'Clamming' from *Reed Whittemore, Poems New and Selected*, copyright by Reed Whittemore. Reprinted by permission of the University of Minnesota Press. 'Our Ruins' from *The Fascination of the Abomination*, copyright © 1961, by Reed Whittemore. Originally appeared in *The Carleton Miscellany*. Reprinted by permission of Macmillan Publishing Co, Inc.

HOWARD NEMEROV – reprinted by permission of Margot Johnson Agency.

CHARLES BUKOWSKI – reprinted by permission of Black Sparrow Press.

RICHARD WILBUR – three poems from *Poems 1943–1956*, 'On the

ACKNOWLEDGEMENTS

Marginal Way' from *Walking to Sleep*, reprinted by permission of Faber & Faber Ltd.

ALAN DUGAN – from *Collected Poems* by Alan Dugan, reprinted by permission of Faber & Faber Ltd.

KENNETH KOCH – two poems, copyright © 1960 by Kenneth Koch, reprinted by permission of International Creative Management.

FRANK O'HARA – from *Meditations in an Emergency* by Frank O'Hara, copyright © 1957 by Frank O'Hara. Reprinted by permission of Grove Press, Inc.

PAUL BLACKBURN – from *In, On, Or About the Premises*, published by Cape Goliard Press.

W. D. SNODGRASS – from *Heart's Needle*, reprinted by permission of The Marvell Press.

A. R. AMMONS – from *Selected Poems*, copyright © 1968 by Cornell University. Reprinted by permission of Cornell University Press.

JAMES MERRILL – from *Nights and Days* by James Merrill, reprinted by permission of Chatto & Windus Ltd.

ROBERT CREELEY – reprinted by permission of Calder & Boyars Ltd.

ROBERT BLY – 'Waking from Sleep' from *Silence in the Snowy Fields*, Jonathan Cape. Ltd, 'The Executive's Death' from *The Light Around the Body*, reprinted by permission of Rapp & Whiting Ltd.

ALLEN GINSBERG – reprinted by permission of City Lights Books Inc.

JOHN ASHBERY – from *The Tennis Court Oath*, copyright © 1959 by John Ashbery. Reprinted by permission of Wesleyan University Press.

W. S. MERWIN – from *The Lice*, Hart Davis MacGibbon, 1969, reprinted by permission of David Higham Associates Ltd.

JAMES WRIGHT – from *The Branch Will Not Break*, copyright © 1961 by James Wright. Reprinted by permission of Wesleyan University Press. 'A Blessing' first appeared in *Poetry*.

ANNE SEXTON – 'Unknown Girl in the Maternity Ward' from *To Bedlam and Part Way Back;* 'All My Pretty Ones' from *All My Pretty Ones*, copyright © 1961 by Anne Sexton, both published by Houghton Mifflin Co. Reprinted by permission of The Sterling Lord Agency.

EDWARD DORN – from *Slinger* published by Wingbow Press, reprinted by permission of the author.

GREGORY CORSO – from *The Happy Birthday of Death*, copyright ©

ACKNOWLEDGEMENTS

1960 by New Directions Publishing Corp. Reprinted by permission of the publishers.

GARY SNYDER – 'A Walk' from *Riprap* reprinted by permission of Laurence Pollinger Ltd. on behalf of New Directions Publishing Corp. 'The Hudsonian Curlew' from *Turtle Island*, copyright © 1969 by Gary Snyder. Reprinted by permission of New Directions Publishing Corp. 'Things to Do Around a Lookout' reprinted by permission of the author.

SYLVIA PLATH – from *Ariel*, copyright © 1965 by Ted Hughes, Faber & Faber Ltd.

ETHERIDGE KNIGHT – from *Poems from Prison*, copyright © 1974 by Etheridge Knight. Reprinted by permission of Broadside Press.

IMAMU AMIRI BARAKA (LEROI JONES) – reprinted by permission of the author.*

RICHARD EMIL BRAUN – from *Children Passing*, University of Texas Press, copyright © 1962 Richard Emil Braun. Reprinted by permission of the author.

ROBERT MEZEY – from *The Door Standing Open*, copyright © 1970 by Oxford University Press. Reprinted by permission of the publishers.

SONIA SANCHEZ – from *We a BaddDD People*, copyright © 1973 by Sonia Sanchez. Reprinted by permission of Broadside Press.

DIANE WAKOSKI – from *Inside the Blood Factory*, copyright © 1967 by Diane Wakoski. Reprinted by permission of Doubleday & Co. Inc.

HAKI R. MAHUBUTI (DON L. LEE) – from *Don't Cry, Scream*, copyright © 1973 by Don L. Lee. Reprinted by permission of Broadside Press.

NIKKI GIOVANNI – from *Black Judgement*, copyright © 1973 by Nikki Giovanni. Reprinted by permission of Broadside Press.

JAMES TATE – from *The Oblivion Ha-Ha*, copyright © 1969 by James Tate. Reprinted by permission of Little, Brown & Co. in association with the Atlantic Monthly Press.

Where no acknowledgement is made, every effort has been made to acquire permission for the right to include the poems.

*A second poem 'For Hettie', by Imamu Amiri Baraka was deleted at the author's request while the book was being printed.

Index of Authors

Index of First Lines

MORE ABOUT PENGUINS
AND PELICANS

Penguinews, which appears every month, contains details of all the new books issued by Penguins as they are published. From time to time it is supplemented by our stocklist, which is our list of almost 5,000 titles.

A specimen copy of *Penguinews* will be sent to you free on request. Please write to Dept EP, Penguin Books Ltd, Harmondsworth, Middlesex, for your copy.

In the U.S.A.: For a complete list of books available from Penguins in the United States write to Dept CS, Penguin Books, 625 Madison Avenue, New York, New York 10022.

In Canada: For a complete list of books available from Penguins in Canada write to Penguin Books Canada Ltd, 2801 John Street, Markham, Ontario L3R 1B4.